The NEW HOLY WARS

The NEW

HOLY WARS

Economic Religion VS. Environmental Religion

in Contemporary AMERICA

ROBERT H. NELSON

The Pennsylvania State University Press
University Park, Pennsylvania

Published in Cooperation with the Independent Institute

Library of Congress Cataloging-in-Publication Data

Nelson, Robert H. (Robert Henry), 1944–
The new holy wars : economic religion versus environmental religion
in contemporary America / Robert H. Nelson.
p.   cm.
Includes bibliographical references and index.
Summary: "Examines economics and environmentalism as competing public religions
that derive from, and continue, a Christian worldview; argues that debates over
global warming and other environmental issues are ultimately based on theological
differences between their respective adherents"—Provided by publisher.
ISBN 978-0-271-03581-9 (cloth : alk. paper)
1. Economics—Religious aspects—Christianity.
2. Environmentalism—Religious aspects—Christianity.
3. Economics—United States.
4. Environmentalism—United States.
I. Title.

HB72.N453 2010
261.8′50973—dc22
2009019054

CONTENTS

IN 1849, PRINCE ALBERT ANNOUNCED in London a plan for a new Crystal Palace Exhibition to be held in 1851 to celebrate the extraordinary recent advances of science and industry. For the prince, as for many other people of the period, it would herald the fulfilment of God's plan for the world. As the prince declared, "So man is approaching a more complete fulfilment of that great and sacred mission which he has to perform in this world. His reason being created after the image of God, he has to use it to discover the laws by which the Almighty governs His creation, and, by making these laws his standard of action, to conquer nature to his use—himself a divine instrument."[1] As would have been unimaginable until recently, the prince was optimistic that human beings by their new powers of scientific knowledge and economic advance would soon be bringing heaven to earth. God, as it seemed, had now chosen in the modern age to reveal to human beings the full secrets of the natural world. In this way, as it seemed, He was finally opening the way to the realization—prematurely forecast in the Christian Bible as imminent—of a divine perfection of the earth.

Today, more than one hundred and fifty years later, things look much different. It has become apparent that the application of human reason, reaching a high point in the scientific method, created powers to control nature that could be used for evil as well as good. Reflecting concerns felt around the world, in 2007 a Philippine newspaper columnist declared that: "Man tends to destroy his natural habitat as he consumes its natural resources in his quest for a better life. The worst environmental damages have been results of major manmade atrocities on land or the waters that veer away from what God designed our planet to be."[2] Reflecting a common fear that God would severely punish those who were destroying his creation, many environmentalists foresaw a future of rising seas, famine, disease, and other natural disasters—environmental calamities virtually biblical in character. There was a wide concern that the rise of modern science and economics might not have been a great gift from God but rather the latest temptation of the devil.

The members of the contemporary economics profession do not use the Christian language of Prince Albert, but they are the heirs to the same belief in scientific and economic progress as the salvation of the world.[3] Environmentalists, by contrast, today reject such progressive religion as a heresy that threatens the human future on earth. As Jesse Ausubel declares, "'Green is the new religion" with its own "environmental shrines" that now "begin to fill the landscape."[4] In the public arena, the most important religious controversy today is the clash between "economic religion" and "environmental religion." The historical sources of the disagreement, to be sure, lie in much older disputes within Christian religion, even when the secular language of the participants may now make little if any specific reference to Christianity or the Bible. In place of Roman Catholicism versus Protestantism, and other Christian religious disputes of the past, the new holy wars are today being fought out—fortunately mostly with words—by two clashing secular religions grounded in the messages of economics and environmentalism.

Whether for good or evil, human beings indisputably are altering the natural world in altogether unprecedented ways. The stakes of human actions have been raised as never before. The answers will in the end have to be resolved by theology. At present, politicians, lobbyists, policy analysts, businesspeople, and other participants in American public debates often have a theology in the back of their minds. Their theological views, however, are largely masked in various outward disguises. Indeed, many of the leading religions in public affairs today deny any religious character. This denial, ironically, is sometimes even an important part of their message. Karl Marx once said that religion is the opiate of the masses, but it can be seen in hindsight that this supposed rejection of religion was actually a main tenet of a new Marxist gospel—in effect, an imperial claim to superiority over other false religions.

Our leading contemporary theologians thus speak publicly in the languages of economics, natural resource management, conservation biology, ecology, sociology, administrative science, and other forms of official policy discourse.[5] Rather than obeying God's commands, in the public arena many Americans are more comfortable communicating their deepest values in languages of technical expertise and rational policy making.[6] Nevertheless, as one American political scientist observed in 2006, it is obvious that "like many other areas of public policy, [environmental policy making] has extremely powerful symbols associated with policy outcomes on all sides." The newer environmental symbols now challenge an older set of economic symbols that venerated "growth and jobs," "private property rights," and other forces of economic progress.[7]

In exploring the disagreements between economic and environmental worldviews, current analysts thus typically make little or no explicit reference to the "R word"—religion. About the closest they get is when they speak in terms of the influence on public policy of an "underlying policy frame," a "policy image," or a "dominant causal logic"; all these outlooks on the world are resistant to any easy change, even in the face of contradictory empirical evidence.[8] If religion is understood, however, as a person's way of framing his or her basic perception of the world and its meaning, as leading theologians such as Paul

Tillich have understood the matter, then these basic perceptual orientations are actually religions in a genuine sense.[9]

Thus, as commonly studied in schools of theology today, a religion does not necessarily have to involve the existence of a transcendent god outside this world. Most people have a set of foundational beliefs that both explains the place of human beings in the world and guides their lives, and the intellectual articulation of these beliefs in a formal way becomes a theology.* Many people now speak of having deep "spiritual" beliefs while denying that they subscribe to any "religious" set of convictions. Indeed, if it makes a reader of this book more comfortable, he or she may think of it as an examination of the "spiritual values" of economics versus the "spiritual values" of environmentalism. For me, though, it is a distinction without a difference.

As William Grassie, the founder of the Metanexus Institute on Religion and Science (sponsored by the John Templeton Foundation), notes, attempts to define precisely the terms "religion" and "spirituality" generally "prove illusive." The term religion not only encompasses the familiar Christian kind but has also been used "to designate a bounded belief system and set of practices, as in the religions of the Greeks, Romans, Jews, Muslims, Hindus, Chinese and others." Recognizing the fact that some actual religions go so far as to deny their religious character, Grassie describes the common worship in modern times of a "God-by-whatever name." Ironically, it is possible to have a "religion of no religion." Grassie observes that the term "spiritual" "derives from the Latin *spiritus*. The Latin verb root is *spirare*, literally, 'to breathe or blow.' The connotation is that we are surrounded by a divine reality as pervasive, intimate, necessary, and invisible as the air we breathe." Whether it is called a religion or a form of spirituality, however, there is one common

---

* Max Stackhouse, a leading professor of theology for many years at Princeton Theological Seminary (now emeritus), defines a religion as "a comprehensive worldview or 'metaphysical moral vision' that is accepted as binding because it is held to be, in itself, basically true and just, even if all dimensions of it cannot be either finally confirmed or refuted." Moreover, such a religion "is functional: it provides a framework for interpreting the realities of life in the world, it guides the basic beliefs and behaviors of persons and it empowers believers to seek to transform the world in accordance with a normative ethic of what should be." As Stackhouse observes,

> By this definition, worldviews such as a philosophical-ethical Confucianism, an atheistic spirituality such as Buddhism, or a secular-humanistic ideology such as Marxism, whenever they form a creed, a code and a cult, and are used to interpret and guide the formation of an ethos, can properly be seen as faiths. They function as "religions," shaping an ethos, even if they are opposed to theistic traditions or do not recognize themselves as religious. They are also subject to theological analysis, for they inevitably contain a "metaphysical-moral vision"—an ontology, a theory of history and ethic—that involves some view of transcendence. (Max L. Stackhouse, *Globalization and Grace* [New York: Continuum, 2007], 7, 8)

See also Robert H. Nelson, "A Covenant for Globalization? An Essay/Review of Max L. Stackhouse, *Globalization and Grace*," *The Review of Faith and International Affairs* 6 (Winter 2008).

element to all these disciplines (offering perhaps the closest that one can come to a definition of religion): "Every religion is . . . making universal truth claims about the fundamental character of the universe as a whole."[10]

Partly reflecting the disguised character of the most important modern religions in matters of public affairs, most of our leading public intellectuals have not committed much time or effort to formal theological reflection. This is partly because, as Grassie comments, "the social sciences—psychology, sociology, economics, and anthropology—were largely founded by thinkers who took for granted that there was no truth content or value to religions, that religions were irrational, superstitious, regressive, and dysfunctional." Indeed, "the social sciences were founded with a lot of *anima* toward religion, so it is little wonder that the faith factor is the forgotten variable in the social sciences in the decades that followed."[11] In retrospect, it now appears that the dismissive attitude of the social sciences toward religion was actually the disdain of one faith as expressed toward a religious competitor.

Although attitudes have begun to change, the greatest efforts of social scientists and policy analysts—the priesthood to the dominant religion in the public arena of the twentieth century—have been devoted to studying and promoting the mechanisms of scientific and economic "progress." In some private universities, there are schools of theology, but they are commonly separated from the main areas of study in the physical sciences, social sciences, and humanities. In public universities, religion can be a legitimate object of "scientific" study, but the "nonsectarian" mission precludes a full range of theological debate. Social science's claims to "value-neutrality" thus produce virtually the opposite of their professed intent, serving to privilege modern religion at the expense of traditional religion, and thus setting tight boundaries on acceptable religious discourse in officially "public" settings.

Our critical theological debates therefore have been driven underground. The camouflaged form of contemporary theological debate is preferable to no debate at all, but the quality of the argument inevitably suffers. There can be large confusions introduced when questions that are essentially religious have to be explored in a "value-neutral" language of economics, ecological science, or other "technical" fields. The very claims to value neutrality inhibit closer examination of the powerful normative assumptions and the processes of theological reasoning that underlie the thinking of economists and environmentalists alike. Yet if these elements remain unacknowledged, conversations between economists and environmentalists will often be like ships passing in the night.*

---

* The *Economist* magazine observes that "academic disciplines are often separated by gulfs of mutual incomprehension, but the deepest and widest may be the one that separates most economists from most environmentalists." In the name-calling and other nasty disputes that often break out between

A New—or Post?—Christianity

Whereas economic religion and environmental religion typically make little if any explicit reference to a god, both are derived (to a much greater degree than many of their followers are aware) from Christian sources (as originally derived from and subsequently blended with Jewish sources). Indeed, allowing for the outward differences in vocabulary and metaphor, the underlying messages are sometimes little altered from the original Christian statements. Economic religion and environmental religion may be talking about a Christian God; they may be describing the character and thinking of this God; they may be locating the original source of sin in the world; they may be describing God's commands; and they may be prophesying a final, divinely determined outcome of history, but all this is left implicit. For the many people skeptical of institutional Christian religion but seeking greater religious meaning in their lives, that is no doubt part of the attraction of secular religion.

The American theologian Max Stackhouse thus comments that, even when they were expressed through various forms of "civil religion," it remained true that the core beliefs "incarnate in most of the various spheres of life in the world of Western modernity remained basically Christian (or Judeo-Christian)." The basic worldview of Christian religion continued to prevail even among many people who were "forgetful or ignorant of its dominant religious vision embedded in the fabric of . . . civil society." Although the most influential belief systems of the modern age often "became secular," they were "secular in a Christian (or Judeo-Christian), not in a Confucian, Hindu, Buddhist, or Islamic, way." Among the core modern beliefs rooted originally in Christianity are "the ideas of human rights, based in the idea that each person is made in the image of God, and that each is endowed by our Creator with certain inalienable rights," and "the idea that there is an ultimate end for humanity beyond death, and that the vision of the end is the New Jerusalem"—as given new expression by many modern prophets announcing one or another vision of the arrival of a new heaven on earth.[12]

Economic and environmental religion follow closely the patterns of secularization, as described by Stackhouse. The American historian Thomas Dunlop thus wrote in 2006, with respect to environmentalism, that:

> religion, from that perspective [of William James], flowed from humans' need to make sense of their lives in this world, and beliefs that gave

---

economists and environmentalists, "what underlies rows like this, as well as the more insidious refusal even to engage with the other side, is not so much disagreements about facts as disagreement about how to think" about the world. See "Never the Twain Shall Meet," *Economist*, February 2, 2002, 74.

answer to those questions were religious ones, though they might not
be complete (in the sense of answering all important questions), might
deny deities or even the possibility of transcendence, might even rely on
other systems they called religion (as the American Way of Life did) to
supplement their creeds. Environmentalism fell into that category.

[Environmentalism] offered (in those first years somewhat too enthusiastically) jeremiads—warnings of disaster if we followed our sinful ways, directions to the path of righteousness, and the promise of an
Earthly Paradise if we reformed our ways—and told us how we should
live. Like an established religious tradition, pointing the path to saint-
hood, offering comfort to the masses, and holding open the door to the
repentant sinner, it had ways of work for all. It offered the committed bio-
regionalism, a life lived on the land, learning its possibilities and building
a community that would unite humans and nature and heal them.[13]

Besides economic and environmental religions, there have been other influential secular religions at work in the modern age. Freudianism and other
schools of psychology, for example, have often been described as powerful
religions.[14] They have less to say, however, about the organization of society
or the capacity of human beings to alter the natural world. Their greatest influence has been in private matters such as marriage, child rearing, sexual
morality, and other aspects of personal life. For many people, it has been left
to economic and environmental religion to address the wider truths of human society and the natural world. One might say that, in general, the secular
religions of the modern age are a new stage in the long history of religion.
For some, secular religion may be a new legitimate form of Christianity; for
others, it may be a new Christian heresy; and for still others, it may even be
the beginning of a post-Christian era, if still deriving many of its core beliefs
from the original source.

Over the course of its long history, Western religion has evolved frequently.
Christian theology, as it is said, emerged from a synthesis of Jerusalem and
Athens almost two thousand years ago. Islam was an offshoot from Christianity in the seventh century, since regarded historically as a separate religion
even while sharing a common monotheism, a strong missionary impulse,
and many other important features. Protestantism broke away from Roman
Catholicism in the sixteenth century and was initially regarded in Rome as
a great new heresy. One might see "secular religion" in the West as the next
great historical stage of this long historical evolution from the biblical Abraham, now characterized by an outward denial of a Christian status even as
modern secular religions have implicitly reworked traditional Christian messages. As the British political philosopher John Gray comments, "The political

religions that wrought such havoc in the twentieth century," most of them grounded in one or another vision of economic progress, "were secular versions of the Christian promise of universal salvation." Yet the Christian roots of modern political and economic thought have "not been much studied," partly because "amongst analytical philosophers, ignorance of religion is a point of professional honor, while social science continues to be dominated by theories of secularization that were falsified generations ago."[15]

By the standards of at least some leading theologians, a secular religion that implicitly reflects closely a Christian set of precepts might be deemed an actual form of Christian belief, capable of showing the way to salvation, even when there is no explicit mention of the Bible or other historical Christian teachings.* Indeed, in Europe today, one might argue that the secular character of society has reached such an all-encompassing extent that—much as would have been true historically of a primitive tribe—there is little real exposure for many people to the historical teachings of Christianity. For those people who live their whole lives outside any traditional Christian experience, they might thus be regarded as actual Christians even without realizing this themselves, believers in one or another of the secular faiths of the modern age that follow closely in the historical path of Christianity.

---

*Whether a secular religion can be considered a legitimate new form of Christianity is itself a theological question. As in many areas, there is a wide diversity of Christian opinion on the range of acceptable beliefs that can still be considered to fall within the actual realm of "Christianity." This issue was explored in 2008 by the Fordham University theologian Avery Dulles (a cardinal of the Roman Catholic Church), partly in the context of the possibility of salvation for those people who could not in principle have had any knowledge of either the past existence or the message of Jesus Christ (for example, people who lived before Christ was born or people who lived in the Americas before the arrival of Europeans). Dulles notes that one main historic line of Catholic thought would deny any possibility of salvation to such people—that salvation is possible only within the Catholic Church and that, as an early Christian theologian declared, "not only all pagans, but all Jews, and all heretics and schismatics who are outside the Catholic Church, will go to the eternal fire that was prepared for the devil and his angels."

But the thinking today has often changed. This harsh (at least to contemporary eyes) view has increasingly been rejected in "modern theology [which], preoccupied with the salvation of non-Christians, has tended to neglect the importance of explicit belief in Christ." As Dulles notes, the Second Vatican Council "did not indicate whether it is necessary for salvation to come to explicit Christian faith before death, but the texts give the impression that implicit faith may suffice"—thus suggesting that an implicit Christianity, as found in many secular religions such as economics and environmentalism, may be sufficient for salvation. Modern Catholic theology tends toward a view that "the traditions of all peoples contain elements of truth imbedded in their cultures, myths, and religious practices. These sound elements derive from [the Christian] God, who speaks to all his children through inward testimony and outward signs," even when the outward language may not be that historically of Christianity. The German Catholic theologian Karl Rahner goes so far as to argue that "those who accept and live by the grace offered to them, even though they have never heard of Christ and the gospel, may be called anonymous Christians." An American environmentalist who has never learned about the life of Christ but behaves in a "Christian" way, it would seem, could in these terms be an actual Christian. See Avery Cardinal Dulles, "Who Can Be Saved?" *First Things* 180 (February 2008): 20–21.

The rise and further development of secular religion over the past three hundred years has been perhaps the central event of Christian history since the Protestant Reformation. It is in any case impossible to imagine a vital Christianity of the future that does not take account of and somehow achieve a synthesis with the messages of secular religion. Another way of saying this is that secular religion represents the most influential effort to reconcile Christianity and modern science, and no widely followed religion of the future will be able to escape the need for a successful reconciliation of these two leading sources of legitimacy and authority of our time.

Playing God

The central role of economic and environmental religion in contemporary public life reflects the fact that, less than two hundred years ago, an event altogether unprecedented in the four-billion-year history of the earth occurred. As economic historian Gregory Clark reports, there was no large improvement in the living standards of the great majority of the people living in England until 1800. Indeed, for the world as a whole, "the average person in . . . 1800 was no better off than the average person of 100,000 B.C." Life expectancy was thirty to thirty-five years, "no higher in 1800 than for hunter gatherers." It was not until the arrival of the Industrial Revolution that there occurred "the first break of human society from the constraints of nature, the first break of the human economy from the natural economy"—the moment when human beings first clearly came to resemble God in their powers of control over nature.[16]

Indeed, as Clark acknowledges, the truly decisive breakthrough both in terms of growth in physical outputs and in human living standards may not have occurred until after 1850. Until then, mechanical invention had typically been the product of individual tinkerers working outside the realm of the theoretical sciences. In the seventeenth and eighteenth centuries, the greatest scientific discoveries (such as Sir Isaac Newton's explanation of the workings of the solar system) had greater theological than practical significance. But the new scientific understanding of electricity, and the rise of applied scientific fields such as chemistry, changed all this. From around 1850 onward, technological advance increasingly depended on improved scientific understandings and their application by trained engineers and others with specialized scientific expertise. In the Progressive Era in the United States, older universities such as Harvard and Yale rapidly retooled from educating Protestant ministers to producing the professional experts needed to create a new world. As the new modes of technological advance were incorporated into the routine life of universities, businesses, governments, and other leading institutions, to say that the results were extraordinary is an understatement.

For the first time ever, one of the earth's creatures—human beings—had literally acquired the capacity to remake "the creation." Atomic bombs could destroy entire cities in an instant, potentially spreading radiation over the entire planet, and a few human actions could eliminate whole plant and animal species. This new human power over nature was bound to be of immense theological as well as practical significance. Astonishingly enough, human beings had now acquired knowledge and powers previously reserved for God. It had become possible in practice (and human capacity seemed to be growing by the day) for human beings to "play God" in the world. Theologically, as most of the visitors to London's Crystal Palace saw matters in 1851, this might be seen in the most positive terms as part of a divine plan for saving humanity, involving the perfection of the world by means of the use of human reason, the one faculty that human beings (uniquely among the creatures of the earth) share with God.

As noted above, a less favorable theological response, however, was also possible. In their hubris, human beings might once again be challenging God's authority. If that was the case, it would surely bring on His severe punishments—as happens repeatedly in the Old Testament when sinful human beings seek to defy God's commands. For human beings to try to take the place of God is the gravest sin of all. Mankind might have been tempted once again to pursue forbidden forms of knowledge properly reserved to God alone, and might now face travails and punishments even more severe than those that were visited upon the successors to Adam and Eve.

A very large number of previous writers have, of course, addressed the moral, philosophical, and religious implications of modern scientific and economic progress.[17] The religious side of environmentalism has been less studied but is attracting growing attention. The contribution of this book is to explore these issues by comparing and otherwise examining in depth the conflicts between economic and environmental religion. Explicitly identifying economics and environmentalism as secular religions helps to understand the difficulties they have experienced in working together in many practical areas of government policy and management. In the public arena over the course of the twentieth century, it was economic religion that had the greatest influence in shaping government policy. In the last few decades of the century, however, environmental religion increasingly challenged economic religion. It may turn out that the most influential public gospels of the twenty-first century—religions that seek to provide answers to basic questions of public policy, leaving aside matters of personal salvation in the hereafter—will offer some kind of religious synthesis of these two leading public theologies of the previous century.

The Origins of This Book

Perhaps surprisingly, this book emerged from practical experience in the trenches of government. I am trained in economics and much of my professional life was spent as a working government economist. In 1975, I took a job on the economics staff of the Office of Policy Analysis in the Department of the Interior in Washington, D.C., one of the main federal agencies responsible for policy and management of the lands, minerals, and other natural and environmental assets of the United States. This office provided policy studies and advice and otherwise served as an in-house think tank for the Office of the Secretary of the Interior.*

It soon became apparent to me that policy making in the Interior Department involved more than such traditional rational economic goals as maximizing benefits minus costs. It was also more than simply adjudicating among competing private interests. The Interior Department was also a prominent forum for resolving fierce value conflicts within American society. Moreover, these value clashes in many cases had an underlying religious quality. Sociologically, the leading participants in Interior Department policy controversies frequently exhibited a righteous—a "religiously certain"—character. As applied to Interior Department matters, they had few doubts about the correctness of their way of "framing" central human concerns of the treatment of the natural world. They were anxious to apply, and to convert others to, their own convictions in these matters.

As I delved further into the character of Interior Department policy making, I gradually realized not only that the participants behaved religiously in a sociological sense, but also that each group literally possessed and advocated an actual religion. I was often witnessing in the making of government policy a new form of holy war. Any full understanding of Interior Department policy making would necessarily involve the study of the religious claims that commonly underlie the beliefs of the key actors. The most important of these systems of religious truth, one or the other informing the thinking of most leading policy makers at the Interior Department, were economic religion and environmental religion. Outside groups were similarly divided, helping to explain the intensity of the policy disagreements.

---

* After joining the Interior Department in 1975, I remained in the Office of Policy Analysis for eighteen years, eventually working for seven Secretaries of the Interior, ranging from Tom Kleppe in the Ford administration to Bruce Babbitt in the Clinton administration. (The most colorful was James Watt in the Reagan administration; perhaps the most practically effective was Cecil Andrus in the Carter administration.) I left in 1993 to join the School of Public Policy at the University of Maryland. See Robert H. Nelson, "The Office of Policy Analysis in the Interior Department," *Journal of Policy Analysis and Management* 8 (Summer 1989).

As Daniel Fiorino (a working political scientist for many years at the highest levels of the Environmental Protection Agency) has similarly observed, environmental policy making in the United States has a "long history of adversarial relationships and distrust" among the participants, resulting in frequent stalemate and tending toward outright administrative and policy dysfunction at times.[18] Law professor Richard Lazarus comments that in many cases "the choice between one environmental standard and another poses no less than a choice between competing moral absolutes," partly reflecting the tendency of participants in environmental debates to perceive "policy disputes as always presenting starkly contrasting images of good versus evil."[19] Achieving religious compromises is a more difficult problem than the more traditional task in American government of reaching compromises among contending private interests.

For many years after I arrived at the Interior Department, I felt unprepared to write about such issues. I had been brought up in a largely secular home environment and had almost no previous training in philosophy or theology.[20] By the mid-1980s, however, my curiosity was getting the better of me. A more carefully developed analysis also offered a way of working out my own thinking. After several years of intermittent efforts, a book on economic religion finally emerged in 1991, *Reaching for Heaven on Earth: The Theological Meaning of Economics*. With respect to environmental religion, I first publicly examined its tenets in a 1990 article, "Unoriginal Sin: The Judeo-Christian Roots of Ecotheology."[21] Many other writings on economic and environmental religion followed over the next decade and a half, including *Economics as Religion*, a 2001 sequel to my 1991 book.[22] Although I have written many articles on the subject, the present book is my first to include an extended theological analysis of environmental religion.[23]

The Plan of the Book

The majority of the chapters below are updated and adapted (sometimes with very substantial revisions) from previous writings of mine (which are credited in the endnotes), leaving four chapters, dealing mainly with environmental religion, that are brand-new. The introduction describes how economics and environmentalism are modern secular religions, the latter having emerged in part as a reaction against the excesses of the former. Part I focuses on the basic tenets of economic religion, highlighting its areas of disagreement with environmental religion. For those readers who may already be familiar with my previous books on economic religion, the central theme will not be new. Some readers may therefore want to skim over Part I. Many of the illustrative details and the manner of development of the argument, however, have been updated.

Part II turns to environmental religion, finding that in the United States its sources are predominantly found in American Protestant Christianity—offering a new "Calvinism minus God." In fact, the environmental movement has increasingly adopted the language of protecting "the creation." Part III shows that this "environmental creationism" is more than simply a powerful metaphor. Environmentalists experience a sense of religious reverence and awe in the presence of nature "untouched by human hand," which is a modern equivalent of devout Christians in previous centuries encountering the "Book of Nature" as written by God at the creation.

In contrast to environmentalism and its Protestant roots, economic religion—especially in its claims to a scientific status, its methodology, and its institutional structure—owes more to the heritage of the Roman Catholic Church.[24] But there have been a few leading economists, as Part IV examines, who had a more typically Calvinist understanding of the economic world. A possible synthesis of such "economic Calvinism" with "environmental Calvinism" may offer important clues to the future development of public religion in the twenty-first century. Despite the great optimism at the beginning of the twentieth century, its subsequent history raised again the question of the real origins and sources of human depravity. Calvinism may have especially important things to say on this subject.

Both economic and environmental religion can learn from a greater recognition and study of their Christian religious origins. American environmentalism in particular might be described as a "populist" faith; it has been more successful in attracting followers and influencing U.S. government policy than in the formulation of a logically developed body of thought—that is, a coherent theology. It is time for environmentalism to enter into a more "mature" stage of its development, both as a matter of achieving greater intellectual integrity and in its understanding of the requirements for improving environmental policy in the real world.[25]

Traditional Jewish and Christian religions may also benefit from a greater dialogue with the secular economic and environmental gospels. Economic and environmental religion both arose in part from a perceived inability of the older faiths to answer basic religious questions for the modern era in a manner that would be consistent with a rigorous scientific understanding of the world. Therefore, in the public arena at least, the most vital parts of theology moved outside the institutional Christian churches.

In this book, I thus propose to develop, compare, and contrast the systems of thought of economics and of environmentalism as an exercise in theological analysis. For many people this may be their first exposure to such an undertaking in "secular theology" (the study of secular systems of thought in an explicitly theological way).[26] As other students of secular religion have also found, this inquiry reveals that both economic and environmental religion have deep roots in Western civilization. Indeed, economic and environmental religion, like most of the secular religions of the modern age, to a significant extent rework in a new language the earlier messages of Jewish and Christian faiths. In many cases the greatest change is not the core religious truths being developed but rather the recasting of these traditional Jewish and Christian understandings in a new (ostensibly more modern and scientific) vocabulary—thus disguising the origins, lending them greater authority in an age that gives greater public legitimacy to scientific methods than the reading of the Christian Bible.

ACKNOWLEDGMENTS

TWO PEOPLE IN PARTICULAR played an important part in the writing of this book. The environmental philosopher Mark Sagoff occupies an office on the same floor as mine at the School of Public Policy of the University of Maryland. Since I arrived at the school in 1993, Mark and I have carried on a running discussion of many subjects addressed in the following pages. Mark made special efforts to expand my horizons beyond the education I originally received in the field of economics. Since the publication in 1991 of my book *Reaching for Heaven on Earth*, Max Stackhouse, one of the leading U.S. theologians, has offered much-appreciated encouragement for my efforts to examine economics from a religious perspective. Both Mark and Max read the full manuscript of the present book and provided extensive reactions and comments.

Herman Daly, a founding figure in the field of ecological economics, is another colleague of mine on the third floor of the Maryland School of Public Policy (who in fact occupies the office to my immediate left).[1] Since he arrived at the school in 1994, he and I have had many informative conversations concerning the limitations of economic analysis; the religious zeal expressed in the pursuit of economic growth; the necessity of a religious basis to justify many environmental values; and many other subjects. These conversations also played a valuable role in the development of my thinking, as reflected in parts of this book (not all of which Herman would necessarily agree with).

Long before I had written anything about economics as a religion in disguise, Deirdre McCloskey had pioneered such an approach—although her emphasis was more on seeing economics as a disguised metaphysics rather than religion per se.[2] Over the years, Deirdre has been exceedingly generous in her encouragement of my explorations of this topic. She also provided detailed comments on a draft manuscript of this book. I thank also Kathyrn Blanchard, Robert Geraci, Paul Oslington, and Larry Witham, who read and commented usefully on all or significant parts of the manuscript.

The Earhart Foundation provided valuable support for the planning and other early stages of development of this book. Large parts of the book were written during my 2006–7 sabbatical year from the University of Maryland. I thank the School of Public Policy for the generous assistance and encouragement offered for this and other writing efforts. During my sabbatical year, I was hosted for six months as a visiting professor at the Universidad Torcuato Di Tella in Buenos Aires, Argentina, and then for six months at the School of

Economics of the University of the Philippines in Manila. I had opportunities there to give seminars based in part on the book and enjoyed many conversations with fellow faculty on matters relating to economics and religion. I have also benefited from discussions with fellow scholars at the Mercatus Center of George Mason University, where I am an affiliated senior scholar.

This book is dedicated to James W. Michaels (1921–2007), whom I was privileged to know as a personal friend for almost thirty years. Jim was known to the rest of the world as the man who remade business journalism as the legendary editor of *Forbes* magazine from 1961 to 1999. He was a source of unfailing wisdom for me as well as many others around him. His courage in pursuing inconvenient truths in the pages of *Forbes* was inspiring to millions of readers. In the current financial crisis (I write in early 2009), many of us are wishing that he could be here to offer his counsel. This book, I hope, follows in the path of Jim's commitment to pursue the real story wherever it may take us.

Economics and environmentalism are types of modern religions. This observation is not as controversial as it might seem. Although few economists see a religious purpose to their professional activities, a number of outsiders have characterized their efforts in such terms. John Cobb, a leading Protestant theologian, writes that in the twentieth century "neoclassical economics became the theology of those who saw economic growth as the savior of humankind." Although economic religion "does not dominate the spirituality of all peoples, it is the 'religion' that governs planetary affairs," based on a righteous "devotion" to the "increase of economic production."[1] The environmental historian J. R. McNeill writes similarly that "communism aspired to become the universal creed of the twentieth century, but a more flexible and seductive religion succeeded where communism failed: the quest for economic growth. Capitalists, nationalists—indeed almost everyone . . . —worshipped at this same altar." Economic growth promised not only to deliver material comforts but also to solve all "social, moral, and ecological ills." The economists "who promised to deliver the holy grail became [the] high priests" of the United States and other societies around the world.[2]

Like the members of the economics profession, most leaders of American environmental organizations have sought to distance themselves from religion. Explicitly acknowledging the religious character of environmentalism would have posed a host of complicated, and potentially politically damaging, issues concerning the role of these organizations in the public arena (how to explain, for example, their strong support for the active proselytizing of an environmental "religion" in the public schools). Many individual environmental advocates, however, have been more forthcoming.[3] John Muir, the founder of the Sierra Club in 1892, preached that visitors should come to "holy Yosemite" to "worship with Nature."[4] In the 1990s, Steven Rockefeller and John Elder stated that "the global environmental crisis, which threatens not only the future of human civilization but all life on earth, is fundamentally a moral and religious problem."[5]

In assessing the character of contemporary environmentalism, the leading U.S. environmental historian, William Cronon, finds that it shares "certain common characteristics with the human belief systems and institutions that we typically label with the word *religion*." Indeed, the parallels were so striking, extending to so many features traditionally associated with religion, that Cronon in the end found literally the presence of a new gospel, following in the Jewish and Christian religious heritage of Western civilization:

> [Environmentalism] offers a complex series of moral imperatives for ethical action, and judges human conduct accordingly. The source of these imperatives may not appear quite so metaphysical as in other religious traditions, but it in fact derives from the whole of creation as the font not just of ethical direction but of spiritual insight. The revelation of seeing human life and the universe whole, in their full interconnected complexity, can evoke powerful passions and convictions ranging from the mystical to the missionary. Certain landscapes—usually the wildest and most natural ones—are celebrated as sacred, and the emotions they inspire are akin to those we associate with the godhead in other faith traditions. Much environmental writing is openly prophetic, offering predictions of future disaster as a platform for critiquing the moral failings of our lives in the present. Leave out the element of divine inspiration, and the rhetorical parallels to biblical prophecy in the Hebrew and Christian traditions are often quite striking. Maybe most important, environmentalism is unusual among political movements in offering practical moral guidance about virtually every aspect of daily life, so that followers are often drawn into a realm of mindfulness and meditative attentiveness that at least potentially touches every personal choice and action. Environmentalism, in short, grapples with ultimate questions at every scale of human existence, from the cosmic to the quotidian, from the apocalyptic to the mundane. More than most other human endeavors, this is precisely what religions aspire to do.[6]

To be sure, the environmental movement is large and diverse with many varieties of environmental religion—just as there are multiple understandings of Christianity (and of economic religion).[7] A few environmental groups have core beliefs that are in fact closer to economic religion than to the prevailing tenets of environmental religion.[8] Often labeled as a "moderate" environmental organization, Resources for the Future (RFF) in Washington, D.C., for example, is largely staffed by economists, who are frequently at odds with environmental true believers. Indeed, many of the RFF staff are economic true believers—followers in a religion of economic progress, now reworked to include much greater attention to environmental amenities in the overall economic calculus. As such, members of RFF, and some other environmentalists, might say that economic religion should not be abandoned, but rather revised and reworked to reflect new environmental concerns and ecological understandings.[9]

There are also branches of environmentalism that may not involve any significant religious elements at all.[10] A desire simply to reduce levels of air and water pollution, to curtail exposure to toxic substances, and in these and other ways to reduce cancer rates and otherwise improve the health of the American people is not a religious belief in and of itself. The distinctive feature of the contemporary environmental movement, however, is not its goal of improving public health but rather its rethinking of the basic relationship between human beings and nature—a central topic of religion for thousands of years.*

Economic Versus Environmental Religion

Although there are thus some exceptions, the mainstream of American environmentalism is significantly defined by its opposition to economic religion, and is thus part of a wider reaction against what many now see as the excesses of modern optimism.† One hundred years ago in the Progressive Era, the most powerful new religious force in American life was the economic "gospel of efficiency."[11] An American historian, Samuel Haber, wrote that the Progressive Era was characterized by an "efficiency craze" that represented "a secular Great Awakening."[12] A leading political scientist, Dwight Waldo, commented that "it is yet amazing what a position of dominance 'efficiency' assumed, how it waxed until it had assimilated or over-shadowed other values, how men and events came to be degraded or exalted according to what was assumed to be its dictate."[13]

---

*Concern to improve the health of Americans, moreover, is much older than the environmental movement that emerged in the 1960s. Indeed, the public health movement achieved its greatest successes in the United States in the nineteenth century, cleaning up rivers and other water supplies, for example, that had previously often spread cholera and other fatal diseases to thousands. See Richard N. L. Andrews, *Managing the Environment, Managing Ourselves: A History of American Environmental Policy* (New Haven: Yale University Press, 1999), chap. 7.

†The members of the economics profession, it might be said, do not quite reciprocate the strong feelings—they are an older and more jaded group. Some of the leading critics of the environmental movement, nevertheless, have been economists. See, for example, Julian L. Simon, *The Ultimate Resource* (Princeton: Princeton University Press, 1981); and Wilfred Beckerman, *A Poverty of Reason: Sustainable Development and Economic Growth* (Oakland: Independent Institute, 2002).

In the American Progressive Era, "efficient" and "inefficient" came to replace for many modern men and women the older Christian categories of "good" and "evil." Efficiency was so important because it was the operative measure of economic progress, and, as J. B. Bury would write in 1932, the idea of progress "belongs to the same order of ideas as Providence or personal immortality."[14] Actions that were efficient or inefficient served to advance or impede the arrival of a new heaven on earth, much as good or evil actions in an earlier time had been said to move Christians closer to or further from God.

Economic religion preaches that sin in the world has material causes—the severe poverty and deprivation in which the great majority of people lived for most of human history.[15] In the theology of economic religion, if it came down to a choice between lying and stealing, or letting your children starve, most people throughout history would have chosen to lie and steal. Nations have gone to war with one another for economic reasons, fighting for control of scarce resources. In short, the economic faith assumes that the true causes of sinful behavior in the world are ultimately material. By contrast, the biblical story of Adam and Eve and the fall of man in the Garden of Eden is just another ancient myth that preceded the modern era of scientific enlightenment.

If the economic assumption is valid—if past evils in the world arose from a human condition of dire poverty and material desperation—it creates a whole new prospect for humankind. Human beings by their own efforts may now be able to save themselves and the world. In the modern age, as economic religion preaches, scientific and economic progress have advanced to the point that they create the possibility of abolishing material scarcity. If scarcity can be eliminated, the true cause of sin in the world will be eliminated as well, thereby opening the way to a whole new earthly circumstance.

In the Marxist branch of this economic religion, for example, the arrival of total abundance and the end of material struggle would yield a "new man." Human beings would no longer be fundamentally "alienated" from themselves and their surroundings—the Marxist way of saying that they would no longer be fundamentally corrupted by original sin. A distinguished theologian wrote in 1956 that "Marxism was in a real sense a Judeo-Christian heresy" whose appeal lay in "its affirmation of certain prophetic emphases of the biblical tradition."[16] In an age when scientific knowledge was undermining traditional Christian religion for many people, large numbers turned to the "scientific laws of history" as a barely disguised substitute for the traditional Christian God. The contemporary philosopher Alasdair MacIntyre declares that "Marxism shares in good measure both the content and the functions of Christianity as an interpretation of human existence, and it does so because it is the historical successor of Christianity"—or at least so it appeared for much of the twentieth century.[17] Although the specific theologies are very different,

Marxism and environmentalism have at least one important element in common: they both owe a large debt to Christian sources.

In the United States, rather than Marx it was John Maynard Keynes who held out the greatest hope of heaven on earth, once declaring that continuing rapid economic growth—based in part on the application of Keynesian economic methods—would soon "lead us out of the tunnel of economic necessity into daylight." In the new world of the future, perhaps not even one hundred years away, Keynes prophesied in 1930 that we shall finally be "free, at last, to discard" the uninhibited pursuit of self-interest, the obsessive accumulation of capital, and other "distasteful and unjust" features of our present-day economic system.[18] Because the path of salvation would be economic, the followers of Keynes in the American economics profession soon become the leading priesthood, the moral guides and guardians, of American society.[19] Economists would possess the technical expertise to guide society along a path of economic progress, and thus of earthly perfection.

Even when specific details of the Keynesian economic prescriptions would later be challenged in the 1970s, new economists with new theories stepped forward to fill the priestly role. Indeed, progressive beliefs that saw economic growth and development as the path to earthly salvation were widely shared across much of the world in the late nineteenth century and throughout the twentieth century. Economists were the leading theologians of the times.

The Dam and the Wilderness

As I have said, the American progressive movement sought to advance the goals of a powerful secular religion of economic progress. It was based on the new power of human beings to control nature, as this power had been created by modern science and economics. Progressive religion also had its artwork and cathedrals that served to provide religious inspiration. Many Americans made pilgrimages to places such as Hoover Dam on the Colorado River or Grand Coulee Dam on the Columbia River. Such modern pilgrims experienced a sense of awe and reverence in seeing the dramatic evidence before them of the newfound power of human beings to bring wild nature under control for human benefit. With this power, as it appeared, humanity was no longer dependent on God to save the world, but rather could achieve this wondrous result through its own efforts.

It is easy to forget that the current era of human control over nature commenced only two hundred or so years ago with the rise of organized technological advance based on the systematic development and application of physics, chemistry, and other theoretical sciences. It was in the Progressive

Era—typically dated from 1890 to 1920—that American intellectuals first sought to come to terms with the full implications of these developments. If the initial response was a burst of optimism, today the reaction often is more pessimistic. Former executive director of the Sierra Club David Brower once declared that "I hate all dams, large and small."[20] Brower was not concerned that many dams were pork barrel projects that served narrow interest groups and could not pass a simple benefit-cost test. Rather, he hated dams for the very fact that they powerfully symbolized the new human power to control nature—the very opposite of the old progressive feeling of reverence in the presence of a dam. Involving the most threatening form of human mastery of nature, for many people the development of nuclear power now provokes even stronger negative symbolic associations.[21]

Although their language is less certain and less righteous, economists to-day are by and large still true believers in progressive religion. This goes far to explain the tensions often seen when economists and environmentalists come together: they are waging a new version of religious warfare (fortunately without bloodshed). The Roman Catholic theologian Robert Royal writes that "in the modern environmental debate, those who would permit use and those who advocate wilderness preservation have become virtual warring denomi-nations."[22] For many environmentalists such as Brower, a symbol of human control over nature filled them with disgust and regret. In recent years, more-over, the environmental antagonism toward dams has been winning. Congress is still fully as addicted to pork barrel in other areas of government spending, but it has largely stopped funding new dams. Indeed, a recent trend is to tear some of them down—as evidenced by the planned removal (as I write) of the Elwa River Dam in Olympic National Park in Washington State, for one.

Instead, "antiprogressive" symbols have become the leading religious objects in American life. In the theology of environmentalism, wilderness areas are the new "cathedrals."[23] Like a dam, a wilderness area makes a symbolic statement about the goal in human interaction with nature. In this case, however, rather than showing an aspiration to greater mastery of nature, the creation of a wil-derness area renounces such human powers. As defined by Congress in the Wil-derness Act of 1964, a wilderness area is a place "untrammeled by man" where any signs of a past human presence should be at a minimum. The protection of the Arctic National Wildlife Refuge (ANWR) in Alaska has been so vital to the environmental movement because it is said to be one of the last remaining places on earth still "untouched by man."

Economic religion for much of the twentieth century exalted human con-trol over nature; environmental religion today offers a precisely opposite view. The *Washington Post* editorialized in 2008 that the management goal for the surrounding state governments should be to "turn the dream of a pristine

Chesapeake Bay into a reality."[24] Innumerable similar illustrations could be offered from recent popular and professional literature—expressing a great hope that a true "natural" condition, reflecting a minimum of human influence, can be established and maintained across the world (or at least as much of the world as might be practically feasible).

A Double-Edged Sword

Why has this large shift in religious thinking taken place? One reason is that the products of science have proved less unambiguously beneficial than the true believers in economic progress once advertised. The development of modern chemicals, for example, was regarded initially as a wonderful scientific blessing; the use of DDT helped eradicate malaria in many parts of the world. In 1962's *Silent Spring*, however, Rachel Carson portrayed these chemicals in a new environmental light; the use of DDT and other toxic chemicals was poisoning some of the nation's most important bird wildlife.[25] More broadly, as the new environmental prophets began to preach in the 1960s, the modern spread of industry and commerce over the entire globe was wiping out vast areas of plant and animal habitat, posing for many species a threat even to their very existence on earth.

The powers of modern science and economics were proving to be a mixed blessing in many other areas as well. For progressive optimists, the Holocaust was perhaps the most troubling event of the twentieth century. There had been terrible bursts of anti-Semitism in Europe before, but they had never been married to modern economic efficiency. Contrary to the core tenets of economic theology, all this had occurred in Germany, one of the more economically advanced nations of the world. The atomic bomb and the control over nuclear energy raised a possibility—unimaginable until the mid-twentieth century—of the extinction of human beings from the earth by their own actions. As the twenty-first century opens, an exploding capacity for bio-engineering and other genetic manipulations may soon challenge traditional understandings of what it means to be a human being.[26] Rather than a new heaven on earth, in the worst case modern science and economics could even bring a new hell on earth.[27]

Even small groups of people—perhaps even lone individuals in the future—would hold the power to do great harm to a whole society. Both environmentalism and the war on terror involve an attempt to protect the world from potentially harmful products of modern technological "progress." The war on drugs has similar origins, and its supporters appeal to related public fears and anxieties. If environmentalism is concerned with chemicals in the external environment, the war on drugs is concerned with the internal environment of the human brain and body. Cocaine, heroin, LSD, amphetamines, and other mind-altering substances are all products of modern scientific discovery. They are also capable of changing nature, in this case human nature, creating an altered biological working of the brain.

Together, environmentalism, the war on terror, and the war on drugs are having a great cumulative impact on American life. Although they are sustained by much different coalitions, and their advocates are often critical of and politically opposed to one another, these outward differences mask a fundamental underlying similarity. Environmental threats, terrorist attacks, and mind-altering drugs are all products of modern technologies that are now seen to pose grave dangers. In the face of both the deep public fears that have been aroused in these areas and the extraordinary pace of technological change, these three leading moral crusades of our time seek to offer the hope of restoring—however improbably—the past certainties of a true "natural" order in the world.

Environmentalism and Libertarianism

The likely consequences of the new human powers over nature cannot be separated from the political institutions that will oversee the use of these powers. Here again, the history of the twentieth century was discouraging for progressive true believers. In economic, environmental, and other areas of concern, there was a sharp loss of confidence in the capacity of governments to act "in the public interest"—or even to identify any set of generally accepted public goals within a large nation-state. Modern science and economics were increasingly making it possible for governments to put nature to use for human purposes, and yet these governments seemed unable to exercise such new, large powers over nature with appropriate care and responsibility.

This was all the more reason for environmentalists to doubt the gains from "the modern project." Interestingly enough, another group, seldom associated with environmentalism, reacted in a similar manner: libertarians were more concerned about the impact on human freedom of the newly powerful governments of the twentieth century than they were about impacts on the natural world.[28] Here again, the history of the twentieth century offered deep cause for concern. In the worst cases, heads of government such as Adolf Hitler and Joseph Stalin killed millions of their own citizens—their ability to do so magnified by modern scientific and economic "advance."

Economic religion might speak of marrying modern technology with modern industry for the salvation of all mankind. The reality was that control over the new instruments of scientific and economic power rested with ordinary politicians. Scientific and economic developments had greatly escalated the stakes with respect to the decision-making capabilities of governments. There seemingly had been little corresponding improvement, however, in governing skills.[29] Environmentalists feared for the future of the natural world, and even for the future of human existence on earth. Libertarians feared for the future of individual rights and human freedom.

Environmental Calvinism

The roots of modern libertarianism trace to the writings of John Locke and the struggles of the Puritans—the English branch of Calvinism—to maintain their religious freedoms. It is less widely recognized, but contemporary environmentalism also has Calvinist roots. The environmental movement is more than simply a reaction against the progressive gospel of efficiency. Its beliefs derive from Western religion well preceding the rise of the secular gospels in the modern age. The founders of the Massachusetts Bay Colony in the seventeenth century were also Puritans. Throughout American history, the Puritan influence in American life has been—and still is—extraordinarily great.[30] As the environmental historian Mark Stoll now observes, "The moral urgency that animates the environmental movement is also a direct legacy of Calvinism and Puritanism. . . . The activist wing of environmentalism traces its roots through the Puritans directly to God's holy self-appointed instruments, the committed Calvinists."[31]

In contemporary environmentalism, one learns again of human corruption by greed, of an excess of human pride, of a desire of humans to possess forms of knowledge that must be reserved for God alone, and of punishments that God will inflict on those sinners who have violated His commands. The source of temptation, to be sure, is no longer a snake in the Garden of Eden; it is modern science and economics, which have led human beings— encouraged by the various forms of economic religion—to believe that they can assume God-like powers on their own. Indeed, many modern men and women have ceased to believe in God at all, in effect substituting their own thoughts and actions for His commands.

In the beginning, as Christianity has long taught, God created the world according to a divine plan.* Modern human beings, however, are now acting

---

* Daniel Migliore, a professor of systematic theology at Princeton Theological Seminary, observes that "creation may be called 'necessary'—that is in the sense that God creates in total consistency with God's nature. Creation fittingly expresses the true character of God. . . . Creation is not an arbitrary act, something God just decided to do on a whim, as it were. On the contrary, God is true and faithful

to remake the natural order according to their own designs. Yet in the Christian tradition there can be no greater sin than to challenge the place of God. As the Oxford theologian Alister McGrath comments, "The fundamental element of original sin . . . is a desire to 'be like God' and to be set free from all the constraints of creatureliness"—to exhibit a "human self-centeredness, which causes people to develop a skewed relationship with each other, with God, and with the environment."[32] As foretold in the Bible, there will be a certain outcome when God is confronted with direct challenges to His authority—those usurpers will soon be punished severely.* Indeed, the punishments in the Old Testament generally take the form of environmental calamities very much like those that our contemporary environmental prophets foresee.[33]

In Deuteronomy, for example, we learn in chapters 28 and 29 of the wrath of God that will be inflicted on those who have defied His commands. As Moses tells his fellow Jews:

> If you won't listen to the Lord your God and won't obey these laws I am giving you today, then all these curses shall come upon you.
>
> He will send disease among you until you are destroyed from the face of the land you are about to enter and possess. He will send tuberculosis, fever, inflections, plague, and war. He will blight your crops, covering them with mildew. All these devastations shall pursue you until you perish.
>
> The heavens above you will be as unyielding as bronze, and the earth beneath will be as iron. The land will become as dry as dust for lack of rain, and dust storms shall destroy you.
>
> You will sow much but reap little, for the locusts will eat your crops. You will plant vineyards and care for them, but you won't eat the grapes or drink the wine, for worms will destroy the vines. Olive trees will be growing everywhere, but there won't be enough olive oil to anoint yourselves. For the trees will drop their fruit before it is matured.

---

to God's own nature in the act of creation." See Daniel L. Migliore, *Faith Seeking Understanding: An Introduction to Christian Theology* (Grand Rapids, Mich.: Eerdmans, 1991), 84.

*Migliore states that God is offended by "the sin of presumption, the violent effort to bring in God's Kingdom with or without God. In this spirit of presumption and violence, there is limitless confidence in ourselves and our goodness." On the essence of sin, Migliore observes that:

> we misunderstand the depth of sin if we see it only as a violation of a moral code; it is, instead, primarily the disruption of our relationship with God. . . . This disruption . . . that is the essence of sin appears in vastly different forms. . . . Sin may take the form of rejecting God's grace and absolutizing ourselves. Declaring our freedom to be infinite, we proclaim ourselves God. This is the sin of the prideful, titanic, egocentric self. . . . In our insecurity, we seek to be our own God [thus harmfully separating ourselves from God]. (Migliore, *Faith Seeking Understanding*, 134, 130–31)

All these curses shall pursue and overtake you until you are destroyed.

"Why has the Lord done this to his land?" the nations will ask. "Why was he so angry?"

And they will be told, "Because the people of the land broke the contract made with them by Jehovah, the God of their ancestors. . . . For they worshipped other gods, violating his express command."[34]

In our own time, environmentalism is in effect telling us, humankind has once again turned to worship other gods—above all, in the twentieth century, the god of economic progress. And, as environmentalists now warn, terrible punishments on a biblical scale surely lie in store. With the rise of modern industry, for example, and the resulting great increase of carbon dioxide and other greenhouse emissions into the atmosphere, human actions have been literally changing the climate of the earth. But this domain must be reserved to God, and therefore global catastrophes on a worldwide scale loom. Following the rise of the earth's temperatures, the oceans will rise and flood the land; new famines will threaten the world; severe hurricanes and other terrible weather events will increase in frequency; and malaria and other pestilences will spread and worsen.* As one might say, climate change is the new book of Deuteronomy, the biblical passage above now rewritten with the vocabulary of greenhouse gases and global warming.

Robert Mendelson is a well-regarded American economist and professor at Yale University. According to his analysis, as presented in a host of books and articles, higher average temperatures in Canada and Siberia might actually open up large new areas for both human settlement and more productive agriculture. In the United States, since air conditioning became available a half century ago, many people have been moving to the South in search of warmer weather. If the climate of the earth warmed somewhat, they might be able to enjoy milder winters without having to move as far, or perhaps at all. Indeed, taking the full range of impacts of global warming into account, and the many opportunities for human adaptation and substitution, Mendelson has estimated that the residents of the United States, northern Europe, Russia, China, and Japan—essentially the entire temperate zone of the Northern Hemisphere—might well see their welfare little affected by a moderate degree of warming of the climate of the earth, and for many there might in fact be a benefit.[35]

---

*In 1992, former U.S. vice president Al Gore thus warned that "artificial global warming" was looming and "threatens to destroy the climate equilibrium we have known for the entire history of human civilization. As the climate pattern begins to change, so too do the movements of the wind and rain, the floods and droughts, the grasslands and deserts, the insects and weeds, the feasts and famines, the seasons of peace and war"—all such changes threatening the human future on earth. See Al Gore, *Earth in the Balance* (Boston: Houghton Mifflin, 1992), 98.

Mendelson is speaking in the voice of economic religion, for which events in the world are measured by their direct impacts on human welfare. Such arguments, however, have had almost no influence on the thinking of contemporary environmentalism. Mendelson's writings have been ignored, if not spurned outright, by the environmental movement. In environmental religion, global warming is a sin against God, not an issue to be resolved by economic calculations of possible future benefits and costs to human beings. The Endangered Species Act—a modern Noah's Ark, as some have called it—directs the federal government to spare no costs in seeking to ensure the survival of every plant and animal species.[36] It is a new and secular way of saying that, in obeying a command of God, ordinary, crass political and economic calculations can have no place—any more than Noah could have decided to exclude some species from his ark because he perhaps found himself short on space.

Surface mining of coal alters the shape of tall mountains, dams divert the course of great rivers, greenhouse gases change the chemical composition of the earth's atmosphere, and toxic chemicals contaminate the soil. Such God-like acts would have been impossible until very recently in human history. For the past two hundred years, however, human beings have increasingly been able to remake the natural world by their own actions. From the perspective of environmental religion, they are overstepping their proper bounds, and God will surely be offended. Indeed, the wrath of God will soon be upon us, and, as the Bible says, it will frequently take the form of an environmental disaster.

In the modern age, science displaced religion as an ultimate source of authority for many people.[37] Yet religious yearnings seemingly diminished little if at all. The result has been the translation of biblical messages into "scientific" messages. The language of mathematics replaced Hebrew and Latin. Old-fashioned religion today masquerades as science—the modern rise of secular religions can be regarded as only in a limited respect a truly "secular" phenomenon.[38]

Environmental Creationism

According to the Puritans and other Calvinists, there were two "books" that provided a correct knowledge of God and his ways. The most important was the Bible, but there was also the "Book of Nature." Puritans encouraged the study of the natural world as a religious exercise.* When Henry David

---

* Abraham Kuyper—a leading Dutch Calvinist of the late nineteenth century—commented that historically in Calvinism "cosmical life [in nature] has regained its worth not at the expense of things

Thoreau in 1845 moved to Walden Pond, he was following a path already well blazed by his Puritan predecessors in New England.[39]

Until the nineteenth century, it was generally believed that the earth was still found as it had originally been created—an event of only about six thousand years ago. There was no thought that the earth might be four billion years old, or that it had been transformed by vast geological upheavals and the biological evolution of dinosaurs and many thousands of other plant and animal species, most of which had long ago become extinct. A good Christian thus believed that in visiting nature he or she was encountering "the creation" in its original character. God was not actually in nature—that would be the heresy of pantheism—but God had created the natural world as an expression of his true thinking and essence. God was like the painter of a picture that, amazingly enough, could now still be seen here on earth. One could thus discover in nature literally a product of God's own handiwork in the first six days.[40] For the Christian faithful it would be hard to imagine a more inspirational thought.

John Muir was in his early twenties when Charles Darwin's *On the Origin of Species* was published in 1859 yet seemingly was little influenced by the Darwinist ways of thinking that were spreading with a revolutionary force in the second half of the nineteenth century. Thus for Muir, the present rocks, plants, and other features of the natural world were "the terrestrial manifestations of God." In visiting wild nature, it was possible to find a "window opening into heaven, a mirror reflecting the Creator." Of the Sierra wilderness, Muir declared that "everything in it seems equally divine—one smooth, pure, wild glow of Heaven's love." The trees in nature were "psalm-singing"; the primeval forests were "temples"—and for an age increasingly skeptical of biblical revelations, these phenomenon were perhaps the leading means by which God still communicated with the faithful.[41] As historian Roderick Nash comments, it therefore "followed that wild nature provided the best 'conductor of divinity' because it was least associated with man's artificial constructs." Going to a wild area for Muir revealed the "fundamental truths of existence" in God's given universe.[42]

---

eternal, but by virtue of its capacity as God's handiwork and as a revelation of God's handiwork and as a revelation of God's attributes." For John Calvin, as Kuyper writes:

> instead of simply treating Nature as an accessorial item as so many Theologians were inclined to do, [Calvin] was accustomed to compare the Scriptures to a pair of spectacles, enabling us to decipher again the divine thoughts, written by God's hand in the book of Nature. . . . Thus vanished every dread possibility that he who occupied himself with nature was wasting his capacities in pursuit of vain and idle things. It was perceived, on the contrary, that for God's sake, our attention may not be withdrawn from the life of nature and creation. (Abraham Kuyper, *Lectures on Calvinism* [Lafayette, Ind.: Sovereign Grace Publishers, 2001], 72, 73; these lectures were originally delivered at Princeton Theological Seminary in 1898)

In environmental religion today, although the explicit references to "God" are many fewer, nature is still seen much in this way. The contemporary environmental philosopher Holmes Rolston—a winner of the Templeton Prize in religion—declares that "with [its wild] forests, America is even more of a promised land than is Palestine. . . . Such forests are a church."[43] Environmental writings are filled with statements of the urgent need to protect "the creation." While he was secretary of the interior, Bruce Babbitt explained in 1996 to his fellow Americans that "all the plants and animals in the natural world are together a direct reflector of divinity, that creation is a plan of God."[44] Then, since "God put them there," there was a moral imperative for human beings that "we ought not to recklessly destroy the patterns of creation."[45]

In such thinking, wilderness and other "untouched" areas are among the last remaining places where God's original artwork still remains visible. If we were to destroy all the remaining wild areas of the earth, we would in effect be defacing the places where God has revealed Himself most visibly to the world. It would be almost like a giant fire in which all the Bibles of the world were being burned; only the devil could hope for such a result. In seeking the economic development of the wilderness, often following the tenets of economic religion, modern men and women are thus—from the perspective of environmental religion—committing a terrible sin against God. In the pursuit of economic growth and development, they would even go so far as to erase some of the main remaining evidences of God's own plans for the world.

Two Understandings of Nature

Environmental creationism has great religious appeal, yet this correspondence subjects the environmental movement to the charge of exhibiting a basic theological confusion. Perhaps the greatest source of difficulty for environmental theology—which carries over to environmental policy making as well—involves the idea of "nature." Environmentalists often speak of the "nature" of God's original creation, as depicted in the Bible. But environmentalists also often speak of another nature, in which there is a constant struggle among plant and animal species for survival. In this Darwinian world, there is unremitting conflict, with different species often killing one another; on the whole, it is a cruel and heartless place.

Environmental religion generally offers the more romantic vision of nature, the wonderful happy harmony of "the creation" at the beginning, as an appropriate benchmark for the setting of public policy. Environmental policy making now often seeks to accomplish the virtual restoration of the Garden of Eden on earth.* Yet modern biological science tells us that the Darwinian vision of an unremitting, harsh struggle for survival is a more valid depiction of the natural world. In this outlook, the recent human development of modern scientific and economic powers to control nature represents the ultimate Darwinian triumph of the human species. Why is it not an extraordinarily happy event to be celebrated that human beings have emerged as the greatest victors ever in the evolutionary struggle (exceeding even the dinosaurs in their dominance of the earth's landscapes)? Why should this great Darwinian triumph of our own species be lamented, as environmentalism is wont to do?

This raises a related question: which nature is environmentalism speaking about? Environmental religion and the corresponding environmental ethics are drawn from one understanding of nature: the world of a happy harmony that represents the artwork of God at the creation. The biological and ecological sciences, however, describe a much different natural world. Although many environmentalists simply seek to have it both ways, compartmentalizing their scientific and religious lives, this is not an intellectually—or theologically—workable solution. Other environmentalists seek to escape the dilemma by arguing that protecting "the creation" is also an evolutionary requirement for future human survival. But this is too clever by far. It is most unlikely that the number of wilderness areas set aside for protection from human impacts since the 1960s will have much—if any—effect on the Darwinian prospects for survival of the human species. Environmentalists may argue that maintaining the gene pool of wild plant and animal species will have a high future practical value to society. But the rapidly growing human ability to play God in genetic domains makes this ever less likely. Those species of greatest value to human beings have already been domesticated; there is no danger of their extinction. Indeed, even if a benefit-cost test came out decisively against the protection of an individual species, few environmentalists would be prepared to accept this economic verdict.

Implicitly, environmentalism thus rejects Darwin and embraces a morality outside the strictly scientific realm. But most environmentalists—wanting to maintain their scientific credentials—are unwilling to say so. As this book

---

* As the environmental philosopher Mark Sagoff has observed, "Ecology in large part has become the science of Eden." If outwardly proclaiming a strict scientific status, there is an underlying ecological belief that "Nature has ecological integrity and design because it is directed by an independent Force"—that is to say, by God. In the present day, "it is our ecologists and philosophers who now impute overarching order, purpose, or design to the natural world." The contemporary science of ecology offers new metaphors by which environmental religion speaks to modern men and women who otherwise have rejected traditional religion in its older Jewish and Christian forms. See Mark Sagoff, "Ecosystem Design in Historical and Philosophical Context," in *Ecological Integrity: Integrating Environment, Conservation, and Health*, ed. David Pimentel, Laura Westra, and Reed F. Noss (Washington, D.C.: Island Press, 2000), 74–75.

will argue, if they did, it would come close to professing a belief in God's commands as the basis for current environmental policies. Because that is not acceptable to many current environmentalists, many of whom question or deny outright the existence of God, the actual ethical grounds for environmental policies must remain hidden. Theological confusion for many people is preferable to a loss of faith altogether.

The "Lurking Inconsistency"

In an article in the journal *Conservation Biology*, University of Maryland economist Herman Daly, a founder of the field of ecological economics, described such tensions within environmental religion. He noted that many working conservation biologists and other leaders in the field of ecology believe, on the one hand, that virtually everything important in the world is the product of a Darwinist outcome of "random mutation and natural selection." On the other hand, they also put great energies into fighting in the public arena for government "policies to save this or that species." But why? In a strictly Darwinist world, as Daly says, any ethical goal (including saving a species) is itself no more than an "'epiphenomenon'—an illusion which itself was selected for because of the reproductive advantage that it chanced to confer on those under its influence." Logically enough in Darwinist terms, "most leading biologists claim not to believe in purpose (in the sense of either cosmic telos or mere individual preferences that are causative in the physical world)."[46]

Yet, if there is no "purpose," Daly asks, what is the need to make valiant efforts to preserve species—and to take all the other heroic measures to protect nature sought by the environmental movement, often at large costs to society. Without purpose, these environmental goals would make little if any sense at all. Yet environmentalists who claim that the lens of Darwin and biology informs their understanding of the world are also fierce partisans for such causes. This is the "lurking inconsistency" that, Daly writes, renders the thinking of much of contemporary environmental religion theologically incoherent.

Of course, as noted above, environmentalism has a great deal of company. It has been characteristic of the entire modern age—from nineteenth-century Marxism to deep ecology today—that powerful religious beliefs, in most cases derived from Jewish and Christian sources, have been translated into a new positivist language of science. As Daly notes in his article, the British philosopher Alfred North Whitehead was critical of this modern "radical inconsistency" as long ago as 1925. As Whitehead put it, "A scientific realism, based on mechanism, is conjoined with an unwavering belief in the world of men and of the higher animals as being composed of self-determining organisms" and whose actions are actually directed to the realization of "final causes." But the scientific materialism that underlies modern thinking offers no justification for such "final causes"—or for the actions of noble men and women who sometimes have even been willing to die for their causes. The result, Whitehead concluded, and Daly finds matters little changed today, was an "absolute contradiction" that underlay much of modern thinking.[47]

When Daly says that there must be a "purpose" in the world to justify saving plant and animal species, he does not mean that a saved species must be useful for finding new pharmaceutical drugs or some other such practical goal. It is not a utilitarian matter of determining that species preservation is dictated by the maximization of some economic or other "objective function" (reflecting some given social "purpose"), subject to a set of constraints. Indeed, it is not that environmental actions must serve any practical purpose of advancing the interests of the human species itself. When Daly says a "purpose" is required, he really means a source of religious authority and legitimacy that transcends the daily experiences of human beings. In Western civilization that has generally meant a Christian (or Jewish) God. Thus, Daly's required "purpose" is really God's purpose; like so many others involved in economic and environmental debates, however, he does not say so explicitly. Perhaps this is because it would have put him beyond the pale with many of the fellow biologists and ecologists he hopes to influence (and *Conservation Biology* might not have published his article with too much explicit "God talk" in it).

Conclusion

As this book will argue, contemporary environmental religion can be seen not only as a secular extension of Jewish and Christian religion but also, more specifically, as an offshoot of Protestantism and especially Calvinism.[48] The Calvinist elements go far to explain the attraction of environmentalism for so many Americans. Based on an ostensibly "scientific" body of thought, environmentalism has reasserted the powerful U.S. Puritan heritage in a form free of the historical baggage of institutional Christianity. As historical Puritanism waned, its main religious convictions proved more resilient in American life. But the new Calvinists were determined to distance themselves from the old wars among competing denominations, the petty squabbles, and the many other historical failings of institutional Christian religion; they found a means to do so in the new secular religion of environmentalism.

PART I

THE FALSE GOD OF ECONOMIC SALVATION

INTRODUCTION

A contemporary economist and former staff member at the Council of Economic Advisers in the White House, Ray Squitieri, finds that the Council's members and many other economists in the federal government today play a role that is "Scholastic" in character, following in the tradition of Thomas Aquinas and other Scholastic theologians of the Roman Catholic Church. Grounded in concepts of natural law, as Squiteri explores the parallels, the Catholic Scholastic tradition seeks to apply "logical rules that rational men could all agree on." It prescribes "certain formal methods of inquiry," and the adherents of these methods seek to "present and debate our results with others who are bound by the same methods." In this way, the hope is to provide "an orderly, logical and systematic way to understand the world," based on the application of rational methods of analysis. In these and other respects, as Squiteri declares, current "economists are [the] scholastics" of our time.[1]

Emerging in Germany in the early sixteenth century, the Protestant Reformation was much more skeptical of the rational methods of Scholastic theology.* Today, again in Germany, a platform adopted by the Green Party states that "the prevailing economic rationality must be replaced by a policy guided by long-term and ecological goals. We must stop the violation of nature" in

---

* This is not to say that there was no scholastic tradition in Protestantism. Calvinism carried on much of this scholasticism (among English and French "puritans," for example), but typically did so by creating complex structures of thought to interpret individual Bible texts. Nevertheless, they relied mainly on the original "sources," namely the Bible texts, and sought to explicate their literal meaning, rather than looking to apply the logic of Aristotle's physics or to develop traditional Catholic natural law teachings.

the name of rationally guided economic progress.[2] In language as harsh as that used by Martin Luther, American environmental philosopher Bryan Norton finds that there are good reasons why "environmentalists hate mainstream economists." One of the main sins of economists is that their standard methods of rational analysis assume a "static character" of the world, one that accepts tastes ("preferences") as given, thus standing in the way of the necessary environmental conversion of American society. In the name of science, economists assert a value-neutrality that accepts "all demands as equally valid" when the survival of the natural world depends on making strong value judgments that will lead to "reducing demands" for many less worthy goods and services.[3]

In *Deep Ecology*, a leading 1980s manifesto of environmental religion, Bill Devall and George Sessions complain that professional economists are possessed by a "secular religion of faith and hope—a faith in never-ending technological progress" as the salvation of the world. In their blindness, professional economists see nature as "primarily a storehouse . . . for humans. The intrinsic value of Nature, or the spirit of a place, has no sanction." When "resource economists look at wilderness," the filters imposed by their lifelong professional norms are so powerful that they are incapable of truly "seeing it."[4] Luther also saw the rationalism of Scholastic theology as a barrier to "seeing it" religiously—to fully experiencing God's love powerfully, personally, and without any church intermediaries. For Luther, personal salvation did not depend on any arid processes of Scholastic reasoning, but rather was "by faith alone." Like the Protestant Reformation in the sixteenth century, the environmental movement is today again protesting against and seeking its own "reformation" of the most powerful (and "catholic") world religion of our time, economic religion.

Indeed, in the public life of the United States and Europe, environmentalism has emerged as the leading voice in attacking the technological optimism and modern faith in economic growth and development as the path of world salvation. For many environmentalists, it is the false doctrines of economic religion that have justified the many terrible assaults against the natural world of modern times. For much of the twentieth century, the great public debates concerned the merits of alternative forms of economic religion—capitalism versus socialism, Marxism versus Keynesianism, social Darwinism versus the progressive gospel of efficiency, and so forth. From the viewpoint of environmental religion, however, they are all false gospels. In the United States and the former Soviet Union alike, the environment was severely abused in the name of economic progress (although the communist nations were the worst offenders).[5]

Few present-day economists have thought much about the religious side of their profession, and fewer still are inclined to join a theological debate.

They are content to leave questions of the foundational beliefs and values of economics to philosophers and theologians. A few economists, however, have themselves acknowledged that a literal theology underlies the efforts of economists and that it is necessary to explore its tenets. Paul Oslington is an Australian economist who has published well-regarded professional articles in the field of international trade. In a side of his career less familiar to his fellow economists, Oslington argues for "a theological economics" that should be developed explicitly as such. This is partly because of the "existence of theological structures within economic theory" that should be better understood, criticized, and, as necessary, reconsidered. As Oslington writes, "If there is economic analysis implicit in theology, as well as the theological in economic theory, this strengthens the case for fruitful links between theology and economics, and the admissibility of economic arguments in theology and theological arguments in economics."[6]

Economic religion and environmental religion are relative newcomers to the long history of religion. Yet, to a significant extent, economic and environmental religions are secularizations (if, for many orthodox Christians, heretical ones) of core messages of Christianity. As a secular religion, the novel element of environmentalism today is its negative verdict on the consequences of the modern worship of economic progress. Here again, as in so many other respects, its message can be seen as a new Christianity without the historical institutional settings and language of Christianity. In 1986, cardinal Joseph Ratzinger (now Pope Benedict XVI) declared that Christianity must be vigilantly "opposed to the false worship of progress, the worship of changes that crush humankind, and the calumny against the human species that destroys the earth and creation." In place of Notre Dame, Chartres, and other inspirational sites of Catholic worship, the economic heresies of the modern age proposed that "the cathedral of the future will be the [scientific] laboratory, and the Basilicas of San Marco of the new age will be electrical plants," such as the massive dams on many great rivers of the world, symbols of the overriding goal to "transform nature itself" for human purposes alone.[7] Few environmentalists would find much here with which to disagree.

Part I explores the tenets of economic theology, in opposition to which environmental theology significantly defines itself. Chapter 1 briefly reviews the underlying theological logic of economic religion and its large influence on government policy and administration over the course of the twentieth century. Chapter 2 illustrates these core tenets of economic religion by exploring recent efforts to understand the rise of Islamic terrorism, contrasting the economic understanding with a biblical understanding grounded in original sin. Some economists have proposed new methods of analysis that could incorporate environmental values within the framework of economics, making use of the concept of "existence value." Chapter 3 shows how this project to extend the domain of economic rationality to encompass environmental religion has been theologically confused and practically unsuccessful.

Chapter 4 examines how, in response to the perceived failures of mainstream economics, environmental economists have attempted to replace traditional economic judgments based on "efficiency" with new ethical standards of "sustainability"—and the large difficulties that they encountered. Finally, chapter 5 shows how the all-out pursuit of economic progress in the twentieth century all too often ignored various types of social and environmental consequences, resulting in wide abuses in the name of religion.

1

WHAT IS "ECONOMIC THEOLOGY"?

FOR MANY PEOPLE, "economic theology" may seem an oxymoron—that economics is the science of the mundane, whereas theology is the study of the transcendent. It might seem that two areas of inquiry could not be more distinct. Yet surprisingly many writers have found a large theological dimension in economics. Critics of the contemporary economics profession—many of them in the environmental movement—often say that it is "theological." Among a large number of examples that could be offered, Sallie McFague states that the world needs to turn away from "the theology implied by the neoclassical model of economics. . . . [which] assumes that God . . . controls the world through laws of nature. This God is like a good [economic] mechanic."[1]

Admittedly, few current economists think of their profession as connected to religion.* That does not mean, however, that theology has been altogether absent from their professional efforts. When William Baumol—a former professor at Princeton University and a prominent American economist—was asked a while ago to recall why he had entered the economics profession, his response was that "I believe deeply with Shaw, that there are few crimes more heinous than poverty. Shaw as usual, exaggerated when he told us that money is the root of all evil, but he did not exaggerate by much."[2]

---

* One exception was Paul Heyne, who taught in the economics department of the University of Washington for many years and was the author of *The Economic Way of Thinking*, an introductory economics textbook that appeared in nine editions (and has now reached its eleventh edition with new coauthors following Heyne's death in 2000). Almost uniquely among contemporary economists held in high regard by the economics profession, he held postgraduate degrees in theology. Heyne was also unusual among economists in his stated view that "any economics which purports to be relevant to policy-making contains a hidden (and not even well-hidden) theology." See Paul Heyne, "Reply" (to Martin E. Marty), in *Religion, Economics, and Social Thought: Proceedings of an International Symposium*, ed. Walter Block and Irving Hexham (Vancouver: Fraser Institute, 1986), 161.

In the Bible, of course, original sin in the Garden of Eden is the "root of all evil." In Baumol's alternative economic explanation, characteristic not only of George Bernard Shaw but also many other people over the course of the twentieth century, there is a new explanation for the presence of sin in the world: material deprivation—the dire poverty in which human beings have lived for almost all human history—has oppressed people, driving them to lie, cheat, steal, and commit other sinful acts. If poverty is the actual explanation for evil in the world, the economic success of the modern age has created a radical new possibility for human beings. If poverty—indeed, all material shortages—can be eliminated, the biblical God will no longer be needed; economic progress will lead us to a new heaven on earth.*

At the annual meetings of the American Economic Association, the Richard T. Ely Lecture is one of the most prestigious platforms in economics. Ely is remembered today as the leading early American economist who in 1885 co-founded the American Economic Association. Few current economists know much of this history, but twenty of the fifty founding members of the Association were former or practicing ministers. Ely was himself a leading member in the 1880s of the social gospel movement, better known at that time to the American public in this capacity than as an economist. In those early years, Ely argued that economics departments should be located in theology schools. Although he regarded himself as a devout Christian, the kingdom of heaven for him was to be achieved in this world, not in the hereafter. As Ely would write, "Christianity is primarily concerned with this world, and it is the mission of

---

* It was admittedly not until the nineteenth century that economic theology typically offered the promise of heaven on earth through the achievement of a state of full abundance and the elimination of all material deprivation in the world. The full scope of the new scientific and economic powers to control nature for human purposes had not become apparent until the second half of that century. In the eighteenth century, there were still forms of economic theology, but they were developed more in terms of perfecting a divine harmony on earth. If the natural laws governing the physical and social worlds could be understood with increasing perfection through the application of scientific methods, all the ills of the world that had been grounded previously in an ignorance and misunderstanding of God's true purposes could be abolished. Adam Smith offered the most influential statement of such a theology. As the theologian Paul Tillich wrote, in the Enlightenment the secular idea of the "harmony" of nature replaced the earlier transcendent role of "supernatural authority" as revealed in the Bible. Tillich considered that "the first clear expression . . . can be seen in the area of economics. It was expressed by Adam Smith . . . in his idea of harmony as yield by the workings of the natural forces of self-interest in society." When Smith refers to the necessity of human beings behaving according to the requirements of "Nature," it is another modern way of saying that human beings must act according to God's commands. Throughout the modern age, many people would find their God and his commands without making any explicit reference—which might have turned such people away—to the traditional Christian and biblical language. See Paul Tillich, *A History of Christian Thought: From Its Judaic and Hellenistic Origins to Existentialism* (New York: Simon and Schuster, 1967), 338, 334. See also A. M. C. Waterman, "Economics as Theology: Adam Smith's Wealth of Nations," *Southern Economic Journal* 68 (April 2002).

Christianity to bring to pass here a kingdom of righteousness." As a "religious subject," the teachings of economics were to provide the expert knowledge base for "a never-ceasing attack on every wrong institution, until the earth becomes a new earth, and all its cities, cities of God."[3]

A Hidden Theology

A core theological purpose was thus explicit in the early days of the American Economic Association. The early founders of economics were part of the first wave of social scientists, many of whom who were making the transition from the Protestant ministry to the social science professions. In fact, president Woodrow Wilson, who studied political economy as a graduate student and later served as president of the American Political Science Association in its early years, was the son of a Presbyterian minister and in his youth was interested in entering the ministry himself. The transition would occur in two key stages. At first, the Christian trappings would remain, but the focus of this new Christianity, as in the social gospel movement, shifted from heaven in the hereafter to a new heaven right here on earth.

There was, however, a deep tension present in this process. True believers could be confident that economics would lead the way to heaven on earth because it was a "scientific" field of study, said to be capable of providing accurate scientific knowledge of the laws of economic growth and progress. But Christianity and science had often been at odds since at least the days of Galileo, and the discoveries of Charles Darwin had served to widen the separation. Economists wanted to distance themselves from the internal disputes within Christianity and the old religious tensions with Jews and members of other religions. Hence, in a second stage, the outward appearance of Christianity was gradually abandoned altogether as unnecessary to the enterprise. This was evident in the career of Ely himself, who increasingly placed his social gospel religion and his economic research in separate spheres.

New forms of secular religion—frequently one or another form of American progressivism—took the place of Christianity for many people. To be sure, the change was greater in form than in substance.[4] There was no God explicitly mentioned, but in other respects the American secular religions of economic progress followed closely in the Christian (and Jewish) traditions. Like Christianity, history was seen linearly as a transition from a humble beginning to a final glorious ending. During most of history, human beings had lived in sin and deprivation. A new age would soon be arriving, however, as human beings could be sure from the revelations of an authoritative—now economic—priesthood. All men and women of good faith were to work together for the coming salvation of the world, based on the good news recently and astonishingly revealed to mankind—now being delivered by the economic and other professional experts in the ways of economic progress.

Thus, as one historian writes, "the social gospel . . . was, in a sense, the religion of the progressive movement."[5] Arthur Vidich and Sanford Lyman comment that leading social scientists were making a "shift from the old Social Gospel to the new statistical positivism."[6] Nobel Prize–winning economist Robert Fogel explains that in the Progressive Era there emerged among many Americans "a modernist enthusiasm for the imminent realization of God's kingdom on earth," based on the "new doctrine that poverty was the source of sin"—and thus that the end of poverty would mean the end of sin in the world.[7] Dorothy Ross comments that progressive social scientists "still spoke in the idiom of Christian idealism" until World War I. The useless deaths of eight million men on the battlefields of Europe, however, dealt progressive optimism a blow from which it would never fully recover. Not only in the United States but also throughout the rest of Western civilization, the years after World War I saw a rapid growth in the political and economic influence of secular religion.*

---

* The Italian historian Emilio Gentile finds that there has been a widespread "*sacralization of politics* . . . in the modern era." It has involved "taking over the religious dimension and acquiring a sacred nature, [by means of which] politics went so far as to claim for itself the prerogative to determine the meaning and fundamental aim of human existence for individuals and the collectivity, at least on this earth." Politics as religion has yielded "an elaborate system of beliefs, myths, values, commandments, rituals and symbols, and consequently [has become] an object of faith, reverence, veneration, loyalty, and devotion." In this respect, the various modern political religions displaced Christianity, all this coming to a head in the twentieth century, which was "the most fertile period for the sacralization of politics," all too often inciting terrible religious warfare and violence:

> The First World War, which was fought as an apocalyptic struggle between Good and Evil, exalted the nation and thus intensified the sacralization of politics in its nationalist manifestation. This then favored the creation of the new political religions of fascism and Nazism, while the Bolshevik Revolution, which was another child of the war, engendered an internationalist version of the sacralization of politics, and indeed it attracted an enthusiastic response and proselytized in every corner of the globe. Between the wars, Europe experienced the bewildering spectacles of great seas of people acclaiming the dictators of new totalitarian states as terrestrial demigods. These regimes were the churches of the new intolerant religion of politics that claimed to determine the meaning and ultimate end of individual and collective existence through an obligatory system of beliefs, myths, rituals, and symbols. The perception of fascism and bolshevism as political religions goes back to the 1920s. The concepts of "secular religion" and "political religion" were coined precisely in order to describe the novelty and originality of the totalitarian regimes that sprung up between the two world wars. (Emilio Gentile, *Politics as Religion*, trans. George Stanton [Princeton: Princeton University Press, 2006], xiv, xvii)

The Economic Priesthood After World War II

A graduate student in economics is not required to study the history of the economics profession. Historians and other researchers in noneconomic fields, however, have explored the origins of American professionalism, including economics, in considerable detail.[8] As they have shown, the rise of the economics profession was closely linked to a wider professionalization of American life and other important developments of the Progressive Era.[9] For the students of the early years of American social science, little of the above would be either new or controversial. The transition from Protestant Christianity to the new progressive religion of the social sciences has been widely documented.[10]

Much less has been said and written, however, when it comes to the history of the economics profession in the second half of the twentieth century. Although the story is not as well-known, economists after World War II were the leading modern priests of economic progress. The economists of that generation still largely understood human history as being driven by economic factors. Many of them still believed, like the Princeton economist William Baumol, that the elimination of economic deprivation would lead to a great improvement in the human condition, morally as well as materially.* That was a main reason in many cases for their entering economics in the first place. The role of economists as the preeminent profession among the social sciences was justified by economists' possession of the key scientific knowledge required to bring about a future heaven on earth.[11]

In support of this argument, it is possible to find additional revealing quotes, similar to those of Ely, Keynes, and Baumol above. The economist Robert Mundell (a Nobel Prize winner in 1999) argued that, if economic policy had been handled more scientifically in the past, and as one can hope it will be in the future, "there would have been no Great Depression, no Nazi revolution, no World War II."[12] A better application of economic knowledge, in short, could prevent the kinds of horrible events that occurred in the world in the first half of the twentieth century.

Another leading contemporary economist, Charles Schultze, argued that economists serving in government should not be value-neutral—in fact, this

---

* Reflecting perhaps a new willingness among American economists to address the moral and theological side of their traditional strong advocacy of economic growth, and perhaps also a recognition that the actual social benefits of growth have been coming under increasing challenge in recent decades, the Harvard economist Benjamin Friedman in 2005 put the moral case for growth in a newly comprehensive and explicit form (at least for a prominent member of the economics profession). See Benjamin M. Friedman, *The Moral Consequences of Economic Growth* (New York: Knopf, 2005).

would be impossible—but rather should serve as "partisan advocates for efficiency." That is to say, economists should work diligently for the economic policy measures that would in the end lead to a secular salvation of the world.[13] Earlier Christian priesthoods advised governments on the commandments of a biblical God; the economics profession has advised on the necessary efficiency steps on the path of economic progress, the reigning gospel of the twentieth century. In the daily affairs of twentieth-century government, the terms "efficient" and "inefficient" became the operative substitutes for "good" and "evil."

Paul Samuelson's famous introductory textbook *Economics* has now appeared in eighteen editions (with Yale economist William Nordhaus as a coauthor in the more recent versions). The first edition appeared in 1948 and was the model for many other introductory textbooks in economics in the years to come. From the first edition, Samuelson advertised *Economics* as a value-neutral study of a technical field. Yet it is more appropriate to regard *Economics* as a new "bible" of economic theology, which was dominant in this role for decades following World War II.

The new understanding of good and evil in economic theology can be found in many passages throughout *Economics*. Whenever a political or economic institution infringed on the efficiency of the economic system, Samuelson was surprisingly prone to make an explicit moral judgment—indeed, sometimes to state directly that this result was "evil." Thus, monopoly pricing results in a "wastage of resources," which for Samuelson puts it in the category of the genuine "economic evils" of society. On another occasion, Samuelson says that "competitive advertising" is economically "wasteful," creating yet another of the unfortunate "evils" that continue to distort the efficient functioning of the American economic system.[14] Economic progress will lead to heaven on earth, and a morally upright person will do everything possible to avoid creating any obstacles to this wonderful outcome.

Most economists today employ less reverential tones in describing the glories of economic progress. Yet, in his "brief economic history of the world" from 1200 to the present, University of California economist Gregory Clark in 2007 declares that he "make[s] no apologies for focusing on income" in his historical interpretation. "Over the long run income is more powerful than any ideology or religion in shaping lives. No God has commanded worshippers to their pious duties more forcefully than income as it subtly directs the fabric of our lives."[15] The Christian God, in short, is false; an economic god is the deity truly controlling our lives and fates. Clark is unusually explicit, but large numbers of his fellow economists today would still in essence agree.

Other evidence in support of my thesis is found in the behavior of many economists. Some individual economists such as Milton Friedman showed an obvious messianic character. His fellow economist at the University of Chicago Gary Becker has written approvingly that throughout his career Friedman exhibited "a missionary's zeal in the worship of truth," dedicated to the improvement of public policy.[16] The former Harvard economist Albert Hirschman has written of the actions of American economists who sought to spread Keynesian economics in the aftermath of World War II, holding that they functioned as "a band of sect-like initiates and devotees." Driven by "an exhilarating feeling of possessing the key to truth," they undertook with great energy and commitment to "spread the message" and "to preach their gospel to a variety of as yet unconverted natives"—not only in the United States but also throughout the world.[17]

Belonging to the economics profession creates a sense of common bonds and solidarity. It is much like belonging to a priesthood, and at least a few economists have approached a saintly standard of behavior. Thus, in his remembrance for the University of Chicago economist Harry Johnson, Edward Shils noted that, even though Johnson died before he was fifty-five, he produced twenty books and 525 articles. Shils relates the story of encountering Johnson still working at his hospital bed in Italy after suffering a stroke. For Johnson, "economic analysis" was not merely a practical tool but something in which he "believed" in a fundamental way. The study of economics was essential to his basic "intellectual integrity" in the pursuit of truth. Indeed, like other saintly figures, Johnson "gave his life" to this cause; Shils relates that Johnson himself considered it all part of his "missionary" commitment in life.[18]

Many economists thus do not behave like the economic maximizers of their own models. It is true that a university life as an academic economist offers a decent salary, a great deal of personal freedom, and the opportunity to enjoy intellectual pursuits. But many economists—especially the top economists who have been the leaders of the profession—work much too hard to take full advantage of the opportunities for personal enjoyment and pleasure. Given their talents, and if they worked as diligently, many of them could have made much more money in other pursuits. The majority of them, it seems, chose to enter the profession of economics because they had a strong commitment to economic progress as the essential route of the common good.

Few economists, however, have had any great interest in formally proclaiming on such subjects. The central importance of economic progress to society was considered so obvious that there was no real need to talk about it (now that environmentalists and others often attack economists—sometimes on explicitly theological grounds—this circumstance has changed considerably).* It

---

*There may also have been a loss of economic faith among some economists themselves. An economist today may be more likely to declare him- or herself "agnostic" with respect to economic

is sometimes said that a religion encompasses those things that are so obvious that they can simply be taken for granted. In the medieval period this included the existence of God. For much of the twentieth century, for a large part of the American population, including its economists, it included the redeeming benefits of economic progress.

"Legitimate" and "Illegitimate" Costs

An economic critic might say that the evidence above of an important theological element in economics is thus far "anecdotal." It is far from meeting any standard of rigorous "proof," as a professional economist would expect to see a formal analysis developed. If the arguments thus far have been "soft," it is also possible to make a "hard" argument. Indeed, some of the most important conclusions of economic theory could not be sustained without certain theological assumptions. It is as though a mathematician had developed the proof of a theorem in which some of the essential steps had been left implicit. Upon close inspection, moreover, the omitted steps in this case turn out to have a special feature—they are religious in character. Their omission may further reflect both an unacknowledged understanding among economists that these steps cannot be defended in "scientific" terms, and an unwillingness to defend them explicitly on religious grounds.

Economists almost universally argue that a market system leads to an efficient allocation of resources. In making this argument, most economists of the twentieth century compared one equilibrium state of the economy with another—the approach of "comparative statics." As they argued, the "efficient" states of the economy will be characterized by the condition that it is impossible to make any change to improve the welfare of one party without damaging the welfare of another party. So far, there is nothing theological in this.

If we are not at present at an efficient state of the economy, however, it will be necessary to move from our current position. This movement will itself involve real transitional costs. In deriving the central theoretical and policy

---

progress. More economists may say that they simply do economics as an "intellectual puzzle" or a "mental game." The idea that consumer demands may be insatiable—contrary to the core assumption of economic religion—is also probably held more widely today among economists (perhaps as a result of the empirical observation that the extraordinary growth of U.S. incomes seems to have done little to curb the appetite for more goods and services). Although these views may be more widespread among current economists, the potentially radical consequences have not been much internalized. If the wider society came to share these views, or to realize that many economists hold such views, the current priestly role of economic professionals in American society might well come under greater challenge.

conclusions of economics, these transitional costs were long ignored—in effect treated as nonexistent. Even if it is perhaps less true today, they are largely still ignored when economic thinking is applied to real-world policy issues.

For example, if a new and more efficient firm moves into a market and displaces another firm, the owner of the losing firm will very likely suffer some significant burdens, both financially and in many cases emotionally. Economists may recognize the financial side of this but usually do not include it in the calculations of total social welfare (it is regarded as a non-compensable "pecuniary externality") or the related policy recommendations. They ignore the potentially large emotional burdens altogether. Economics graduate students are taught to ignore—to treat as zero—these kinds of transitional costs. If they were actually given full account, it would be impossible to say in principle whether a market system is economically efficient. Indeed, it might just as well be highly inefficient—there would be no basis for making a judgment.

In the real world, large resources are used up and other transitional costs incurred in moving toward new equilibria (of course, society never actually gets there and is constantly in motion toward new destinations). From a strictly scientific viewpoint, these transitional costs demand some accounting. Why should they be implicitly treated as having a zero cost to society, as the main corpus of economic theorizing long did—and still does for most policy purposes, as in the advocacy of an open market economy? One might argue that they are small and thus need not be included in the analysis—as friction is typically ignored in working out the laws of physics. Economists make no effort, however, to provide strong evidence that this "economic friction" is in fact inconsequential. A priori, it seems likely that the individual and social burdens of economic transitions will be large. The biggest losers in the economic system are likely to feel bruised and battered—at least for the length of a "healing period," which could last many years or even a lifetime for some people who have seen their whole basis of material livelihood disappear in the face of new market competition.

The true answer—the only good explanation in fact for making such a strong assumption—must be theological. Economists have justified their assumptions with respect to transitional costs by saying that they are only concerned with "the long run." In the long run, a continuing high rate of economic growth will lead to a higher and higher material standard of living—and eventually to a new heaven on earth. Taking account of "short-run" costs may improve the welfare of many individuals for a limited time—even the welfare of some people over their full lifetimes—but it will also delay the perfection of the economic system and thus the arrival of heaven on earth. Ignoring transitional costs makes no sense economically, but theologically it is much more reasonable to assume that anything standing in the way of the salvation of the world must not be given recognition and legitimacy—as the way of thinking of the economics profession normally takes for granted.*

It is thus the religious duty of followers in the economic faith not to interfere in market workings, to halt new technologies, or to block other steps toward greater economic efficiency, steps that might in fact displace large numbers of people. It would be an economic "sin" to stand in the way of the economic progress of the world. The sinful act will be all the more offensive when it serves to benefit privately one or another "special interest." The world of politics is in fact particularly likely to be filled with such selfish motives; although it will be difficult, the economic priesthood thus must be ever vigilant in seeking to hold politicians accountable to the commandments of a higher economic god. In earlier times, the Christian church was similarly often required to seek to contain the "wayward" impulses of kings and other political leaders, who were all too willing to ignore a higher set of religious commands.

In Christianity through most of its history, the events of the world were to be regarded as a minor concern, at least as compared with the attainment of a heaven in the hereafter. A pleasure of the moment might be a great temptation to sin, but no person would rationally endanger his or her eternal soul for a fleeting moment of satisfaction. So it is today with economic theology; the faithful must not lose sight of the glorious destination in the future, even as they are tempted by "politicians" and others who offer short-run pleasures and other diversions from a long-run economic progress of society. In short, there may not be good scientific reasons but there are sound religious reasons—from the perspective of economic theology—to pay little or no heed to the large stresses and strains of economic transitions along the road of economic salvation.

Prominent economists have in recent years acknowledged that, as a matter of science alone, there were in fact severe technical problems with Samuelson's mainly static framework of economic analysis. Indeed, a former MIT student of Samuelson, Joseph Stiglitz (winner of the Nobel Prize in Economics in 2001), comments that a new understanding has developed among economists since the 1970s that "the analysis of how the economy allocates its resources

---

* It is true that a "new institutional economics" has emerged since the 1970s within the economics profession that focuses on the central role of "transaction costs" in shaping economic institutions. The transaction costs that receive the most attention, however, are things like the information costs of searching for the lowest prices of goods and services or of verifying product quality, or the legal costs of writing and enforcing contracts. Few if any economists have entered into their consideration of transaction costs the emotional pain of economic loss resulting from competitive market failure. Moreover, when it comes to making actual policy recommendations, most economists revert to models of an economic system in which transaction costs play a small role that can be disregarded for practical purposes. Achieving the competitive market outcome, and ignoring most transaction costs, becomes the template for policy judgment.

is far more complicated, and far more interesting, than the engineering approach that prevailed in the decades following Samuelson's *Foundations of Economic Analysis*"—an approach that was offered in a simplified, nonmathematical form in Samuelson's introductory 1948 textbook, *Economics* (and then in many subsequent editions).[19] By focusing mainly on equilibrium states of the economy, Stiglitz finds, it was possible for economists to ignore issues of the availability and production of information that inevitably must be central to the workings of the economy in a more dynamic setting. Indeed, the economists of Samuelson's time typically went so far as to assume "perfect knowledge" of fully rational economic actors, in effect dismissing the practical difficulties of the transitional processes by which information in the real world must be acquired and communicated. As Stiglitz has stated, reflecting the new mainstream economic view of the 1990s,*

> The competitive paradigm [of *Economics* and other similar if more technical works] not only did not provide much guidance on the vital question of the choice of economic systems but what "advice" it did provide was often misguided. The conceptions of the market that underlay that analysis mischaracterized it; the standard analyses underestimated the strengths—and weaknesses—of market economies, and accordingly provided wrong signals for the potential success of alternatives and for how the market might be improved upon.
>
> The fundamental problem with the neoclassical model [is that it fails] . . . to take into account a variety of problems that arise from the absence of perfect information and the costs of acquiring information, as well as the absence or imperfections in certain key risk and capital markets.[20]

---

* Stiglitz won the Nobel Prize in Economics for his many refined technical analyses, at which he was exceptionally skillful and prolific. Perhaps recognizing that the technical economics that won him so much praise is of limited practical application, Stiglitz himself has moved well beyond such efforts in recent years. In 2008 Robert Skidelsky (a British economist and the leading biographer of John Maynard Keynes) reviewed a recent book, *Making Globalization Work*, commenting, "Stiglitz is an economist turned preacher, one of a new breed of secular evangelists" in the economics profession. As Skidelsky notes, in his recent writings "Stiglitz wants to stop the rich countries from exploiting poor countries. . . . His missionary fervor . . . is very American. 'Saving the Planet,' one of this new book's chapter headings, could have been its title."

Yet it is difficult for a person trained in the technical abstractions of formal economics to shift to such a radically new mode of religious communication. Skidelsky is of the opinion that Stiglitz in his newer proselytizing "lacks the eloquence, urgency, and passion of the preacher, while he has too often abandoned the rigor of the scientist." If some economists are now beginning to acknowledge their religious purposes more openly, and wish to become effective preachers in a more traditional manner, they may have to begin the learning process before receiving tenure. See Robert Skidelsky, "Gloomy About Globalization," *New York Review of Books*, April 17, 2008, 60, 64.

The writings of Stiglitz and other "new institutional economists" have undermined the intellectual foundations of the neoclassical economics that Samuelson and other leading economists developed over many years.[21] It is not that they have shown that these older economists were making any serious errors of logic or major failures of reasoning. Indeed, many of the economists of Samuelson's generation were quite skilled in mathematics and such errors would have been unlikely. Rather, they have shown that the perfect knowledge, perfect rationality, and other assumptions generally made by the economists of Samuelson's day were so far from reality as to be economically "uninteresting." An economic analysis based on these assumptions could not illuminate the central economic questions that the members of the economics profession are expected to answer.

The deficiencies in economic reasoning and practice admittedly became disturbingly apparent to many observers of the severe economic contraction of 2008 and 2009, involving a set of economic events that most current economists would have said is virtually impossible—until they actually happened. As economic columnist Martin Wolf wrote in the *Financial Times* in March 2009, "Another ideology has failed. . . . The financial system is the brain of the market economy. . . . If the financial system has failed, what remains of confidence in markets?"[22] Despite their importance, few economists had devoted significant amounts of time to understanding the real-world details of derivatives and other recent workings in the U.S. financial system (which, given the complexities, would probably have required that the economists actually work inside the system for at least some time). Given their propensities to think of economic systems as mechanical objects governed by objective "laws" analogous to the natural world, most economists generally neglected psychological elements such as can give rise in the real world to bubbles, panics, and other forms of social hysteria. Economists were even less likely to study the sources of the powerful bonding agents of mutual trust that are necessary to the workings of Wall Street and other markets. Although they have made some tentative steps in this direction with a recent growing professional interest in the economic role of "social capital," the actual origins of social capital—likely to be in part a religious phenomenon—have remained almost a complete mystery to the economics profession. Such matters were simply considered outside the scope of legitimate profession concern, however central they were to actual economic outcomes.

But the assumptions underlying economic reasoning were more interesting theologically. By assuming an enormously simplified world of perfect information and perfect equilibrium, the economic models in effect made a powerful symbolic statement that transitional costs were of no great consequence to society. Samuelson's *Economics* may have been gravely flawed in terms of the scientific understanding of the economy it offered, but as a work of religious art it was much more successful. Employing economic imagery in place of older biblical language, *Economics* successfully conveyed the message that the long-run salvation of the world was the only object of real concern. In the long run, in which the highest state of "perfect equilibrium" would be attained, guided by the expert knowledge of the contemporary economics profession, economic progress would lead to a new heaven on earth. Americans could be assured of a glorious future, if only they kept the faith in the knowledge and advice of their economic priesthood.

Economic Commandments

There have been other heroic assumptions in economic reasoning that most economists have regarded as virtually self-evident and have not thought necessary to defend. The basic framework of economic analysis assumes that human welfare is a product of the consumption of goods and services alone. Other matters, such as the institutional arrangements of the economy that produce those goods and services, for example, are not included among the key variables that influence the welfare—economically speaking, the level of "utility"—of individuals. Thus the use of interest rates as a device for rationally allocating the use of capital is not in itself considered as having any impact on the sense of well-being of members of society. This is a strong assumption, however, in light of the deep moral disapproval of "usury" during most of the history of Western civilization—an attitude that still exists today in parts of the Islamic world and other societies.

Economists of course are well aware that usury historically has been prohibited in many times and places. They reject such old attitudes not as a matter of rebutting the historical facts, however, but as a matter of introducing "modern" views that are not based on "superstition" and that take only "legitimate" factors of production into account. In his textbook *Economics*, Samuelson thus writes dismissively of anyone who would apply a normative perspective to the role of interest rates in the economy, who might regard usury as properly "a philosophical question" that might be answered by studying "what Aristotle had to say about it." Rather, for Samuelson the question of usury "simply boils down to" the important practical role that interest rates play in bringing the demand for financial capital into balance with the supply of such capital—thus working to maximize the efficient use of the total investment resources of society.[23]

Medieval Christians, as one might say, saw usury in light of the commandments of a biblical God; Samuelson now sees usury in light of the commandments of an economic god. The reality is that there are two forms of religious value judgment here, although Samuelson claimed the exclusive authority of "scientific truth" for the ethical commandments of his economic god. Without the use of interest rates, the economy would perform poorly and the rate of economic progress would be significantly diminished, thereby impeding the salvation of the world—ample grounds for Samuelson and virtually all other economists to consign the old attitudes about usury to the historical dustbin.

Samuelson is equally dismissive of more recent "reactionary beliefs," such as the old thinking that "that government is best which governs least." Writing in 1948 in the first edition of *Economics,* he is contemptuous of Friedrich Hayek (who would later win the Nobel Prize in Economics in 1974, four years after Samuelson received his prize), declaring that "no immutable 'wave of the future' washes us down 'the road to serfdom.'"[24] Samuelson here makes yet another powerful value judgment. If there is a conflict between economic liberty and economic efficiency, the efficiency considerations trump the liberty considerations. Again, there is nothing scientific about Samuelson's values in this respect—which are admittedly shared by most other mainstream economists even today. Science in itself does not reveal anything about whether economic growth is more or less important than individual freedom.

Rather, Samuelson is affirming the message of economic theology, which tells us that economic progress is the correct route to the salvation of the world. Abolishing economic scarcity will abolish sin—and in this sense might even be said to guarantee long-run human freedom in the most important sense. And Samuelson is of the view that an undue emphasis on liberty today might impede the rate of economic progress. The degree of efficiency, by contrast, is the operative measure of an action's contribution to the advance of world and national economic growth—and thus in this framework must command the highest obedience of all, superseding other potential values, such as the degree of human freedom in current society.*

Samuelson makes other powerful value judgments throughout his economic analysis. Indeed, like many other economists of his generation, Samuelson was very much a product of the intellectual climate of American progressivism that was dominant in the university world throughout his most professionally productive years. Despite his frequent claims to being a value-neutral scientist, the religious truths of the progressive "gospel of efficiency" lie just below the surface of his writings and thinking. Like other progressives, Samuelson sought to advance the "scientific management" of American society. This depended on the existence of a powerful national government to

---

*Since he wrote in 1948, to be sure, the University of Chicago school of economics has argued that there is less tension between efficiency and liberty than Samuelson then considered to be the case (and Samuelson has revised his own views somewhat, as reflected in later editions of his textbook).

oversee the comprehensive application of expert knowledge. Any undue deference to property rights might well crimp the efforts of economic and other social science professionals, the legitimate social engineers of American life, the new high priests with the most relevant knowledge to ensure economic progress and thus save the nation—and, in the long run, the world.

It is an ideology—a religion—of tight social control by a new priesthood of experts. Society is like a well-crafted computer or other finely tuned machine, in which every part must play its scientifically determined role.* Even when advocating the old-fashioned pursuit of self-interest in the marketplace, as he does for ordinary goods and services, Samuelson introduced a new "scientific" way of describing all this—the socially engineered "use of the market mechanism," spurning any use of the old laissez-faire terminology of "the free market." As Samuelson himself acknowledged, he was in such respects a disciple of John Maynard Keynes, who had shown how the unregulated market might spin out of control save for economists, who could now apply appropriate macroeconomic methods to eliminate unemployment and otherwise manipulate the market to the ends that society might choose.

Samuelson of course had a great deal of progressive company. Progressive ideas created the intellectual foundations for the development of the twentieth-century American welfare and regulatory state. American universities in those days were filled with the heirs to the progressive tradition.† Large numbers of ordinary Americans in fact "believed in" the goal of economic progress as a matter of their own basic faith. Samuelson did not cre-

---

* The earliest statements of this new religion of the scientific management of society—serving the goals of a perfectly ordered rationality and a maximum economic production—can be traced as far back as the French socialists Henri de Saint-Simon and disciples such as Auguste Comte. Saint-Simon declared, with respect to his positivist plans for the scientific management of society, that "the golden age of mankind is not behind us, [but rather] is in the [future] perfection of the social order" through the application of expert knowledge by the qualified social science and other engineers of society. On his deathbed, he declared that "religion cannot disappear from the face of the earth; it can only undergo transformation." His followers would shortly announce that "Saint-Simon will be chief of religion, the Pope" of the new positivist faith. See J. L. Talmon, *Political Messianism: The Romantic Phase* (Boulder, Colo.: Westview Press, 1985), 70–71.

† The progressive assumptions of economics were shared widely among the other social sciences, including psychology and sociology. Writing one year before Samuelson's first edition of *Economics*, the prominent German psychologist Erich Fromm declared in 1947 that:

a spirit of pride and optimism has distinguished Western culture in the last few centuries. . . . Man's pride has been justified. By virtue of his reason he has built a material world the reality of which surpasses even the dreams and visions of fairy tales and utopias. He harnesses physical energies which will enable the human race to secure the material conditions necessary for a dignified and productive existence, and although many of his goals have not yet been attained there is hardly any doubt that they are within reach and *the problem of production*—which was the problem in the past—is, in principle, solved. (Erich Fromm, *Man for Himself* [New York: Rinehart, 1947])

ate this faith, but his and the work of other economists served to guide and affirm it. These economists gave it a new symbolic and rhetorical expression. Whatever the many large deficiencies of economic science, which have been now exposed by the next generation of professional economists, the efforts of American economists from the 1940s to the 1960s did in fact work very well for a time as a form of modernist religious art. It is possible to draw compelling pictures with a mathematical brush.

To be sure, Samuelson, and many others like him, defended the "gospel of efficiency" as a matter of genuine scientific truth. Christianity is a monotheistic religion; there cannot be plural religious truths. The Greeks may have had multiple gods feuding and fighting on Mount Olympus, but the one God of Christianity is omniscient and omnipotent. As in many other respects, economic theology has followed again in the path of Christianity. If only one truth is possible, the methods of economic science alone are capable of revealing an exclusive route to economic progress in the modern age. There is only one economic god and his commands must be followed. Samuelson and his generation converted the entire economics profession to the emulation of modern physics and chemistry—a style of doing economics that continues to the present day. Indirectly, these claims to a scientific status have been a way of saying that the economic priesthood possesses the one valid understanding of the correct material path to the world's salvation.

Nevertheless, as noted above, the verdict of Stiglitz and many other leading professional economists today is that Samuelson failed scientifically; as a theologian, however, he was a much greater success. For several decades his *Economics* bible, and its many textbook imitators and other related writings, dominated the American government's thinking about the proper workings of the economic system. If the conclusions of his economic "science" depended on a host of matters of assumption and faith, the invocation of scientific authority served effectively to give these particular value claims a special place in the American halls of power.

Presidents and members of Congress indeed routinely listened to the members of the economic priesthood, leaving the clergy of old to deliver Sunday morning sermons, to officiate at marriages and funerals, and to fulfil other limited "traditional" functions. Old-fashioned Christian religion, in the words of the theologian Richard Neuhaus, was effectively excluded from "the public square" after *Economics* was published in 1948.[25]

The United States as a Church

Almost every society in the history of the world, from ancient to modern, has had a priesthood. Because the religious claims of these priesthoods are often in conflict, and yet most of them appear to have been important to the functioning of their societies, it is evident that the practical usefulness of a religion and a priesthood can be assessed independently of the exclusive "truthfulness" of the religious message. For this reason, a belief that is widely held can be a powerful instrument of social stability and harmony—and, as a consequence, of economic advance as well.

As the priesthood of the church of economic progress in the United States, the economics profession has thus had an important practical role—if having little to do with the quality of expert economic understanding and advice itself—in the workings of American government and society. If every opinion were equal, social and intellectual chaos would ensue, and that in itself would have powerful negative economic effects. The twentieth-century tendency was to regard matters of religious belief, however, as determined by "subjective judgment"—that is to say, that every opinion is equal. It was thus important that a common church of the United States should be grounded in a more limited claim to authority.

Whatever one might say today of the genuine "truth value" of economics as a body of scientific understanding—and there were many large failings, as noted above—the practical reality is that the economics profession for many years was successful in asserting its scientific status. The economic priesthood could effectively police the dispensation of religious authority in the United States. The modern United States fortunately no longer burns its heretics, but economic censors functioned almost as effectively to dismiss the policy ideas of the many "cranks" seeking to press their ideas in the policy arena.

This policing function, rather than the intellectual content of their ideas, was the largest contribution made by the economics profession to the rapid growth and development of the United States. When economists were called on to provide practical policy advice, many of them fortunately relied heavily on their own common sense, leaving behind the unworldly abstractions of their "scientific" work in economic theory. If the United States required a priesthood, and if the Christian claimants to this role could no longer sustain their previous authority in American life, economists claiming the mantle of true science were able to fill the bill. In this respect at least, perhaps economists played a large—if poorly understood, even by economist themselves—role in the economic successes of the United States in the decades following World War II.

Conclusion

G. K. Chesterton once remarked that the United States is "a nation with the soul of a church."[26] U.S. economic success is attributable in significant part to a high level of "social capital," based on the bonds of a powerful shared national faith. In the twentieth century, that common faith revolved around the core beliefs described above—the progressive economic conviction that sin is a product of external material circumstances, and that economic progress will finally end material shortages in the world, thus leading to a new heaven on earth. If the early Puritans saw Massachusetts as a "city upon a hill," offering a Christian beacon for all mankind, the twentieth-century United States was the place where modern economic progress achieved its greatest triumphs as another form of beacon for the world.

As suggested above, however, the time of American economic religion may be dwindling. There was great economic progress in the twentieth century in the developed nations of the world, but at the end of the century the results did not seem to point to heaven on earth. Indeed, it increasingly appeared that the sources of individual happiness and spiritual contentment might lie elsewhere. In emphasizing economic elements, the modern age might have fundamentally misconstrued the essential nature of a human being. Economic religion, it increasingly appeared, was another false religion in the long history of misguided faiths to which so many human beings have so often been powerfully drawn. As Robert Fogel commented in 2000, sounding notes of an old-fashioned Protestant vision of individual responsibility for salvation (again, by faith alone), and standing against the progressive collectivism of the American welfare and regulatory state:

> Failure to recognize the enormous *material* gains of the last [twentieth] century, even for the poor, impedes rather than advances the struggle in rich nations against chronic poverty, whose principal characteristic [now] is the spiritual estrangement from the mainstream society of those so afflicted. . . .
>
> The proposition that material improvement would ennoble the masses, so widely embraced by modernist reformers, did more to promote the consumerism of the 1920s and 1930s than to produce spiritual regeneration. . . .
>
> Realization of the potential of an individual is not something that can be legislated by the state, nor can it be provided to the weak by the strong. It is something that must develop within each individual on the basis of a succession of choices. . . .
>
> The quest for spiritual equity [among the members of society] thus turns not so much on money as on access to spiritual assets, most of which are transferred and developed privately rather than through the market. . . . Some of the most critical spiritual assets [are] . . . a sense of purpose, self-esteem, a sense of discipline, a vision of opportunity, and a thirst for knowledge.[27]

Although Fogel does not characterize his efforts in these terms, he is writing in such passages as a theologian as well as an economist—as a contributor, as I would say, to "economic theology." The old progressive economics was also concerned with spiritual themes, believing that spiritual advancement was the product of material advance. Material gain in economic religion was never the main purpose, but rather the means to a much higher end. But Fogel, along with many others outside economics, has now come to believe that the most important sources of individual growth and well-being actually lie elsewhere. A clinical psychologist writing in the *Washington Post*, Patricia Dalton, observes that "there is ample evidence, both anecdotal and scientific, that once people attain a reasonably good standard of living, making more money and buying more has no appreciable positive effect and in some cases has negative effects" on individual happiness. A report issued by the Alfred E. Sloan Foundation "found an inverse relationship between self-reported child happiness and parental income. Blue-collar and middle-class kids identified themselves as happier than wealthy ones."[28]

It is not as though economics is becoming altogether irrelevant. In modern society, a detailed understanding of its economic workings will always be an important form of knowledge, even if the economic god has failed. Economic journalist Robert Samuelson (no relation to Paul) perhaps most aptly characterized the new view: "Prosperity is a necessary—but not sufficient—condition for solving most serious social problems."[29] The great material gains of the human species over the past two hundred years might be seen as a positive step, even if well short of sufficient to bring heaven to earth.

2

THEOLOGIES OF 9/11

FOR MUCH OF THE TWENTIETH CENTURY, social scientists neglected religion. By the end of the century, however, it was evident that religion was once again playing a growing role in the world.[1] As they rediscovered religion, economists typically approached the subject in one of two ways. The largest body of economic writings examined the impact of religious ideas and institutions on economic and political affairs. Max Weber had pioneered this approach early in the twentieth century, arguing that specific tenets of the Calvinist theology of salvation encouraged an ascetic dedication to hard work and the rise of capitalism.[2] At the end of the twentieth century, a new economic literature similarly sought to explore the impact of "social capital"—often the product of religious influences—on economic outcomes.[3] A "new institutional economics" focused on transaction costs that might be higher or lower, according to the level of social capital.[4] Religious beliefs might be particularly important economically—a religion could be more or less "efficient"—simply because they could foster trust and otherwise significantly reduce the level of transaction costs in society.[5] Whether a religion was practically useful thus did not necessarily depend on the validity or correctness of the religious truths being proclaimed.

Asking a much different set of questions, another new area of economic study of religion concerned the impact of economic and social variables on religious behavior.[6] Are people with higher incomes more likely to go to church? What is the relationship between income and the size of church donations? Economically, membership in a religion can be understood as a way of maximizing individual "utility" and thus can be placed under the same economic lens as other forms of individual "consumption." For those who believe in life after death, some economists even argued that calculations of the benefits of long-run consumption—and thus the total long-run individual level of "utility"—might be conceived to include expected events in the hereafter (properly discounted).[7]

On the supply side, a church was a special form of "business," and the "market for churches" offered a potentially interesting case study in the field of industrial organization.[8] In this body of analysis, economists assumed that leaders of religions and organized churches acted according to the standard economic assumptions of the marketplace. Contrary to the usual assumption, a religion and a church were not distinguished by the benevolent motives of their participants, but rather by the unusual setting in which private profit seeking took place. A religion could be a good business as well, from this perspective including the economic "monopoly" that the Catholic Church had long sought to protect itself from religious competition.[9] By comparison, Protestantism could be described as a "free market" system of religion with many fewer barriers to entry.

In my own writings, I have explored another side of the interaction between economics and religion, one that has received less attention. The past indifference of social scientists to religion might have reflected a disdain for a religious competitor. The social sciences—with economics leading the way— might have themselves challenged traditional Jewish and Christian faiths to become the most powerful religions of our time.[10] But it was not necessarily a matter of outright rejection of these older faiths. Secular religions might have cleverly borrowed from historical Jewish and Christian themes, adapting the older messages to a newly scientific and economic language.[11] Indeed, now taking secular forms, such a disguised Christianity in the twentieth century was often more influential than the old-fashioned versions. If economics is now to be seen as a religion, one approach to its study might be described as "comparative theology." How do the religious explanations of economic theology compare with those of other faiths? Chapter 2 will develop a case study of this kind. The attacks on the World Trade Center and the Pentagon on September 11, 2001, and other subsequent terrorist actions, raised disturbing questions for many people at the beginning of the twenty-first century. Why did the terrorists do it? Why did they hate Americans to such an extent that they would plan carefully for years and then slaughter several thousand innocent people on 9/11? Why did normal moral restraints, generally assumed by Americans to be present in all people and in every community, not inhibit the evil actions of terrorists?

Historically, explaining the presence of evil in the world is a main question for religion. Thus Americans have recently looked to various religions, including economic religion, for explanations of the terrorist actions on 9/11, and these explanations have influenced the resulting government policies to deal with terrorism. As a group of prominent figures in American theology declared, "We believe our response to terrorism is a religious issue."[12] Surveying the alternative explanations for terrorist actions also serves to illustrate the specific theologies of the main competing religions—including economic religion—from which Americans seek answers regarding the presence of sin in the world.

Experiencing the Wrath of God

If well out of the mainstream, one of the first religious responses to 9/11 came from the Reverend Jerry Falwell and Pat Robertson. As with other believing Christians, for them terrorism was ultimately attributable to original sin in the Garden of Eden. It is because of the transgressions of Adam and Eve that all human beings—and not just terrorists—are capable of and in fact often have and still do commit sinful acts. The overall concept of original sin, however, did not give a specific answer to the timing of 9/11 and how this might fit with God's grand plan for the world.

In the Bible, as Falwell and Robertson knew well, there are repeated episodes of God visiting severe punishments on a society that has fallen into evil ways. These punishments often take the form of earthquakes and other natural calamities, but God also sometimes works through human agency. As Falwell and Robertson now interpreted the events of 9/11, the United States clearly qualified as a nation that had fallen into evil practices, allowing a million or more abortions each year and in many other ways abandoning God. Thus, as Falwell stated on September 13, 2001, with Robertson on a televised religious program, *The 700 Club*, "What we saw on Tuesday, as terrible as it is, could be miniscule if, in fact, God continues to lift the curtain and allow the enemies of America to give us probably what we deserve." Elaborating on this, Falwell declared that "the abortionists have got to bear some burden for this because God will not be mocked. . . . The pagans, and the abortionists, and the feminists, and the gays and the lesbians . . . all of them who have tried to secularize America, I point the finger in their face and say, 'You helped this happen.'" Robertson agreed, saying that "God almighty is lifting his protection from us."[13] As the *New York Times* noted, although such comments proved deeply offensive to large numbers of Americans, they were in fact "based in theology familiar to and accepted by many conservative evangelical Christians, who believe the Bible teaches that God withdraws protection from nations that violated his will."[14]

If this was the correct way of understanding the 9/11 terrorist attacks against the United States, the policy response should be directed inward— to cure the spreading sinfulness in American life. Terrorism was a sign of a nation having fallen out of God's favor, and the policy response must be to recommit to a life in the service of God. Despite the ample biblical pedigree, however, Falwell and Robertson were soon denounced across much of the United States as religious crackpots. Facing such intense criticism from so many quarters, they soon retracted their statements. Apparently even many devout American Christians no longer looked to the historical biblical understandings to explain the occurrence of calamitous events in the world.

In a way, ironically, it confirmed Falwell's and Robertson's point—Americans had abandoned the traditional Christian God, as they increasingly understood the world around them through the lens of secular gospels such as economic religion.* Whatever the Bible might say, and however consistent Falwell's and Robertson's interpretation, for most Americans God would never have been so capricious as to determine that thousands of people—people who had done nothing special to deserve this fate—should pay with their lives for the sinfulness of other fellow Americans. As Falwell and Robertson were learning, perhaps to their surprise, many traditional Christian formulations had long ago been abandoned, even by many "devout" American Christians who regularly attended church.

9/11 in Economic Theology

In seeking to understand the presence of sin in the world, the most widely accepted explanation in American life is economic rather than biblical. For many Americans, and for many other people around the world as well, the most convincing explanation for terrorism is to be found in the economic backwardness of the Muslim world. It was the extreme poverty of many people in Yemen,

---

* Interestingly enough, some prominent American intellectuals took a view similar to Falwell and Robertson, also attributing the 9/11 attacks to American sinfulness—but in their cases to the strong U.S. support for Israel and to U.S. worldwide "imperialism." Writing in the New Yorker shortly after 9/11, Susan Sontag asked, "Where is the acknowledgment that this was not a 'cowardly' attack on 'civilization' or 'liberty' or 'humanity' or 'the free world' but an attack on the world's self-proclaimed superpower, undertaken as a consequence of specific American alliances and actions?" Noting the American sanctions applied to Iraq in the wake of the 1991 war, Sontag asked, "How many citizens are aware of the ongoing American bombing of Iraq? And if the word 'cowardly' is to be used, it might be more aptly applied to those who kill from beyond the range of retaliation, high in the sky, than to those willing to die themselves in order to kill others."

The United States, Sontag was saying, in almost a secular echo of Falwell and Robertson, was being punished for its recent sinful behavior (although they had very different evils in mind). The solution for Sontag would also have to be found internally—in the reform of American aggression against other innocent peoples and nations. It was another illustration of how traditional Christianity can be adapted to a secular guise. Sontag was actually closer in her thinking to old-fashioned Puritans such as Cotton Mather than to most mainstream Protestant theologians of today. See Susan Sontag, "Talk of the Town," New Yorker, September 24, 2001.

Egypt, Pakistan, Afghanistan, and other Muslim nations that had bred deep despair and fanaticism leading to 9/11.

One observer thus commented that "more than 90 percent of Yemen's 20m people live in squalor, providing fertile breeding grounds for militant Islam"; as a consequence, "Yemen is a frontline state in the US war on terror," where it is necessary to maintain an active "hunt for al-Qaeda terrorists."[15] In Indonesia, another commentator noted, "Islamic militant groups [were] attracting more young men radicalized by poverty."[16] The prime minister of Malaysia warned that terrorism would continue until its "root causes" were addressed, reflecting a common view that "the destruction of the twin towers was caused by global poverty."[17] British prime minister Gordon Brown, then chancellor of the exchequer, declared that "the international community will have to confront the world's other war, the global war against poverty, a war that must be won if we are to succeed in our war against global terrorism."[18]

Columnist Thomas Friedman of the *New York Times* (a former Middle East correspondent for the paper) wrote in 2003 that "the U.S. war on terrorism suffered a huge blow last week—not in Baghdad or Kabul, but on the beaches of Cancun," where world trade talks had broken down. As Friedman saw matters, the best hope for alleviating poverty in less developed nations was an expansion of world trade. As Friedman described his views of the fundamental causes of terrorist events such as 9/11, "Sure, poverty doesn't cause terrorism—no one is killing for a raise. But poverty is great for the terrorism business because poverty creates humiliation and stifled aspirations and forces many people to leave their traditional farms to join the alienated urban poor in the cities—all conditions that spawn terrorists."[19] Concerned as well that trade talks were not making sufficient progress, the president of Brazil, Luiz Inácio Lula da Silva, stated in 2006 that global economic progress based on widespread international trade was essential because, "if we want to combat terrorism . . . we have to give the people the opportunity to survive [economically]. That's the challenge of the twenty-first century."[20]

Matthew McHugh, chair of Bread for the World, similarly stated that "reducing poverty, not just feeding the hungry," is the true means to curb the threat of terrorism. "If you have impoverished people, it promotes helplessness, instability and radical solutions."[21] Indeed, an almost limitless number of statements of this kind could be cited. In the wake of 9/11, Middle East poverty was the one explanation for terrorism given most widely by leading journalists, politicians, and other mainstream figures in the United States and elsewhere around the world. This reflected the pervasive economic determinism and materialism of contemporary thinking, a worldwide common faith in the tenets of economic religion, held among many people who may not explicitly recognize the large religious implications. Human beings do not go wrong, as Christianity taught for almost two thousand years, because they are afflicted by original sin. Rather, they are led astray by the damaging economic circumstances of their external environment, especially the dire poverty in which so many live.*

The corollary is that the problem of sin in the world can be solved by economic actions. If the material conditions of life can ultimately be perfected, as contemporary economists profess to know how to do, there will no longer be any basis for terrorism or other such sinful acts. Indeed, in the longer run, as economic abundance reaches higher and higher levels, the result will be a new heaven on earth. Economics will save the world. This is the core message of economic religion, as illustrated in the most common explanation given, not only in the United States but around the world, for the events of 9/11.

American Political Religion

Applied to 9/11, however, the specific details did not fit very well the causal model of economic theology. Osama bin Laden came from one of the richest families in Saudi Arabia. Many of the people surrounding him were Islamic radicals originally from Egypt, including Ayman al-Zawahiri, a graduate of a medical school and for a time a practicing doctor. As Lawrence Wright explained in his comprehensive study of the origins of al-Qaeda, "The men who came to train in Afghanistan in the 1990s were not [the] impoverished social failures" that many people assumed (and that economic religion would

---

* Although there are significance differences, and Adolf Hitler had much greater impact on world history, the popular perceptions of Hitler and Osama bin Laden are similar in important ways—both as evil geniuses who somehow led large numbers of people to lose their collective sanity. Yet, although it is a minority view, a number of scholars have attempted to understand Hitler within the narrower framework of economic religion alone. He was not mindlessly irrational, somehow possessed by a modern equivalent of the devil, but was actually following a clearly identifiable economic logic. A 2002 book thus rejects the leading historical treatments that find the origins of World War II in "political or diplomatic" causes, or that the war may even have "personal origins in the form of Hitler." Rather, the book concludes "that economic rivalries among interventionist . . . governments formed the essential and primary cause of World War II." A key factor was that "with colonization cut off as a means of gaining raw materials, the Germans turned to the east," part of a wider "competition for eastern European trade and resources [that] shaped the outbreak and course of the war." It was "Hitler's desire for 'living space' and for resources in Poland [that] prompted the war that Germany launched in 1939." Then, the competition for "Yugoslavian and Romanian resources affected the expansion of the war two years later, as the Germans prepared to attack the Soviet Union in 1941." In was the terrible culmination of an "intense struggle for trade and market share" among Germany, Britain, France, and other Great Powers during the 1920s. Thus, in a world of total economic abundance, among the many other wonderful benefits, events such as World War II would never occur. See T. Hunt Tooley, review of *A Low Dishonest Decade: The Great Powers, Eastern Europe, and the Economic Origins of World War II, 1930–1941*, by Paul N. Hehn, *Independent Review* 9 (Fall 2004): 293–96.

have predicted). Indeed, it was just the opposite; as Wright reported, they had typically been "model" citizens in their countries of birth. Most "were from the middle or upper class, nearly all of them from intact families. They were largely college-educated, with a strong bias toward the natural sciences and engineering." Those who joined bin Laden's jihad were characterized by "their urbanity, their cosmopolitan backgrounds, their [high] education, their facility with languages, and their computer skills."[22]

It was much the same with the 9/11 hijackers, many of whom had studied in Germany and were well-off economically with promising futures. Later, the London terrorists who bombed the subway system in July 2005, killing fifty-two and injuring seven hundred, had been born and raised comfortably in Britain. A difficult upbringing in dire poverty might explain the actions of some terrorists, but the correlation was weak at best.* At a minimum, it would be necessary to look in other directions as well.[23]

Former president George W. Bush professes to be an evangelical Christian and has a masters degree from the Harvard Business School. Yet, at least in his public statements in the years after 9/11, Bush was seemingly less influenced by the teachings of traditional Christianity or of conventional economic religion, and most influenced by a strong commitment to the tenets of an American political religion (to which elements of economic religion contribute). Some of the key tenets of Bush's political religion were revealed in a 2004 speech at Oak Ridge National Laboratory in Tennessee, in which the president stated that "the rise of democracy, and the hope and progress that democracy brings, [are] . . . the alternative to hatred and terror in the broader Middle East. In democratic and successful societies, men and women do not swear allegiance to the malcontents and murderers" who make up terrorist groups. As Bush elaborated, "democratic governments do not shelter terrorist camps or attack their neighbors," partly because they are genuinely committed to "building better lives."[24] As he stated on another occasion, Americans could be certain that, "as [political] freedom advances in the Middle East, those societies will be less likely to produce ideologies of hatred and produce recruits for terror."[25]

Bush explained his pursuit of the Iraq war in these terms. But he did not explain exactly why political freedom would have such a powerful influence in inhibiting terrorism. Perhaps he believed that an external environment of

---

* For those seeking to uphold the message of economic theology, it was still possible to argue that many terrorists, while not poor themselves, might be motivated by a horror of the oppression of the poor elsewhere. In this way terrorism would still have an economic explanation, even if the terrorists themselves were not economically deprived. Even if this view is accepted, however, such an explanation is ultimately grounded in the character of the values and beliefs of the terrorists. Why are rich terrorists so concerned for the condition of the poor? Such a concern, as well as the consequent terrorist actions, are not easily explained by material circumstances alone.

political repression could be as psychologically damaging—as alienating—to an individual as an economic environment of poverty and other material oppression. Perhaps regimes that imprison and torture their political opponents inevitably foster hatred and a desire for revenge. Whatever the precise reason, for Bush the saving character of democracy was a core element of faith, like the Christian beliefs to which he also subscribed.

On at least one occasion, however, the president did address a specific objection—that Iraqis might not be prepared for free political institutions, that they might be so bruised and battered from years of Saddam Hussein's rule that the preconditions for democracy might not be present in Iraq. Addressing a gathering of Iraqi Americans in Dearborn, Michigan, in 2004, Bush stated that "you are living proof the Iraqi people love freedom and living proof the Iraqi people can flourish in democracy." For Bush, the love of liberty was not limited to any one or a few cultures or religions; it could be found everywhere on earth as a simple matter of basic human nature: "I believe that God has planted in every human heart the desire to live in freedom. And even when that desire is crushed by tyranny for decades, it will [soon] rise again."[26] Thus, in Iraq and other parts of the Middle East, "whether you're Sunni or Shia or Kurd or Chaldean or Assyrian or Turkoman or Christian or Jew or Muslim—no matter what your faith, freedom is God's gift to every person in every nation," and the real experience of political freedom will save individuals, nations, and eventually the whole earth.[27]

If the political—and the economic would then follow as well—sources of individual repression in the Middle East were lifted, as Bush was saying, the original and true inner nature of each person would be released to do great things in the world.* God created human beings in his image, but sin had entered the world in the Garden of Eden. And ultimately, of course, only God could end the condition of human sinfulness that traces to man's rebellion

---

*In Great Britain, it should be noted, former prime minister Tony Blair advocated much the same political religion with a similar enthusiasm. Blair was more articulate, but the core principles he defended were similar to those of President Bush, partly explaining why their alliance in Iraq held together so long. As Blair declared in a postmortem on his years in office, "There is nothing more ridiculous than the attempt to portray 'democracy' or 'freedom' as somehow 'Western' concepts which, mistakenly, we try to apply to nations or peoples to whom they are alien." Rather, democracy and freedom are "universal" values. The key to defeating terrorism was to spread the values of democracy and freedom in opposition to the Islamic "ideology of the extremists." In opposition to their false "world view," Blair saw the necessity of fighting for "our own world view, no less comprehensive." Valiant efforts were called for to show an "even-handed commitment to our values, for the world as it changes to adopt these values, universal as they are, to guide us" into the twenty-first century. Blair, in short, and no less than Bush, saw the path to the salvation of the world in the political and economic religion of Great Britain and the United States, a set of secular religious beliefs—derived ultimately from Christian sources—that must extend over the whole earth. See Tony Blair, "What I've Learned," *Economist*, June 2, 2007, 27–28.

in the Garden. Perhaps God had decided that his will should be exercised through political and economic means, saving the world through lifting the external oppressions that had afflicted human beings throughout all of previous human history. It was not an exact biblical account, but Bush seemingly was open to a more modern reinterpretation of the core Christian message.

For Bush as a Christian, it was also possible for him to believe that God had perhaps chosen him to be a chief agent of His will in this regard. According to a larger design, Bush had become president and was now critical to implementing God's plan to save the Middle East through political and economic progress, a key step toward a future heaven on earth. Bush was not the first American president to think in such messianic terms. The events of World War I had resulted in an even much greater sacrifice of lives on the battlefields of Europe, done in the name of American political and economic religion, as Woodrow Wilson personally led a grand crusade to save the world for democracy.

Wilfred McClay comments that it is traditional for an American president to "convey a strong sense of God's providence, His blessing on the land, and of the Nation's consequent responsibility to serve as a light unto other nations." Ronald Reagan liked to invoke such themes in his presidential speeches, and his skill in using the language of the redemptive role of the United States in the world played a part in his many political successes. But McClay finds that President Bush "surpasses even that standard and puts forward the civil-religious vision of America with the greatest energy of any president since Woodrow Wilson."[28] Unfortunately, also much like Wilson, his sense of a divinely appointed mission was considerably greater than his own skills in implementation. Perhaps God's ways are, as the Bible says, ultimately inscrutable, and those who claim to know His design—including many of the political and economic true believers of our time—may be among the deluded.*

---

* In *The Bush Tragedy*, published toward the end of the George W. Bush presidency, Jacob Weisberg sought to identify the roots of its many large "failures." Some of the difficulties started with Bush's desire to adopt transformative missions, reflecting the pursuit of "a clear moral goal, [thereby proclaiming] the ambitious work of a consequential presidency." As Weisberg comments, in his second inaugural address in January 2005, Bush dramatically "announced the goal of abolishing oppression on planet Earth." The message was that "democracy is God's gift to humanity . . . and the United States would help extend its blessings" to all other peoples. In this and other ways, "his inaugural address sounded religious." Indeed, "it was as if Bush now . . . identified his democratic crusade with the will of God."

Admittedly, and to a greater extent than Weisberg acknowledges, Bush in this respect had a great deal of company among previous American presidents. In broad terms, he was simply restating core tenets of the American civil religion. The real problem for Bush was that he tragically lacked the executive capacities, and the broad understanding of the world and its limits, required to advance such a world redemptive goal in practice. Bush seemingly suffered from the illusion—reflecting a serious misreading of Christian theology—that God would automatically guide his decisions, thereby requiring minimal

Muslim Infidels

Among the competing theologies of 9/11, there was yet another traditional Christian explanation in addition to that of Jerry Falwell and Pat Robertson.* Although it was sometimes also harshly criticized, this theological line of reasoning was not so offensive that it could not be raised openly in mainstream U.S. culture. Many Christians have long believed that Islam is a dangerous religion—a great false heresy. Among the criticisms, it is said that Islam preaches war and violence as a principal means of religious conversion. In contrast to the spread of Christianity in the Roman Empire, Islam did in fact spread across the southern Mediterranean in the seventh century on a great wave of military conquest. Today, once again, a new drive for Islamic conquest is threatening Europe—and the United States as well. Militarily unable to challenge the West directly, Islamic terrorists have turned to the one effective means available to them of applying force.†

Franklin Graham (who gave the benediction at President Bush's 2001 inauguration and is the son of the Reverend Billy Graham) stated in November 2001 on national television that Islam is "a very evil and wicked religion."[29]

---

independent intellectual exploration and other efforts on his own part. See Jacob Weisberg, *The Bush Tragedy* (New York: Random House, 2008), excerpted in *Newsweek*, January 28, 2008, 33–34.

* In still another biblical explanation, also well outside the mainstream of American public opinion, many millions of evangelical Christians believe—drawing on the book of Revelations—that history is on a course toward an apocalyptic set of events that will usher in a Second Coming. Moreover, for some of these American evangelicals, the fate of Iraq and Israel are central portents of things to come. As the *Christian Century* (a longtime leading voice of liberal Protestant Christianity) commented, "Millions of Americans believe that the Bible foretells regime change in Iraq, that God established Israel's boundaries millennia ago, and that the United Nations is a forerunner of a satanic world order," all this presaging the arrival of the millennium. Osama bin Laden and the terrorist actions of 9/11 thus might be God's way of giving president George Bush a justification and the means for a "regime change" in Iraq—a necessary step in the millennial process. Because Bush considers himself a devout evangelical Christian, the *Christian Century* editorialized that "the American people have a right to know how the President's faith is informing his public policies, not least his design on Iraq." Did Bush see the war in Iraq as a part of the fulfillment of biblical prophesy? Quoted in Alan Cooperman, "Openly Religious, to a Point," *Washington Post*, September 15, 2004.

† In a recent example of this assessment of the dire threat to the West posed by Islam, Frank Gaffney Jr., the president of the Center for Security Policy, declares with respect to "Islamofascism":

> Adherents to this totalitarian political movement are determined to destroy the Free World, whose nations, values and institutions are seen as impediments to the to the global triumph of the Islamists' preferred Taliban-style religious rule. For our enemies, Iraq represents but one front in a world war. And we, too, must recognize it as such.
>
> [It is supported by] various state-owned and terrorist-sponsored television outlets. . . . It features imams calling for death to America; officials of Mideast governments making plain the destruction of the United States is God's will; even tiny children regurgitating their desire for death while killing Israelis, Americans and other infidels. (Frank Gaffney Jr., "What We Fight For," *Washington Times*, March 21, 2006, A16)

It has warped the minds of its believers against the teachings of the Christian God, causing them to commit evil acts.* Graham elsewhere declared that "I believe it is my responsibility to speak out against the terrible deeds that are committed as a result of Islamic teaching," and that "the persecution or elimination of non-Muslims has been a cornerstone of Islamic conquests and rule for centuries." The events of 9/11 were particularly horrifying—and new in occurring on American soil—but otherwise fell within a long history of Islamic attacks on the Christian world. In Muslim nations, Graham said, deep intolerance is the norm and "conversions from Islam to any other faith are often punishable by death."[30] It is not a marginal feature of Islam, according to Graham; rather, "persecution is taught by them, it's in their Koran."[31]

Both economic and political religion are in significant part secularizations of messages that can be found historically within the wide range of Christian belief. The Christian message that the content of Islamic religion is the fundamental source of terrorist actions in the world also has a secular counterpart. According to Middle East historian Bernard Lewis at Princeton University, Islamic terrorism is part of "a religious war, a war for Islam and against infidels, and therefore, inevitably, against the United States, the greatest power in the world of the infidels." In centuries past, Muslims had interpreted their military successes and their acquisition of great empires as a sure sign of God's favor. In the twentieth century, as the Islamic world was helpless before the military power of the West, Muslims felt growing concern, fear, and even humiliation and rage. Osama bin Laden in one of his videotapes rails against the "humiliation and disgrace" that Islam has experienced for "more than eighty years." As Lewis comments, "We can be fairly sure that bin Laden's Muslim listeners . . . picked up the allusion immediately and appreciated its significance. In 1918, the Ottoman sultanate, the last of the great Muslim empires, was finally defeated—its capital, Constantinople, occupied, its sovereign held captive, and much of the territory partitioned between the victorious British and French Empires."[32]

Now Islamic terrorists were finally lashing back at the Christian West in the only practical way available to them, fighting a new battle to evict the latest Christian crusaders. It was all the more dangerous because the new Christian crusaders often adopted the scientific disguises of secular religion. But in reality, now justified by economic and political religions, as many Muslims saw the matter, self-righteous Christians were still seeking to conquer their lands.

---

* Graham has not backtracked since he offered these views in the wake of 9/11. He repeated them in 2006 in a *Nightline* broadcast aired by ABC News. See Richard N. Ostling, "Graham Still Calls Islam Evil: Defends Words Said in 2001," *Washington Times,* March 16, 2006, A2.

Antiterrorism as Religious Policy Making

As this review finds, there have been four main competing lines of theological explanation for 9/11. Two are explicitly grounded in the tenets of traditional Christian religion, and two look to modern reinterpretations as provided by secular economic and political religions. As described above, they are:

1. God is punishing the United States for its recent sinful behavior and defiance of His biblical commands.
2. The United States and the West once again confront the menace of a false Islamic religion, one that in its religious zeal has always sought to conquer and defeat the Christian world, and is still doing so.
3. Terrorists were driven to their evil actions by the desperate poverty and dire material deprivation in which they lived in Islamic nations.
4. Terrorists were spawned by the rage and humiliation of people living in dictatorial Islamic societies that repressed their individual rights and denied them basic human freedoms.

These understandings are not, of course, mutually exclusive. It is possible that all contain partial elements of truth; each in concept could be a contributing factor in explaining the rise of Islamic terrorism. Although not the standard biblical understanding, a Christian God might in fact have chosen in the modern era to employ economic means to guide human actions. Yet the leading advocates tend to see one or another as the sole correct answer. According to the choice of a true answer, there will be profound implications for American policy with regard to world terrorism. Although the theological elements are often left implicit, the devising of public policies to address Islamic terrorism has in fact spawned a fierce religious debate within American society. In the end, to ask why 9/11 occurred and how similar events can be prevented is virtually to seek an explanation for the presence of evil in the world—to ask what is the original basis for the continuing large presence of sin in the modern age, despite the enormous "progress" in many areas (even in most of the poorest countries today, people have more food and receive better medical care, living to a much older age on average).

The Bush administration, as noted above, largely based—at least in its public rhetoric—its antiterrorism policies on the tenets of American political religion. To end the threat of Islamic terrorism, it would be necessary to transform the Middle East according to the democratic principles of the American civil religion. Yet the subscribers to economic religion would respond that the oppressive political institutions are themselves the products of the severe poverty and other adverse economic circumstances in the Muslim world. As long as the Middle East remains economically backward, they would say, it will be impossible for the people there to remove their corrupt and dictatorial governments. Economic reform thus must precede political reform.

If that is a correct diagnosis, if economic religion reflects the most essential religious insight, then the key element in American antiterrorism policy should be the promotion of Middle East economic growth and development. This might include large elements of foreign economic assistance, in both infusions of capital investment funds and technical economic advice. Islamic nations might be encouraged to develop rules of law, well-defined property rights, fair and independent judiciaries, and efficient civil services, and to take other steps to promote their economic advance.* The Bush administration gave some lip service to such messages of economic redemption yet did not show great enthusiasm. At least in public statements, its real faith was in the "spread of freedom and democracy."

Perhaps this is because examples such as Saudi Arabia—the leading source of manpower and funding for world terrorism—seem to belie the tenets of economic religion. Despite the presence of enormous oil reserves, annually yielding many tens of billions of dollars of oil revenues, Saudi Arabia has failed to transform itself either democratically or economically. Hence, the core problem might in fact be the tenets of Islamic religion itself. Perhaps the adverse political and economic outcomes in Muslim nations are a direct consequence of failings of Islam as a religion. Islam may encourage poor governance, which then spawns negative economic outcomes. Or perhaps it is the reverse: Islam may contribute to economic backwardness that then creates an insuperable obstacle to any real political reform.

Either way, Islam would be the problem. If this is a correct religious diagnosis, perhaps the American government should then invest heavily in the study of Islamic theology and take steps to encourage the spread of new and more truthful religions—as, for example, heroic efforts were made during the

---

* In yet another example of the influence of economic religion, two leading Democratic members of the U.S. House of Representatives, Jim Turner and Jane Harman, in 2004 released a report titled "Winning the War on Terror." The report expresses the bottom-line conclusion that in the Middle East, "the primary hope for heading off this explosive situation is economic growth." They concede that economic failure alone "does not make poor people into terrorists." "Poverty" and the conditions that cause it, however, "can make weak states vulnerable to terrorist networks within their borders." Indeed, there was wide bipartisan agreement among past and current members of Congress on this diagnosis of the roots of terrorism. Jack Kemp, the former Republican member of the House of Representatives, and former secretary of housing and urban development, declared his full agreement with the urgency of a "dramatic and massive commitment, on the scale of the Marshall Plan, to the future of the Arab children, and to the economic prosperity of the Middle East." Combating the evil of terrorism in this part of the world, as it seemed to many leading American policy makers, required a rededication to applying the messages of economic religion. See Jack Kemp, "Middle East Peace and Prosperity," *Washington Times*, May 6, 2007, A19.

Cold War to combat the false messages of Marxist religion. Awkward as it may be for many Americans to consider the prospect, an effective antiterrorism policy thus could require public proselytizing by the American government to promote religious transformation throughout the Muslim world.

Thus far, I have been neglecting the first of the religious explanations described above for 9/11 and other Islamic terrorism—that God is acting to punish the United States for its recent evil ways. As noted above, this theology finds wide support in the language of the Bible and in historical Christian teachings. The difficulty even of raising such arguments in public today offers testimony to the advanced state of secularization of American society. Although the majority of Americans profess to be Christians, in many cases they have modified their "Christian" beliefs to such an extent that the resulting religion would not be recognizable to Martin Luther, John Calvin, and many other leading Christians of the past.*

Roman America

Duke professor of religion Stanley Hauerwas, one of the leading Protestant theologians in the United States, sees the recent blending of traditional Christian and secular religion as resulting in a theologically incoherent and indeed frequently heretical set of beliefs. It is not up to the United States to save the world; this is a task reserved to God, whose ways are often unknowable—and God's plans are certainly not to be given their definitive statement by U.S. political leaders. Harking back to Martin Luther's criticisms of the Roman Catholic Church, the United States may be in danger of substituting its own words and actions in place of God's. In 2004, Hauerwas thus signed a statement criticizing any American politicians who "adopt the dangerous language

---

* Christian theologian Sallie McFague, professor emeritus at the Vanderbilt Divinity School, finds that many Christian faithful have religious convictions grounded in implicit ideas about the world whose source and central importance remain unknown to them. Thus, even as they formally profess to accept fully biblical sources of authority, the messages of economic religion—often in fundamental conflict (at least outwardly) with biblical understandings—may also have thoroughly infused their thinking. As McFague explains:

> Christian theology is the attempt to think about God and the world—who God is and who we are. . . . Every Christian is a theologian; each of us has a theology. That is, each of us has a picture, a set of assumptions, usually not conscious, of how we think God and the world are related. And all of us can and do express through our words and actions who we think God is and who we think we are. These unconscious or implicit theologies are very powerful. They control many of our decisions and actions; we rely on them as justification for what we do personally and as a nation. Theology matters. (Sallie McFague, *A New Climate for Theology: God, the World, and Global Warming* [Minneapolis: Fortress Press, 2008], 5)

of righteous empire in the war on terrorism and confuse the roles of God, church and nation."[33] He writes that in the United States today,

> theological convictions have lost their intelligibility. They have lost their power to train us in skills of truthfulness, partly because accounts of the Christian moral life have too long been accommodated to the needs of the nation state, and in particular, to the nation state we call the United States of America. As a result the ever present power of God's kingdom to form our imagination has been subordinated to the interest of furthering liberal ideals through the mechanism of the state.[34]

Economic religion and American political religion have long flirted with Christian heresy. It is always possible that God is acting in the world to realize his aims through economic and political means. That would at least potentially be an outwardly Christian viewpoint, as found, for example, in the social gospel movement of one hundred years ago. The Second Vatican Council declared that "earthly goods and human institutions according to the plan of God the Creator are also disposed for man's salvation and therefore can contribute much to the building up of the body of Christ."[35]

But the role of biblical messages and other historic Christian teachings in this process will be small. It is an easy step to abandon the Christian vocabulary and setting altogether, leaving God out of the picture, the salvation of the world to be achieved by American and other human actions alone. Indeed, there are signs today of greater resistance among Christian leaders to the religious claims of the American nation-state. There is a concern that many Americans today are more religiously committed to the secular state—to the "church of the United States"—than to a valid Christian theology. As McClay comments, and although it still represents a minority viewpoint, "For many committed Christians, there has been a growing sense that the American civil religion has become a pernicious idol, antithetical to the practice of their faith."[36] Radical as the thought might seem to many Americans, too many of them may be worshiping the American national state, with the U.S. Constitution as its bible, above their allegiance to any specifically Christian body of teachings.

This is not the first time that such a diagnosis has been offered. The Protestant Reformation said much the same about developments of that era in Rome. The Roman Catholic Church, as religiously dominant then in Europe as the United States is today across the globe, had mistaken its own political and economic advantage for the true Christian faith. The new Rome in the United States, as Hauerwas and McClay are suggesting, is perhaps the greatest heretical threat today to the humble living in the world preached by Jesus

Christ. The economics profession may be the new Roman priesthood, distorting the true Christian faith, substituting arid chains of abstract reasoning—now economic—for a truer knowledge of the world. The top-down hierarchy and sources of authority of the American economics profession do in fact resemble more closely the Roman priesthood than the Protestant ministry.[37]

Conclusion

The members of the economics profession typically dismiss out of hand any suggestion that their chosen field of expertise is a religion. Yet if asked to explain terrorism in the world, many economists would quickly turn to economic answers. In many cases, and like millions of other Americans who are not economists, they would say that material deprivation breeds terrorism. In other cases, the economic explanations might be more technical, seeing terrorism, for example, as a device for creating a powerful set of communal bonds within a group, a form of initiation rite that makes each person a "hostage" to every other person in the group, and thus serves to facilitate collective actions for economic ends.[38] If the goal is to eliminate Islamic terrorism in the world, the followers in economic religion typically argue that the policy solutions must be economic as well. This will include, most importantly, steps to promote rapid economic growth and development throughout the Middle East.

Economists might not be comfortable with the term "sin," but it seems apt in the case of events such as 9/11. Thus, in seeking to explain terrorism, economic religion is seeking to understand one particularly visible and terrible manifestation of human sinfulness. Moreover, in offering an economic understanding it is substituting a competing religious explanation in place of the traditional biblical understanding of the consequences of the original fall in the Garden. The economic explanation given for the events of 9/11, and the resulting economic policy prescriptions to deal with terrorism, is an important story in the modern message of economic religion.

3

HOW MUCH IS GOD WORTH?

RATHER THAN MAXIMIZING economic growth, as will be explored further in later parts of this book, a higher value of environmentalism is to minimize human impacts on the natural world. This means that, to the extent such environmental values come to dominate environmental policy, economists might have little to say. This is not a mere hypothetical possibility. As Stanford law professor Barton Thompson explains: "Many people active or interested in the environment field question the value and even the legitimacy of using economics to decide environmental questions. To them, environmental protection is not about maximizing the economic value of the environment to humans. Rather, it is about honoring rights to a healthy and sustainable environment, maximizing the spiritual potential of humanity, or preserving the integrity of the entire biotic community." Some "environmental moralists" even go so far as to "reject all forms of economic analysis." If less extreme, many other environmentalists still do "oppose market solutions because [they] . . . fear that these solutions conflict with moral, spiritual, or community justifications for environmental protection"—amounting to issuance of economic "licenses to abuse the environment." Still other "environmental moralists . . . are unlikely to find cost-benefit analysis much to their liking" because "cost-benefit analyses do not focus on the ethical considerations that the environmental moralist believes should shape environmental policy."[1]

Some economists, however, also regard themselves as environmentalists. Reflecting their dual identities, they conceived another possibility. What if professional economists could put a dollar value on the very existence of a species, forest, or other object in a "natural" condition, aside from any actual use made of it?[2] If such estimates could be made, they could then be factored into overall economic analyses, and government decisions could still be shaped by benefit-cost calculations—now extending over a newly enlarged range of environmental values and benefits. In this way, the challenge that the rise of environmental religion posed to economic religion perhaps could be averted; professional economists might continue to be the unchallenged high priests of American society, encompassing even ethical considerations relating to the environment within the domain of economic calculation.

Valuing Images in the Mind

In *Encounters with the Archdruid*, the distinguished *New Yorker* writer John McPhee relates a discussion with David Brower, regarded by McPhee—and many others—as among the leading American environmentalists of the second half of the twentieth century. Talking about the real meaning of wilderness, Brower notes, "I have a friend named Garrett Hardin, who wears leg braces. I have heard him say that he would not want to come to a place like this by road, and that it is enough for him just to know that these mountains exist as they are, and he hopes that they will be like this in the future." As Brower said of his own views, "I believe in wilderness for itself alone."[3]

Economics as traditionally practiced, however, cannot accommodate this perspective on the world.[4] Economics assumes that human beings live for happiness ("utility"), and that happiness is a result of consumption. As the economist Stanley Lebergott says, "The goal of every economy is to provide consumption. So economists of all persuasions have agreed, from Smith and Mill to Keynes, Tobin, and Becker."[5] Historically, there has been no place in economic thinking for the idea that something that is never seen, touched, or otherwise directly experienced—that is not consumed in any way by any person—can have an economic value to an individual or to society.

Yet, as McPhee's discussions with Brower indicated, the economic way of thinking was at odds with an emerging environmental ethos that in the 1960s and 1970s was beginning to spread widely in American society. Instead of a "natural resource" to be used to increase the production—and ultimately the consumption—of goods and services, the natural world was increasingly seen as something to be protected and restored for its own sake, even if there was no direct consumptive benefit. Nature was said by many environmentalists to have an "intrinsic value" independent of any tangible benefits to human beings. Although obviously not a practical possibility, one environmentalist went so far as to assert that "every intervention in nature that cannot be rectified is a sacrilege."[6]

Economists, it appeared, might therefore be faced with an awkward choice: either reject their own economic perspective on the world or find themselves disagreeing frequently with a powerful new ethical movement in American life. It is also probably fair to say that some economists experienced an internal tension within themselves, feeling personally drawn to environmental values that were impossible to express in their own professional language. In 1967, a leading environmental economist at Resources for the Future, a Washington research institute, proposed a solution. John Krutilla suggested that the scope of economics should expand to include a new concept that has since come be known as "existence value."[7] The enjoyments of life need not be limited to things that can be directly seen and touched. Consumption, even as economists think about it, should extend as well to the simple fact of knowing that a rare geologic formation, a wild tiger, a dense rain forest, or some other object in nature continues to exist.

Formally, the "variables" in a person's "utility function" would include not only the amounts of food, clothing, and other ordinary goods and services directly consumed, but also the various states of knowledge that each person has of the existence of plant, animal, and other natural features in the world. Implicitly at least, consumers would be willing to pay something for this latter form of "consumption," the existence of a pleasant thought in their mind, thus giving rise to efforts by economists to calculate existence values in precise dollar terms.[8]

By the 1980s, the concept of existence value was coming into use by a number of environmental economists for purposes such as estimating the benefits of government actions or calculating damage assessments against business corporations whose actions had harmed parts of the natural world. A federal appeals court in 1989 directed the Department of the Interior to give greater weight to existence values in its assessment of money payments for damages to public resources under the Superfund law.[9] The concept even received favorable notice in literary circles, such as in the *New York Review of Books*, where the author of one article argued that it should be central to achieving world biodiversity objectives: "Why should citizens of industrialized countries pay to preserve resources that are legally the domain of other countries? An obscure tenet of economics provides a rationale. Certain things have what is known as an 'existence value.'"[10] More recently, an MIT economist finds that the economic profession is concerned with studying three types of value— "use value, option value, and existence value." Although there may be many conceptual issues to resolve, economists cannot continue to ignore the fact that "consumers may want [that] some good or state of the world continue to exist, and be willing to pay something to sustain it, even though they know they will never experience it directly, or 'consume' it in any normal sense."[11]

The potential policy impact of calculating existence values was emphasized by the very large dollar magnitudes—implausibly large, as they have sometimes seemed—that environmental economists were finding in this new source of economic benefit. Knowledge of the preservation of the northern spotted owl in the Pacific Northwest was estimated in one economic study to have a total existence value for all U.S. households of $8.3 billion per year. Yet another economic study found still higher numbers, asserting that the preservation of a population of whooping cranes would be worth $32 billion per year in total existence value for the United States.[12] If they were taken seriously, such high dollar estimates raised the possibility that their application in benefit-cost assessments might significantly alter government environmental policies.

A Growing Debate

When the idea of calculating existence values was raised, most mainstream economists at first paid little attention. As the potential uses widened and as the policy stakes escalated, however, an active professional debate developed in the 1990s.[13] Noneconomists also entered the controversy.[14] As some suggested, it appeared that environmental economists were attempting to calculate the economic value of obeying an ethical command, which necessarily transcended dollars and cents. Many environmentalists recognized the potential political gains from showing high dollar estimates of existence values but otherwise found the concept offensive to their own environmental values.[15]

The Exxon Corporation, facing large potential damage assessments as a result of the *Exxon Valdez* oil spill in Alaska, and believing that these assessments might be based in part on existence value estimates for the loss of natural features in Prince William Sound, committed large financial resources to studying the issue. Exxon hired a number of leading economists—many whom were not environmental economists and were new to this subject—to examine whether the calculation of existence values was an appropriate economic method. Their critique, on the whole, was negative.[16] In response, the State of Alaska and the federal government hired several leading environmental economists who took a much more positive view.[17]

Hoping to resolve the issue, the National Oceanographic and Atmospheric Administration (NOAA) convened a panel of leading economists, chaired by two Nobel Prize winners in economics, Kenneth Arrow and Robert Solow. In 1993, the NOAA panel declared that, although there were significant practical problems in estimating existence values, and much care must be exercised to prevent their misuse, the concept should in principle be incorporated into the acceptable set of professional economic tools.[18] The controversy, however, has continued.[19] As economist Henry Jacoby commented in 2002, when it comes to the use of "techniques of contingent evaluation" (for estimating existence values), the majority of economists did not have much confidence in them—even as they were reluctant to concede that important domains of social choice fell outside the realm of legitimate economic calculation.[20]

From a narrower standpoint, there were a number of technical problems with existence value calculations in terms of traditional methods of economic analysis.* Moreover, those who have actually attempted to measure existence values have thus far studied mostly wilderness areas, threatened species, and other environmental concerns. The application of the concept, however, is potentially much wider. Tropical forests may have an existence value, but there will also be an existence value in knowing of the higher incomes of poor people in less developed countries—some of whose jobs may depend on cutting the forests. Indeed, there is virtually an endless set of possibilities for the calculation of existence values.[21] Almost any state of the world invested with symbolic significance by significant numbers of people will have a nontrivial existence value. For example, the very presence of an abortion clinic in a community will cause some of the residents of the community to feel psychic pain, whereas others will feel good about it, giving rise to abortion-related existence values. An act of burning the American flag will have a large negative existence value for many patriotic citizens, and a large positive value for others who may "enjoy" the symbolic assertion of free speech rights in American political life.

Once the full scope of existence values was recognized, it could be seen that environmental economists were in effect proposing to substitute formal economic calculations as a way of resolving basic value controversies within American life. Essentially religious questions in many cases would be decided by public answers to economic survey instruments, administered by economists, asking how much was the dollar worth to a person of one mental image in their mind versus another. And it was not merely a few environmental economists but a number of leading members of the economics profession, including Nobel Prize winners, who were giving their blessing to this new form of professional practice.

---

*Peter Diamond and Jerry Hausman, economists at MIT, concluded in 1994 that "surveys designed to test for consistency between stated willingness-to-pay and economic theory have found that contingent valuation responses [used to estimate existence values] are not consistent with economic theory." Other critics found that in practice existence value studies often yielded estimates that were altogether implausible. For example, respondents to survey questionnaires sometimes gave almost the same dollar estimates for saving wild animals from human harm even when the number of animals saved might vary from one survey to another by several orders of magnitude. See Peter A. Diamond and Jerry A. Hausman, "On Contingent Valuation Measurement of Nonuse Values," in *Contingent Valuation: A Critical Assessment*, ed. Jerry A. Hausman (New York: North Holland, 1993), 46.

Negative Existence Value

The concept of existence value faced other problems as well. Environmental economists focused almost entirely on mental images, such as the protection of a beautiful mountain view, that invoked positive feelings—and thus would involve positive dollar benefits. In any diverse society, however, it is almost inevitable that cultural or religious symbols regarded favorably by one group will be regarded negatively by other groups. Indeed, negative existence values—costs imposed on a person by an unpleasant image in the mind—are likely to be almost as common as positive existence values.

In the specific case of a wilderness, for example, environmentalists will view it positively, but there are many other people who may regard the existence of a newly created wilderness area as a symbolic affront to their own core values. It is for some of them offensive in the manner of throwing away good food—a deliberate waste of good timber, minerals, and other natural resources. As a result, the knowledge of the creation of the wilderness might make them feel worse (experience "disutility"). A leader of the "wise-use" movement, Ron Arnold, thus writes that wilderness and other curbs on development "have bit by bit impaired our productivity with excessive and unwise restrictions on forest and rangelands, on water and agriculture, on construction and manufacture, on energy and minerals, on every material value upon which our society is built."[22] Some true believers in economic religion may be just as upset about the creation of a wilderness area as other true believers in environmental religion have strong positive feelings about this same government action.

In general, the legal setting aside of nature, free of human influence (to the extent practically possible), represents symbolically a testimony to the glory of one faith, but this faith may be at odds with the beliefs of other Americans (further, these people may thereby feel their own religious convictions offended). It is not simply an issue of a secular economic versus secular environmental religion. One analyst characterized the fierce policy disputes over the creation of wilderness areas in southern Utah as, at their core, a clash between the Mormon beliefs of many Utah natives and a competing set of secular religious environmental beliefs found among many newcomers to the area.[23]

Another aspect of existence value is that some people may find it unpleasant to contemplate the increasing secularization of American religion.[24] The rise of environmental religion, with its secular cathedrals in the wilderness, might be seen as an indication of a growing threat posed to many traditional Christian religions.* Probably reflecting the fact that most advocates of exis-

---

* The Catholic League for Religious and Civil Rights, for example, reacted to speeches by interior secretary Bruce Babbitt defending the Endangered Species Act in biblical terms with a press release,

tence value calculations have been environmental economists, no professional economist thus far has proposed to calculate negative existence values of this kind, even though the omission may significantly bias the overall process of economic calculation. It seems that environmental economists are happy to put their professional skills at the service of creating more wilderness areas— and to experience a negative existence value of their own with respect to the very thought of assisting the enemies of wilderness.

Finding God's Hand in Nature

As John McPhee related, David Brower had for many years been touring lecture halls on college campuses and other places across the United States preaching an environmental gospel. Of course, there had been previous environmental prophets, great texts, and sacred sites. According to McPhee, "Throughout the sermon, Brower quotes the gospel—the gospel according to John Muir . . . the gospel according to Henry David Thoreau."[25] As a former executive director of the Sierra Club for seventeen years in the 1950s and 1960s, Brower was a direct follower in the line of Muir, who had founded the environmental organization in 1892. For Muir, wild areas had an explicitly religious significance as the visible places on earth showing the handiwork of God at the creation. Thus, as Roderick Nash wrote in *Wilderness and the American Mind*, Muir considered that the "wilderness glowed, to be sure, only for those who approached it on a higher spiritual plane. . . . In this condition he believed life's inner harmonies, fundamental truths of existence, stood out in bold relief," reflecting Muir's belief that in the natural objects of wild areas it was possible to find "terrestrial manifestations of God." They provided a "window opening into heaven, a mirror reflecting the Creator," making it possible to encounter in wild nature some true "sparks of the Divine Soul."[26]

For Muir, a wilderness area was literally a kind of church. A church is a place of spiritual inspiration, a place where people come to learn about and to know God. A wilderness church, further, is in one sense more awe inspiring than any human-built church could ever be. In environmental religion, a wilderness—as a part of nature untouched by human hands—is a church literally built by God. Today, these religious convictions that inspired Muir often still lie behind the protection of wilderness. Roger Kennedy, while he

---

"Bruce Babbitt Maligns Catholicism." Babbitt had said in his speech that he found more spiritual inspiration in nature than in the Catholic Church of his youth. The president of the League, William Donohue, declared that the secretary's explanation of his religious turn away from Catholicism showed political "stupidity as well as unfairness." See *Human Events*, January 12, 1996.

was serving as the director of the National Park Service in the Clinton administration, stated that "wilderness is a religious concept . . . we should conceive of wilderness as part of our religious life." Wilderness puts us "in the presence of the unknowable and the uncontrollable before which all humans stand in awe"—that is to say, although Kennedy did not put it in just these words, in wilderness we stand in the presence of God's creation.[27]

How Much Is a Church Worth?

If the concept of existence value were extended into every possible area of life, it would be possible to ask: How much is a belief in God—yet another image in a person's mind, if historically for many people the most important image of all—worth in dollar terms? Although leading members of the economics profession endorse the concept of existence value, even the boldest economists stopped short of putting a dollar value on the existence in a person's mind of the knowledge of God's commands and powers (however consistent this step might have been with the logic of their argument in other contexts). Yet calculating a monetary value for the existence of a wilderness area comes close to the same thing. Nature untouched by human hands, as found in a wilderness area, is for the John Muirs of the world a means of instruction in the ways of God. In environmentalism today, this message comes in only a modestly revised form; any explicit mention of God is often left out, but wild nature is described in terms such as "the true source of values for the world" or other such paraphrasing of traditional Christian messages.

Admittedly, to value a wilderness as a type of church is to value the earthly means of communication of religious truth rather than the pure mental act of knowing about God. Thus, a more precise analogy would be: How much is the existence of a church worth—including the dollar benefits to those who come to the church to discover a new faith or to reaffirm their old faith? There may also be an additional existence value gained by others who do not visit the church, knowing that the church is helping to spread the true faith to more people throughout the community and the world. The total dollar value of a church is, at least in concept, an answerable question. Economists can validly point out that, although leaders of organized religions may well be offended by the question, they do in fact routinely make such calculations. Other things equal, the existence of more churches is likely to be better for religious people everywhere, but more churches also cost money. In making a decision about whether to build another church, a religious organization is in effect saying that the money benefits of an additional church are, or are not, worth the cost of building and maintaining it.

So how would one go about putting a marginal value to society of the existence of one more church (i.e., one more wilderness "cathedral")? Answering this question, assuming that a person is willing to think about the matter in these economic terms, would involve multiple concerns. One would have to consider: How much does a particular new church (wilderness) add to the religious education of the faithful and the total existence value that they experience in further contemplating God? How many new people might it draw into the faith? Related to this would be the question: How many churches (wildernesses) should a religious denomination ideally maintain, and how many does it already have? This obviously depends on the total number of faithful, their geographic distribution, and the expected growth of the religious group in the future. In the end, all these religious dollar benefits will be derivative of the ultimate existence value derived from large numbers of people believing in God—the main reason for building the churches (adding to the national wilderness system) in the first place.*

Yet another factor, to be sure, is that the building of a church is not just a way to be spiritually uplifted; it can also be a way of publicly and symbolically announcing a depth of religious commitment, a way of formally taking an action for the greater glory of God. Building a grand cathedral, such as Notre Dame in Paris, can take on a special religious significance when it involves a great sacrifice of human effort and cost—as religions have historically found meaning in making large sacrifices of many kinds as a way to express their great devotion. Many primitive tribes, for instance, have had religious rites in which they sacrifice their best cow, goat, or other animal to honor their god.

A wilderness area thus might become all the more meaningful in much the same way: the more valuable the mineral, timber, and other natural resources given up, the greater the sacrifice made and the greater the symbolic statement of devotion to the faith. The dollar value of the existence of a belief in God, as an environmental economist might put it, may be increased by the heightened religious experience following the making of a religious sacrifice. Indeed, this may be why the Arctic National Wildlife Refuge (ANWR) in northeast Alaska has become so religiously important to the environmental

---

* As mentioned above, there is also the possibility of negative existence values associated with protecting wilderness areas and other parts of wild nature. One possible source of negative existence value for some people—libertarians, for example—might be that a wilderness area is in effect a government-owned church. For those who believe in a strict separation of church and state, it may be unpleasant to think about this violation of their basic constitutional principles. Indeed, if the principle of separation of church and state were strictly applied in the case of wilderness areas, this would be an area of activity precluded from government involvement. All wilderness areas—at least in their capacity as cathedrals of environmental religion—would have to be acquired and maintained privately by environmental organizations and other environmental true believers.

movement.* It is not just the on-the-ground environmental features of the area—in both Alaska and Canada there are in truth many other similarly desolate and isolated places bordering the Arctic. The one truly distinctive feature of ANWR is that there is so much valuable oil and natural gas there—amounts that have an estimated gross worth of as much as one trillion dollars (ultimately depending of course on the future level of oil prices). If this area is instead left "untouched," the ANWR "church" conceivably would be the most expensive cathedral ever dedicated to any faith in the history of the world, forever redounding to the glory of an environmental god and the American environmental movement.

An economic analysis of the benefits and costs of ANWR oil and gas development thus becomes in major part a tradeoff between two alternative "uses" of the energy resources there: (1) as a source of energy for a modern economy, and (2) as a symbol that, left in the ground, would show the willingness of American society to commit vast resources to maintain as much as a trillion-dollar cathedral. In the latter respect, environmental true believers would thus derive two forms of dollar benefit: the knowledge of God in their minds would be heightened (the existence value of knowing God would be higher), and they would also know of the existence of their own heroic efforts (together with other Americans) to make sacrifices for the greater glory of their god.

To be sure, from a wider social point of view, it also has to be taken into account that a church may be valued by many others outside the faith. Like the Vatican and the Sistine Chapel for non-Catholics, they may admire it as a work of art or regard it as an important part of their own cultural history. Many people today regard a wilderness area in much this fashion; it is a museum piece providing a record of one point in the geologic transformation of the earth. Wilderness areas also often have beautiful scenery that can be preserved for the future for people to visit and enjoy; many people can be expected to enjoy hiking in the wilderness for aesthetic and other purposes.

---

* Law professor David Schoenbrod finds a similar motivation in the demands of environmental groups, and the subsequent mandate of the Environmental Protection Agency, that the General Electric Company (GE) spend five hundred million dollars or more to remove PBCs from forty miles of the upper Hudson River, requiring a massive dredging operation involving the removal of more than two million cubic feet of sediment. There was little real evidence of any potential public health benefits, and the dredging itself would be disruptive for the local communities along the river (most of which opposed the action). Instead, as Schoenbrod concludes, the EPA was "basing policy on religious doctrine," requiring the dredging as an act of religious penitence. It reflected a strong conviction of "a moral imperative to bruise the head of the industrial serpent. GE must be made to suffer, regardless of whether science shows that the dredging does any good." In other words, the larger the amount of money GE was required to waste, the greater the demonstration of religious commitment—and the larger the total existence value for all Americans of knowing that GE was being punished. See David Schoenbrod, *Saving Our Environment from Washington: How Congress Grabs Power, Shirks Responsibility, and Shortchanges the People* (New Haven: Yale University Press, 2005), 86, 100.

There is little controversy among economists, admittedly, about the need to incorporate such tangible benefits of direct visits to wilderness areas in government decision making. For both museum and recreational benefits, and unlike calculations of existence values relating to the pleasures experienced from positive mental images, there is a direct use by individuals that can be assigned a monetary value by economists according to long-standing economic methods.

Yet many devoutly religious people (in a conventional sense) will resist putting a dollar value on even the direct "use value"—to say nothing of the existence value—of a wilderness or other church. Assigning such a dollar value would be to regard a visit to a church (or wilderness) in the same category as, say, attendance at a football game. Indeed, most religious leaders would reject such a suggestion out of hand. A church involves an element of the sacred; to put a monetary value on the physical existence of a large number of churches and worshippers profanes the faith.

In considering proposals by economists to measure the existence value of a wilderness, many environmental leaders do in fact commonly react much as other traditional religious leaders would. While recognizing a potential gain in political support in putting their case in conventional economic terms, environmentalists have on the whole been cool if not antagonistic to efforts by economists to calculate existence values. The environmental philosopher Mark Sagoff, a past president of the International Society of Environmental Ethics, writes that the calculation of existence values is "an attempt to expand economic theory to cover environmental values. . . . But what makes environmental values important—what makes them values—often has little or nothing to do with 'preferences,' with perceived well being, or with the [economic] 'satisfaction' people may feel in taking principled positions." Aside from the many practical analytical problems, Sagoff rejects existence value in principle as an imperialistic attempt by economists to substitute clever analytical techniques for "the role that the public discussion of values should play in formulating environmental policy" in American society.[28]

As Sagoff and others are saying, a religion must be judged by the validity of its claims to offer "the truth" about the world, not on the basis of the dollar value of the pleasures found in thinking about the existence of God, its churches, or other leading public symbols of the religion. Over the course of history, surprisingly many people have even chosen martyrdom over a coerced renunciation of their individual understanding of religious truth. When religions offer different basic orientations to the world, various ways of framing the meaning of human existence, the matter cannot be resolved by dollar calculations of the relative pleasures found in thinking about alternative forms of such mental imagery.

That even some leading members of the economics profession would endorse such a bizarre course of action suggests the high level of anxiety that environmental religion was provoking among the economic priesthood and other followers in economic religion. The stakes involved nothing less than their own religious self-identity. For a true believer in economic religion, the god of economics in fact does control the whole world, including all matters relating to the environment as well. To argue otherwise was virtually equivalent to asserting that the economic god was yet another of the many false idols of history.

Conclusion

The story of existence value is a small part of contemporary economic history. Yet it is especially revealing of the character of economic religion. The core purpose of economics is to provide the expert knowledge for American society to maximize total production and consumption of goods and services—thus revealing a path of economic progress that will in the end lead to a new heaven on earth. Given the transcendent purpose of economics, all important things in life then should fall within the scope of economic calculation. When confronted with a rival environmental gospel that explicitly challenged the imperial claims of economics—that often suggested in fact that the god of economics was a false god—the members of the economics profession found it difficult to defend themselves. They could not offer a theological defense, partly because they knew little about theology, and also because they typically denied the religious character of their own professional activities. In the past, economists had faced similar challenges to their authority from traditional Christian critics, but the swelling popular enthusiasm for the environmental cause now made this challenge much more difficult to ignore.

When attacked on such religious grounds, economists could think of only one legitimate response. Environmental religion must somehow be incorporated within the framework of economic religion. The higher religious goals sought by the environmental faithful must be reinterpreted in terms of dollar benefits and costs. The creation of a wilderness must be assigned a monetary value, including not only the benefits to future recreational visitors but also the (presumably) much greater value to all Americans everywhere in simply knowing of the existence of the wilderness. By resolving the claims of environmental religion with dollar calculations, however, it was like resolving the claims of Christian religion by asking: How much is God worth (in existence value)?

4

AS THE MEMBERS OF THE ECONOMICS PROFESSION faced the rise of environmental religion, another challenge was to understand the meaning of new social objectives such as "sustainability." In many ways the goal of economic religion was the opposite of sustainability—to move as rapidly as possible along the route of "progress," often involving major social transformation. What would it mean to have a "sustainable" economic system? From one perspective, this might mean a slower rate of growth or even the absence of economic change. Indeed, the highest purpose of environmentalism was not rapid economic progress but the protection of nature from undue human impacts. The language of "sustainability" might be a way of symbolically communicating this new value. If that were so, it might be another area of deep conflict between economic and environmental religion. How, if at all, might a reconciliation be achieved?

The Economic Way of Thinking

Mainstream economics' framework of thought begins with the fact that economics is a social science, and thus it is about the interactions of people in society and their welfare. Animals, plants, the physical state of the world, and other material conditions do not enter into consideration, except insofar as they provide a backdrop to increasing human well-being. It is in this sense similar to the biblical view that human beings alone are made in the image of God, and that God created the world both for His enjoyment and human dominion.

That is not to say that sustaining nature in a wild condition necessarily commands a low priority in the economic value system. If people derive much pleasure ("utility," to use the economists' term) from the direct experiencing of wild nature, then preservation of natural conditions may be a high individual and social priority. But it is the fact that people directly benefit, or chose to protect nature for practical reasons of their own doing, and not the intrinsic merits of sustaining elements of nature per se, that counts in economic thinking.

Another key feature of the economic way of thinking is that the factors entering into human welfare are regarded as substitutable. Thus, no one good or service—no one biological or natural unit or system—has any automatic claims. If any one item is not available for human use in the future, economists expect that people will be able to turn elsewhere to find substitutes. By the essence of its method, economics is concerned with tradeoffs. Given that item A costs so much, economists ask whether consuming more of A will add or detract from individual and social well-being, recognizing that producing or maintaining A requires giving up the "opportunity cost" of other items that could alternatively have been obtained for the same commitment of resources. For society as a whole, the goal is to maximize the total value of all human consumption, not the social gains from any one particular item.

Another way of saying this is that the economic way of thinking rejects the idea that some things are literally "priceless."[1] Many people will say that preserving a species, saving a human life, or some other goal is beyond the consideration of costs, but economists regard such assertions as merely a rhetorical and political ploy. They are actually strong claims on resources being made by partisans of particular causes, rather than a reasonable basis for any society as a whole to set its priorities. Adding up all the claims made for "priceless" objects, or even for perfectly realizing one "priceless" goal, economists suggest, could well exceed the total resources available to society.[2] It is thus not only objectionable in concept but also in practice, as it is often impossible to deliver on any such utopian set of aspirations.

In standard economics, the economic world is thus divided into acts of production and acts of consumption, and it is only the latter that enter into the "utility functions" by which economists rank one overall individual consumption set—and in the aggregate, one overall social outcome—relative to another. In policy making, this way of thinking translates into opposition by economists to preserving particular industries, jobs, communities, and other portions of the social and physical infrastructure of production for their own sake. If the making of textiles in the United States is economically inefficient, then this activity, and any local communities that depend on it, should fade into American history. Any transitional stresses and strains felt by the current residents of the losing communities are simply part of the price of a greater progress of the whole. Economists have similarly opposed the many proposals that society should chose a social infrastructure of production—a set of laws, regulations, and other institutional mechanisms—on the basis of the specific ethical claims made for and against such particular mechanisms. What counts is whether the legal and other institutions of society most effectively advance total production, and in the long run total consumption—and thus the most rapid economic progress of the world.

The wage level, for example, is an important part of the arrangements for production and thus is not in itself an item of consumption. Hence, most economists criticize government interference with market wages, opposing the many people who have sought on social equity grounds to require a "just wage"—or more recently the payment of "comparable worth" to different types of job holders. Similarly, economists argue that the best way to control pollution is to allow the market system to function, requiring the creation of systems of rights to pollute that can either be temporarily "rented" by the government (i.e., polluters pay a tax) or transferred into private ownership for market trading among rights holders (a "cap and trade" pollution rights system).[3] Economists rejected the moral objections made by some leading environmentalists that such a policy would amount to the official sanctioning by government of morally unethical behavior.

The mainstream economic way of thinking thus argues that achieving efficient use of resources to maximize the total value of economic output, not the moral desirability of the physical methods of production or of the social institutions for ordering the economy, should determine public policy. In considering whether current levels of total consumption in society should be reduced, as many environmentalists have said is required for reasons of sustainability, the economic way of thinking thus finds that there is only one sound reason for doing so. It might be desirable to reduce present-day consumption only if this reduction will allow for greater efficiency in the long-run allocation of production and consumption. That is to say, it might be desirable to reduce consumption today because this will make possible investments that yield greater future consumption tomorrow worth more in the future. The possibility that consumption should be reduced because this act is good for the soul, or because consumption is not what actually makes people happy, has no place within the standard methods of economics.

Economists as Advocates

A powerful set of value assumptions—an economic religion—thus underlies the methods and the thinking of professional economists. Yet for many years, dating back to the Progressive Era early in the twentieth century, professional economists argued that their policy efforts were those of a "value-neutral" expert.[4] Governing was to be divided into separate realms of objective professional expertise and subjective value systems. These corresponded to the two governing domains of politics and of administration. The social value judgments—based on religion, ideology, or perhaps some other normative basis—should be made by politicians in the democratic process, setting the broad policy directions for the whole society. Economists, along with other expert professionals, should frame the policy options for consideration and, once politicians had chosen among these options, should put the political choices into practice. But this would involve only the undertaking of "technical" tasks. Economists were not to press their own religious or any other individual personal values, as the reigning economic orthodoxy went for many years, because that would be an improper "advocacy" role for a professional expert.

Economists began entering government in large numbers first in the New Deal years and then during World War II. They found, in many cases, that they could not reconcile their actual experiences in the policy-making process with the understanding of proper professional conduct in which they had been educated. Indeed, well before the recent discussions of sustainability, many leading policy economists were led to abandon the claims previously made to value-neutrality. In 1968, the Harvard economist Carl Kaysen observed that "the role of the economist in policy formation in these areas is almost diametrically opposite to that envisaged in the formal theory of policy making. . . . He functions primarily as a propagandist of values, not as a technician supplying data for the pre-existing preferences of the policy makers."[5]

Charles Schultze, a former director of the federal Bureau of the Budget in the 1960s, and chair of the Council of Economic Advisers in the 1970s, has said that "political values permeate every aspect of the decision-making process in the majority of federal domestic programs. There is no simple division of labor in which the 'politicians' achieve consensus on an agreed-on set of objectives while the 'analysts' design and evaluate—from efficiency and effectiveness criteria—alternative means of achieving those objectives."[6] Within this framework, as Schultze understood and approved, economists acted as strong efficiency advocates in government.[7] In the 1980s and 1990s, the inevitability of an advocacy role when economists entered the policy process was increasingly accepted. In 2002, MIT economist Henry Jacoby stated that within the economics profession, "it is understood by all but the shallowest practitioners that, particularly when applied to public choice, prevailing economic methods are anchored in a web of (often unstated) moral propositions and assumptions about political values and institutions."[8]

The work experiences of economists in government also revealed other tensions with their original professional training. For working government economists, it soon became apparent that most of the details of higher economic theory were often too removed from the real world to have practical consequences for policy decisions.[9] The statistical results of econometrics were typically too fragile to be relied on in setting policies where government actions could affect millions of people. Instead, it was a few key ideas—"Just common-sense economics . . . the kind of basic analytical framework that we all sort of got in Econ. 101," as one former staff member at the Council of Economic Advisers put it—that were usually the greatest source of economic influence in policy making.[10]

Alec Cairncross similarly wrote of his long experience as a leading economic policy adviser to the British government that it was the overall economic "way of thinking" that had the greatest impact.[11] In general, as Carol Weiss wrote, the key policy role of the social sciences is that they provide "the intellectual background of concepts, orientations and intellectual generalizations that inform policy."[12] Although Weiss did not speak explicitly of a religion, she was effectively saying that the tenets of an economic religion were being communicated by the members of the economics profession. It was this basic economic way of thinking about the world, and the powerful belief system underlying it, that in the 1970s and 1980s increasingly put the mainstream of the economics profession at odds with many of those most concerned about the environmental "sustainability" of the natural world.

More recently, some economists have themselves acknowledged that even the higher reaches of economic theory are not truly separated from strong implicit value elements. Extending the thinking of philosopher Richard Rorty into economic domains, economist D. McCloskey argued in 1985 that economic theorizing, with its scientific claims, "promises knowledge free from doubt, free from metaphysics, morals and personal conviction. What it is able to deliver renames as scientific methodology . . . the economic scientist's metaphysics, morals and personal convictions"—his or her religion, as one might say, recognizing that religion can take many different forms in contemporary life, secular and traditional alike.[13]

The professional economists' claims to scientific objectivity thus are, as McCloskey and others have said, a rhetorical device, not to be taken literally. If perhaps not by conscious calculation, economists are effectively seeking to exclude noneconomists from the debate and to stake a claim to greater policy legitimacy and influence in society, based on their asserted exclusive scientific authority. In the medieval period, the Roman Catholic priesthood sought to impress and exclude ordinary people by communicating in Latin; today, an economic priesthood speaks in mathematics and other technical languages. Yet it is the underlying religion of economics, more than the specific applications of the expert methods themselves, that in the end is the driving force in shaping most economic policy recommendations.

Solow's Vision of Sustainability

In a 1991 lecture to the Woods Hole Oceanographic Institution, the MIT economist Robert Solow (winner of the Nobel Prize in 1987) applied the economic way of thinking to the subject of sustainability.[14] First, Solow acknowledged that, like most economists, he started off skeptically. Even where an effort had been made to develop "carefully thought out definitions and discussions" of sustainability, the fact was that "they all turn out to be vague."* Indeed, Solow was of the opinion that "sustainability is an essentially vague concept, and it would be wrong to think of it as being precise." If there was a meaning, it belonged more to the realm of ethics than of science: "It says something about a moral obligation that we are supposed to have for future generations." As long as sustainability was understood as merely a declaration of such a broad social value, Solow could admit that sustainability "is not at all useless."[15]

A more substantive understanding, however, might be sought. Taking up this challenge, Solow observed that sustainability cannot literally mean "to leave the world as we found it in detail." This would be something that would not only be physically "unfeasible" but also "when you think about it not even desirable"—here reflecting the economist's commitment to continuing rapid social change and economic progress. Solow stated that instead sustainability must be understood in the terms of "an obligation to conduct ourselves so that we leave to the future the option or the capacity to be as well off as we are."[16] Thus, society is morally obligated to act to ensure that the economic welfare of future generations will be at least as high as that of the present generation.

As noted above, the economic way of thinking considers that there is no reason in principle why any one form of consumption should not be able to substitute for another, all as part of the effort to maximize the overall level of well-being. As Solow thus said at Woods Hole, "What about nature? . . . I think that we ought, in our policy choices, to embody our desire for unspoiled nature as a component of well-being. But we have to recognize that different amenities really are, to some extent, substitutable for one another." If people will feel happier going to baseball games (now and in the future) than in visiting wilderness areas, then building baseball stadiums should command a higher social priority. As Solow elaborated, economically, "sustainability doesn't require that any *particular* species of owl or any *particular* species of fish or any *particular* tract of forest be preserved."[17]

---

* John Pezzey surveyed the definitions given in a review of writings on the subject of sustainable development and found more than fifty, covering a wide range. See John Pezzey, "Economic Analysis of Sustainable Growth and Sustainable Development" (working paper 15, World Bank Environmental Department, Washington, D.C., 1989).

Thus sustainability, as Solow understood it, did not require that the natural world be preserved in any one specific form or another. Nature for economists is a "natural resource" that embodies in its various forms productive potential to increase total national product—the real final goal. Hence, in Solow's understanding, there was no necessary justification for complete protection of every individual species, as under the Endangered Species Act. As a follower in economic religion, Solow followed the commands of a god who differed not only with a secular environmental god but also with the God of the Bible, who instructed Noah to build an ark for all the species of the earth.

Sustainability as Growth Theory

Unlike some economists, Solow did not believe that the welfare of future generations could simply be entrusted to the workings of the private market; active government policy interventions might be necessary. Indeed, it was not only a matter of macroeconomic goals of avoiding unemployment and holding down inflation to stimulate rapid economic growth, but also of achieving social equity. Solow thus also urged his audience to think about what government policy measures might be needed to ensure "sustainability as a matter of distributional equity between the present and the future." In this framework, sustainability becomes "a problem about savings and investment. It becomes a problem about the choice between current consumption and providing for the future."[18] And government, as economists have been arguing at least since the writings of John Maynard Keynes, can play a major role in determining levels of total social consumption and investment. Thus, the issue of sustainability is incorporated as an important topic within the broader subject of macroeconomics and government management of the processes of economic growth and development.

To be sure, by this definition of sustainability, the protection of the welfare of future generations had never been much of a problem in the modern era and would not be unless future developments caused a drastic reversal of the economic trends of the nineteenth and twentieth centuries. Indeed, for two hundred years in the West, the material welfare of each generation has improved significantly over that of its predecessors. As Solow observed, as a matter of social equity, "you could make a good case that our ancestors, who were considerably poorer than we are . . . were [therefore] probably excessively generous in providing for us."[19] In other words, past generations saved and invested so much, sacrificing their own consumption for our benefit, that they ironically ended up accomplishing a large transfer of income from a relatively poorer group of people at that time to a relatively richer group of people living today. Based on this past precedent at least, and given a presumption in favor of a more equal distribution of income, past generations should have consumed more, and the current generation perhaps should also be looking to increase its levels of consumption relative to the future.

Few economists, admittedly, advocated such a course of action. They were less concerned with equity among generations and more concerned with reaching heaven on earth as soon as possible, a goal that required a maximum rate of economic growth and development (as Solow had in fact long personally advocated). Social equity can be important in economic religion, but it is a short-run and lesser consideration that should not impede the much greater long-run goal. Indeed, when scarcity is abolished, and a state of full abundance is reached—perhaps not so far away for the developed nations of the world—social equity will no longer be an issue at all.

Solow's transformation of sustainability into an issue of savings and investment obviously is not what many environmentalists concerned about sustainability had in mind. His concerns reflected in part the long-standing, strong interest of professional economists in the determinants of economic growth. Indeed, early in his career, Solow was a leading professional developer of "growth theory," which addressed much the same policy questions of determining appropriate levels of investment and consumption over the long run.[20] In policy-making circles, economists generally have been prominent as advocates for high rates of economic growth. The Council of Economic Advisers, the leading vehicle for transmitting the views of professional economists to federal policy makers, was created in 1946 expressly for the purpose of maintaining full employment and setting the economy on a path of long-run rapid growth.

Sustainability and Climate Change

When environmentalists advocate the sustainability of the world's climate, they mean that the climate should be changed as little as possible, ideally avoiding any "anthropocentric" interventions and seeking to sustain the climate indefinitely at a "natural" temperature. Here again, however, most economists had a much different way of thinking about the future of the earth's climate. Within the economics profession, the leading analyst of climate change is Yale economics professor William Nordhaus (also coauthor, with MIT economist Paul Samuelson, of the more recent editions of the classic introductory textbook *Economics*). Following many other books and articles on the subject, in 2008 Nordhaus authored *A Question of Balance: Weighing the Options on Global Warming Policies.*[21] Princeton physicist Freeman Dyson reviewed it in the *New York Review of Books*, generating an unusual number of reader responses, a few of which, including that of Nordhaus himself, were printed in subsequent issues.[22]

For Nordhaus, similar to the earlier thinking of Solow, it would make no sense to spend money to mitigate climate change in pursuit of a goal of future climate stasis pursued for its own sake. Rather, climate change mitigation is a form of economic investment. Like other investments, the core question is the rate of future return. In the particular case of climate change, the returns from mitigation come mainly in terms of avoided future damages to society—economic, environmental, or whatever (there could also be positive aspects to a warmer climate, but these tend to receive less attention). As in other investment analyses, the costs and the returns do not all occur at the same time. Indeed, a special feature of climate change is that many of the largest costs of mitigation will be faced in the next few decades, whereas the largest benefits would not be obtained until much later. Nordhaus himself is broadly in agreement with other analysts who have concluded "that there would be relatively little damage from climate change over the coming century and that most damages would occur after 2200."[23]

To compare near-term costs with benefits that may not be realized until 2200 and later, economists employ "discounting" methods to calculate "present values." Nordhaus suggests that an appropriate discount rate will fall between 3 and 6 percent, and he uses 4 percent for his own analyses. As he points out, if a person invested $39,204 today and left the money in a bank account earning 4 percent per year, his or her investment would have grown to $100 million by 2200. Economically, this implies that an investment today of, say, $1 billion for climate change mitigation would have to generate future climate benefits of $2.6 trillion in year 2200 (assuming for the purposes of analysis that all the benefits were accrued in a single year) to be economically justified. If the future benefits in 2020 were less than $2.6 trillion, the return from simply putting the money in the bank would be greater. To put this in some perspective, $2.6 trillion is more than 15 percent of today's total U.S. gross national product.

By this standard, many of the possible current investments to mitigate future climate change will fail an economic test. Nordhaus acknowledges that many ordinary people would be "shocked" by this economic way of approaching the issue. But, as he states, society has available to it "a vast array of productive investments in an economy with rapid technological change. The power of compound interest turns tiny investment acorns into giant financial oaks over a century and more."[24] Moreover, much as Solow also saw matters at Woods Hole, any specific results for the world's climate, like any (or most) other specific features of the environment (or other features of society), are not valuable in and of themselves. Rather, what is important about the climate is its impact on the total national income in the future. By maximizing national income, the greatest total funds can then be applied to any priorities (including the environment as one possible competing claim on resources) that society may set when the time comes.

It would be "truly bizarre," as Nordhaus thinks, to reduce total future national income in the name of maximizing a single item of production and consumption such as the world's climate condition. Even if redistributional concerns are factored in, and as Solow also noted before him, the future is likely to be richer than the present, so making large current sacrifices to benefit a richer future would be socially regressive. Rather than wasting money on excessive climate mitigation, it would be economically more rational to invest it today in a range of high-yield investments that Nordhaus suggests—although he does not develop specific numbers—would on balance do more to "improve the quality of life for future generations at home and abroad." Nordhaus mentions several possibilities, including "investments in health systems at home, cures for tropical diseases, education around the world, basic research on new energy and low-carbon technologies, and infrastructure in war-torn countries such as Afghanistan."[25] In his Copenhagen project, Bjorn Lomborg has sought to refine the numbers, calculating specific priority rankings of the best ways to invest world resources today. Investments in climate change mitigation tend to fare poorly in comparison with a number of other current investment alternatives.[26]

But what if an unchanging world climate is an ethical imperative in and of itself? There may be a moral injunction to protect and preserve the "natural" climate that transcends economic calculations. Changing the climate is "playing God" in an especially dramatic way. There are many other things in the world that are pursued as a matter of basic moral principle—abolishing slavery, for example, came to be seen in these terms in the nineteenth century. In his book review, Dyson concludes that Nordhaus simply fails to understand the environmental argument. As a scientist whose feels compelled to see the world accurately, even if he may personally have some regrets, it is quite clear to Dyson that, not only Nordhaus, but also:

> all the books that I have seen about the science and economics of global warming . . . miss the main point. The main point is religious rather than scientific. There is a worldwide secular religion which we may call environmentalism, holding that we are stewards of the earth, that despoiling the planet with waste products of our luxurious living is a sin, and that the path of righteousness is to live as frugally as possible. The ethics of environmentalism are being taught to children in kindergartens, schools, and colleges all over the world.

Environmentalism has replaced [the economic religion of] socialism as the leading secular religion. . . . Environmentalism, as a religion of hope and respect for nature, is here to stay. This is a religion that we can all share, whether or not we believe that global warming is harmful.[27]

Commenting on Dyson's review in a later issue of the *New York Review of Books*, Nordhaus stated that he found "little to quarrel with."[28] Nevertheless, as most economists probably would, he chose not to address Dyson's finding that climate change policy is fundamentally a religious question.[29] Economists are typically uncomfortable with the very subject of religion. This raises an interesting question in its own right: Why, even when they know that the impact of religion is often large (as many economists would acknowledge informally when they are outside a professional setting), do economists so typically neglect the subject in their professional writings? Perhaps it is simply that they do not want to acknowledge formally and explicitly even the existence of a legitimate competitor such as environmental religion. The medieval Roman Catholic Church could burn heretics at the stake, but the professional economic priesthood today is limited to ignoring them.

The Biblical Treatment of Sustainability

As compared with economic religion, the environmental religious understanding of sustainability is closer to the Old Testament treatment. In the Bible, the question of the sustainability of society comes up many times and has powerful religious connotations. Early in Genesis, chapter 6, verse 1, in the King James version notes that "men began to multiply on the face of the earth, and daughters were born unto them." We learn shortly thereafter that God, looking down on the spread of humankind over the earth, was mightily displeased with this and other elements of his creation—that "the wickedness of man was great in the earth" (6:5). Indeed, God's displeasure was so great that he resolved to "destroy man whom I have created from the face of the earth; both man, and beast, and the creeping thing, and the fowls of the air" (6:7). It was, to use more contemporary language, a negative verdict on the sustainability of the human condition of the time.

In a more recent translation of the Bible, the same verse is given in present-day English. God is said to be displeased with the fact that "now a population explosion took place upon the earth." As a result of this and other signs that human beings were failing to fulfill his intentions, he resolved to "cover the earth with a flood and destroy every living being." He recanted later only to the extent of allowing Noah to save two of every species, as the Endangered Species Act today seeks to sustain the plant and animal heritage of the earth in the face of an unsustainable loss of habitat and other threats arising due to the spread of human population and economic development.

After the six days of creation, the first time that the question of sustainability comes up is in the Garden of Eden, where Adam and Eve lived in harmony and bliss but could not sustain this condition, and instead were cast into a world of pain and suffering. Later books of the Old Testament are filled with other places and societies that, owing to their wickedness, suffer again the wrath of God. This divine retribution usually takes the form of an environmental disaster—if not a great flood, then famine, drought, pestilence, earthquake, or other natural calamity. The greatest environmental threats with respect to the spread of greenhouse gases and resulting global warming are today seen—perhaps coincidentally, perhaps not—in terms of many of the same calamitous consequences: the onset of flooding, famine, drought, pestilence, and other natural catastrophes. The environmental god apparently thinks along the same lines as the Christian God—or perhaps it is the same God, described now in a different language.

In our secular age (at least in the leading universities and in general among elite segments of society), people are not likely to speak in mainstream policy circles of the "wickedness" of mankind. Yet among some members of the environmental movement—who express the strongest doubts about the sustainability of our current civilization—there is a strong sense of current human depravity. David Brower argued in his standard "sermon" that: "we're hooked. We're addicted. We're committing grand larceny against our children. Ours is a chain letter economy. . . . When [such] rampant growth happens in an individual, we call it cancer."[30] Absent some radical change in the human condition, and like other cancers, the progressive spread of the disease could be fatal to the host—that is, the human presence on earth might not be "sustainable."

These, to be sure, are some of the more extreme views. Yet large numbers of people today do believe that the moral condition of the world is bad and getting worse. In secular circles, while people no longer typically believe in divine retribution, they often do have a vague sense that some form of disaster might be a consequence of the many moral transgressions of human beings against other species, against nature, and against the earth. Perhaps what we are seeing in current environmental discussions of "sustainability" is the reappearance in secular language of an old biblical message. The biblical commands were, of course, delivered by priests, ministers, and other clergy. Today, the discussions of sustainability are carried on mostly by physical and social scientists. In the modern age, they have assumed the role of the priesthoods of old.

Scientists of the Apocalypse

Echoing many biblical prophesies, the Stanford biologist Paul Ehrlich wrote in the late 1960s that widespread world famines were likely within a few years and certain within a few decades.[31] The Club of Rome in 1972 published *The Limits to Growth*, a volume that eventually sold twelve million copies, employing elaborate computer simulations to predict that the world system faced imminent physical collapse if existing economic growth patterns were not substantially altered. By the 1990s, a new field of "ecological economics" had joined the discussion, rejecting the mainstream economic understanding of sustainability.[32] The United Nations Educational, Scientific, and Cultural Organization published in 1991 a collection of explorations by ecological economists on the subject of sustainability. As Federico Mayor summarized the overall conclusions, "Unless development is distinguished from economic growth, the turn-off towards sustainable development will be missed." Time was running short to avert grave environmental and social damages to the very fabric of the earth because "too many warning signs have already been ignored suggesting that, in North and South alike, we are moving in the wrong direction and that there may be few, if any, short-cuts back."[33]

The Report of the World Commission on Environment and Development in 1987—the "Brundtland Commission"—indicated that the total world economy might have to grow to about five to ten times the current size; without such growth, the poor would be unable to come up to the living standards of existing developed nations, leaving the world with unacceptable long-run inequalities.[34] The editors of the UNESCO report found, however, that an attempt to achieve "anything remotely resembling" this magnitude of economic increase would "simply speed us from today's long run unsustainability to imminent collapse" of the world economy and environment. To avoid the permanent maintenance of large disparities of income between rich and poor countries, the scale of economic activity of rich countries would therefore have to decline sharply: "Ecological constraints are real and more growth for the poor must be balanced by negative throughput growth for the rich."[35]

Other major institutional changes, including curtailments in world trade, would also be necessary conditions to achieving a sustainable future. From the viewpoint of such spokespeople for ecological economics, achieving sustainability is not simply a tenet of environmental religion that rejects the necessity of economic growth and seeks a higher moral standard in the human relationship with nature. Rather, the arguments for sustainability are fundamentally practical as well. Without newly sustainable economic policies, the world faces potentially catastrophic consequences in economic, political, and other realms.

As in the Bible, if the wicked of the world do not reform their ways—and today that includes a wholesale reworking of the world's economic system—they will face severe punishments not only in a hell in the hereafter but right here on earth in the next few years to come.

Economic Versus Environmental Religion

Partly reflecting their general aversion to engaging in religious and other forms of values debates, mainstream economists did not address directly the religious elements that underlay the sustainability discussions—the growing doubts that modern economic progress was all it was cracked up to be and the possible punishments of human beings for their moral transgressions against the earth. They did effectively communicate a negative verdict in a more "technical" manner, however, applying the lens of conventional economic analysis to the forecasts of looming environmental destruction. Economists pointed out that the prices of most minerals and other natural resources had shown a fairly consistent trend of downward movement for more than a hundred years.[36] Indeed, an excess of food and minerals supply, and associated employment losses, price fluctuations, and other disruptive transitional effects, rather than shortages of these items, had been the greater economic policy concern of world governments. There might be large price increases again in the future (as in fact happened in 2007 and 2008), but they would probably then be followed by later price declines, following a long-standing cyclical pattern of natural resource prices.

The existing trends in environmental degradation were less favorable, but full awareness of the air quality, water quality, and other environmental problems was more recent and institutional adaptation could be expected to occur gradually. As the economic way of thinking set the framework of analysis, the "sink capacity" of the environment has in effect been treated as a free good. Given a price in effect of zero, it should not be surprising that the demand for sink capacity for the world's pollutants would eventually overwhelm supply. The wide development of regulatory and pricing mechanisms to bring under control access to the environmental commons is only about thirty-five years old in economically advanced nations and is only beginning in the less developed countries. Reflecting this mainstream economic perspective, the World Bank stated that "the environmental debate has rightly shifted away from concern about *physical limits* to growth toward concern about incentives for *human behavior* and policies that can overcome *market and policy failures*." As the mainstream way of thinking of economics explains, as expressed in a 1992 World Bank report, "The reason some resources—water, forests, and clean air—are under siege while others—metals, minerals, and energy—are not is that the scarcity of the latter is reflected in market prices and so the forces of substitution, technical progress, and structural change are strong" in the latter areas.[37]

In the former areas, by contrast, these elements are often still missing, and the environmental resources as a consequence are still being misused and abused. As economic religion tells us, the past deterioration of air quality, water quality, and other environmental assets was not due to any moral or ethical failure associated with the false worship of economic growth—or any other god—but was simply due to a practical failure of economic pricing policies. In many cases, all that might be needed is the development of an appropriate set of property rights, abolishing the commons circumstance of free access that has characterized so many environmental assets. In the 1980s, deregulation of oil and gas ended the "energy crisis" of the 1970s after some unsatisfactory earlier attempts by governments to apply price controls and other regulatory devices. Most economists have argued that improved pricing policies would work just as well today in environmental realms.

The Bible, of course, is filled with messages of hope and redemption, as well as messages of the wrath of God being visited on the earth. And today both messages can be found within the wider profession of economics. The mainstream view of the large majority of economists holds out a path to heaven on earth through rapid economic growth and development. Indeed, in economic religion the best way to improve the environment is to put the current economic system to work for environmental purposes. Not only will prices then reflect true scarcities, but rapid economic growth will make available more total resources to society that then can be put to good environmental purposes.

A dissenting group of ecological economists warned prophetically, however, that continuing current rates of economic growth would bring on large environmental disasters and, if no reform of our economic system takes place, eventually a new hell on earth.* Unlike many faithful of environmental religion, however, ecological economics argues that the future achievement of a

---

* Such concerns among economists, to be sure, date back to at least the early part of the Industrial Revolution. Thomas Robert Malthus contended that exponential population growth was sure to outrun the arithmetic increase of agricultural production. Population might grow initially but wide starvation and many deaths would eventually result from the inevitable resulting shortage of food supplies. Later in the nineteenth century, William Stanley Jevons, another prominent figure in the history of economic thought, argued that coal was certain to run out in England, and that no other energy substitute would be available to sustain the existing standard of living. The most famous statement of all was that of Karl Marx, who saw the economic processes of the time plunging human beings into ever-greater class struggle, alienation, and destructive warfare. Marx, however, gave it all a biblical twist that proved to be of immense historical significance, prophesying that, out of the earthly apocalypse toward which the economic system was surely headed, there would in the end emerge a new heaven on earth.

sustainable earth must be informed by detailed knowledge of the workings of supply and demand, the impacts of environmental "externalities," and many other technical economic subjects. It would be a new kind of marriage of the values of environmental religion with the methods of economic expertise.[38] Whether economic methods can be separated from economic ends, to be sure, remains an open question.

Sustainability as Environmental Justice

The analysis above finds that sustainability has more to do with the ultimate goals than the practical means of achieving them.* To declare that an action should be "sustainable" is to insist that the action—whether informed by a technical economic understanding or not—should in the end serve the values of environmental religion. Indeed, it is similar to the use of the term "efficient"—which in many cases also has been surprisingly lacking in substantive content—in economic religion. For the economic priesthood, to describe some action as "efficient" is a way of saying that it will work to advance the cause of economic progress. As noted above, working government economists have typically found that it is the way of thinking of economics, rather than any technical models or other elaborate calculations, that in practice informs economic policy decisions.

The environmental advocate Wes Jackson thus writes that "my six grandchildren range in age from two to nine. I have tried to imagine what they will need to know if 'sustainability' were to become as central to their lives as, say, the concept of justice." Acknowledging that the idea of justice is "imperfect" and hard to define, Jackson notes that we have nevertheless "built much of our society around it." Although it is thus far a "mere fledgling" by comparison, Jackson hopes that the idea of "'sustainability,' [which is] also a value term," will come to be as important to future generations as the idea of justice has been to past ones.[39] Indeed, sustainability might be described as the extension of ethical concerns and the principles of justice from the arena

---

* It is partly for this reason that policy analysts who expect a precise meaning are often critical of the use of the term sustainability. Indeed, it may be close to worthless for policy purposes if the goal is to actually distinguish between better and worse government actions in specific circumstances. Harvard law professor Cass Sunstein writes that it is easy to agree that "everyone should support sustainable development." Unfortunately, however, "support for sustainable development does not answer any of the hard questions. It is important to ensure that policies are sustainable rather than the opposite. But in poor nations as well as rich ones, regulators need much better guidance than that." See Cass R. Sunstein, *Risk and Reason: Safety, Law, and the Environment* (New York: Cambridge University Press, 2002), 106.

of human dealings with one another to a wider arena of human interactions with the natural world.

If the precise meaning still remains vague, Jackson argues, the goal of "just" dealings with nature should be at least to maintain a relationship that does not impose human "dominance" over nature. We should not "oppress" nature by asserting human control to remake nature according to our own designs. We should not "play God" in the world. In the Progressive Era, the newfound human ability to change nature according to human purposes was seen as opening the way to rapid economic progress and the salvation of the world. Jackson and many others were now seeking to renounce that human capacity—to abandon as far as practically feasible the human use of new scientific and economic powers to remake nature for society's material benefit. Human control over nature had become too great and too dangerous. Human beings must learn to respect the "integrity," the "health," the "naturalness" of the plant and animal worlds—to treat them justly according to a new ethical standard encapsulated in the term "sustainability."

Conclusion

In current policy discussions, to say that an action is sustainable is in essence to declare that it has been blessed by a new environmental god who is concerned to protect and preserve the natural world. It is to reject an economic god who seeks efficiency and the pursuit of economic progress as the highest ethical command. Terms such as "providence" in the medieval era, "natural law" in the Enlightenment, "efficiency" in the Progressive Era, and now "sustainability" at the beginning of the twentieth-first century tell us more about our basic belief systems—the gods we worship and who must bless our actions—than they do about the character of any specific government policies or actions to be followed.

To a remarkable degree, our current economic policy debates owe their assumptions and moral perspectives to the Jewish and Christian heritage of the West. If they are outwardly secular, it often takes only a modest probing beneath the surface to find large biblical elements. Sustainability is perhaps a new word in current policy debates, but there is no more value-charged question in the writings of the Bible. To ask whether a society is sustainable is to ask whether its people are living according to God's commands.

5

ALL IN THE NAME OF PROGRESS

MODERN SCIENCE AND ECONOMICS have given us the capacity to alter nature in fundamental respects—to "play God" with the natural world. Is this good, or bad? The leading public religions for most of the twentieth century assumed that it was for the good. They carried on in the tradition of what James Scott in *Seeing Like a State* describes as "high modernism."[1] Scott explains, however, that the results often had significant and unexpected consequences:

> Much of the great state-sponsored calamities of the twentieth century have been the work of rulers with grandiose and utopian plans for their societies. . . . There is no denying that much of the massive, state enforced engineering of the twentieth century has been the work of progressive, often revolutionary elites. Why?
>
> The answer, I believe, lies in the fact that it is typically progressives who have come to power with a comprehensive critique of existing society and a popular mandate (at least initially) to transform it.
>
> What is high modernism, then? It is best conceived as a strong (one might even say muscle-bound) version of the beliefs in scientific and technical progress that were associated with industrialization in Western Europe and in North America from roughly 1830 until World War I. At its center was a supreme self-confidence about continued linear progress, the development of scientific and technical knowledge, the expansion of production, the rational design of social order, the growing satisfaction of human needs, and, not least, an increasing control over nature (including human nature) commensurate with scientific understanding of natural laws. *High* modernism is thus a particularly sweeping vision of how the benefits of technical and scientific progress might be applied—usually through the state—in every field of human activity.[2]

The carnage of World War I first brought all this great optimism into question among many leading Western intellectuals. But the progressive convictions continued to exert a powerful influence in the practical affairs of government throughout the remainder of the twentieth century. The proselytizers of high modernism, moreover, extended their influence beyond western Europe and North America to encompass the entire world.[3] This was reflected, for example, in the construction of the Aswan Dam on the Nile River in Egypt in the 1960s; the Itaipu Dam on the Parana River between Brazil and Paraguay in the 1970s and 1980s; and, most recently, the Three Gorges Dam on the Yangtze River in China (completed in 2006).*

By the end of the twentieth century, however, more and more people were finding that the promise of economic salvation had been false. Immense material advances over the course of the century, for one thing, had not transformed the human condition in basic ethical and spiritual ways. Large-scale planning of the economy and of the natural world, moreover, often turned out to be a much more complicated and difficult task than the progressive optimists had believed.[4]

What is less appreciated, however, is that many of the negative consequences were—or at least could have been—easily anticipated. In some cases they were even sought—although, of course, not originally seen in a negative light. As previous chapters have discussed, economic religion involved applying a powerful value lens on the world as found in the economic way of thinking. According to their special economic way of thinking, economists excluded many things—those that did not contribute to the economic progress of the world—from even receiving consideration. Mainstream economics, as explained in chapter 1, effectively defined categories of "legitimate" and "illegitimate" costs, leaving the latter out of the calculations (or, as one might say, effectively treating them as having zero costs). Indeed, many—perhaps most—policy conclusions of economic analysis depend critically on this set of assumptions. Once large categories of costs (or benefits, as costs avoided are sometimes defined) are excluded from consideration, the final economic result is often foreordained.

---

* Although a latecomer in the competition to demonstrate great national power and prestige through the building of giant dams, China was determined to outdo its predecessors. When finished in 2006, the Three Gorges Dam represented "the biggest engineering feat in China since the Great Wall." Despite earlier warnings of major environmental problems, it had been pushed forward by an entire "generation of party leaders trained as engineers and eager to demonstrate the country's prowess in taming nature." Like American, Soviet, and other engineers and economic planners around the world, they were focused on "the economic benefits and national prestige that would grow from such an accomplishment." See Edward Cody, "In Chinese Dam's Wake, Ecological Woes," *Washington Post*, November 15, 2007, A1.

For most economists, the identification of the exact categories of legitimate and illegitimate costs remains largely implicit; it has essentially been taken for granted since their graduate school days. At least one leading economist, however, has been more forthright. As Charles Schultze once put it, the greatest "advantage of the market as a means of social organization is its 'devil take the hindmost' approach to questions of individual equity"—and by equity he meant a much wider range of social impacts than the measured distribution of income alone. As Schultze elaborated, if a social value judgment of "do no direct harm" to anyone—as was typical in the workings of ordinary "politics"— prevailed throughout American society, many of the most efficient actions in the market and in government would be blocked.[5] By excluding consideration of such "equity" impacts in the social decision calculus, however, it was possible to render a positive verdict and for American society to advance rapidly along the route of economic progress.

The number of social costs that are automatically excluded from mainstream economic calculations is large. It includes, among others:

1. The loss of community when the market, operating nationally and internationally, renders a negative verdict on the mainstays of the local economy—and, if they want to have a job, most people have no choice but to move away to another place.
2. The individual financial and psychic losses when a person, owing to the workings of market forces, loses a job and has to look for another one.
3. The individual sense of anxiety about possible losses of a community or a job, even when such losses never actually occur.
4. The sense that a precious social asset is devalued by the very fact of entering it into the price system (occasionally, as in the case of prostitution, government may intervene to limit such costs, but there are no restrictions in the great majority of cases).
5. The loss of personal freedom when economically efficient actions require collective organization by governments—often large governments, such as the national government in Washington, D.C.—that then must employ powers of coercion to collect income and other taxes to fund these efforts (including even from people opposed to the actions).
6. The sense of personal powerlessness when large private organizations are the winners in the market, leaving many people to work as small parts in a large and often impersonal business enterprise.
7. The sense of personal, community, and national disappointment when a person realizes that he or she is a relative loser (or belongs to a group of relative losers) in the competition for greater profits, higher paying and

more prestigious jobs, and other indicators of social rank, as established by market and other economic forces.

8. The sense of loss when homes, streets, farms, and other historic reminders of the past are swept aside by the workings of the market (or by "efficient" government actions and programs).

9. The sense of individual and community loss when plant and animal species habitats, wild areas, and other parts of nature are transformed from their earlier condition to become "natural resources," sources of the energy and other material requirements to power a modern economy.

10. The feelings of loss when the defense of private property rights is perceived to encourage strong feelings of individual possessiveness and a weakened sense of communal bonds (violating, among other ethical systems, many Christian biblical injunctions).

11. The sense of offense when particular instruments of market economic efficiency—such as the charging of interest for loans—violate religious (as in parts of the Islamic world today) or other ethical principles.

12. The loss of traditional tribal, religious, and other cultures that are disrupted and otherwise swept aside by the forces of economic progress.

13. The overall sense of loss among those people who believe the world is captive to a heretical religion of economic progress that has taught many people to worship a false god.

Most mainstream economists, to be sure, are well aware that such costs do exist. But they would argue that the enormous benefits of modern economic progress more than amply justify the need for society to bear such burdens—that they are necessary parts of the "price of progress." Admittedly, the large net benefits to society resulting from economic progress (taking into account the actual full range of all possible costs) are never actually calculated or scientifically demonstrated. Rather, they are simply a core element of economic faith. Indeed, if economic progress does lead to heaven on earth, as economic religion has long taught, it would follow directly that society as a whole—if not every individual or group—will benefit overwhelmingly from the long-run economic progress of the world. If some individual people do in fact have to make large sacrifices today for the progress of society in the future, they should know that it is for a grand and glorious cause.

By the end of the twentieth century, however, there were rapidly growing doubts among many people that economic progress would save the world. The history of the twentieth century, if perhaps not finally resolving the matter, had offered abundant evidence to the contrary. As chapter 3 discussed, a few economists, perhaps sensing that the core tenets of economic religion were coming under growing challenge, proposed that "existence values" should be calculated. If this could be done, calculations of economic efficiency could then be extended to include most of the above costs, which are now generally left out of economic calculations (since most of these costs relate to thoughts or feelings in the mind, whose very existence does in actual fact frequently generate pleasure or pain).[6]

Even leaving aside the practical impossibility of making such calculations, however, if the real goal is to save the world by economic progress, attempts to calculate existence values are a hopeless detour. In economic religion, the salvation of the world is to be achieved by abolishing material scarcity, not by economists encouraging the development of more pleasant images in the minds of as many people as possible (a task perhaps more suited to psychologists or to advertising executives). The advocates of existence value in effect proposed to redefine economic progress in new terms, now including publicly popular steps to impede progress as part of their new definition of progress—an impossible contradiction.

It is a distinct sign of a loss of self-confidence when even some of the most prestigious members of the American economics profession are willing to bless such silliness.[7] Apparently, some economists no longer believe that economic progress will save the world, even as they are still hoping to remain the leading priesthood in American society, leading them to embrace such strange professional directions. Others outside economics, however, are not as charitable. If the economic god is a false god, his commands deserve little respect. Indeed, there will be many who will see in them the latest temptations of the devil, who has always worked in devious ways.* The world will always need economists because economic matters are too important to ignore.

---

* Highlighting the concern that the all-out pursuit of economic progress, following the methods of economics, has led mankind astray, the environmental philosopher Holmes Rolston related in 2006 that:

> after four centuries during which economics has progressively illuminated us about how we can transform nature into the goods we want, the value questions raised in economics too are as sharp and as painful as ever. Economics can, and often does, serve noble interests. Economics can, and often does, become self-serving, a means of perpetuating injustice, of violating human rights, of making war, of degrading the environment. Nothing in economics ensures against philosophical confusions, against rationalizing, against mistaking evil for good, against loving the wrong gods. The whole economic enterprise of the last four centuries could yet prove demonic, a Faustian bargain in the next millennium. As good an indication as any of that is our ecological crisis.

Finding that there is a pressing need for much greater attention to religion, Rolston goes on to say: "What kind of planet ought we humans wish to have? One we resourcefully manage for our benefits? Or one we hold in loving care? Science and economics can't teach us that: maybe religion and ethics can." See Holmes Rolston III, "Caring for Nature: What Science and Economics Can't Teach Us but Religion Can," *Environmental Values* 15, no. 3 (2006): 308–9, 312.

It may not need, however, an economic priesthood that claims the highest moral ground in American society.

In a 2002 book, *Industrialized Nature: Brute Force Technology and the Transformation of the Natural World*, Paul Josephson takes this view. He develops a graphic portrayal of the environmental destruction, loss of community, and many other evils that have followed in the wake of the false worship of economic progress in the twentieth century. His book might be taken as a partial catalogue of the "illegitimate costs" that economists historically have ignored. Rapidly growing numbers of people, as Josephson's book now illustrates, are demanding that in the future they be taken into much greater account.

"Brute Force Technology"

The worldwide worship of economic progress in the twentieth century, as Josephson finds, yielded in practice a commitment to "brute force technology"—the physical means by which "the corridors of modernization" were spread over most of the earth. Some of the main products of modern technology were "roads, highways, power lines, and railroads"; others were "power generators—dams, boilers, reactors"; still others were "processing plants—the industrial farms, forests, stockyards, and animal cages"; and one should not leave out "the iron, copper, and aluminium factories." Whether these were found "within socialist or capitalist systems" was not critical; in either case there was a technological imperative at work that sought—and frequently achieved—"the transformation of nature." It was of no great significance that in capitalism the justification was "the pursuit of profit" whereas in communism it was "the glorification of the state (or the proletariat)." Public decision makers everywhere agreed that "nature is something that can, even must, be exploited, and that we will find solutions for the unanticipated costs of that exploitation" as necessary.[8]

The result, as Josephson believes, was a fierce assault on nature throughout the developed parts of the world, justified "in the name of civilization" and "in the name of progress." If a person sought to resist the workings of economic progress, that person—in capitalist and socialist states alike—would be labeled as "obstinate, self-interested, unpatriotic." People in the less developed parts of the world who resisted the introduction of the modern management of nature were "considered backward, illiterate, ignorant." The leading advocates of progress everywhere were professional economists, planners, and engineers. In looking back on the history of the twentieth century, Josephson says, "There is little difference between the claims of the engineers on planning boards in Washington State," who promoted the Grand Coulee Dam project; the "engineers from Brazil's state electrification company, Electrobas," who sought to develop the Amazon basin; and "the Soviet nature planners," who sought massive dams and other projects to transform the Volga, Ob, Enisei, and other Russian river basins. All these professionals were motivated by an "identification of progress and [material] plenty with their work." Because progress for them was the one path of earthly salvation, "they refuse[d] to go slow when promoting geo-engineering projects," using the most powerful technologies of their time.[9]

The fiercest assaults on nature, officially justified in such terms, were found in the former Soviet Union. In 1948, the Communist Party released the "Stalinist Plan for the Transformation of Nature." As Josephson explains, this plan "involved geological engineering to maximize productive capabilities on a scale never before imagined. Visionaries proposed turning nature itself, its lakes, ponds, rivers, forests, and plains, into a giant factory." The ability to transform nature advantageously would prove pivotal in the struggle between communism and capitalism. As one Soviet defender of the system argued, "Complete mastery of nature was simply impossible under capitalism. A socialist order was required to ensure 'complex rational utilization of resources.'"[10]

Capitalist countries, the Soviets believed, faced two obstacles. First, capitalism had an "anarchic distribution of property and monopolies," whereas in the Soviet Union central planners could efficiently coordinate the use of state resources to maximize the human use of nature. Second, capitalist countries often had democratic political systems, while the most intensive uses of nature often required large displacements of people. In building the Kuibyshev project on the Volga River, for example, around five hundred thousand people were relocated. Soviet engineers and planners were less constrained than their democratic counterparts by the possibility of strong public complaints and political opposition from the "losers" in such projects. In their pursuit of the scientific management of society, Soviet authorities, as Josephson observes, "viewed public involvement in decisions about whether to proceed with the diffusion of a new technology as at best a necessary evil; as for the environment, it was simply something to be managed."[11]

In a capitalist system, economic feasibility might also restrict the application of brute force technology. As Josephson writes, if the government did not provide subsidies, "market forces . . . might have damned fiscally and environmentally expensive projects." For the Soviets, however, ordinary economics imposed few limitations—partly because the transformation of nature had itself become a symbol of the triumph of state socialism. As Josephson notes, Lenin had "embraced electricity . . . as a panacea for the country's backwardness." A hydropower station would then become one of "Stalin's icons." Soviet leaders after Stalin would compete to surpass his accomplishments in these regards, seeking to affirm that the "creation of the material basis for communist society" was occurring under their guidance. From Stalin to Khrushchev to Brezhnev, "the engineering organizations responsible for water melioration projects in the USSR seemed only to gain in hubris. In each year of Soviet power, the quantity of manipulated water increased, from 70 billion m³ in 1937 to 125 billion in 1957 and to 450 billion by 1967."[12]

Although economists and engineers in the United States had to work within the limits of a democratic political system, to a surprising degree this nation followed a similar path. The Progressive Era, Josephson writes, introduced the conceptual schemes for the scientific management of American society—once again in the name of modern economic progress. Under the banner of progressive ideas, professional classes of economists, engineers, and planners in the United States likewise played an increasing leadership role. Resistance to growth of the federal government declined during the severe economic depression of the 1930s, opening the way for implementing the scientific design of American progress on a nationwide scale.

In 1935, for example, the first concrete was poured in the construction of the Grand Coulee Dam on the Columbia River, designed to supply vast amounts of power and to irrigate more than a million acres of farmland in Washington State. As Josephson explains, it was motivated by a vision of "the transformation of the Pacific Northwest into a utopia of economic growth and American democratic ideals . . . tied to technological advance." The goal was to "improve on nature" and thus encourage the spread of thriving "economic activities" throughout the region. Josephson sees close parallels to the efforts of the Soviet dam builders. "As in Soviet Russia, [American] advocates of progress became convinced that electricity, more than the railroad, was the key to further economic development" of the Pacific Northwest. The construction of dams to produce electricity became more than a practical device. Indeed, American engineers, like their Soviet counterparts, "spoke about the huge dams in unbounded metaphor." As Grand Coulee became a great cathedral, modern pilgrims streamed to the site to witness a glorious triumph of engineering skills, experiencing a feeling of deep national pride and religious devotion in the presence of the new human ability to control nature for human benefit— and thereby to lay through economic progress the basis for "'a new civilization of mankind' based on electricity." As they would later compete in space travel, Americans earlier had competed to build the largest dams as part of "an ideological contest with the USSR"—another holy war, on this occasion fought among competing branches of economic religion—to demonstrate which economic system could do more to rapidly advance economic progress in the world.[13] Russians for centuries saw Moscow as the "Third Rome"; from the first years of Puritan Massachusetts, Americans saw themselves as building a "city upon a hill," offering a beacon for all mankind to follow. In the twentieth century, the worship of economic progress took the place of Christianity—or perhaps reshaped Christianity to a new secular form, as it may be more accurate to say—in the affairs of state.

Toward Heaven on Earth

An economic religion in one or another form indeed held sway in most of the nations of the world over the course of the twentieth century. Josephson examines a number of national applications of this religion in *Industrialized Nature*, including the efforts of the Brazilian government to develop the Amazon basin and the Norwegian government to manage ocean fisheries. Josephson has little to say about the prophetic assumptions and reasoning that underlie economic religion. As a result, his modern economists and engineers are often presented as a befuddled and sometimes evil group whose operatives seemingly enjoy committing grave sins against the natural world. More accurately, if less conventionally, they were zealots of a new fundamentalist economic faith. Human beings cannot live without religion, apparently, but sometimes they can hardly live with it.

A leading American progressive and founder of the U.S. Forest Service, Gifford Pinchot, declared that he had been motivated to enter public service by the desire "to help in bringing the Kingdom of God on earth."[14] The social gospel movement provided much of the moral energy for American progressive causes. As one scholar describes this movement, it sought the "social salvation" of mankind and hoped to achieve "the coming to earth of the kingdom of heaven."[15] Over time, however, leading progressives increasingly abandoned the Christian religious trappings, although the change was less substantial than it appeared at the time.

By the later part of the twentieth century, however, economic hopes for a new heaven on earth were fading. Human beings lived longer and healthier lives, but no wholesale transformation in the degree of happiness or spiritual contentment was apparent. Indeed, some people argued that the material wealth of modern life was alienating. By the end of the twentieth century, new forms of Christian, Islamic, Hindu, and other religious fundamentalism were arising, partly reflecting a turn away from the communist, socialist, and other modern religions of economic progress.

As long as progress had a transcendent purpose, the burdens of economic growth and development could be ignored. If no heaven has yet or will come to earth, however, the economic system must have a more prosaic purpose. An honest accounting, moreover, will have to include any transitional adjustments as real costs. As Josephson explains, in mainstream economics "the true costs of the well-intended efforts to understand nature and to transform it into readily available commodities, and to force nature to become more machine-like, more predictable, and a human construct more readily recognizable, are difficult to establish." For example, "to quantify the costs to local fishing communities of their loss of livelihood to modern technology, which harvests cod, haddock, and the like so much more efficiently," is difficult. Also difficult or impossible to quantify are "justice, beauty, morality and ethics," so such factors often fell "outside the scope of consideration" in the economic, engineering, and planning professions' modernist ways of thinking.[16]

For example, Grand Coulee, along with other dams in the Pacific Northwest, devastated the region's salmon populations. In the old Soviet Union, the sturgeon of the Caspian Sea were reduced to a tiny faction of their former populations in part by damming the Volga River. The achievement of the future "material basis of society" did not depend on individual fisheries. Salmon and sturgeon, however, were core parts of the cultural identity of their regions. Incorporating this identity into economic models—giving it a dollar value—was ignored in making economic calculations of dam benefits and costs. Even if economists and planners had sought to do so, it would have been practically difficult if not impossible. Yet, in a broad understanding of "welfare," the loss of the salmon and the loss of the sturgeon imposed large human costs; people really felt badly, suffering a real loss of "utility" (as the proponents of existence value calculations, in at least this respect correctly, are quick to point out).*

As Josephson reviews the consequences of progressive religion, some of the biggest losers were the indigenous peoples of Siberia, who were subject to "a program of forced assimilation." The Soviet government sought to educate the Nenets, Khanty, Mansi, and other Eskimo peoples in "the glories

---

* Josephson, it should be noted, is hardly alone. Many other critiques of the destructive influence of economic religion have been authored in recent years. In *Caring for Creation*, the environmental philosopher Max Oelschlaeger, for example, laments the unhappy consequences of a false gospel:

> Americans are embedded in a *final vocabulary* that offers ready-made descriptions of our relations with nature in a way that closes rather than opens discourse about caring for creation. We have collectively become Homo Economicus. . . . Our preferences as consumers are institutionalized in the marketplace. . . . Our first language, the discourse that binds secular society, is the language of utilitarian individualism. Insofar as Americans have a common faith, it is the belief that the good life is tied to an ever increasing quantity of life. The high priests of this [economic] civil religion are embedded in the citadels of power. . . . These experts maintain and periodically refurbish the legitimating narrative of economics . . . that tells us that the Gross National Product and Rate of Economic Growth are holy, unqualified, and absolute social goods. This secular narrative has, ironically, became a cultural absolute, defining Americans collectively, as a people. (Max Oelschlaeger, *Caring for Creation: An Ecumenical Approach to the Environmental Crisis* [New Haven: Yale University Press, 1994], 95)

of the Communist Party." The "new enlighteners were radicals fully steeped in Marxist-Leninist values, which they intended to instill in the ignorant masses." Consistent with the tenets of their economic religion, these enlighteners professed that the salvation of indigenous groups would be achieved by economic means. Indigenous peoples "would be civilized through material change—through the building of apartment houses, roads, and schools and more generally through Moscow-derived public health programs, economic development and educational programs." The goal was "to modernize—that is, change forever—the culture of indigenous peoples." Such policy reflected "an ideology of progress . . . [in which] the indigenous peoples were seen as backward and uncivilized, if not innately hostile to Soviet power." They would have to abandon their old ways of thinking and living to adapt to a world of "central industrial planning," including an abandonment of their old tribal beliefs in favor of Marxist "atheism."[17]

Not only indigenous Siberians would have to serve the cause of economic religion; millions of political prisoners from European Russia were sent to the Gulag in Siberia. Indeed, given the transcendent religious stakes, the Soviet Union was willing to sacrifice almost any of its citizens for the greater glories of economic progress. Dams, nuclear stations, and brand-new cities were rushed to construction in Siberia. As Josephson reports, "Whatever the climate, whatever the design of the station, the steepness of the valleys, or the difficulty of building the foundation, the political indoctrinators were more concerned with progress at any cost than with safety." The arrival of heaven on earth should not be subject to delay. In the calculations of Soviet planners and engineers, "the workers, no less than the lands, were peripheral." The ordinary workers were required to labor "without hard hats, without safety ropes, without any safety culture whatsoever, at high spots hooking wires, at low spots near rushing water pouring concrete and setting charges." All this was necessary for the realization of the overarching goal: "to transform rivers, taiga, and tundra and to enter the earth's crust in search of fossil fuels and mineral ores" across Siberia, thus advancing the material productivity of Soviet society as rapidly as possible.[18]

There was a similar indifference to human costs in the development of the Amazon basin. Indeed, as Josephson argues, national economic planning "for nature transformation was under way for much of the twentieth century, and not only in the USSR but also in Brazil, in China, in Norway, and above all in the United States."[19] In seeking the salvation of mankind, indifference to the transitional burdens of economic progress was a worldwide phenomenon over the course of the twentieth century. As Josephson summarizes:

> Nation-states [of all stripes] became major actors in forcing the pace of resource development in the twentieth century. Whether essentially

capitalist or socialist, the governments of those states supported the costly diffusion of large scale technologies to provide access to extensive resources in previously inaccessible or inhospitable regions. The highways, railroads, hydropower stations, smelters, and combines brought much of the world's forest and its core into the hands of processing industries. But as the cases of Amazonia and Siberia show, significant social and environmental changes, some of them highly destructive, accompanied the expansion of civilization into the rain forest and taiga. The forests have disappeared hectare by hectare, and with them have gone endemic species and indigenous people. The earth has been scarred by mining and oil extraction. Hazardous wastes associated with industrial manufacturing now fill soils, lakes, rivers and valleys, even in the center of "undeveloped" regions.[20]

These outcomes, however, were not mere random acts of selfish or evil individuals. To the contrary, the economists, planners, and engineers here were working for a great religious cause. Many were willing to inflict a pain and suffering on fellow citizens that was justified as being done in the service of the highest of purposes. If the natural world suffered severe assaults, these were the temporary costs that served a more wonderful long-run goal. If many workers suffered and died, the same reason could be given.

Restraints on the exercise of religious zeal were greater in the United States, where realities of the private market limited some of the grander designs and where the presence of a political democracy inhibited the power of government to ignore the short-run welfare of the citizens. In the former Soviet Union, successor state to long traditions of autocracy and serfdom, few restraints existed, and the willingness to sacrifice the present for the future reached its apogee. As Josephson reports, "What the Soviet Union lacked in technological sophistication its engineers and policy makers made up for in unbridled enthusiasm" for the socialist transformation of nature.[21]

Has Economic Progress Been Worth It?

Along with many other writers, Josephson makes a persuasive case that the pursuit of economic progress failed to account for many large costs that were being imposed on many victims—human and nonhuman alike.[22] The question, however, remains whether modern progress has been finally worth it. Perhaps, when all the warts and blemishes, all the miscalculations, have been accounted for, the benefits of economic progress have been greater than the costs. Certainly, for many human beings, it would seem that the benefits must be greater. Until the modern age, the population of the world comprised a few hundred million people. Absent the products of modern science and economics, most people on earth today would not be present at all. If the world were to revert to premodern conditions, most of current humanity might well soon expire.

In the summer of 2003, I spent five weeks in Moscow. I was surprised to find that Stalin was still held in rather high regard by many Russians. One town was proposing to restore an old statue of Stalin to its former place of honor. I encountered businesspeople and other worldly Russians who described an admiration for Stalin. He ranks highly today in polls of great Russian figures of history. Of course, he did make enormous "mistakes," it is said; but Stalin, as many Russians still seem to believe, even if he sometimes used unnecessarily brutal methods, was successful in his efforts to force march a backward, semifeudal society into the modern age. At the end of communism in 1991, whatever the savagery involved in the transition, the average Russian lived much better than his or her counterpart one hundred years earlier. Whether it was all worth it cannot be resolved by any "scientific" or "value-free" analysis. (And, of course, a complete analysis would also have to ask whether the same economic gains could have been achieved by happier means—especially given the realities of Russian culture and history.)

In the United States, a middle-class person now lives in matters of health, food, transportation, and communications far better than just a few generations ago. If the presence of sin in the world actually had material causes, as economic religion preaches, ordinary existence in the United States by now should be getting close to heavenly. Given the abundant evidence to the contrary, salvation apparently depends on more than economic factors alone. Nevertheless, few Americans today seem willing to give up on economic progress. Politicians still compete on the basis of their ability to devise public policies that will spur growth. The fate of the world aside, many Americans would like a new forty-two-inch plasma television set, or would like to spend another week in Cancún during the winter. And, seemingly violating the economic law of diminishing returns, Americans work harder than Europeans, even though Americans are, by standard measures, somewhat richer than Europeans.

Josephson has raised, even as he does not answer, profound questions—what is the purpose of our economic gains, and how does this purpose affect the way we organize the economy? Until nearly the end of the twentieth century, the answer was clear for the intellectual leadership of the Western nations: they hoped to save the world by economic progress. The economics profession symbolically reinforced this conviction with formal economic models that ignored the burdens of progress—the many "losers" in economic growth and development, who did not even exist in the schemes by which economists purported to represent the real world. As the leading priesthood in the public arena, economists provided moral blessings for "efficient" economic systems—capitalist and socialist alike. They legitimized it all. Now that progress no longer seems to have a religious blessing, however, many economists are as uncertain as the rest of the population as to the ultimate purpose of the economic system.

Clearly, the losers in progress can no longer be ignored. To impose large sacrifices on people and the environment in the name of a great religious cause is one thing; to impose such sacrifices in the name of some people having larger cars is quite another. Yet if the losers in the workings of the economy must be compensated for all their losses in all the many forms in which they can occur, the vaunted efficiency of the market—and of other economic systems as well—would be significantly undermined. Contrary to the claims of many economists, the success of the market is not primarily due to its technical workings. The market succeeds because it incorporates a profound moral judgment: no one can be allowed to stand in the way of economic progress as the market transforms society by the workings of economic competition. If each loser in the market could file, say, a "nuisance" claim for damages to him or her by a more successful competitor, the market would soon grind to a halt. In the all-out pursuit of economic progress, however, the legal system also played its part, and virtually any judge would have dismissed such a nuisance claim out of hand.[23]

Conclusion

To ignore the costs of losers in the pursuit of "progress" is a social decision. No divine command—no religion of progress—requires a market system as the means of organizing society. Herein lies a dilemma that current economists have scarcely even recognized. One solution might be to justify the market in terms of the preservation of individual freedom—that would be the libertarian solution. But mainstream members of the economics profession, by contrast, still assign today the highest ultimate value to economic efficiency. Economic progress—not the maximization of liberty, or the preservation of any other particular good or value—is for them still the legitimizing goal of economic activity. But if—the assumptions of economic religion to the contrary—rapid economic growth and development is a false path of salvation, it would be impossible to give efficiency such an exalted status.

If the struggle between communism and capitalism was a holy war fought fiercely in the decades following World War II, the new holy wars of the twenty-first century are no longer likely to be mainly among different branches of economic religion. Rather, the greatest religious struggles of the future may be waged between economic religion and other types of noneconomic religious competitors, such as evangelical and Pentecostal Christianity or Islamic fundamentalism. There may also be new holy wars among religions that are altogether secular. Indeed, the deepest religious conflict in the American public arena at present is being waged between economic religion and environmental religion.

Turning from economic religion, parts II and III of this book will focus on environmental religion, applying the methods of "secular theology" to explore its foundational assumptions and the logic of its way of thinking.

PART II

ENVIRONMENTAL CALVINISM

INTRODUCTION

The daily existence of ordinary human beings in the world changed more in the past two hundred years than in all previous human history. Until the modern age, sheer survival was the greatest challenge for the great majority of people—beginning with finding enough food to eat and keeping warm at night. Today, however, the greatest eating problem facing most Americans is an excess of calories, and it is the poor, not the rich, who typically face the highest likelihood of obesity. This and other elements of the "Great Transformation" in the modern age, as Karl Polanyi once labeled it, raised a host of questions.[1] Would the moral character of human beings improve at the same rate as the physical quality of their lives? Would people be happier? Where was all the extraordinarily rapid pace of scientific and economic change, seemingly occurring even at an accelerating rate, leading?

The task of confronting such questions began in the Enlightenment, when at least the potential for such a transformation in the human condition was first coming into view. For the most part, the leading thinkers of the age saw the future with great optimism; indeed, for many a new heaven on earth seemed possible.[2] There was, however, at least one great dissenter: Jean-Jacques Rousseau. Whereas other Enlightenment figures viewed the eighteenth century as the moment of a great human triumph, Rousseau strenuously argued otherwise. A better world was not resulting; rather, the workings of science and industry and other elements of the new conditions of life were warping and corrupting human nature to an even greater extent.

Rousseau's perspective, however, was less novel than many people believed at the time. It was essentially a Christian understanding, the biblical story of the fall reworked in a secular vocabulary. Rousseau's message, moreover, was more appealing to his time, an age becoming more skeptical of the authority of the Christian Bible and often exhibiting an antagonism to traditional religion. The fall from the Garden of Eden thus appears in Rousseau's rendition as a terrible decline from a happy "natural state" that once existed in the world. There was no apple, but other temptations appeared. To their great misfortune, men and women were determined to apply their rational faculties to acquire new knowledge and put it to practical use—they were tempted by a new kind of economic snake in the Garden. The first sign of the fall, many thousands of years ago, was the rise of organized agriculture, which was then followed by the spread of ancient cities. The consequences of the fall had now reached the most advanced stage of sinfulness with the scientific and industrial "progress" of the eighteenth century.

As Jean Starobinski, a leading interpreter of Rousseau's thought, explains, "The cost of intellectual and technical progress has been moral degradation." The Enlightenment is for Rousseau a time in which "the human mind triumphs but man has lost his way"—humanity has succumbed to a new form of excess of pride and ambition. Although many people in the eighteenth century failed to notice, the biblical parallels have become increasingly obvious with time. As Starobinski now observes, Rousseau "takes the religious myth and sets it in historical time." In order "to explain the fall of man, no demon tempter or tempted Eve—no supernatural intervention—is required; human causes [alone] will suffice." As a result of misguided human actions in the world, for Rousseau there has been an "ever-increasing burden of human artifice" that in its consequences has "accelerated the fall into corruption: such is the history of mankind." The disastrous outcome has been a loss of that original "state of nature [in which] man lived happily in peace. Appearance and reality [then] were in perfect equilibrium. Men showed themselves and were seen by others as they really were. External appearances were not obstacles but faithful mirrors, wherein mind met mind in perfect harmony."[3] Rousseau had rewritten the book of Genesis in a naturalist language more suited to his time—and, as it would turn out, for the nineteenth and twentieth centuries as well.

It was not only Rousseau, however, who remapped the Christian message to a secular vocabulary. As Starobinski comments, intellectual historians of the twentieth century increasingly recognized that in the Enlightenment "the philosophes' major ideas are for the most part secularized religious concepts." The disagreements among Enlightenment philosophies, moreover, often reflected past controversies within Christian theology. For example, Rousseau was born in Geneva, where John Calvin had ministered to the faithful for many years, and Rousseau's family had been followers in the Calvinist faith. Calvin's theology saw the state of human depravity and corruption, owing to the original fall, in especially severe terms. Although success in a calling was to be sought, Calvinists condemned the pursuit of wealth and consumption for their own sake. Rousseau in this respect offers not only a generally Christian but a specifically Calvinist version of the terrible consequences of the fall. As Starobinski thus comments, Rousseau sees historical "change as corruption. As time goes by, man becomes disfigured and unrecognizable. This drastic (and, if you will, Calvinist) version of the myth of origin" shaped the very core of his thought.[4]

The genuine novelty of Rousseau's view of the world thus was not to be found in its essential contents but rather in its manner of expression. That may be a characteristic of religion, especially in the modern era, as traditional religion has been discredited for many people and yet the religious impulse seems not to have declined at all.[5] Rousseau and other Enlightenment thinkers inaugurated a modern tendency in which the messages of Christianity were increasingly divorced from the original biblical sources, only to be reappear in a new secular language—a formula repeated time and again among the leading thinkers of the West over the next three hundred years. If the modern age was characterized by remarkable scientific advances in understanding the physical workings of the natural world, it was also an age of self-deception—perhaps more of regress than of progress—in matters of theology.

In the nineteenth century, Karl Marx followed closely in Rousseau's footsteps. Although claiming a scientific status, Marx substituted the all-determining economic laws of history in place of an all-controlling Christian God. For Marx, once again, there had been a much simpler and better state of nature, but human aspirations for material gain had plunged the world into fierce economic conflicts among classes, yielding a terrible state of "alienation" (the Marxist translation of "sinfulness"). Compared with Rousseau, however, Marx shows much more confidence about the final result—the end of the class struggle, itself a certain outcome in economic history, has already predetermined the arrival of a new heaven on earth. In this respect, he was more faithful to his Christian predecessors and, ultimately, and at least partly for this reason, exceeded Rousseau in historical impact, as his writings became the new bible of a worldwide communist religion.

The United States shares a Calvinist history with the Geneva of Rousseau's early years. The Puritans were the English branch of Calvinism and many arrived in seventeenth-century Massachusetts as refugees from religious persecution. A hundred and fifty years later, Ralph Waldo Emerson, Henry David Thoreau, and other American transcendentalists were products of this same New England culture. They also reworked elements of the Calvinist story of the fall to a new secular vocabulary, again questioning the benefits of scientific, industrial, and other powerful forces of economic "progress" in their own time.* Like the Romantic movement in England, they looked to encounters with the natural world, rather than the all-out pursuit of economic growth and development, as a main source of religious understanding and inspiration.

John Muir, the founder in 1892 of the Sierra Club, saw Emerson as his mentor and inspiration. The religious roots of contemporary American environmentalism trace directly to Concord. Environmental historian Mark Stoll thus comments that today's "environmentalists rally in defense of virtuous nature against the amoral forces who let themselves be overcome by greed." This reflects the "Calvinistic moral and activist roots" of the contemporary environmental movement. Indeed, recasting in new language "the doctrines laid down by John Calvin," one finds today in the environmental movement a "moral outrage, activism, and appeal to government intervention [that] draw on the same account. [In this vision] the world has been transformed with new answers that are often only old ones rephrased" from past American religious history.[6]

A remarkable number of American environmental leaders, including John Muir, Rachel Carson, David Brower, Edward Abbey, and Dave Foreman, were brought up in the Presbyterian church (the Scottish branch of Calvinism), or one or another of its other American offshoots. In Europe, environmentalism has also exerted a large influence in Germany, Denmark, Sweden, and Norway—all nations with a Lutheran Protestant heritage. Finding that all these Protestant connections are more than a mere coincidence, the distinguished environmental historian Donald Worster identifies four key ways in

---

* The term Calvinism can be used narrowly to apply to a specific theology or, as employed in this book, more broadly to refer to certain broader tendencies of religious thought. There are, moreover, many specific interpretations of Calvinism, and it is even possible for a leading historian of American religion to write that in the nineteenth century, "the Baptists stepped in to spread Calvinist theology to a large segment of the population." Traditionally, theories of predestination and an elect few were identifying characteristics, but equally important to the Calvinist way of thinking were ideas of "the crippling effects of original sin and depravity, the power of grace to transform the sinful heart, the value of divine law as a guide to the Christian life, the insistence that the saving truth came through scripture alone, and the necessity that the church order its ministry and structure in close accord with scriptural instruction." Other identifying features of Calvinist religious practice were an emphasis on hard work, the pursuit of a calling, commitment to a sparse and disciplined lifestyle, a tendency to see the world in terms of good and evil, and a heroic effort to seek perfection in this world as well as in the hereafter, at least insofar as this was possible for such deeply corrupted human beings. See E. Brooks Holifield, *Theology in America: Christian Thought from the Age of the Puritans to the Civil War* (New Haven: Yale University Press, 2003), 11.

which environmentalism has followed in a Protestant path.* First, present-day American environmentalism exhibits an attitude of profound "moral activism," in this respect following the legacy of Calvin, Ulrich Zwingli, and John Knox—all major figures in the history of the Protestant Reformation who were "energetic radicals hacking away at obstacles to social change."[7]

This intense desire to purge the world of its evils was combined in early Protestantism with a strong sense of "ascetic discipline." There was, as Worster explains, "a deep suspicion in the Protestant mind of unrestrained play, extravagant consumption, and self-indulgence, a suspicion that tended to be very skeptical of human nature, to fear that humans were born depraved and were in need of strict management." Worster finds echoes of this more pessimistic way of thinking prominently featured among current environmentalists, for whom "too often for the public they sound like gloomy echoes of Gilbert Burnet's ringing jeremiad of 1679: 'The whole Nation is corrupted . . . and we may justly look for unheard of Calamities.'"† Worster suggests that in our own time

* In the United States, even at the beginning of the twenty-first century, the Protestant way of thinking still exerts a powerful influence in many areas of American life, not only the environment. Protestantism, for example, encourages a strong sense of individual autonomy and skepticism of any hierarchy, whether it is a church or government body. Indeed, in Rome some Vatican observers were expressing concerns as recently as 2004 with respect to the Protestant tendencies of the United States, including even many American Catholics who had become captive to the prevailing Protestant ways of seeing the world. Despite the best efforts to educate them otherwise, it seemed in Rome that "Calvinism fuels the subconscious of many Americans, including Catholics." There were "more than a few Vatican officials [who were] accusing American leaders of harboring a Calvinist streak," influencing them to perceive the United States in terms of "a purely good people chosen by God" who have a divine command to overthrow others who may be "perfectly evil"—as in the decision to go to war in Iraq. According to John Allen, a leading media commentator on Vatican affairs, all this was seen by many in the Vatican as reflecting the continuing strong influence among all Americans, Protestants and Catholics alike, of "Calvinist concepts of the total depravity of the damned, the unconditional election of God's favored, and the manifestation of election through earthly success" in a calling. The Calvinist "heresy" persisted in the United States, perhaps most dangerously in disguised forms of American secular religion. Quoted in Douglas Todd, "GOP and Vatican Divided by Iraq War," *Christian Century*, November 16, 2004, 15.

† By the middle of the first decade of the twenty-first century, climate change had become the leading source of the expected future biblical calamities for the earth. As a columnist for the *Los Angeles Times* commented in 2007, a Calvinist sense of the pervasive spread of human sinfulness was demanding reforms throughout American life, frequently expressed as a necessity to impose a powerful moral discipline to restrain the continuing sinful emission of greenhouse gases:

> Global climate change—along with terrorism—has replaced the Soviet Union as the Monster Under the Bed in our national consciousness. It has reached the level of a full-blown zeitgeist social issue, with far-reaching moral and religious undertones.
> Because global warming and the efforts to halt it touch on nearly every realm of policy, the environment has become a moral prism through which all other issues are being filtered. Regardless of whether they actually care about the environment, partisans of all stripes are using the issue to gain the moral edge.
> A green think tank in London has urged British couples to think of the environmental consequences of having more than two children. It released a paper showing that if couples

of seemingly ever-expanding devotion to personal pleasures and consumption, "the Protestant ascetic tradition may someday survive only among the nation's environmentalists, who . . . compulsively turn off the lights."[8]

Yet another large debt to Protestantism is found in a powerful sense of "egalitarian individualism." Worster writes that Protestantism "originates in the conviction that God's promise is to the individual, freed from the bonds of tradition and hierarchy," such as were prominent features in the Roman Catholic Church. This nonhierarchical view of the world was applied in Protestant societies to defend fiercely the individual rights of human beings—John Locke, for example, was closely reflecting his Puritan roots in his libertarian defense of private property. In environmentalism, it was possible to extend such thinking to protect new "rights of nature." Protestant principles, Worster suggests, could "lead not only to elevating the poor and despised in society but also to investing whales, forests, and even rivers with new dignity."[9] While many Protestant ministers have joined the environmental crusade, many fewer Catholic bishops and Jewish rabbis historically have unrestrainedly embraced the environmental cause.*

A final main inheritance from Protestantism is labeled by Worster as "aesthetic spirituality." It involves a rejection of narrowly utilitarian purposes that suggest an appropriate goal of "using" nature, and instead sees the value of nature lying in its inherent worth. In the Protestantism of old, and now in environmentalism, it is important "to see beyond instrumental values, to find beauty in the unaltered Creation, and to identify that beauty with goodness and truth."[10] The leading American theologian of the eighteenth century, Jona-

---

had two children instead of three, "they could cut their family's carbon dioxide output the equivalent of 620 return flights a year between London and New York."

Similarly, last month a London tabloid featured a 35-year-old environmentalist who asked to be sterilized so she could contribute to the effort "to protect the planet." "Having children is selfish," she insisted. "It's all about maintaining your genetic line at the expense of the planet."

Environmental rhetoric . . . constantly reminds us of our own culpability. For that reason, environmentalism is more akin to a religious awakening than to a political ideology.

Like evangelicals, environmentalists speak, in their way, of fire and brimstone. Like the preacher, the environmental activist demands that we give ourselves to something beyond ourselves and that we do penance for our wasteful, carbon-profligate sins.

And like any religion that emphasizes sin, devotees will find all sorts of ways to prove their personal righteousness. (Gregory Rodriguez, "Greenness Is Next to Godliness," *Los Angeles Times*, December 10, 2007)

* Mark Stoll comments that the members of the small set of influential "Jewish environmentalists" have often bemoaned the apparent absence of prominent Jews in the environmental movement," in large contrast to the disproportionate presence of Jews in many other areas of American intellectual and political life. See Mark Stoll, "Green Versus Green: Religions, Ethics, and the Bookchin-Foreman Dispute," *Environmental History* 6 (July 2001): 419. This is not to say, however, that Jewish writers have ignored environmental matters altogether. See Hava Tirosh-Samuelson, *Judaism and Ecology: Created World and Revealed World* (Cambridge: Harvard University Press, 2002).

than Edwards, preached "God's excellency, his wisdom, his purity and love, [which] seemed to appear in everything, in the sun, moon, and stars; in the clouds and blue sky; in the grass, flowers, trees; in the water, and all nature."[11] Worster finds such a Calvinist religious appreciation for nature reappearing in new forms among such twentieth-century environmental leaders as Rachel Carson, William O. Douglas, and David Brower. As he explains, it had been "learned in New England pastures or Wisconsin oak openings, [but] this Protestant tendency to go back to nature in search of divine beauty could be exercised in an infinite number of landscapes" across the United States.[12]

In the secular climate of the late twentieth-century American public arena, the essentially Protestant roots of the American environmental movement could be awkward.[13] Because of the religious diversity of the nation, and looking back to many past wars and other fierce conflicts among competing branches of Christianity, Americans have long been wary of debating religion in public. In the twentieth century, Americans thus typically disguised their main religious arguments as conflicts among secular religions, and typically without even any explicit mention of God. Worster notes that even most of the "the histories of environmentalism in the United States have so far been preoccupied with politics and careers, with public ideas and debates. Nowhere near enough attention has been given to the inward drives of reformers, to the elusive and hidden patterns of temperament and motive, to the shaping forces of religion, family and class"—all this typically derived from Protestantism and very often from specifically Calvinist understandings of Protestantism.[14]

In some cases there might have been elements of willful deception. To the degree that religious origins have come up at all, there has been a tendency in the environmental movement to look to more exotic sources of inspiration, such as Buddhism, Hinduism, American Indian religion, and primitive paganism. Believing that they have rejected Christianity, many environmentalists might be uncomfortable in hearing that, truth be told, they are still in essence Christian followers, if now receiving the message in a new and disguised (and heretical by orthodox Christian standards) form. Indeed, in many cases the changed vocabulary might have been intended precisely to obscure the actual origins, thereby making Christian religion accessible to many people who might well have rejected it altogether in a more overt and explicit form.

Newly expressed in the secular metaphors of environmental religion, it is possible today to proselytize familiar elements of Protestant religion in Ivy League and other settings where the original versions would never be allowed into the public discussion—unless they were presented as part of an historical or "scientific" study of religion. In a 2008 interview, Gus Speth, dean of the Yale School of Forestry and Environmental Studies, warned of the dire consequences if human beings continuing their wasteful ways: "If we just keep doing what we're doing today, releasing the same amounts of greenhouse gases, the same impoverishment of ecosystems, the same toxification, you know, well in the latter part of this century the planet won't be fit to live on." The fact is that our profligacy is "on the verge of ruining the planet." Our failures were at heart moral, a failure to recognize and respect essential limits that now had reached the point of threatening our civilization. And the solution thus had to be found in the moral reform of our lives. As Speth declared, the "next steps are to begin to question our obsessive concern with economic growth so that it trumps everything. . . . We have to question our own pathetic capitulation to consumerism." The signs of our increasing failures of will were all around us: "We've had our home size in the U.S. go up 50 percent in the last few decades. . . . And yet we still don't have enough space for all of our stuff. So, we've had to create this self storage industry in the United States." Like others of the past who had sunk into excess, our commitment of our lives to greater and greater riches—our fall into material consumption and pleasure seeking for its own sake—was a failure even on its own terms: "It's all illusory . . . in terms of real human happiness and real well being, because . . . buying more and more stuff doesn't work."[15] True fulfilment would come only from obeying higher sources of authority, learning to show a genuine respect for the planet earth—or in the language of Protestantism of old, making a renewed commitment to live our lives according to God's commands.[16]

In expressing ancient religious truths in new secular metaphors, environmentalists may find some comfort in recognizing that they have a great deal of company. In the United States, like Western civilization as a whole, the range of powerful secular religions extends well beyond the environmental movement.*

---

* Some observers have asserted that secular influences are much exaggerated in the United States, which remains a deeply religious nation—and in this respect much in contrast to European developments. In his 2008 visit to the United States, however, Pope Benedict XVI saw matters differently. After addressing the American bishops assembled in Washington, D.C., he was asked by his audience to assess "the challenge of increasing secularism in public life and relativism in intellectual life." He noted that religion had traditionally been a powerful influence in the United States, but that "its foundations are being slowly undermined," reflecting the "real challenges the Gospel encounters in contemporary American culture." Indeed, "America's brand of secularism poses a particular problem" because it is less overtly hostile to religion, including the Catholic Church, and thus its insidious effects are less obvious. For many Americans, however, including many Catholics, "faith becomes a passive acceptance that certain things 'out there' are true, but without practical relevance for everyday life. The result is a growing separation of faith from life: living 'as if God did not exist'"—leaving it to secular systems of belief to be the actual definers and shapers of individual American lives and of the whole society. All this was exaggerated by the historical Protestant individualism of American life, in which "each person believes he or she has a right to pick and choose, maintaining exterior social bonds but without an integral, interior conversion to the law of Christ" as universally proclaimed in the teachings of the Roman Catholic Church. See "Prepared Text of Pope Benedict XVI's Speech Before the Bishops of the United States at the National Shrine of the Immaculate Conception," Washington, D.C., April 17, 2008, as provided by the U.S. Conference of Bishops.

The clashes today between two of them, economic and environmental religion, may go far to shape the history of the twenty-first century. If environmentalism owes much to Protestantism, the messages of the American progressive economics of the twentieth century owed more to Roman Catholic religion.[17] Protestantism and environmentalism, for example, rejected the special religious authority of any single clerical hierarchy, even as the expert professionals of economic religion had became a new authoritative "Roman" priesthood.[18]

Although Calvin took the distinctive features of Protestant theology to more radical lengths, the Reformation of course began with Martin Luther. In this book I will draw especially on the more "libertarian" and "dissenting" aspects in both of their worldviews. This is the individualism of the Protestant tradition, what Luther called a "priesthood of believers," each of whom had a direct relationship with God outside the intermediation of any church or other hierarchy. Calvin and Luther both protested against the ruling order. It should also be recognized, however, that Calvinism and Lutheranism later sometimes became state churches themselves in European nations. Calvinists and Lutherans were perfectly capable of using the powers of state coercion to require dissenters to conform. Nevertheless, in this book "Calvinism" will refer to the libertarian and dissenting side of the Protestant tradition, as would be seen in its later application to the ideas of covenant agreements, democratic deliberation, and God's "judgments" of government. We also know English Calvinism as Puritanism, a way of life that emphasized human imperfection (original sin), self-restraint, the moral urgency that prompts activism, and the sovereignty of God in nature. As we shall see, all these Puritan traits have deeply influenced American culture, which includes its secular ideologies and modern movements such as environmentalism. When I speak of secular religion, or "Calvinism minus God," it will mean a similar way of framing events in the world, even when there may be no explicit religious doctrines attached.

Part II examines the Calvinist roots of American environmentalism. Chapter 6 shows how environmentalism revived the old Calvinist sense of a fundamental corruption of human nature since the fall. Chapter 7 traces the religious significance of the natural world in Calvinist thought, beginning with the central role of the "Book of Nature" in John Calvin's theology. Calvin's message was elaborated by Jonathan Edwards and other Massachusetts Calvinists; it was prominently secularized for the first time in the United States in New England transcendentalism; the founder of the Sierra Club in 1892, John Muir, wrote about going to nature to find God; and, finally, "deep ecology" in the 1980s reflected a powerfully renewed Calvinist outlook on the world.

6

UNORIGINAL SIN

MANY POPULAR ENVIRONMENTAL WRITINGS have been filled with a moralistic language reminiscent of the Ten Commandments, now applied as well to human relationships with the natural world. Wild areas are being "raped," trees are being "murdered," "greedy" corporations are "assaulting" lakes and rivers, and nature in general is being "ravaged" by the economic forces of the modern world. It is a familiar story of a rapidly spreading evil in the world—in this case, of big corporations and other sinful agents violating the innocence of nature. In 1997, an environmentalist, Julia "Butterfly" Hill, climbed two hundred feet to the top branches of a redwood tree in the Headwaters Forest in northern California and remained there for two years, hoping both to protect the tree from timber harvesting and to protest publicly the further cutting of redwoods. In the Middle East, devout monks long ago climbed stone pillars, where they sometimes remained for years, demonstrating in this way their complete devotion to God.*

---

* In another interesting parallel between environmentalism and Christianity, the Roman Catholic Church once sold indulgences to relieve sinners from their guilt (and the fear of divine punishment). Today, there is a rapidly growing market in a contemporary equivalent—voluntary carbon offsets. More and more people, even though they have no legal obligation to do so, are purchasing offsets to the greenhouse gases that they create in the course of their own lives (the carbon dioxide released in driving a car, for example). The offset takes the form of new activities (which would not otherwise be undertaken) that reduce greenhouse gas levels (such as planting a new forest, which will capture carbon dioxide). The *Washington Post* reported in a 2008 front-page story that "in the Washington area and across the country, there is . . . a bull market in environmental guilt. Sales of carbon offsets— whose buyers pay hard cash to make amends for their sins against the climate—are up," even while the stock market was falling. One buyer calculated that his vacation travel had generated 52,920 pounds of greenhouse gas emissions over the course of the previous year. He paid $240 to purchase offsets from Carbonfund.org, a Maryland seller. The *Post* commented that, because there was no personal profit or other financial gain, the benefits of such offset purchases "must be psychological, moral." In a "cultural shift" that reflected a new "guilt boom" in American society, "the American public has become accustomed to feeling guilt about climate change, and, instead of writing letters to members

Environmental theology typically says little about God; it offers no answers concerning the hereafter; it is vague about the route of personal salvation; and in other respects it departs from basic tenets of Christian religion. Yet present-day environmentalism also derives large parts of its message from Christianity. Indeed, like other secular religions of the modern age, a main source of the appeal of environmentalism is that it offers traditional religious messages of the West in a new "scientific" form. This is a main source of their success because, in an age of wide questioning of biblical authority, the scientific claims give these traditional messages greater authority for large numbers of people.*

Devil's Design

Present-day environmentalism draws on the long and powerful tradition within Christianity that regards wealth and riches, sophisticated reasoning, the structures of the law—all the formal institutions of society and of the good life—as dangerous and corrupting influences. These instruments all too often serve not the will of God but reflect the devious designs of the devil. Since the fall of man from the Garden, human weakness has rendered the products of human reason unreliable, often deluding human beings into false optimism and excessive confidence in their own powers. Perhaps the foremost American Catholic theologian of the twentieth century, John Courtney Murray,

---

of Congress or donating to an environmental group, they have learned to buy their way out." If events were now taking place in Washington rather than Rome, Martin Luther would have found it familiar. See David A. Fahrenthold, "There's a Gold Mine in Environmental Guilt: Carbon-Offset Sales Brisk Despite Financial Crisis," *Washington Post*, October 6, 2008, A1.

  * Among leading American politicians, former vice president Al Gore, for example, has been at the forefront of the effort to spread the environmental gospel. Although he has shown little interest in exploring the precise contents of the religious views he espouses, he has been unusually explicit—especially for a person so much in the public eye—in declaring that his environmental beliefs do in fact have a religious basis. In his 1992 book *Earth in the Balance*, Gore stated that "the more deeply I search for the roots of the global environmental crisis, the more I am convinced that it is an outer manifestation of an inner crisis that is, for lack of a better word, spiritual." The "growing struggle to save the earth's environment," reflecting an "ungodly" turn of events in human history, required "an investigation of the very nature of our civilization" and its core values. Gore has had remarkable success with his new religious crusade, as reflected in his winning of the Nobel Peace Prize in 2007. The *Washington Post* reported that in 2007 "former vice president Al Gore screened his film, 'An Inconvenient Truth,' at the [Wal-Mart] company's headquarters [in Arkansas] to a standing ovation. Michael Marx, head of the Business Ethics Network, an umbrella organization of several [environmental] activist groups, likened it to a 'religious revival'" of leading American business executives. See Al Gore, *Earth in the Balance: Ecology and the Human Spirit* (Boston: Houghton Mifflin, 1992), 12, 13, 1; and Ylan Q. Mui, "Wal-Mart Extends Its Influence to Washington: Under Siege, Retailer Engages Opponents," *Washington Post*, November 24, 2007, A1.

once labeled this powerful tradition within Christianity as one of "contempt of the world," and found that it characterizes "sin as a permanent human fact that casts a shadow over all human achievements." This main Christian tradition encourages asceticism (and had an important influence on a number of monastic orders), spurns the attempt to perfect an earthly existence, and suggests that human beings "should by right neglect what is called the cultural enterprise—the cultivation of science and the arts, the pursuit of human values by human energies, the work of civilization." Such an outlook often asserts that the world is about to be overcome by the forces of evil—but also that there can still be hope that "in that moment [of collapse] the light disperses the darkness."[1]

Contemporary environmentalism shares a closely related outlook: a sense that modern civilization both tempts human beings to sinful acts and represents retrogression rather than progress; an apocalyptic foreboding concerning ecological catastrophe and the near-term future of the earth; an attitude that human reason, as today most importantly embodied in science, offers false promises and separates humanity from its true self; a view that a widespread sinfulness has infected the world (now seen in the rampant destruction of nature that meets popular indifference); a condemnation of the pervasive greed that motivates current evils (found especially in corporate "profiteers" who abuse nature); a view that urban and industrial civilization cuts human beings off from their deeper and truer natural selves; and a desire for a return to an earlier primitive and more natural existence—the existence of the earth thousands of years ago—in which the corrupting products of modern science and economics were absent. In short, the deliverers of such environmental messages today issue a new call for human beings to renounce their evil ways and to live in a simpler harmony with their truer natures and with the divine order that governs the universe—much as Christianity has long preached obedience to God and repentance and deliverance from sin.

The Wicked World of John Muir

The idea of human beings as fundamentally corrupt and sinful, fully capable of defiling the earth—and that, in fact, little else should be expected—is a staple of old-fashioned Protestant religion. (Original sin was of course also part of Roman Catholicism as well, but Rome's understanding of the consequences for human behavior tended to be less dire.) As the leading advocate of the preservationist cause of the late nineteenth and early twentieth centuries, John Muir saw his mission in characteristically Protestant terms: "to save humans from their depravity, indifference, and destructiveness," which was now manifested in their treatment of not only fellow human beings but also fellow creatures in the natural world.[2] Muir thus described the "barbarous wickedness" of both buffalo hunters and the "temple destroyers" who sought to build Hetch Hetchy Dam in Yosemite National Park.[3] He encouraged Americans to "cleanse your soul of worldly evil" by experiencing the handiwork of God in nature.[4]

Robert Royal is a contemporary Catholic theologian who comes from a religious tradition that historically has shown greater tolerance for human foibles and frailties. He finds in Muir a characteristically Protestant view of the world (speaking here of Protestantism in the original sixteenth and seventeenth century versions, not the optimistic "liberal" Protestantism of the social gospel movement and of many late twentieth-century denominations, which often departed radically from the original). In understanding the relationship of human beings and nature, Muir brought the "same prophetic fervor, antihuman bent, and moral absolutism that his [Calvinist] ancestors had brought to the ancient faith. For him, what was human was corrupt, as only a Calvinist can construe corruption, and the human was corrupting nature" totally, and with ever increasing power, due to the unhappy confluence of modern science and industry.[5]

Although its roots lie in Protestant Christianity, mainstream environmentalism, of course, is no longer explicitly Christian—or at least in any orthodox form. As Donald Worster writes of Muir, he "invented a new kind of frontier religion: one based on going to the wilderness to experience the loving presence of God. Only corrupt, ignorant, arrogant human beings stood outside that divine beauty, spoiling and abusing it. Separating himself from human corruption, Muir found redemption in the wild and he called the rest of the nation to join him." Muir had been raised in a devout family environment within the Campbellite branch of American Protestantism, a faith to which Muir's father had turned after leaving a more orthodox Presbyterianism. As Worster finds, throughout his life and preaching Muir powerfully exhibited the influence of his early immersion in the Campbellite faith. As an environmental prophet, he offered a novel religious blend of "Scottish and Campbellite mentality, out of left-wing Protestantism, out of Enlightenment rationalism, and out of frontier evangelism."[6]

Yet it was not something that Muir readily admitted, perhaps even to himself. Taking Muir too much at face value, Worster comments, his leading "biographers neglect this religious background because Muir himself never quite acknowledged its hold on him. On the contrary, he insisted that he had broken free from it at an early age"; there are many other environmentalists today of whom this could be said. "Muir has become a hero for many Americans who made a similar transition from Judeo-Christianity to modern environmental-ism. Their new faith grew up within the shell of the old"—or perhaps it was more than just a shell that remained.[7]

From Plato to Deep Ecology

The idea of human alienation from their true nature existed in the Western world well before Christianity. For Plato, the undermining and corrupting power of greed and other economic influences—destroying the virtues of the citizenry—explained the increasingly degenerate character of Greek society. In the later part of the Roman empire, Augustine brought together the Platonic tradition and Christian theology. For Augustine, life on earth offered an existence of sin and depravity, characterized by "the love of self" and the all-consuming pursuit of a hedonistic life, as exemplified by the corruption and debauchery of ancient Rome.

In the history of Western religion, Martin Luther and the Protestant Refor-mation represented the next great statement of such a theology—all followers in the "contempt for the world" tradition described by John Courtney Murray. The greatest objects of their scorn were once again to be found in Rome, now the headquarters of the Roman Catholic Church, successor to the Roman Em-pire and still a great corrupting influence in Western civilization. Luther also continued the Platonic and Augustinian tradition of seeing economic compe-tition and the pursuit of self-interest as forces of darkness, perhaps temporarily necessary in a sinful world, but only as a result of the deeply fallen condition of present-day human beings. It was better that private property should divide one man from another than that sinful human beings should engage in endless strife and internal warfare.

In many important ways, Marxism is a secular variation in the same tradi-tion of Plato, Augustine, and Luther—and now this tradition can also to be found again in some important segments of environmentalism.[8] The Marxist concept of alienation was derived, as the political philosopher Isaiah Berlin commented, from what "Rousseau and Luther and an earlier Christian tradi-tion called the perpetual self-divorce of men from unity with nature, with each other, with God." Although there is no similar certainty with respect to a glorious ending, as decreed by the Christian God, many leading figures in the American environmental movement have also seen the contemporary world in much the same terms.

The ideas of "deep ecology" are not widely known to the American pub-lic but have exercised a significant (if often unacknowledged) influence, even within the mainstream environmental movement. Deep ecology takes some of the core premises of contemporary environmentalism and extends them to their full logic, reaching radical conclusions that more timid—or more politically practical—environmentalists are reluctant to examine or defend. In their 1985 environmental "catechism" *Deep Ecology*, Bill Devall and George Sessions develop a new portrayal of the fall of man in secular terms—the story of human history as one of decline from an original existence in true harmony with nature. In their version, and echoing Rousseau and Marx, the causes of human alienation are to be found in "technological society [that] not only alienates humans from the rest of Nature but also alienates humans from themselves and from each other."[9] Thus, deep ecology challenges "not only the growth addict and the chronic developer, but science itself."[10]

Dave Foreman was the founder in 1980 of Earth First!, a self-described "radical environmental" organization that drew heavily on the ideas of deep ecology. It received wide media attention later in the decade for its activist campaigns, which included the engaging in "monkey wrenching"—the sabotaging of heavy machinery and other acts of destroying the instruments of economic development. Partly owing to the national publicity generated (this was before 9/11, when terrorism could still hold a romantic appeal for many Americans), Earth First! helped to bring about the sharp curtailment of federal timber harvesting on the public lands of the Pacific Northwest in the late 1980s and early 1990s.

Foreman preached to his environmental followers that "human destruction of the wild" is the "keystone to understanding our alienation from Nature, which is the central problem of Civilization." Foreman followed the standard secular and environmental formula in locating the fall of man in recorded human history.* He wrote that it was the "nascency of agriculture" about ten

---

* In a book published by the Sierra Club, environmental writer Paul Shepard similarly refers to a much happier time in history when human beings could "live at peace with their world, . . . feel themselves to be guests rather than masters" of the earth. It was a simple life in harmony with nature that fostered "mental growth, cooperation, leadership, and the study of a mysterious and beautiful world where the clues to the meaning of life were embodied in natural things, where everyday life was inextricable from spiritual significance and encounter." But this was all lost over the course of "these ten millennia since the archaic foraging cultures began to be destroyed by their hostile, aggressive, better-organized, civilized neighbors." Shepard identifies four stages of this terrible fall into the current stage of "ontogenetic crippling" in which the old "humility and tender sense of human limitation is no longer rewarded," having been replaced by a sense of "moral superiority, masked by the psychological defenses of repression and projection," and in which "the childish will to destroy and other useful regressions" are socially encouraged. The first stage, the initial moment of the fall, was the rise ten thousand years ago of the "earliest agriculture," followed by the gradual further decline of the human condition with "the era of the desert fathers, the Reformation, and [culminating in] present-day industrial society." We have reached today a world in which "madness" prevails. It is Jean-Jacques Rousseau in the 1980s language of American environmentalism. See Paul Shepard, *Nature and Madness* (San Francisco: Sierra Club Books, 1982), 6, 14, 15, 16.

thousand years ago that first left human beings "apart from the natural world," and there soon followed the evils of "city, bureaucracy, patriarchy, war, and empire."[11] This had caused "an ever widening rift . . . between the wilderness that created us and the civilization created by us."[12] In the gospel of Foreman, man was born in innocence but has now rebelled against his primitive naturalness and fallen into a state of deep sinfulness and alienation. Foreman had been brought up in the same Campbellite branch of Presbyterianism as Muir, and to similar effect.

Many other environmentalists today preach similar messages. Wes Jackson is the director of the Land Institute in Salina, Kansas, long dedicated to reorganizing American society according to "sustainable" principles. In a 2005 tribute to Jackson in *Smithsonian* magazine, Craig Canine commented that "farming, in Jackson's view, is humanity's original sin." Developing a chronology similar to Foreman, Jackson dates the fall to around ten thousand years ago, when "people first started gathering and planting the seed of annual grasses, such as wild wheat and barley."[13] As Jackson elaborates on the message, "that was probably the first moment when we began to erode the ecological capital of the soil," the point in time when "humans first started withdrawing the earth's non-renewable resources."[14] This set in motion historical forces that have now led to the vastly destructive impacts for the earth of "fossil fuel dependency, environmental pollution, overpopulation and global warming."[15]

Jackson seems to depart from Christian theology in that, as he says, "it didn't require . . . the devil to make us do it—we just did it."[16] As in other secular religions, there is no god outside history; it is human beings, for better or for worse, who make their own history, even as that experiencing of the world then turns out to be remarkably similar to earlier Christian understandings. Moreover, even in Christianity, the devil does not actually make us commit sinful acts; he tempts us, but we always have the ability to refuse. Human beings are made in the image of God; as a result, and unlike any other creature of the earth, they have the capacity to reason and to decide between good and evil—they have free will. Jackson might have employed a new set of metaphors, and said nothing about a god or the hereafter, but otherwise his vision of errant choices made by sinful human beings would be quite familiar to a Christian listener.

Apocalypse Without Purpose

Such religious similarities were apparent to conservation biologist David Orr, as he described in 2005 in the professional journal *Conservation Biology*. As

Orr comments, there is "an interesting convergence of views between conservation biologists and religious fundamentalists." As many Protestant ministers have been preaching since the Reformation, and now many environmental preachers were following in their steps, "both agree that things are going to hell in the proverbial handbasket."* Conservation biologists today, Orr comments, see clearly that "whether by climate change, biotic impoverishment, catastrophic pollution, resource wars, emergent diseases, or a combination of several, the end is in sight, although we can quibble about the details and schedule." With a few changes in terminology, as Orr acknowledges, "evangelicals would most likely regard these [same] data as a sign of the end times," when terrible evils will be spreading across the earth. Admittedly, for devout Christians this moment of environmental calamity will also presage "the imminent return of Christ, which is to say the fulfillment of prophesy."[17]

Lacking the Christian message of such a wonderful ending, however, the many current signs of the end times become for Orr a potential source of deep pessimism. If sinful human beings cannot turn to any all-powerful god to save them, Orr can hope only for a new worldwide recognition among all people and nations of the necessity to "recalibrate human numbers, wants, needs, and actions with the requisites of ecology within a finite biosphere."[18] This, to be sure, seems an unlikely possibility within the framework of his own thought. Why should sinful human beings so suddenly become rational and ethical when they have never been so before throughout recorded human history, and when environmentalism itself casts strong doubts on the more recent progressive hopes for a new era of great scientific and economic progress?[19]

Noting the many similarities between biblical messages and those of secular religions, Donald McGregor comments that, if there is no God to ensure a happy final outcome, "secular apocalypticism appears devoid of an underlying redemptive meaning and moral order, and thus is 'characterized by a sense of hopelessness and despair.'"[20] That is a fair characterization of the outcome in Orr's case; his environmental history offers little basis for hope, leaving

---

* Indeed, the environmental messages often sound remarkably similar to such preachers as Billy Graham. In *How to Be Born Again*, Graham explains that "something has gone wrong with our jet age." He offers a litany of evils to show the spiritual failings and the severe moral decline of our time (including the fact that "the atmosphere [is filled] with waste products that nearly obscure the sunset"). In a typical Graham sermon, the message was of terrible statistics, such as that "in the U.S. in the past 14 years, the rate of robberies has increased 255%, forcible rape 143%, aggravated assault 153% and murder 106%. . . . There is no longer a safety zone in any city." Our environmental prophets have used different examples and different numbers but to the same effect—to emphasize the current gravely fallen condition of humanity and the urgent necessity of a spiritual renewal. See Billy Graham, *How to Be Born Again* (New York: Warner Books, 1979), 76–77.

worldwide catastrophe as the most likely outcome, a terrifying prospect whose meaning—or lack of such—Orr himself seems to be struggling with.*

In another statement of environmental religion, Bill McKibben in *The End of Nature* identifies a severe "crisis of belief" at the end of the twentieth century but asserts that "many people, including me, have overcome it to a greater or lesser degree by locating God in nature." When Europeans first arrived in North America, as McKibben tells us, they found a "wilderness" that was a "blooming, humming, fertile paradise," very much like the biblical one. But Europeans were the descendents of Adam and Eve and were soon spreading their evil ways to the new world as well. Human sinfulness by now has reached almost every corner of the globe, destroying wilderness wherever it had existed, and thereby rapidly erasing the final visible traces of God's handiwork in creating the world. As McKibben warns, modern men and women are now everywhere following an agenda of "making ourselves gods." If we succeed entirely, reflecting the deep pessimism to which a secular environmental theology can easily lead, there will be no "hope for a living, eternal, meaningful world."[21] If wild nature should in the end somehow disappear from the earth, "one of the possible meanings . . . is that God is dead."[22] Friedrich Nietzsche once said much the same thing, although he was more ruthlessly honest and fearless in confronting the abyss.

The Cancer of the Earth

Absent a Christian or other god to give meaning, the reasoning of secular environmental theology in fact easily leads to the conclusion that the world might be better off without the continued presence of the human species. If environmentalism is a "Calvinism minus God" (see chap. 7 for more on this),

---

*In a study of the apocalyptic tendencies in American history, Daniel Wojcik notes that there is a "process of innovation within apocalyptic traditions: prophesy interpreters and believers have inventively reformulated and updated their belief systems to incorporate new technology, current crises, and perceived threats." Among the more recent arrivals in the American apocalyptic tradition, "environmental destruction has been viewed as an endtimes sign. . . . Humanity is powerless to save the earth and will inevitably destroy it." For some people "the suffering occasioned by ecological crises is the result of divine judgment upon humanity's careless destruction of the earth." For others who are less traditionally devout and believe in a "secular apocalypticism," the human destruction of the earth will simply expose the "meaninglessness and randomness" of human existence; it will be "an unjust catastrophe without purpose." Whatever specific form such visions may take in the future, Wojcik sees no end to apocalyptic prophesies in Western civilization: "The fact that Christian traditions have flourished at a grassroots level for two millennia demonstrates their enduring relevance and explanatory power and portends the continued appeal of such beliefs well into the third millennium"—in many secular and Christian forms alike. See Daniel Wojcik, *The End of the World as We Know It: Faith, Fatalism, and Apocalypse in America* (New York: New York University Press, 1997), 173, 172, 146, 174.

that is a bleak vision indeed. Calvinism preached the overwhelming sinfulness of human beings and the deep depravity of their existence on this earth, but, as in other Christian messages, this would be overcome in the end and given meaning by the final intervention of a God in heaven. With this God removed from the picture, however, the only prospect would seem to be an endlessly continuing human depravity on earth.

Perhaps it should not be surprising, therefore, that some leading environmentalists have spoken of human beings as a malignant presence in the world. Dave Brower once said in the 1970s that the human race was a spreading "cancer" that threatened to destroy all the other plant and animal species.[23] More recently, Dave Foreman has similarly described human beings as "the cancer of the earth."[24] Paul Watson, a founder of Greenpeace, altered the metaphor slightly, in 1988 labeling humanity as the "the AIDS of the earth."[25] One of their followers, Anne Peterman, although she has now recanted somewhat (although still a self-professed radical environmentalist), describes her original exposure to environmental religion: "When I was a teenager, I was deeply misanthropic. I loved nature and spent as much time as possible out of doors. But at night, I would look out the window at the Burger King across the street, at the gas stations on all sides, at the noisy stinking stream of traffic, and I would loathe humanity, dreaming of its demise. When I found Earth First!, the campfire chants of 'Billions are living that should be dead' or 'fuck the human race' appealed to me. Yes, I thought, humans are a cancer on the earth."[26]

It is not only impressionable teenagers who can come to think this way. Eric Pianka is an ecologist at the University of Texas who was named Texas Distinguished Scientist of 2006. In a speech to the Texas Academy of Sciences, he looked favorably on the possibility that a viral epidemic might accidentally depopulate much of the earth. Although he was not advocating any positive steps to bring it about, he stated that "things are gonna get better after the [impending ecological] collapse because we won't be able to decimate the earth so much. And, I actually think the world will be much better when there's only 10 or 20 percent of us left." A university student who was present at the speech wrote shortly thereafter in her personal blog that "he's a radical thinker, that one! I mean, he's basically advocating for the death of all but 10 percent of the current population! And at the risk of sounding just as radical, I think he's right."[27]

Such blunt statements are of course exceptional. Only a few people are personally willing to confront the logical endpoint of these widely held positions. Indeed, in a perfect environmental world, it does follow from these assumptions that the best outcome for the earth might actually be the end of the human presence—a complete radical surgery to remove altogether the rapidly spreading human destruction that now threatens every other living creature with a nonhuman holocaust. The earth without any human beings, from this perspective, would be a much better place.* Nature would then be allowed to be truly "natural"—the highest value in environmental religion— in an all-encompassing way that otherwise will never be. British philosopher Kate Soper thus comments that some of the basic premises concerning the role of human beings in the world, as widely accepted in contemporary environmentalism, lead to "the logical conclusion . . . that it would have been better by far had the [human] species never existed."[28]

One of the foremost U.S. environmental historians, William Cronon, finds this logic, as he agrees is embodied within the core tenets of environmental theology, significantly problematic for the environmental movement. Environmentalism seeks to protect wilderness areas from human impacts as a core statement of its religious convictions. But, as Cronon notes, if the main message of environmental theology is carried to its full extent, "it is hard not to reach the conclusion that the only way human beings can hope to live naturally on the earth is to follow the hunter-gatherers back into a wilderness Eden and abandon virtually everything that civilization has given us." Indeed, it might be even more logically coherent to conclude that, "if nature dies because we enter it, then the only way to save nature is to kill ourselves." Although the vast majority of environmentalists would no doubt reject this conclusion, if presented so baldly, Cronon finds that the line of thinking of "radical environmentalists and deep ecologists all too frequently come[s] close to accepting" an ending of the human presence on earth "as a first principle," the ultimate goal.[29]

Illustrating Cronon's point, as mainstream an environmental writer as Bill McKibben can declare that "it is not utter silliness to talk about ending— or, at least, transforming—industrial civilization." McKibben is prepared at least to hope for "a different world, where roads are torn out to create vast new wildernesses, where most development ceases, and where much of man's imprint on the earth is slowly erased."[30] Another prominent figure in mainstream environmental thought, the distinguished historian of the American

---

*Utopian literature has always been a good indication of the temper of the times. In what may be an historical first, a 2007 book (which sold quite well) portrays a utopian future characterized by the disappearance of the human species. In *The World Without Us*, Alan Weisman explores the many wonderful consequences "on the day after humans disappear [from the earth, as] nature takes over and immediately begins cleaning house." As the new utopia without humans is reached, "the thought of rural Europe reverting one day to original forest is heartening." Of course, the full benefits will not be realized immediately, and the earth may in fact never be totally restored because, even "if we were to vanish tomorrow, the momentum of certain forces we've already set in motion will continue until centuries of gravity, chemistry and entropy slow them to an equilibrium that may only partly resemble the one that existed before us." Weisman describes his overall project as offering a "view [of] our Earth's current myriad stresses from the disarming vantage of a fantasy in which we . . . no longer exist." See Alan Weisman, *The World Without Us* (New York: St. Martin's Press, 2007), 15, 14, 19, 277.

wilderness movement Roderick Nash, declared in 1991 that "I'm sorry people are starving but I'm much more concerned with members of the species smaller than Homo sapiens."[31] In the twentieth century, the number of human beings on earth expanded exponentially, whereas the presence of other living creatures—the wildest ones especially—decreased correspondingly. The latter, therefore, must now be our priority, over human welfare.

The possibility that the earth might actually be better off without any human beings at all reflects a fundamental dualism that Cronon finds both pervasive and troubling in environmental religion. On the one side, there is nature; on the other side, there are human beings, who are unnatural. But natural and unnatural are virtually synonymous with good and evil in environmental theology. It would therefore seem that a new human devil has triumphed in the past few thousand years over the entire earth, spreading an unprecedented worldwide eruption of unnatural forces that has been accelerated by the rise of modern civilization. Unlike many environmentalists, Cronon sees the danger of the full consequences of such a basic environmental way of thinking about nature becoming more widely recognized among the mass of the American public. Because few people are prepared to embrace the suicide of the human race, or to regard human beings as such a malevolent force in the world, it would be severely damaging in practice to the environmental cause. Hence, even though his views have been harshly attacked by many fellow environmentalists, Cronon argues forcefully that the natural-unnatural dualism at the heart of environmental religion must be abandoned.*

Radical as the prospect sounds to many environmentalists, Cronon goes so far as to declare that "the time has come to rethink wilderness" as a basic environmental value.[32] Moreover, the common environmental way of thinking about nature, which "encourages us to believe we are separate from nature . . . ,

---

* The ambiguities and confusions in the use of "nature" have long been noted (although seemingly without having much influence in clarifying future discussions). In his 1874 essay "On Nature," John Stuart Mill discussed similar issues. Mill wrote there that:

> "NATURE," "natural," and the group of words derived from them, or allied to them in etymology, have at all times filled a great place in the thoughts and taken a strong hold on the feelings of mankind. That they should have done so is not surprising when we consider what the words, in their primitive and most obvious signification, represent; but it is unfortunate that a set of terms which play so great a part in moral and metaphysical speculation should have acquired many meanings different from the primary one, yet sufficiently allied to it to admit of confusion. The words have thus become entangled in so many foreign associations, mostly of a very powerful and tenacious character, that they have come to excite, and to be the symbols of, feelings which their original meaning will by no means justify, and which have made them one of the most copious sources of false taste, false philosophy, false morality, and even bad law. (John Stuart Mill, "On Nature," in Nature, The Utility of Religion, and Theism [1874; repr., London: Rationalist Press, 1904])

is likely to reinforce environmentally irresponsible behavior" in many human domains. The natural-unnatural dualism works to deflect attention from a wide range of environmental concerns, including those in many ordinary places on earth where humans and nonhumans alike have a significant presence. The environmental movement, Cronon argues, should devote more attention to urban parks and gardens, and turn away from the impractical, religiously confused, and ultimately untenable goal of separating virtuous nature from unnatural ("sinful") humanity—as reflected in the pursuit of the "wilderness" goal of nature untouched by human hands as the place where the highest ideals of environmentalism are realized.

The natural-unnatural dualism that so troubles Cronon is not just an obscure matter of environmental theology; it has been enacted into law by the U.S. Congress, including in the Wilderness Act of 1964, which defines a wilderness as a place "untrammeled by man." The National Park Service in the 1960s adopted a similar policy to avoid interfering with nature and to seek to return the national parks to their "natural" conditions preceding human—in practice European—influence (thus, "unnatural" fires caused by humans should be put out, but "natural" fires caused by lightening should be allowed to burn). In the 1990s, such thinking was increasingly extended to the national forests, managed by the U.S. Forest Service.[33] In another area of government policy, the government endorses heroic efforts to keep out "invasive" species that have arrived due to human actions, even as a "natural" movement of species from one place to another does not call for any special actions at all.* The government goes to great lengths to regulate very small quantities of man-made pesticides but sees few problems with the widespread presence of equally dangerous pesticides in the environment, as long as they are created "naturally" as part of the evolutionary defense mechanisms of vegetables and other plants.[34] Global warming due to natural causes would be a cause for concern but would arouse much less public alarm than the same degree of warming demonstrated to be due to "unnatural" human activities. A large number of other examples could be offered, and in each case it is the human, and thus the unnatural, violation of nature that is at the heart of environmental policy concern today, rather than the precise statistical health risks posed or other direct threats to human well-being.

---

* The National Park Service has had a policy to exterminate mountain goats in one part of Yellowstone National Park because they had moved into the park from nearby goat populations introduced by hunters in the early twentieth century—and were thus an "artificial" population. At the same time, the Park Service actively protected another group of Yellowstone mountain goats in another area of the park because they were deemed to have entered naturally from historically long-standing goat populations outside its boundaries.

A Part of Nature

If Cronon is correct, if the mutually exclusive categories of the "natural" and the "unnatural" are to be abandoned, this might be accomplished by seeing human beings as simply another species in nature. Indeed, a strictly scientific approach would presumably require this. The same laws of physics and chemistry govern the flow of blood, the transmission of neural signals, the digestion of food, and other workings of human bodies along with the bodies of other animal species. Biologically, science tells us that human beings are the product of the same Darwinist evolutionary processes, beginning with a common chemical origin several billion years ago. In these ways, no valid scientific distinction could be made between "unnatural" human beings and the rest of nature.

Many environmentalists, however, see human beings as appropriately being brought into the category of the "natural" in a much different way. They note that all species of life on earth are "interconnected." Human beings in the past have sought to master and control nature for their own use, but now they must learn instead to renounce this hubris and to be "a part of nature." Although they may be much more intelligent and powerful, human beings have no special claims or rights to the fruits of the earth. They must share it equally and fairly with all its other creatures. They must come to understand that everything in nature, including the human presence, is part of one great cosmic unity.

According to some proponents of such thinking, this may require a rejection of biblical teachings. In Genesis, we are told that God has given the earth to human beings for their use and enjoyment—for their "dominion." This Christian message, as it is said, became in the modern age an outlook of vast human arrogance; human beings have aggressively sought to "dominate" the world without any consideration of the legitimate claims—perhaps even the core "rights"—of other parts of nature. In a much discussed 1967 article in *Science* magazine, historian Lynn White Jr. developed this line of thought, suggesting that the environmental movement might have to make a decisive break with the Judeo-Christian tradition (White seemingly failed to recognize that environmentalism itself is fundamentally a Judeo-Christian offshoot).[35]

The need for human beings to submit themselves to the dictates of nature— to become a humble member of the community of all things in nature, rather than seeking to exist "apart from" nature—was powerfully stated by Aldo Leopold in 1948 in *Sand County Almanac* and would become a staple of environmental writings over the second half of the twentieth century. J. R. McNeill in 2000 said that contemporary American environmentalism "loosely defined [is] the view that humankind ought to seek peaceful coexistence with, rather than mastery of, nature."[36] In a 2005 article in *Conservation Biology*, two environmental spokespeople declared that a new "essential message of respect" toward nature is required. In the past, partly reflecting the progressive tenets of economic religion, American society sought "to use better science and economics to get nature's resources" to produce ever greater human benefits, paying little attention to the potentially harmful consequences for the rest of the natural world (except insofar as any potential future direct human uses of it might be negatively affected).[37]

In the future, it will be necessary instead to acknowledge that "our powers over nature are vast but not unlimited, which means we need to accommodate ourselves to nature more than we do." Indeed, we must reject the false thinking of the past, which suggested that "people run the planetary system . . . and are empowered to act as they see fit." Instead, human beings must modestly recognize that their greatest concern must not be their own welfare but rather the future of "the planet" for its own sake. Moreover, this future "will come upon us whether we like it or not. Our control over it is modest. As for the planet, our most misguided machinations are unlikely to imperil its multibillion year prospect." Rather than the anthropocentric values of the past, environmental religion now requires "something quite different, perhaps to modify our actions so that the future is maximally shaped by nonhuman forces."[38]

Theological Confusions

From the standpoint of positive science, however, this argument makes little or no sense at all. To suggest that humans should renounce their power over nature is virtually a self-contradiction—it would be merely a different way of exerting power. In seeking to expand their numbers and assert ever greater control over the resources of the earth, human beings individually and collectively are behaving in a natural way by any Darwinist standard in biology. The Darwinian laws of nature are not typically the laws of an idyllic or pastoral world; more often, they are the laws of the jungle—"nature, red in tooth and claw," as Lord Alfred Tennyson famously put it. Nor does there seem to be any way that human beings in the twentieth century could have moved outside the natural laws of physics and chemistry. Indeed, rather than newly becoming a part of nature, as so many environmentalists seem to suggest, the actual goal of the environmental movement is the very opposite: to inculcate a new morality with respect to the natural world that is found nowhere else in nature. No other creature is obligated to protect other species, as the Bible says that Noah was once commanded to do, and as the Endangered Species Act of 1973 again seeks to accomplish. Human beings, in short, must be unnatural, but they must cease being unnatural in the evil ways of the past, which reflected—to put it in Christian terms—the fall in the Garden.

By suggesting that the goal is the opposite, to become a part of nature, environmental theology ends up in a self-contradiction: human beings are to look to the current natural world for their values and spiritual sustenance, yet are instructed to behave and are to be judged by a standard found nowhere else in nature.* If the lion is not to be condemned morally for wanton acts of cruelty against other creatures, why, then, should mankind be judged harshly for behaving in an equally "natural" fashion to dominate the earth. In strictly evolutionary terms, human beings are a great triumph—perhaps the greatest ever. As philosopher Kate Soper notes, "Since any eco-politics . . . accords humanity responsibilities over nature, it presumes the possession by human beings of attributes that set them apart from all other forms of life." Philosophically, she says, many environmental thinkers become incoherent at this point because the common tendency among them has "rejected [a] dualism" of human beings and nature "as inherently un-eco-friendly and even incompatible with support for their objectives."[39]

Obeying God's Commands

It does not require years of theological or philosophical training to see the problem here. Why, then, would such a great number of environmentalists, many of them obviously intelligent and of high integrity, offer such a confused and even illogical set of arguments. I submit that they are driven to it by a wider confusion that they are unwilling to confront directly. What these environmentalists are really saying is that human beings should submit to God's

---

* This theological problem has been noted by a number of others. The Protestant theologian John Cobb, for example, while stating his sympathy for many of the goals of deep ecology, finds the arguments made by deep ecologists frequently to be confused and contradictory. As Cobb states, the reality is that human beings are "the one species that plays the dominant role in the whole [of the earth] and which, therefore, has responsibility for the well-being of the whole," including the rest of the plant and animal species. As a result, "the fate of the earth lies in human hands." Cobb acknowledges the danger of an apocalyptic outcome if human beings do not change their past ways: "It is certainly true that unless there are basic changes in the way human beings behave, we are destined for a terrible end." But the solution is not to become part of nature and thus to act like all the other species—"the abandonment of the dominant [human] role for which deep ecologists sometimes seem to call." Rather, as Cobb says, it is just the opposite; what is necessary is a new "mentality of responsible concern" for nature, which in reality is one particular and much better "way of exercising dominion" over the earth. Only human beings have it within their capacity to save the earth from their own unique sinfulness. See John B. Cobb Jr., "Protestant Theology and Deep Ecology," in *Deep Ecology and World Religions: New Essays on Sacred Ground*, ed. David Landis Barnhill and Roger S. Gottlieb (Albany: State University of New York Press, 2001), 222.

commands. Becoming "a part of nature" really means something much different than being natural in a biological or any other scientific sense. The actual message is that human beings must abandon their false pride and learn a new humility; they must accept that they are insignificant creatures in relation to a wider universe and a much greater power in the world. A new human unity with nature really means a new human unity with God. Human beings must be "born again," environmentally, renouncing both their past sinful preoccupations with self and their petty existences, and take God into their lives, including exercising a proper stewardship over God's creation.

This is not just a matter of an apt set of Christian metaphors that have been conveniently borrowed by a separate environmental religion; environmentalism may be literally in the process of inventing a new form of Christianity. The arguments of environmental religion would make little or no sense without the presence of a Christian God (or something closely equivalent), even when the "God word" is never used. If the result is perhaps heretical by orthodox Christian standards, it may be no more heretical than Martin Luther seemed to observers in Rome in the sixteenth century. The large problem this poses for many environmentalists today, however, is that many do not consider themselves Christian; indeed, quite a few would say that they do not believe in any god at all. A certain number proudly advertise their atheism and their certain conviction of the falseness of the Christian message.

Nevertheless, however large the confusions that may be involved, when environmentalists speak of subordinating human concerns to the dictates of "the planet," there is no other coherent understanding except to say that they are talking about submitting to God. Rather than confronting their own internal religious misunderstandings, many contemporary environmentalists apparently prefer to resort to large doses of rhetorical camouflage and other obfuscations of their own state of confusion. It also helps that many environmentalists have little knowledge of religious history and thus can remain blissfully unaware of the fact that their own environmental messages—with some changes in language—have been a staple of Protestant teachings for centuries. George Marsden describes one of the most famous statements of human corruption, as found in Jonathan Edwards's Northampton sermon of 1741, "Sinners in the Hands of an Angry God." The world, Edwards warned, was full of people who were "in rebellion against God" and who had a "love of evil."[40] Some of them were in the church right at that moment and exhibiting a "sinful wicked manner of attending his solemn worship"—just as many sinful Americans at the end of the twentieth century were entering, abusing, and destroying God's great cathedrals in nature.

If they did not mend their evil ways, all these infidels in Edwards's time would be punished severely, but God was still holding out hope. Invoking an image of impending environmental calamity, Edwards declared that "the wrath of God is like great waters that are dammed for the present; they increase more and more, and rise higher and higher."[41] But if current sinners would repent—would give up their arrogance and their false pride, their conviction that they can live happily and well separate from God—they could still be saved. As Marsden comments, "The whole point of a sermon like this was to reduce sinners to a sense of their utter helplessness" in the face of divine wrath. God sees them as no better than a "loathsome insect," but if they will simply accept the justice of this harsh verdict, renouncing their own past false pridefulness, it will paradoxically be at that moment that they can be saved by "strenuous spiritual efforts" that require "throwing themselves entirely on God's grace." In this process, the prideful human "must be radically transformed from its natural self-love to love of God."[42] Or, to put it in contemporary environmental terms, human beings must cease being "outside of" and instead must become "part of" the much greater cosmic unity of "nature"— they must cease their rebellion against God and his commands.

Many current environmentalists no doubt would be greatly surprised to hear that they are such "neo-Christians." One might speculate that many environmentalists want to believe in God, and perhaps do actually believe in God, but simply cannot bring themselves to state their own beliefs in such explicit terms. Moreover, it might violate other elements of their own self-image, raising the possibility that they might have to address awkward contradictions within their own thinking about the world and their place in it. There would also be difficult questions of how all this de facto environmental Christian reverence can be accommodated within the framework of the modern sciences of physics, chemistry, and—above all—Darwinist biology. The secular vocabulary of many environmentalists may, in short, be a linguistic subterfuge to avoid all these potentially irresolvable—at least for secular environmental true believers—theological conundrums.

The tensions in environmental thought that trouble William Cronon, and many other less-articulate observers, do raise profound theological questions that are not easily answered. As we can presumably all agree, human beings have often behaved sinfully throughout history. In the Garden of Eden before the fall, and in heaven in the hereafter, there was and will be no sin. For many environmentalists, this may be what they mean by striving for the "wilderness" goal—being "natural" means rediscovering the happier and purer self that existed before being corrupted by original sin, before human beings tragically rebelled against God. But how is this to happen? How is sin to be newly banished from the world? Unless it is set within a Christian context, and an all-powerful God is the agent of change, environmentalism in fact has no answer. Environmentalism may be offering merely a brand-new form of wishful thinking, yet another modern utopian scheme following many other such impractical—if perhaps morally uplifting and inspiring—hopes for a coming perfection of the world.

Hence, perhaps an environmentalism that has any theological coherence cannot simply be metaphorically Christian; it may have to be literally Christian—or conceivably some other religion of an all-powerful god that can successfully address the theological issues raised here. This does not necessarily mean, however, that environmentalism must employ all the old Christian language of the past. Christianity has often evolved over the centuries. Whether contemporary environmentalism should, or would want to, continue to employ a secular vocabulary to disguise an essentially Christian message, however, is a question beyond the scope of this book.

Conclusion

In an analysis of "the meaning of wilderness," the chair of the Sierra Club, Michael McCloskey, identified twenty-four reasons to support the creation of wilderness areas. The reasons were classified into four main categories: biocentric; anthropocentric but not utilitarian; anthropocentric and utilitarian; and, least valid, commercial. The utilitarian reasons included "watershed function," "education," "science and research," "therapy," and "recreation." U.S. wilderness areas can be seen as a museum of the geological and biological past, especially important to a nation that lacks a lengthy history (as in Europe) to put on display. But McCloskey concluded that the core justification for creating wilderness areas was that they provide "beacons of hope for all those whose lives are oppressed by lines of traffic, layers of smog, piles of trash, and the menace of toxics. At last, perhaps, we can understand what Thoreau meant when he said: 'In wildness is the preservation of the world.'" Stated in more traditional terms, however, perhaps Thoreau was really saying that "in God is the salvation of the world."

7

CALVINISM MINUS GOD

A LEADING AMERICAN HISTORIAN of environmentalism, Mark Stoll, comments that "natural theology lay much of the groundwork for European natural science in general and ecology in particular, and justified and encouraged the study of nature as a religious activity."[1] It was, moreover, a process dominated by ecologists with Protestant—and in the United States, mostly Calvinist—backgrounds:

> Virtually all founding ecologists, the theorists of the communities of nature, had Protestant backgrounds. Prior to the Second World War, American and European Protestants very nearly monopolized ecological theory: first German and Scandinavian Lutherans, then Swiss Reformed, English Anglicans, and American Protestants. American Protestants from only certain denominations participated in developing this new science: ecology as a science crystallized mainly out of the Calvinist Puritan tradition that planted Congregationalism and Presbyterianism in America. Within the general attitudes toward and doctrines of these and their daughter churches, and not within the much larger Catholic, Methodist, and Southern Baptist denominations, lay the taproot of modern American ecological science.[2]

Ecology was the scientific branch that provided many of the concepts and explanations of the world that would later be adopted by the environmental movement. But it was not only ecology that had strong Calvinist ties; environmental philosophers Baird Callicott and Michael Nelson observe that "many of the most notable and most passionate . . . defenders of the wilderness faith have a direct connection to Calvinism."[3] The Calvinist roots of American environmentalism go well beyond certain cultural or behavioral similarities (e.g., a common disdain for luxury consumption or a shared drive to save the world). From the beginning, nature occupied a central place in Calvinist theology, and there were powerful religious reasons to visit and experience nature. As Calvinism evolved, and especially when it moved to the United States with the arrival of the Puritans in Massachusetts, these themes were reasserted by many other writers, including Jonathan Edwards in the mid-eighteenth century.

In the nineteenth century, Ralph Waldo Emerson, Henry David Thoreau, and other New England heirs to the Calvinist tradition adapted it to a new transcendentalist setting. The members of the transcendental movement were absorbed with visiting, studying, and appreciating nature as the best way of learning about "the universe" and its meaning. John Muir, founder of the Sierra Club in 1892, popularized but did not significantly alter this set of understandings. Later in the twentieth century, however, many environmental followers in the Calvinist tradition—like other intellectuals throughout the twentieth century—claimed a more "scientific" status. The result was a newly secularized environmental religion—a "Calvinism minus God."[4]

This is not to suggest that every environmentalist is a disguised Calvinist. Moreover, Calvinism has multiple interpretations, and the environmental movement has a similar diversity. Other branches of Protestantism, such as Lutheranism, have contributed significantly to environmental thought. There are also some environmentalists who have been almost exclusively concerned with the most practical of matters, such as public health, pursuing objectives that will be supported by virtually any religion—Christian, economic, environmental, Buddhist, or whatever. Nevertheless, the essential character of American environmentalism is not to be found in the fulfillment of a public health agenda. Rather, it lies in a historically Christian, and especially Calvinist, outlook as now applied to age-old questions of the appropriate relationship of human beings and nature.*

---

* The historical roots of environmentalism traced in this chapter, going back to Calvinist theology, also should not be taken to suggest that similar thinking cannot be found in the long history of the Roman Catholic Church. Understanding the Calvinist influence is especially important in understanding American environmentalism for two reasons. First, Calvinism, as expressed in the thinking of the early Puritan settlers, has had an extraordinary impact on American history, continuing to the present time, and the United States was for most of its existence a Protestant nation. Second, the theology of the Catholic Church has traditionally given greater emphasis to social justice, the common good, and other human-centered concerns, as worked out by church authorities over many centuries, and has assigned a lesser religious role to direct forms of communication such as visiting the natural world. In recent years, nevertheless, and reflecting international trends, there has been a rapidly growing attention to environmental issues in the Catholic Church. In the 1990s, for example, the U.S. Catholic Conference released a statement that "the whole universe is God's dwelling. . . . Throughout history, people have continued to meet the Creator on mountaintops, in vast deserts, and alongside waterfalls and gently flowing streams." Unfortunately, most people today increasingly experience their lives in separation from the natural world—which also has frequently been significantly altered by

When the progressive tenets of economic religion were significantly undermined by the many dismal events of twentieth-century history, it was necessary to turn to religions that showed a greater awareness of the potential deep sinfulness of the human condition. Although the doctrine of original sin is found in almost all forms of Christianity, it occupied a particularly prominent place in Calvinism. Given also the enduring power of the Puritan heritage in American history, even up to the present, and the growing evidence of human beings playing God with sometimes disastrous results, the stage was set in the 1960s United States for the rapid spread of a secular environmental Calvinism.

The Environmental John Calvin

In rejecting the historic role of the Roman Catholic Church, the Protestant Reformers taught that a good Christian must read the Bible for him- or herself and will find there exclusively, and without the intercession of centuries of medieval Scholastic and other Church interpreters, God's directly revealed truths to the world. It is less well-known that for the Protestant Reformers there was another main source of direct access to the thinking of God, one that also did not rely on the help of any expert religious authorities of a hierarchical church. As Calvin wrote in his great systematic statement of his theology, *Institutes of the Christian Religion,* "The knowledge of God [is] sown in their minds out of the wonderful workmanship of nature." For those able to turn away from the "prodigious trifles" and "superfluous wealth" that occupy the minds of so many, it will be possible to be "instructed by this bare and simple testimony which the [animal] creatures render splendidly to the glory of God." Human beings must show respect for the natural world because it is especially in its presence that they can find "burning lamps" that "shine for us . . . the glory of its Author" above.[5] As Calvin believed, God had created the world a mere few thousand years ago, and it was still possible to see in nature His handiwork, altered only in minor ways since the creation.

This theological view of the importance of nature as an avenue to the mind of God was not a minor element of Calvinism. Indeed, there were considered to be two great books of authoritative religious truth, the Book of the Bible and the Book of Nature. Both must command the attention of the faithful;

---

past human actions. Nevertheless, as the Catholic Conference stated, "we still share, though [now more] dimly, in that sense of God's presence in nature." See U.S. Catholic Conference, "Catholic Social Teaching and Environmental Ethics," in *This Sacred Earth: Religion, Nature, Environment,* ed. Roger S. Gottlieb (New York: Routledge, 1996), 644.

with the aid of each, as Calvin wrote, "let us study to love and serve him with all our heart."[6] If only people will make the effort, they will be inspired and uplifted in contemplating all of God's creatures and other parts of the creation here on earth. According to Calvin:

> The final goal of the blessed life, moreover, rests in the knowledge of God (cf. John 17:3). Lest anyone, then, be excluded from access to happiness, he not only sowed in men's minds that seed of religion of which we have spoken but revealed himself and daily discloses himself in the whole workmanship of the universe. As a consequence, men cannot open their eyes without being compelled to see him. Indeed, his essence is incomprehensible; hence, his divineness far escapes all human perception. But upon his individual works he has engraved unmistakable marks of his glory, so clean and so prominent. . . . Wherever you cast your eyes, there is no spot in the universe wherein you cannot discern at least some sparks of his glory.
>
> [Thus], there are innumerable evidences both in heaven and on earth that declare his wonderful wisdom; not only those more recondite matters for the closer observation of which astronomy, medicine, and all natural science are intended, but also those which thrust themselves upon the sight of even the most untutored and ignorant persons, so that they cannot open their eyes without being compelled to witness them. . . . Ignorance of them prevents no one from seeing more than enough of God's workmanship in his creation to lead him to break forth in admiration. . . . It is, accordingly, clear that there is no one to whom the Lord does not abundantly show his wisdom.[7]

Yet human sinfulness often limits the ability of the faithful to see the many wonderful opportunities presented in nature to learn from God's workmanship. As Calvin wrote, "Although the Lord represents both himself and his everlasting Kingdom in the mirror of his works with very great clarity, such is our stupidity that we grow increasingly dull toward so manifest tendencies and they flow away without profiting us." Even when it is possible to "grasp a conception of some sort of divinity" in contemplating the creation, yet "straightway we fall back into the raving or evil imaginings of our flesh, and corrupt by our vanity the pure truth of God." Weakened by our fallen natures, "we forsake the one true God for prodigious trifles." This frequently happens not only to "the common folk and dull-witted men, but also the most excellent and those otherwise endowed with keen discernment, [who] are infected with this disease." Because we may find "the eyes to see" when our efforts are "illumined by the inner revelation of God through faith," there is still hope that we can witness "the invisible divinity [that] is made manifest in such spectacles" in nature.[8]

This is all part of the wider circumstance, as Calvin taught, that "our nature, wicked and deformed, is always opposing his [God's] uprightness; and our capacity, weak and feeble to do good, lies far from his perfection." Indeed, it is partly man's misplaced "pride" in his knowledge, skills, and power—in the modern age becoming a supreme confidence in human scientific and economic capabilities exceeding anything that Calvin might have imagined—that is "the beginning of all evils." Calvin warned that, if humanity did not turn away from its evil ways, God's plan for sinners was "wrath, judgment and terror"; their future He "would devote to destruction." The form of God's punishment would often be a natural calamity—a great flood, a drought, a famine, or some other disaster—as foretold in the Bible as the fate of the many sinners of the world. Environmental Calvinism today still foresees much the same divine retributions.[9]

To avoid such a fate, and as present-day environmentalism also instructs us, Calvin said that a person must "indulge oneself as little as possible" and that we must all discipline ourselves and "insist on cutting off all show of superfluous wealth, not to mention licentiousness." Calvin does not of course speak of any requirements for "biodiversity," but he does instruct his followers that God has "wonderfully adorned heaven and earth with as unlimited abundance, variety, and beauty of all things as could possibly be. . . . [They are] the most exquisite and at the same time most abundant furnishings" imaginable. Human beings are told to "follow the universal rule, not to pass over in ungrateful thoughtlessness or forgetfulness those conspicuous powers which God shows forth in his creatures" of the natural world. Given their importance in the divine plan, Calvin also specifies that God intends "for the preservation of each species until the Last Day."[10] It would seem that not only Noah but all the Calvinist faithful have a religious obligation to protect the threatened and endangered species of the world.

The Protestant Reformation banished many of the religious accoutrements of the Roman Catholic Church. There were to be no great cathedrals such as Notre Dame or Chartres; no future Michelangelo or Leonardo would adorn the walls of a bare and simple Calvinist church. God alone and His direct works, as found in the Bible, but also in nature, should be enough to inspire the faithful. As the history of the Roman Catholic Church had all too well demonstrated, human beings who claimed to have their own special access to God's truths were often among the fallen. Their real intent was to substitute themselves in the place of God. In nature, moreover, one could find much greater artwork—more inspiring than any humanly created works—that had been literally made by God Himself at the creation. Like the Bible, the cathedrals of nature were everywhere and freely available, even to the poorest of the earth.

The Book of Nature thus was all the more important because it offered a less harsh and more aesthetically pleasing element within an otherwise austere Protestant faith, which was the most severe of all in the teachings of Calvin. Roman Catholicism, by contrast, had already created its own man-made world of church art, writings, and other religious symbols that could instruct and inspire the faithful. Catholic theology certainly agreed about the divine source of the creation, and also that there could be instructional value in experiencing God's design in nature directly, but it was a lesser part of Catholic religion and practice.* To this day, the Roman Catholic Church has played a less significant role in the development of the environmental movement. In this respect, it has been a recent follower rather than a farsighted leader. Callicott, for example, notes that "the wilderness idea," based on going to wild nature to directly encounter God's essential truths at the creation, "plays no significant role in the intellectual environmental history of Catholic Latin America, only in that of Protestant Anglo-America (and, revealingly, Protestant Anglo-Australia)."[11]

Calvinism and Max Weber

The close affinities between Calvinism and contemporary environmentalism have been noted by a number of authors. Yet, seemingly paradoxically, many people have assigned significant blame to Calvinism for the modern loss of the environment. This is partly because Calvinism also promoted the rapid

---

* In 1898, the famed Dutch Calvinist Abraham Kuyper came to the United States and delivered his *Lectures on Calvinism* at a leading school of the Presbyterian branch of Calvinist theology, Princeton Theological Seminary. Speaking of the role of art in Calvinism, Kuyper explained that:

> if the Sovereignty of God is and remains, for Calvinism, its unchangeable point of departure, then art cannot originate from the Evil One; for Satan is destitute of every creative power. All he can do is to abuse the good gifts of God. Neither can art originate with man, for, being a creature himself, man cannot but employ the powers and gifts put by God at his disposal. If God is and remains Sovereign, then art can work no enchantment except in keeping with the ordinances which God ordained for the beautiful when He, as the Supreme Artist, called this world into existence. . . . The original eye for art is in God Himself, Whose art capacity is all-producing, and after Whose image the artist among men was made. We know this from the creation around us, from the firmament that overarches us, from the abounding luxury of nature, from the wealth of forms in man and animal, from the rushing sound of the stream and from the song of the nightingale; for how could all this beauty exist, except created by One Who preconceived the beautiful in His own Being, and produced from his own Divine perfection? (Abraham Kuyper, *Lectures on Calvinism* [Lafayette, Ind.: Sovereign Grace, 2001], 94)

industrial growth of Europe, which then spread to other continents and has now reached much of the rest of the world.

The relationship between Calvinism and modern industrial development ("capitalism," as it is often somewhat misleadingly labeled)* is a subject that has by now attracted a large scholarly literature, famously inaugurated more than one hundred years ago by Max Weber in *The Protestant Ethic and the Spirit of Capitalism.*[12] Weber argued that specific tenets of Calvinist theology were a main driving force in the emergence of capitalism in the West. Since then, many historians have been critical of Weber's analysis, finding that it was considerably overstated. Sophisticated banking, insurance, and other market practices essential to an industrial economy, for example, were already well advanced in some Catholic areas of Venice, Genoa, and other northern Italian cities centuries well before the Protestant Reformation.

Nevertheless, Calvinism did encourage a commitment to hard work, promote a rational approach to life, and favor the dedicated pursuit in business and elsewhere of a worldly "calling." The real purpose of a calling was the "disciplining [of] their own [sinful] character by patient labor, and of devoting themselves to a service acceptable to God," but it also often made for very good businesspeople.[13] Beginning in the seventeenth century, it seems likely that these and other elements of Calvinism did in fact contribute significantly to the encouragement and eventual wide spread of modern economic growth and development.† Then, as human populations and standards of

---

* The term "capitalism"—made famous around the world by Karl Marx—may have outlived its usefulness. Aside from the immense historical baggage, it lumps together events and economic developments better addressed with greater precision. There was, first, the rise of international trade and the institutions of a market economy, commencing in the tenth or eleventh centuries, and largely occurring well before the Protestant Reformation. Marking a second critical stage, Holland boomed economically in the seventeenth century, and England soon followed with an industrial revolution of unprecedented scope in world history. Finally, a third critical stage emerged over the course of the nineteenth century and continues to the present day. This stage is distinguished from the earlier parts of the Industrial Revolution by the increasing use of technology—especially since 1850—that required the application of scientific knowledge to develop (above all, the various uses of electricity, which continue to proliferate in the present day). It was only during this third stage that the human capacity to manipulate and control nature expanded radically beyond anything previously imagined in human history.

† While the debate continues, Weber's thinking is experiencing a revival. Many economic and other historians continue to find that the rise of the modern industrial system was closely linked to the Protestant Reformation and especially Calvinism. Economic historians Nathan Rosenberg and L. E. Birdzell thus state that "the moral outlook for mercantile capitalism was supplied in the sixteenth century by the Protestant Reformation." The reasons, however, extend well beyond Weber's original focus on elements of Calvinist theology. Protestantism encouraged the individual reading of the Bible and thus higher rates of literacy and the earlier development of human capital. Protestant confiscations of large Catholic properties made them available for commercial use in the market. Protestantism abolished the Catholic separation between the priesthood and the laity—creating a

living rose rapidly, the environmental condition of the natural world often suffered as a result.

It is likely, however, that Calvin himself would have been distressed by all this "progress." From an original Calvinist viewpoint—and as many environmentalists would today agree—the devil has seemingly been given increasing reign over the past three hundred years, and the resulting spread of evils in the world is unprecedented. Indeed, many people ceased to believe in God at all. In the Calvinist view, as Weber states, "you may labor to be rich for God, though not for the flesh and sin," but modern societies are increasingly absorbed with the "flesh and sin."[14] If Calvin could have foreseen that his theology and his followers would contribute significantly to the erosion of Christian faith and the destruction of the natural world, one wonders whether he might have renounced his own religious efforts.

To be sure, while the details were wholly unpredictable, Calvin might not have been altogether surprised with an eventual unexpected outcome. Calvinism also preached the frailty of human reason and the inability of sinful human beings to know the ways of God. In his classic study *Protestantism and Progress*, the great German theologian Ernst Troeltsch observed that the theologies of Luther and Calvin were actually both attempts to turn back the clock against the economic and other forces of modernization. The Catholic Church had been adapting steadily to these forces, but, as Luther and Calvin argued to great effect, the unfortunate result had been to encourage the spread of many evils in the world. Rome for them was now again a place of sinfulness and licentiousness, the abode of the Antichrist. The Protestant Reformers preached instead the necessity of a much stricter piety and a truer Christian way of living, not only for a select priesthood but for all of the faithful of the world. It would be a "revival of the [true] Catholic idea," Troeltsch said, as it had existed in earlier and much simpler times over the first centuries of Christianity, before the corruptions of Rome set in. Many of the environmental faithful today see Wall Street, big corporations such as Exxon Mobil, the Department of Energy in Washington, and other "giant" forms of controlling economic power, justified by a new "Roman" priesthood of American economists, in similar terms.

---

new "priesthood of all believers." The perfection of all society—including its economic elements—became a religious obligation, as seen in the American Puritans' belief that they were a chosen people with a divine mission to create God's kingdom in Massachusetts. This Protestant sense of a great religious responsibility for all matters here on earth would reappear in the American social gospel movement, which played a significant role in the founding of the American Economic Association in 1885. Leading economists such as Richard Ely argued that a valid Christian religion was now about curing the ills of this world, and that scientific knowledge of the workings of society—and especially of the economy—would be essential to fulfilling this profoundly religious task. See Nathan Rosenberg and L. E. Birdzell Jr., *How the West Grew Rich: The Economic Transformation of the Industrial World* (New York: Basic Books, 1986), 129.

Indeed, to some extent the original Protestant Reformers succeeded; Troeltsch found that the actual consequence of the "revolutionary conservatism" of the Protestant Reformation had been that "Europe had to experience two centuries more of the medieval spirit." In the end, however, it was the Reformation, and above all its Calvinist elements, that had played a large and "conspicuous part in the production of the modern world." Protestantism fiercely defended religious freedom, which then spread in later centuries to become political and economic freedom. The seeming paradox, as Troeltsch found, could be explained only by recognizing that the modernizing impacts of Protestantism were "mainly indirect and unconsciously produced effects ... even in accidental side-influences, and again in influences produced against its will."[15]

The greatest economic impacts of Protestantism also often became evident only in the modern era, when the specific character of Protestant theology had been significantly altered. The economic importance of Protestantism may reflect its competitive organizational structure as a religion as much as its specific doctrines. Because Protestantism had many denominations and more religious fluidity, it had a greater ability to accommodate its theology and its practices to rapid social change. If one Protestant denomination was not filling the economic bill, so to speak, another Protestant competitor could rapidly step in. Protestantism sustains a "free market" of religion and thus is more adaptable than the hierarchical religious organization of the Roman Catholic Church—more analogous in many ways to the large and bureaucratic welfare and regulatory states as they developed over the course of the twentieth century (an ironically "Roman" development for a historically Protestant nation such as the United States).[16]

Calvinists in the Massachusetts Wilderness

Calvinism moved to Britain's American colonies when groups of Puritans (the English branch of Calvinism) began settling Massachusetts in the early seventeenth century, often to escape religious persecution. A first order of business for the Massachusetts Puritans was to build their towns and villages. This would mean that forests would have to be cleared, animals killed for food, and fields made ready for farming—nature, in short, would have to be put to use for human purposes. These tasks were undertaken with the usual great energy and firm discipline of the Calvinist faithful.

Many Puritans explicitly saw themselves as repeating the Jewish exodus from Egypt; the trip across the Atlantic was their passage through the Red Sea.[17] And as the Jews had been instructed by God to build a new world in

Israel, the Puritans saw their mission in the New World to build a great society that would shine a beacon to all humankind, a "city upon a hill" in the
words of John Winthrop. Perry Miller, the great Harvard historian of American Puritanism, comments that it was the special religious purpose of "New
England to justify God's ways to man, though not . . . in the agony and confusion of defeat but in the confidence of approaching triumph" in overcoming
the many natural obstacles to building a new, more perfect society in the Massachusetts wilderness.[18] Nature in this respect might be instructive about God,
but it was also something that first had to be overcome and then put to good
use in the New World.

The Old Testament was particularly prominent in Puritan thinking, and a
figure of particular interest to the settlers of early Massachusetts was that of
Job. Further, there are many other stories in the Bible of people going to the
wilderness to be severely tested—for example, Jesus had fasted for forty days
and nights in the wilderness, fighting off the temptations of the devil, before
learning of God's great plans for him. Similarly, if the Puritans could survive
their initial hardships in Massachusetts, as Catherine Albanese explains, the
"wilderness was still a place of testing, the backdrop for a spiritual purification
in which the corruption of old England might be permanently purged. As a
proving ground for the saints, the wilderness might also protect them from
worldly evil and even invigorate them. Indeed, it might become God's chosen
place for conferring religious insight."[19] Echoes of such thinking are still heard
to this day in another side of the American experience of wild nature—as a
place that challenges a person's physical strengths and capabilities and thus
reveals and forges his or her special character.[20]

In his classic study *Wilderness and the American Mind*, Roderick Nash
is critical of what he sees as the Puritan desire to "conquer" the wilderness,
a damaging Calvinist way of thinking that he blames for later encouraging
the wholesale destruction of the natural world.[21] Terms such as "conquer"
and "wilderness," however, have acquired a twentieth-century meaning in
speaking of the human relationship to nature that is difficult to translate to
seventeenth-century circumstances. Given the vastness of the natural areas
that the Puritans were encountering, there were few grounds to be concerned
that the abundant evidences of God's handiwork at the creation might somehow be erased. No early Puritan could imagine the loss of the last remaining
wild areas. The first edition of Nash's book appeared in 1967, the same year as
Lynn White's influential *Science* article blaming Christianity for the modern
indifference to nature.[22] Nash's critique of Calvinist theology seems to reflect a
similarly negative attitude as was then in vogue—and a similar absence of historical recognition of the central role of Christian, especially Protestant, and
above all Calvinist theology in giving birth to American environmentalism.

The Massachusetts Puritans were well aware of, and were inevitably influenced significantly by, theological developments among their brethren in England, for whom the natural setting was more conventional. In England a leading Puritan theologian, John Preston, explained in 1633—sounding much like Calvin a century earlier—that "the heavens are the worke of his [God's] hands, and they declare it, and every man understands their language," and "when a man lookes on the great volume of the world, there those things which God will have known, are written in capital letters."[23] In Massachusetts, Thomas Hooker expressed a similar view, that "there are some things of God that are revealed in the creation of the world. . . . A man looketh into the fabrike of the world, and seeth the making of the earth, and the Sea, and all things therein, hee cannot say but God hath beene here, and infinite wisdom, and an almightie power hath been here."[24] Characterizing the writings of a prominent Puritan theologian of the time, Brooks Holifield states that they "recited the familiar arguments for God's existence—design and order and the need for a sufficient cause to account for the world—and he thought that the 'workmanship' of the creation should prove to any rational person the reality of a God worthy of worship."[25] As Perry Miller stated, "Quite apart from faith, therefore, there are two important sources of truth to which man has immediate access: himself and his experience of the world. Hence secular knowledge—science, history, eloquence, wisdom (purely natural wisdom)—is doubly important for these Puritans; for knowledge is not only useful, it is a part of theology."[26]

By the early eighteenth century, surviving the wilds of Massachusetts was no longer a main issue. Indeed, the colony was increasing in population and wealth, and otherwise was more and more prosperous. With more time to contemplate the larger questions of religion, Cotton Mather authored two major works of theology, the first about the Christian revelations of the Bible, and the second about the Christian revelations to be found in nature. Mather (one of whose descendants, Stephen Mather, in 1916 became the first director of the U.S. National Park Service) informed his readers that nature was a "Publick Library" into which they should "walk with me into it, and see what we shall find so legible there"; it will be a "Temple of GOD, built and fitted by that Almighty Architect." He found in a simple plant seed a wonderful set of qualities—evidence of God's marvelous workmanship—in that this "small Particle no bigger than a Sand" could contain all the information to produce a full "Plant, and all belonging to it," which exhibited an "astonishing Elegancy." Observing the physical properties of magnetism, Mather not only thought them wondrous but also understood that this "leads us to GOD, and brings us very near to him."[27]

As Albanese comments, "Mather's meditations on the physical world pointed to the analogical relationship between nature and human life in ways that would link the Puritan past to the New England Transcendentalist future." The line of thought from John Calvin to Massachusetts Puritanism to New England transcendentalism would eventually reach the American preservation movement of the early twentieth century and then the American environmental movement of the later part of the century.

There was one sense, however, in which Nash's language of a Puritan goal to "conquer" the natural environment in the Massachusetts wilderness was apt. To build a model society for the world, it would be necessary to deal with the Indians. This might not have been a problem if the continent's native inhabitants had been willing to convert quickly and easily to Christianity. But that seldom happened and the Puritans regarded unconverted Indians as uniquely depraved; in colonists' eyes, the Indian lands were the devil's special colonies on earth. This introduced an element of ambiguity in the Puritan experience of nature that was outside European experience. In the end, the Indian populations of New England were expelled and decimated. This was, unfortunately, another side of the Puritan heritage, which showed a continuity even into the twentieth century. In Africa, environmental advocates frequently sought the removal of native Africans from newly designated park areas to protect the "natural" features of these spaces (see chap. 11).

Jonathan Edwards

Jonathan Edwards, by many accounts America's greatest theologian, sought to address the growing religious skepticism of the eighteenth century and the substitution by many of a new faith in science and economics for the old faith in God. If Jean-Jacques Rousseau responded in Europe by translating Calvinist messages to a new secular vocabulary, Edwards took a much different path. Although he was well aware of the latest scientific developments and addressed them in his writings, Edwards stoutly defended traditional Calvinist understandings and conclusions. He represented the American bridge between the traditional Calvinist thinking of the sixteenth and seventeenth centuries and the New England transcendentalism of the nineteenth century.

The subjects of Edwards's most famous writings were matters such as free will, the effects of original sin, and the proper interaction of church and society. But he did sometimes preach about issues relating to the natural world, and in his early years he devoted much thought to theological questions being raised by Newton's discoveries and other increased knowledge of the scientific workings of nature. Partly owing to the transcription and publication in the twentieth century of Edwards's private journals and other writings, it is now possible to study more closely his early thinking on such matters. In a virtual echo of Calvin's *Institutes*, Edwards wrote that when "we look on these shadows of divine things" in nature, it is as "the voice of God [is] . . . teaching us these and those spiritual and divine things." Encounters with nature "will tend to convey instruction to our minds, and to impress things on the mind and to affect the mind, that we may, as it were, have God speaking to us." The Bible and nature are complementary as the two main avenues of God's instruction: to see in nature the creation firsthand "will abundantly tend to confirm the Scriptures, for there is an excellent agreement between these things and the holy Scripture."[28] As Edwards summed up his thinking about the central religious important of nature (in contemporary language, of the "environment"):

> It is very fit and becoming of God who is infinitely wise, so to order things that there should be a voice of His in His works, instructing those that behold him and painting forth and shewing divine mysteries and things more immediately appertaining to Himself and His spiritual kingdom. The works of God are but a kind of voice or language of God to instruct intelligent human beings in things pertaining to Himself. And why should we not think that he would teach and instruct by His works in this way as well as in others, viz., by representing divine things by His works and so painting them forth, especially since we know that God hath so much delighted in this way of instruction.[29]

In his leading biography of Edwards, George Marsden thus explains that, although Edwards's theology of nature involved some changes in emphasis and a few new elements, in most respects it communicated the traditional Calvinist message. In Edwards's "conception of the universe," as Marsden explains, "God had created lower things to be signs that pointed to higher spiritual realities. The universe, then, was a complex language of God. Nothing in it was accidental. Everything pointed to higher meaning."[30] The encounter with nature was not merely educational but for Edwards also a profoundly moving religious experience of the world's wonders:

> [Edwards's] contemplative joys were of a piece with his philosophy and theology. His ineffable experiences as he walked along in the fields were of the beauties of God's love communicated in nature. That created world was the very language of God. As Psalm 19 said, "The heavens declare the glory of God." The beauty of nature proclaimed the beauty and love of Christ. Indeed, in creation, as the Lord declared to Job, "the morning stars sang together, and all the sons of God shouted for joy" (Job 38:7). Enraptured by the beauties of God's ongoing creation,

Jonathan recorded, "it was always my manner, at such times, to sing forth my contemplations."[31]

For many people, Newtonian and other discoveries in science were eroding the older Calvinist sense of religious inspiration in nature. The mechanical Newtonian universe was more like a giant clockwork, operating according to precise mathematical laws of physics. Marsden notes that Edwards resisted the resulting tendencies toward a "desacralization of the New England worldview." Instead, he continued to assert "the immediate presence of God in everything. Rather than allowing the Newtonian universe to lead to a distancing of God from creation, Edwards insisted that the recently discovered immensities and complexities of the universe confirmed God's ongoing intimate expressions of his art and language in all that had being."[32]

These early views—which Edwards held for the rest of his life—were not the main source, however, of his theological fame. Edwards was particularly concerned to combat the many spreading falsehoods of the Enlightenment period. Calvinism from its inception had argued that individual works could have no effect on the prospects for salvation; a truly omnipotent God could not be pressured or even influenced by any human actions whatever. Yet it was increasingly accepted by Americans in the eighteenth century that a person who lived a moral and upright life deserved to be, and could count on being, among the saved. Another increasingly common, and alarming for Edwards, view was that a person is born with, and thus is inherently capable of exercising, a high rational faculty to live a good life on earth. This was in contrast to the traditional Calvinist view that preached the radical corruption of human capabilities, including reason, since the fall, leaving every individual utterly dependent on and subject to God's mercy and saving actions.

But Edwards sought to stand against the new trends; he harshly condemned the new thinking and reasserted traditional Calvinist messages with great force, as illustrated graphically in his most famous sermon, "Sinners in the Hands of an Angry God." At one point in this sermon, he applied his theological views to consider briefly the relationship of human beings and nature, emphasizing that human beings were altogether undeserving and had only God to thank for the many useful things they were able to obtain from the products of the natural world. Indeed, without God's great mercy and assistance, gravely sinful men and women long ago would justly have perished from the earth. As Edwards explained to the congregation sitting before him:

> Your wickedness makes you as it were heavy as lead, and to tend downwards with great weight and pressure towards hell. . . . Were it not for the sovereign pleasure of God, the earth would not bear you one moment

... the creation groans with you; the creature is made subject to the bondage of your corruption, not willingly; the sun does not willingly shine upon you to give you light to serve sin and Satan; the earth does not willingly yield her increase to satisfy your lusts. . . . God's creatures are good, and were made for men to serve God with, and do not willingly subserve to any other purpose, and groan when they are abused to purposes so directly contrary to their nature and end. And the world would spew you out, were it not for the sovereign hand of him who had subjected it in hope.[33]

It is not difficult to notice the parallels when prominent environmentalists, such as David Brower and Dave Foreman in recent years, have pronounced that human beings are a new cancer of the earth. The one large difference, as noted in chapter 6, is the absence now of any mention of a divine plan behind it all. Even though human beings were often loathsome creatures in Edwards's view, God had a purpose for them, and they ultimately would be saved (or at least some of them) and would join with God in heaven. Without God's saving actions, and if there were any justice in the world, it would now seem that the disgusting human creatures that have defiled the natural world, as Edwards so vividly portrayed them, might best rapidly perish from the earth. This conclusion does in fact readily follow from some of the main founding premises of current secular environmentalism, a true "Calvinism minus God"—although pragmatic environmentalists have hardly been anxious to clarify such radical implications of their theology for the American public at large.[34]

American environmentalism has been a populist movement that has not given a high priority to working out a logically well-developed and internally consistent body of religious thought. Environmentalists, like many Americans, regard theology as no longer relevant or necessary, not worth the potentially large amounts of time required. Indeed, environmentalism is typically content simply to live with its contradictions, mostly unaware even that they exist. Thus, environmental thinking assumes implicitly that some modern equivalent to "God's saving actions" does exist, even while saying nothing about its source, or in many cases even denying the existence of any Christian God or other such higher basis for moral authority. That is to say, David Brower, Dave Foreman, and other environmental crusades make no sense outside a religious framework, where ethical rules can be found and there is some basis for believing that the audience is capable of understanding and has some reason for and capacity to respond to higher moral appeals. There must be a god—and the Christian God is at least the leading candidate—somewhere in this equation, or else the argument will collapse of its own weight. It is simply that Brower, Foreman, and their ilk have been unwilling to face all this or to say anything about it explicitly.

The environmental god, admittedly, is sometimes given new names, such as the "planetary unity," the "balance of nature," a worldwide "ecosystem health," a moral priority of "Earth First!," or a host of other environmental synonyms. Moreover, it cannot simply be any god. The environmental god, whatever name he (or she) is given, must have the particular quality of being able to transform human "animals" into moral creatures who are somehow above and beyond the normal Darwinist workings of an evolutionary struggle to survive and dominate all other creatures. If that were not the case, all the environmental preaching would be pointless—the equivalent of preaching to the fox that he must spare the chicken. Raised in devout Calvinist families, the distance Brower and Foreman traveled from the religious training of their youth is seemingly much shorter than they ever admitted to themselves.

Looking back at the end of the twentieth century, Edwards's harsh view of the human condition was unfortunately newly vindicated by much of that century's history. No economic religion or other modern faith that appealed to poverty or other dire external material conditions of life could easily—or perhaps at all—explain the new malignant presence of evil in the world, as exhibited by such individuals as Adolph Hitler in Germany and Joseph Stalin in Russia. It required a theology such as that of Jonathan Edwards to make any sense of it all.

Calvinism Without Original Sin

Edwards, however, was on the losing side of intellectual and theological history for more than two centuries after his death in 1758. The great successors to Edwards in New England religion were Ralph Waldo Emerson and Henry David Thoreau, who offered a more favorable judgment on the human condition. Perry Miller comments that, nevertheless, "certain basic continuities persist in a culture," and this was no less true in New England from the mid-eighteenth to the mid-nineteenth century. Miller expected that "Jonathan Edwards would have abhorred from the bottom of his soul every proposition Ralph Waldo Emerson blandly put forth in the manifesto of 1836, *Nature*." An essential religious connection, however, "is persistent, from . . . Edwards to Emerson [which] is the Puritan's effort to confront, face to face, the image of a blinding divinity in the physical universe, and to look upon that universe without the intermediacy of ritual, of ceremony, of the Mass and the confessional." Emerson no less than Edwards rejected any messages coming from Rome. Both still reflected "the incessant drive of the Puritan to learn how, and how most ecstatically, he can hold any sort of communion with the environing wilderness." One might thus, as Miller states, "define Emerson as an Edwards in whom the concept of original sin has evaporated."[35]

The traditional Christian understanding of original sin was already proving difficult for the modern mind well before Emerson. How could one poor judgment by one man and one woman long ago in a distant garden (assuming that Adam and Eve even existed) have condemned the entire human species to many thousands of future years of terrible sinfulness and depravity? Moreover, because God was omniscient and omnipotent, He seemingly could easily have prevented it. Modern scientific discoveries were also showing that rational human capacities could be extraordinarily great, apparently contradicting Calvin's expectation of the warping and other harmful consequences of original sin. Indeed, it seemed increasingly likely to many people that modern science and economics might enable human beings to build a whole new wonderful world of their own design—that human beings might in fact be acquiring the necessary knowledge to "play God," and thus to build by themselves their own new heaven on earth.

If original sin was removed from the Christian equation, however, and as Edwards had full well understood, the result would no longer be the historical Christian religion. As the Bible taught, Jesus atoned for the sins of mankind, but Christ's life would now have much less meaning in a world without original sin. Emerson was a pivotal figure in American intellectual history because he, and others like him in New England transcendentalism, represented the critical point of transition to a new type of Christianity (many people, in fact, might not recognize it as a legitimate form of Christianity at all).[36] There was much talk of God in many transcendentalist writings, but little of Jesus Christ.

The radical theological implications of discarding the idea of original sin are seen in the much altered significance of "human nature." Calvinism had traditionally looked outward to the natural world—the creation—as an accurate mirror of the mind of God. Looking inward to human nature with the same objective was problematic at best because Adam and Eve's transgression had so severely warped and distorted the original human nature at the creation. A man or woman looking inward thus would find a misleading or even a perverted version of God's original plan. But what if original sin was a false doctrine of superstitious and ignorant centuries preceding the modern era of enlightenment? Looking inward, a person might now find yet another accurate reflection of the mind of God. Indeed, Christianity had always taught that human beings were created "in the image of God," but now this divine resemblance might be much more readily accessible to introspective viewing by uncorrupted human beings.

Emerson thus wrote that "the whole of Nature is a metaphor or image of the human Mind." The natural world was a mirror not only of God's thinking but also of the minds of ordinary human beings as well. Again in Emerson's own words, "The love of nature—the accord between man and the external world . . . is . . . but the perception how truly all our senses, and, beyond the senses, the soul, are tuned to the order of things in which we live. . . . I am thrilled with delight by the choral harmony of the whole. Design! It is all design. It is all beauty. It is all astonishment."[37] There was one great cosmic order of the universe to be found in heaven, in the natural world, and within human beings themselves, available to be seen and experienced by those who merely knew how to look closely. As Emerson wrote in his hallmark 1836 essay "Nature":

> If a Man would be alone, let him look at the stars. . . . One might think the atmosphere was made transparent with this design, to give man, in the heavenly bodies, the perpetual presence of the sublime.
>
> The stars awaken a certain reverence, because though always present, they are inaccessible; but all natural objects make a kindred impression.
>
> In the woods too, a man casts off his years, as the snake his slough, and at what period soever of life is always a child. In the woods, is perpetual youth. Within these plantations of God . . . we return to reason and faith. There I feel that nothing can befall me in life,—no disgrace, no calamity (leaving me my eyes) which nature cannot repair. . . . All mean egotism vanishes. . . . I am nothing; I see all; the currents of the Universal Being circulate through me; I am part or particle of God.
>
> There seems to be a necessity in spirit to manifest itself in material forms; and day and night, river and storm, beast and bird, acid and alkali, preexist in necessary Ideas in the mind of God, and are what they are by virtue of preceding affections in the world of spirit. A Fact is the end or last issue of spirit. The visible creation is the terminus or the circumference of the invisible world.[38]

In *Man and Nature in America*, Arthur Ekirch thus explained that Emerson was a "secular preacher" and that New England "transcendentalism was not a formal philosophy but was rather a faith—one might almost say a religious faith," whose basic tenets provided "substitutes for the teachings of the [Christian] church." In Emerson's new—but in many ways old—theology, "all nature . . . was a unity in which man as an observer played his part—observer being fused with the observed" in a happy mutual interconnection. Invoking a long-standing Calvinist formulation, Emerson still agrees that the natural world is "intermediary between God and man," and thus has "carried a portion of the Divinity to each individual." In a more novel element, however, in seeking to find a mirror of God, "what faculty could be relied on for the finding with more confidence than the intuition of the individual man, made in the image of the Maker." For Emerson and others in New England, "the transcendentalists' God was a God of love, not of hate, who revealed himself in man and nature," as found right here and now on this earth.[39]

Yet there were some discordant notes, if no longer attributed to original sin in the traditional biblical understanding. Indeed, the consequences of original sin had not disappeared altogether. The corrupting influence, however, was no longer to be found in a snake in a garden but in the rapid pace of U.S. economic events in the nineteenth century. Human beings could be led into many evils by the pressures and the temptations of the surrounding industrial world in which they lived. Thus, at times "Emerson was wont . . . to inveigh against society and the uncritical admiration of progress. . . . If society seemed noxious, nature was the antidote against its baleful influence."[40] In this respect, Emerson reflected a new trend to find the main source of corruption of human motives and behavior not in a biblical Eden but rather in the external economic conditions of this world.

Henry David Thoreau was a better writer, a closer observer of the details of nature, and in general showed an iconoclasm with respect to social conventions not found in Emerson.[41] Thoreau was still more skeptical of the directions of modern industrial civilization and all its works of "progress." The rapid rate of economic growth was eradicating more and more of the natural places where the handiwork of God could be seen. In these respects, he was closer to the concerns of the present-day environmental movement, and Thoreau in fact holds a higher position than Emerson among the saints of environmentalism. The language of Thoreau seems contemporary, whereas Emerson, however central to American intellectual and religious history, speaks in an idiom with which most people now have little familiarity. As the environmental philosopher Mark Sagoff puts it, however, both, following in the long Calvinist tradition of New England, "thought of nature as full of divinity," as a "refuge from economic activity, not as a resource for it."[42] Thoreau thus wrote in *The Maine Woods* that the wild moose of the forest "are God's horses, poor, timid, creatures, that will full fast enough as soon as they smell you, though they are nine feet high."[43] If in less reverential language than his Calvinist predecessors, Thoreau also proclaimed that a person entering into a wild area has the opportunity there to learn from God's creation:

> The kings of England formerly had their forests "to hold the king's game," for sport or food, sometimes destroying villages to create or extend them; and I think that they were impelled by a true instinct. Why should not we, who have renounced the king's authority, have

our national preserves, where no villages need be destroyed, in which the bear and panther . . . may still exist, and not be "civilized off the face of the earth,"—our forests, not to hold the king's game merely, but to hold and preserve the king himself also, the lord of creation,—not for idle sport or food, but for inspiration and our true re-creation? or shall we, like villains, grub them all up, poaching on our own national domains?[44]

Thoreau was a fierce individualist who fit easily within a Calvinist tradition filled with rebellion and struggle against higher authorities—resulting on one occasion in a Puritan revolt that beheaded an English king. Not only contemporary environmentalists but also many contemporary libertarians look to Thoreau—who once refused to pay taxes to the government for wars and other projects of which he strongly disapproved—as a hero.* The Calvinists did form powerful bonds of local community within their own churches and villages, although this was admittedly not for Thoreau. In many other respects, however, he was very much a product of the New England heritage of Jonathan Edwards and his other Puritan predecessors.

Emerson's Sierra Disciple

For all his radical language at times, John Muir was well within the American mainstream. He was the founder of the Sierra Club in 1892, helped to bring about the creation of Yosemite National Park, vigorously advocated the preservationist cause in leading national magazines, consorted with American presidents, and was in general a mover and shaker of his times. While some of his writings and lifestyle were closer to Thoreau, his ability to influence American society directly through his public exhortations was closer to Emerson. Muir himself was well aware of the debt, regarding Emerson as his mentor and inspiration.

Well before he became a celebrated national figure, Muir spent much of his thirties wandering through the Sierra Nevada of California, experiencing wild nature directly. He published a few items from these years, but most of his thinking was recorded in personal journals from the 1870s. Although largely unpublished in his own lifetime, they were later assembled in a 1938 publication. As the project's editor, Linnie Marsh Wolfe, comments, they showed Muir developing his "transcendental philosophy [which] he poured

---

* One libertarian think tank, founded in 1994 by Randal O'Toole in Oregon, and a valuable contributor to contemporary public land and other environmental debates, is named the Thoreau Institute.

white-hot into his journals." It provided a written record of how, "when John Muir went into the wilderness, he went in absolute surrender of self and all the concerns of self," experiencing the wilderness as a place "filled with warm God."[45] Muir had been brought up in a devout Calvinist family and never lost the traditional Calvinist celebration of nature as a direct conduit to the mind of God.

Muir also had a characteristically Protestant skepticism of formal theology and other human efforts to communicate the word of God. He explained in 1872 that "I have a low opinion of books; they are but piles of stones set up to show coming travelers where other minds have been, or at best signal smokes to call attention." Having less confidence in the Bible than did his Calvinist predecessors, Muir was preoccupied with nature, the one remaining source for him of direct communication with God, writing that "no amount of word-making will ever make a single soul to *know* these mountains," but a person encountering them directly would discover that "the pure in heart shall see God."[46] Drawing heavily on Emerson, Muir elaborated on the divine messages he encountered in the Yosemite region:

> The glacier-polish of rounded brows brighter than any mirror, like windows of a housing shining with light from the throne of God—to the very top a pure vision in terrestrial beauty. . . . It is as if the lake, mountain, trees had souls, formed one soul, which had died and gone before the throne of God, the great First Soul, and by direct creative act of God had all earthly purity deepened, refined, brightness brightened, spirituality spiritualized, countenance, gestures made wholly Godful!
>
> Not a cloud-memory in the sky. Not a ripple-memory on the lake, as if so complete in immortality that the very lake pulse were no longer needed, as if only the spiritual part of landscape life were left. I spring to my feet crying: "Heavens and earth! Rock is not light, not heavy, not transparent, not opaque, but every pore gushes, glows like a thought with immortal life!"[47]

Muir similarly wrote of the arrival of spring that, "rising from the dead, the work of the year is pushed on with enthusiasm as if never done before, as if all God's glory depended upon it: inspiring every plant, bird and stream to sing with youth's exuberance, painting flower petals, making leaf patterns, weaving a fresh roof—all symbols of eternal love." In urbanized "cities by the sea," by contrast, many people's lives were "choked by the weeds of care that have grown up and run to seed about them." There was hope for them, however, because "earth has no sorrows that earth cannot heal, or heaven cannot heal, for the earth as seen in the clean wilds of the mountains is about as divine as anything the heart of man can conceive." The sinners of the world can be saved, if only they will go to wild nature to see God's creation there. Muir himself saw a close connection to Christian religion in his own brand of proselytizing, writing in 1871 (at the age of thirty-three) that "heaven knows that John [the] Baptist was not more eager to get all his fellow sinners into the Jordan than I to baptize all of mine in the beauty of God's mountains."[48]

The Sierras for Muir thus were a source of religious ecstasy to match that felt by any monk, pilgrim, or other Christian faithful of the past. Describing how he was transfixed by religious enthusiasm, loosing all sense of earthly concerns, in the experience of Sierra wild nature, Muir wrote:

> Mountains holy as Sinai. No mountains I know of are so alluring. None so hospitable, kindly, tenderly inspiring. It seems strange that everybody does not come at their call. They are given, like the Gospel, without money and without price. "Tis heaven alone that is given away."
>
> Here is calm so deep, grasses cease waving. . . . Wondering how completely everything in wild nature fits into us, as if truly part and parent of us. The sun shines not on us but in us. The rivers flow not past, but through us, thrilling, tingling, vibrating every fiber and cell of the substance of our bodies, making them glide and sing. The trees wave and the flowers bloom in our bodies as well as our souls, and every bird song, wind song, and tremendous storm song of the rocks in the heart of the mountains, is our song, our very own, and sings our love.
>
> The Song of God, sounding on forever. So pure and sure and universal is the harmony, it matters not where we are, where we strike in on the wild lowland plains. We care not to go to the mountains, and on the mountains we care not to go the plains. But as soon as we are absorbed in the harmony, plain, mountain, calm, storm, lilies and sequoias, forest and means are only different strands of many-colored Light—are one in the sunbeam.[49]

With Muir, the places for experiencing the transcendent unity of God, man, and nature thus had shifted from the Maine woods, Walden Pond, and other New England landscapes to the California Sierras. Indeed, American preservationists, and more recently environmentalists, would increasingly seek religious inspiration in settings of the American West. The mountains of the West were newer, taller, more rugged, and in many cases less touched by a past human presence. Still, the nature theology of Muir is derived from Emerson, Thoreau, and other New England transcendentalists. Nature is a mirror to the mind of God but also of the mind of man, no longer warped and marred by the consequences of any terrible fall in the Garden. As Muir would write, "So there are no stiff, frigid, stony partition walls betwixt us and heaven. There are blendings as immeasurable and untraceable as the edges of melting clouds. . . . For earth is partly heaven, and heaven earth."[50]

Muir was born in Scotland and came with his family to the United States in his childhood. He was brought up in a devout family of Campbellites, an offshoot of American Presbyterianism (itself the Scottish branch of Calvinism). Having left behind the Calvinist understanding of original sin, however, the meaning of the great sacrifice of Jesus on the cross is lost. Even as Muir's journals are filled with descriptions of finding a reflection of God in nature, there is little mention of the Bible. As a religion, the result might no longer be recognizably Christian, but it nevertheless retained strong Calvinist elements—and these elements would become stronger with the passing years. Muir was particularly distressed when his fellow Americans sinfully resisted his efforts to set aside wild areas. The greatest evil was the congressional decision to construct Hetch Hetchy Dam in Yosemite National Park in 1913, a sacrilege that Muir had fought with all his powers for years.

From 1890 to his death in 1914 (sometimes said to have been partly a result of the Hetch Hetchy loss), Muir was the leading figure in American public life in advocating the preservation of wild nature in parks and other areas specially set aside for this purpose. The national parks, as Muir thought, would be the American cathedrals of an environmental religion in which a person could experience firsthand the artwork of God in nature. As law professor Joseph Sax wrote in 1980, he and other preservationist advocates for the National Park Service were "secular prophets, preaching a message of secular salvation."[51]

Sinners Against the Earth

The high point of American optimism was the Progressive Era, which extended through the first two decades of the twentieth century. The follies of World War I, however, severely challenged the great hopes for human advance, and there would be even more disturbing events to come in the 1930s and 1940s. Besides the many examples of terrible human treatment of other human beings, there were also growing evidences of human sinfulness in the callous treatment of the natural world, including the virtual elimination of some plant and animal species from the earth.

The American environmental movement emerged in its current form in the 1960s but was descended from Muir and his transcendentalist predecessors. A leading figure, David Brower, served from 1952 to 1964 as the executive director of the Sierra Club, the organization that Muir had founded. Yet in environmentalism there was also a new concern for the unhappy state of the human condition and for the world's prospects as a whole. Perhaps the degree of human corruption was worse than Emerson or Muir had believed. Perhaps the old Calvinists were right; whether it was due to events in the Garden of Eden or some other explanation, there were new reasons to believe that total depravity might characterize a surprisingly large part of the human experience on earth.

The organization Earth First! was founded in 1980. Dave Foreman, its founder, had been brought up in the same Campbellite Protestant faith as Muir, and briefly considered becoming a minister; instead, again like Muir, he became an environmental preacher. Reflecting the secular temper of the late twentieth century in environmental circles, Foreman said little about either God (in this respect unlike Muir) or Jesus (more like Muir). As one outside observer commented, however, there was an obvious character of "residual Protestant evangelism" to Foreman's own efforts and the reactions of his followers.[52]

Earth First! never sought to be and never was an important player in the Washington halls of power. In several important ways, however, it had a significant place in the history of American environmentalism. First, important environmental writers such as Edward Abbey identified and worked closely with Earth First![53] Second, Foreman and others in Earth First! pushed logical premises widely accepted throughout the environmental movement to more radical conclusions and outcomes than mainstream environmentalists were willing to reach (whether for reasons of personal timidity, political calculation, intellectual confusion, or simple hypocrisy). And third, by taking radical positions, and gaining wide public attention, Earth First! helped to shift the mainstream center of environmental debate.[54] The leading environmental organizations never came close to adopting Earth First!'s full agenda, but its radical positions made it politically more acceptable for others to move in those directions.* As Susan Zakin reports in her history of Earth First!, for

---

* In 1997 Julia Butterfly Hill climbed to the top of a giant redwood tree in the privately owned headwaters forest of northern California and remained in her precarious perch for two years—in the process becoming a modern saint of the environmental movement. As a media celebrity, she was featured by *Good Housekeeping* magazine as one of its "most admired women of 1998" and was included by *People* magazine in its "Twenty-five Most Intriguing People of the Year" issue, part of a wave of national publicity. After finally coming down, Hill published a testimonial to her convictions. She explains that when she first arrived in the area there were many people sitting in trees—thus preventing them from being cut—but only for a few days at a time. Her own tree initially was part of "an Earth First! tree-sit, [although] I wasn't—and am still not—part of that group." Nevertheless, she shared a common experience of "the earth" as a means "to be alive, to feel the connection of all life and its inherent truth—not the truth that is taught to us by so-called scientists or politicians, or other human beings, but the truth that exists within Creation." The original redwood forests, as she experienced them, were "majestic ancient places, which are the holiest of temples, housing more spirituality than any church."

example, "after the Bald mountain blockades" in 1983, "Earth First! became a prominent feature in the political landscape of the [Pacific] Northwest," helping to set the stage for the large-scale elimination of federal timber harvesting in the region that would occur later in the 1980s and early 1990s in the wake of the northern spotted owl controversy.[55]

Political scientist Martha Lee wrote her doctoral dissertation on Earth First!, based on four years of research, and published it in a revised version in 1995 as *Earth First! Environmental Apocalypse.* As Lee comments, "Throughout Earth First!'s history, its adherents grappled with issues such as the nature of political community, the definition of justice, and the degree to which human life is meaningful." None of their conclusions were written down in any authoritative book, but the members of Earth First! did agree on many things. Lee personally interviewed, sometimes multiple times, the organization's leaders, and studied the many inspirational political and other pamphlets produced by Earth First!. As Lee says, "If we take environmentalism seriously, and follow it to its logical conclusion, we must confront many of the issues" that Earth First! raised for public discussion.[56]

It should also be said that Earth First! was, bluntly, a terrorist organization motivated, like a number of other terrorists, by a powerful sense of religious mission. Again like other terrorists, it was particularly skillful in the use of violent tactics to gain wide publicity. This was before 9/11 and Americans were more tolerant of, and sometimes even fascinated by, such tactics. Earth First! also limited its terrorist acts to destruction of logging equipment, ski lifts, power lines, government offices, housing projects, and other public and private property. It appears that no person was killed by an Earth First! act of "monkey wrenching," although some may have been injured.[57]

In 1980, as Earth First! was being organized, Foreman wrote the following founding "Statement of Principles":

For Hill, as for Dave Foreman, "the Earth," as found in places such as the redwoods, was a literal place of God. Hill relates how she had received an "answer to the prayer I had sent to Creation. . . . I had asked for guidance on what to do with my life. I had asked for purpose. But I had never figured that the revelation I sought would involve taking up residence in a tree." Hill's journey to the headwaters forest was, admittedly, a more radical step in terms of outward form than the inner content of her faith. Like so many other leading figures in the American environmental movement, she substituted the new messages of "the earth" for the old messages of the Christian God of her youth. As she relates, "Even when I was a child, we hardly lived what people would call a normal life. Many of my early memories are full of religion. My father was an itinerant preacher who traveled the country's heartland preaching from town to town and church to church. . . . My parents really lived what they believed; for them, lives of true joy came from putting Jesus first, others second, and your own concerns last." As their true daughter, Hill willingly gave up two years of her life to sit in a redwood tree in the service of "the earth"—a new concept linguistically but in reality not so very far removed from the "God" of her childhood. See Julia Butterfly Hill, *The Legacy of Luna: The Story of a Tree, a Woman, and the Struggle to Save the Redwoods* (New York: HarperCollins, 2000), 24, 6, 9, 2, 3.

—Wilderness has a right to exist for its own sake.

—All life forms, from virus[es] to the great whales, have an inherent and equal right to existence.

—Humankind is no greater than any other form of life and has no legitimate claim to dominate Earth.

—Humankind, through overpopulation, anthropocentrism, industrialization, excessive energy consumption/resource extraction, state capitalism, father-figure hierarchies, imperialism, pollution, and natural area destruction, threatens the basic life processes of EARTH.

—All human decisions should consider Earth first, humankind second.

—The only true test of morality is whether an action, individual, social or political, benefits Earth.

—Humankind will be happier, healthier, more secure, and more comfortable in a society that recognizes humankind's true biological nature and which is in dynamic harmony with the total biosphere.

—Political compromise has no place in the defense of Earth.

—Earth is Goddess and the proper object of human worship.[58]

As Lee comments, "These principles form the basis for a radical critique of the traditional way environmental questions are addressed in American society." They are the core of a "biocentric perspective" that emphasizes the importance of protecting "biodiversity" in the world. The "absolute good," against which "all actions should be judged," is found in "wilderness" values. In terms of the species of the earth, all are "recognized as being equal and of [the same] intrinsic value." Any political or other "compromise" with wilderness goals "becomes an act against good, that is, evil." As a result, because their actions were "destroying the ecosystems that sustained the planet," it was a fit moral judgment to declare that "the American government and corporate infrastructure embodied the evil of human greed." As Lee explains, "Earth First!ers transplanted these ideas from the realm of philosophical speculation to human action" and thus elevated them in public visibility and political impact.[59]

Although Lee labels it a "philosophy," the character of Earth First! efforts is essentially religious; in fact, there were other elements traditionally associated with religion, and specifically Western religion. Earth First! documents were filled with prophesies of the "imminent collapse" of Western civilization. Lee comments that in such writings "the inevitability of the impending crisis is a certainty, but its specifics and the exact date of its occurrence are unknown. The nature of the coming disaster will, however, reflect society's abuse of the environment, and it is understood to be imminent." This was certain because of the total "corruption" of the system. It was also an outcome to be desired because each day that the system's "destruction continues, more irreplaceable wilderness is lost." Without radical change soon, the world faced "biological meltdown."[60] It was the Old Testament rewritten with 1980s environmental metaphors, yet another story of human beings behaving badly and being severely punished by a just earth (God).

The members of Earth First!, like many other religious sects before them, also believed that they had a unique access to the truths that would "dictate the order of the world," and as the "bearers" of these truths they were the "chosen people" whose role would be "pivotal in the history of the world." They could foresee and were urgently warning of the looming "ecocatastrophe" that would cause the loss of one-third to one-half of the earth's species if drastic changes in contemporary ways of living were not made (stated in more biblical terms, if human beings did not curb their wicked ways). Writing in the *Earth First! Newsletter*, for example, one early member described "the salvation that Earth First!ers envisioned":[61] "The Earth is our first love, our first concern. Our children must be imbued with an unswerving sense of responsibility and respect for Her, and a recognition of the significance of *our* role leads to even greater dedication. Grant understanding to our fellows but show no compromise . . . Earth first! . . . [She] must live Her healthy, tumbling life, free from a dread of infestation and misdeed. As Her seed, we become embassadors [*sic*], emissaries in the final drama, and our mission is indeed grand."[62]

The members of Earth First! had the characteristically Protestant skepticism of any formal theology, arguing that the study of books was of limited benefit, that directly experiencing "earth" was central, and that a person either "got it" or didn't, and there were only a select few in the former category, leaving the mass of Americans in effect among the ignorant—the new condemned. Similarly, echoing the traditional Calvinist idea that the elect are predestined, Foreman believed that recognizing and acting on the truths of biocentrism required having the right "gene"—you were either born with it (God had chosen you) or not. The Earth First! theology was in fact Protestant and specifically Calvinist through and through. The powerful Calvinist elements, however, were buried in a torrent of linguistic obfuscation, likely designed to hide the Calvinist origins not only from the American public but also from most Earth First! members themselves.

The translation of the Earth First! religion to ordinary language is less difficult than, say, the deciphering of the hieroglyphics of the ancient Egyptians. In fact, in many cases it requires a mere substitution of the word "God" in place of the word "earth." There is not much novelty in a Western religion of "God First!" Consider a few of Foreman's founding principles as described above and the effect of merely substituting "God" for "earth." The result is a set of religious principles including: (1) "All human decisions should consider God first, humankind second"; (2) "The only true test of morality is whether an action, individual, social or political, benefits God"; and (3) "Political compromise has no place in the defense of God." Or, consider the Earth First! statement above that "the Earth is our first love, our first concern," which would become "God is our first love, our first concern."

When Foreman and others in Earth First! profess to find a basis for a new morality in the defense of mother "earth," it is obvious that they are not listening to anything that the mountains and trees are saying literally in words—since they are saying nothing. What they mean is actually the same message that Muir wrote about, and before him Emerson, and Edwards before that, and still earlier the Massachusetts Puritans, and first of all in this line of theology John Calvin himself (who was giving a new emphasis within a still longer tradition in Christian theology). God created the world, and so one finds in the natural world a mirror or reflection of the mind of God. By entering and experiencing nature, or as Foreman now rephrased it, by heeding the messages of "the earth," one is gaining access to the divine truths of the universe. Obedience to God's requirements as thus revealed must command a higher priority than any mundane concerns of this world.

Compared with Muir, Foreman also added considerably more of the traditional Calvinist sense of a sinful humanity—a significant new dose of Jonathan Edwards for environmentalism, reflecting the increased awareness by the late twentieth century that human sinfulness in the world hardly seemed to be abating and indeed could even be increasing. As noted in chapter 6, when Foreman describes human beings as the "cancer" of the earth, and with some changes in vocabulary, he could almost be Edwards preaching about a state of total human depravity. Foreman also added an element of the old Puritan conviction of being the chosen people, the members of Earth First! again hoping to shine a light for the rest of the world. Finally, and in this respect less distinctively Calvinist, although fully in the biblical tradition, and well represented in American Protestantism, there are warnings by Earth First! of a looming apocalypse. The terrible sinners of the current world will soon be punished severely, and yet in the massive ecological collapse there will be the hope for better things to come—a world that will have seen many of the evils of "the system" washed away by the widespread destruction.

Some people might think that in our modern, "enlightened" age such a transparent blend of Calvinist and other classical Protestant themes would have little impact beyond a few young and naive enthusiasts of an Earth First! sect. In 1990, however, Christopher Manes reported in *Green Rage* that, although most often implicitly and indirectly, "radical environmentalists now exert a growing influence on public land decisions and environmental policy."[63] Manes was a former member of Earth First! and had been an active participant in its internal debates, and thus his judgment might have been biased. I was working in the Office of Policy Analysis of the Interior Department at the same time, however, observing at close hand many of the same public land and environmental controversies of the 1980s. I would on the whole agree with Manes's assessment. As noted above, in one especially importance instance, for example, the members of Earth First! played a significant role in the northern spotted owl controversy in the Pacific Northwest; the organization helped to transform the goal of largely eliminating timber harvesting on federal forests throughout the region from a radical fringe idea to an outcome eventually sought, and then achieved, by mainstream environmental groups. The goals of "ecosystem management," widely adopted throughout the federal government, are not far removed from the theology of Earth First! Ecosystem management seeks to restore natural areas to the conditions that preceded human impacts, before they were marred by the sinful actions of corrupted human beings.

Earth First! broke up into two parts and Dave Foreman severed his relationship with the group in 1989. The two rival factions were divided in particular over the amount of attention that should be devoted to issues of saving nature by creating a more desirable future human society as opposed to an exclusive focus on protecting nature (Foreman supporting the latter view).[64] Thus, although an organization called Earth First! continued for a number of years, its role as an important part of the American environmental scene was significantly diminished after 1989. Foreman himself went on to devote his own efforts to the "wildlands" project, contributing regularly to the journal *Wild Earth*, and thereby remaining one of the more visible American spokespersons for environmental values.[65] Foreman's stated goal was to curtail drastically if not eliminate the human presence and to reestablish new wild areas over as much of the United States as might be politically and ecologically feasible. If obviously a utopian aspiration, the logic of Foreman's message suggested that in a perfect world it would have been better had the millions of immigrants to the American continent remained in Europe, a place already beyond hope of redemption.

Conclusion

Even when it was skeptical of formal theology, as early Protestantism often was, its leading spokespersons still produced a large body of writing that addressed basic religious questions. Martin Luther wrote voluminously and Calvin himself produced *The Institutes of the Christian Religion*, regularly reworking and revising it from the first edition in 1536 to the last in 1559. When historical Christian messages are recast as secular religions, however, often based on pseudo-scientific claims, there is less opportunity to address explicitly the theological issues being raised. In terms of its religious history, the modern age has been characterized by a host of virtual pop religions based on heroic assumptions without much if any further rigorous development of their theological logic. In this respect, owing partly to the refusal to recognize even that it has been engaged in a religious undertaking, modern thinking as a whole, including the many branches of economic religion, has represented a period of theological regression.

As Part III will examine, the theological underpinnings of environmental religion were themselves seriously flawed. A "Calvinism minus God" lacked the coherence of an actual Calvinist theology. It took certain elements of Calvinism, discarded others, and yet did not offer adequate substitutes for the original Calvinist role of a loving and redeeming Christian God that had been lost.

PART III

ENVIRONMENTAL CREATIONISM

INTRODUCTION

The eighteenth century first confronted the religious significance of the startling discoveries of Newton and other scientists. If the natural world—studied previously as part of the subject matter of natural theology—could now be seen to exhibit a universal mathematical order, what did that say about the thinking and character of God? Might God be a mathematician and the mathematicians of this world the highest priesthood, the ones whose reasoning followed most closely among all human beings "in the image of God"? If the physical world had now been shown everywhere and in all times to follow a strictly mathematical set of rules, did the same hold true for the social world of relations among human beings themselves? If not, why would God have made a sharp distinction between the workings of the physical and social worlds—traditionally seen in Christian theology as operating according to natural laws?

The nineteenth century yielded still further startling discoveries for Christian religion, including, most important, Charles Darwin's 1859 *On the Origin of Species.* Even well before Darwin, discoveries of dinosaur bones, new understandings of the world's geology, anthropological and archaeological investigations, and other scientific efforts were revealing that human history was far longer than the biblical six thousand years, and that indeed many strange creatures had once roamed the earth tens and even hundreds of millions of years ago. Again, it raised difficult theological questions: If the Bible contained significant misinformation in Genesis about the origins of the earth, what did that say about the divine authorship and reliability of the remaining parts of the Bible? Why had Jesus been unaware of much of the long natural history of the earth, or, if he had known about it, why had he decided not to reveal this important information to his followers? Because the Christian churches had long made authoritative pronouncements that were not couched in any tentative language, and yet important elements of these pronouncements had now been revealed to be false, what did that say about the place of the institutional churches in God's plans for the world?

A new awareness of the distant origins of the natural world also meant that the historic Christian way of thinking about "the creation" would at a minimum have to be significantly revised. As Part II explored, Calvinist theology had long said that there were two main ways of learning about God: through the study of the Book of the Bible and the Book of Nature. The natural world was thought to provide an accurate indicator of God's thinking because, as Calvinists could believe at least until the nineteenth century, the world was still largely present today as God had made it at the beginning. If the natural world had been evolving for hundreds of millions or even billions of years, however, involving countless geologic upheavals and the emergence and disappearance of innumerable plant and animal species, the very idea of "nature" as a mirror of the mind of God required a significant reinterpretation. It was less religiously inspiring, moreover, to think that God had created the world more than a billion years ago, and since then the laws of evolution as grounded in physics, chemistry, and biology had worked autonomously to create a substantially new world order as encountered in the present time.[1] The precise relationship of the current natural world to God's original act at the creation would be obscured in the mist of so much distant evolutionary history—much of it having occurred even long before there were any human beings on the earth, and which would necessarily remain inaccessible in large part to current human knowledge and understanding.*

Darwin's theories had potentially other radical implications. What counted in a Darwinian universe was the survival of the group—as we now know it to be, a genetic group or species. The existence of an "objective truth" in the traditional Judeo-Christian understanding became more doubtful in a Dar-

---

*One example of the deeply troubling impact of Darwin's thinking on many contemporaries is provided by the writer W. H. Hudson, born in 1841, who reached adulthood just as Darwin's message was becoming widely known. Hudson shared with his mother a passion for wild flowers, seeing them as "little voiceless messengers and divine symbols." Yet, upon encountering Darwin's *On the Origin of Species*, Hudson was plunged into religious confusion and personal despair. Despite its logical persuasiveness, which he could not refute, Hudson later testified that he had "sought to resist its teachings for years, solely because I could not endure to part with a philosophy of life, if I may so describe it, which could not logically be held if Darwin was right, and without which life would not be worth living." See Jason Wilson, "Charles Darwin and W. H. Hudson," in *The Land that England Lost: Argentina and Britain, A Special Relationship*, ed. Alistair Hennessy and John King (London: British Academic Press, 1992), 173.

winist world. What appeared to be "truth" might simply be redefined as a mental instrument that worked as a practical matter to advance evolutionary success. If the members of a genetic group believed X in their minds, and X was harmful to the group prospects for survival, the belief in X would tend to disappear (it would come to be regarded as "untrue"). By contrast, if a belief Y improved survival prospects, it would be more lasting for this reason alone—and would presumably come to be regarded as objectively "true." There was no guarantee, however, that the genuine "truthfulness" of X or Y, as traditionally understood in Christianity (and Western civilization more broadly), would any longer be a matter of great concern (unless, of course, God had somehow arranged the universe so that only "truthful" beliefs also worked in practice to improve evolutionary prospects of survival).

At a simple level, some higher-level animals probably do have ideas in their minds (e.g., the expected behavior of their prey according to the circumstance) and ways of using these ideas that can either advance or detract from their survival prospects. It would appear, however, that only human beings have ethical ideas—often derived from religion—that in the past have been said to be valid or invalid in an absolute sense. The Darwinian system again worked, however, to undermine any such way of thinking. A moral command of God would no longer be absolutely valid (or not); the important thing would be whether it worked to promote species survival. If Cro-Magnon human beings had survived to become modern men and women, and Neanderthal human beings had not, perhaps it was partly because of what was going on in their respective thinking about the world. Even if the Cro-Magnons had believed mistakenly that their ideas had some final truthfulness and validity, that might have only been nature's way of making the evolutionary power of the ideas all the greater.

Human beliefs also came in packages that represented a "culture." Following Darwin, it has increasingly appeared that there might be a powerful predisposition in all human beings to become strongly attached to some culture, independent of any "objective" merits of the culture—other than its actual ability to enhance evolutionary survival prospects. This predisposition to a strong cultural attachment could itself be a powerful evolutionary survival mechanism sustained by genetic factors unique to human beings. When the external circumstances of the world change rapidly, as often happens, it might take a long time for new genes to evolve to alter human behavior. A human culture, however, can change much more swiftly, and human beings might then become attached to their new culture almost as though the culture was part of their genes. In short, the evolution of human societies could occur much more rapidly than could changes in the natural behavior of the other plant and animal species of the earth, which are dependent on actual genetic change. The workings of a uniquely human "cultural gene" (perhaps only evolved in the past one hundred thousand years or so) might have conveyed a large new evolutionary survival advantage, helping to explain the extraordinary, exponential spread of human populations across the earth in that time period.

From a strictly Darwinist perspective, therefore, the whole idea of a culture, including cultures in which religion plays a prominent role, might be seen in newly instrumental and relative terms. People might "believe in" their culture and its moral values ("God's commands") with a fierce passion, but this would be just an evolutionary adaptation. This might be the real explanation for the cultural success of Christianity, Judaism, and other religions—that they advanced the evolutionary survival prospects of Christians, Jews, and other faithful. From a Darwinist perspective, all the devotion to "God" might be a mere convenient fiction that was highly successful in biological evolutionary terms. And Darwinist biology, as modern men and women increasingly were convinced, had developed the most accurate scientific understanding of the workings of the natural world.

Christian theologians had long taught that human beings should learn about God by studying the Book of Nature, but now this core tenet of Christian belief was raising questions that challenged the very truthfulness of the biblical message itself. The result might be a large paradox. It might be that Christianity was indeed a Darwinist success story, actually promoting the survival prospects of Christian nations and societies; yet the discoveries of Darwin might be undermining Christian piety, and thus Darwinism itself might be a negative factor for the long-run survival prospects of the Christian world. Indeed, a new cultural adaptation might be necessary for human survival—the elimination of the newly emergent Darwinist virus from human cultures and societies. Even if Darwinism were true, it might be fatal to the groups of people who believed in it.

Darwinism also posed a grave threat by suggesting that the "natural" order (historically seen as the handiwork of God) might be one of constant conflict—a war of survival of all against all (among genetic groups at least). Darwinism could thus be taken to provide a religious blessing for class struggle, racial hatred and persecution, and other forms of human violence in the world—after all, they were the "natural" forms of human existence, ultimately attributable to God's actions at the creation. But then again, this might be a large negative factor in terms of the evolutionary survival prospects of human beings; in an ultimate paradox, Darwinist biology might itself be a Darwinist loser in the evolutionary struggle. The terrible warfare and destruction of the first half of the twentieth century, often justified in the name of gospels such as Marxism and National Socialism that appealed in part to Darwin for their authority, suggested that this might be much more than a theoretical possibility. In short, rejecting Darwinist thinking, at least as Darwin's ideas were being applied to shape human culture and society in the first half of the twentieth century, might be an evolutionary survival imperative for the Western world.

One main response along these lines, as found in a spreading Christian creationism in the second half of the twentieth century, was an outright rejection of Darwin. The truthfulness of the biblical creation story was simply upheld, regardless of what Darwin might have said. There was typically little sophisticated effort to demonstrate the scientific falsity of the Darwinist theory. The numbers of Christian creationists, most of them in Protestant denominations, moreover, have been rising rapidly since the middle of the twentieth century. They subscribe to a Christian morality of "love thy neighbor" instead of the Darwinist morality of group genetic survival, which could be characterized as a morality of "vanquish thy neighbor" (unless he or she shares at least some genes).

American environmentalism is doctrinally an offshoot of Protestantism, as examined in Part II, and is also structurally Protestant. There are many branches of environmentalism, and they compete with one another for followers; there is no environmental pope. Perhaps reflecting some of the same religious influences that have encouraged Christian creationism within American Protestantism, the environmental movement has also been a leading source of new creationist thinking in the United States. Typical of secular religion, however, the Christian connections are often disguised or even denied outright. Indeed, many environmentalists may be surprised, and some perhaps disconcerted, to find their beliefs identified below as secular variations on Christian creationist themes.[2]

Admittedly, the separation has been narrowing as secular environmental writers increasingly have been more explicit in invoking the historical Christian language of "the creation." Two 1990s books by environmental authors, for example, are entitled *Caring for Creation* and *Covenant for a New Creation*.[3] The journal of the Natural Resources Defense Council (NRDC) describes the need for a greater "spiritual bond between ourselves and the natural world similar to God's covenant with creation."[4] Natural environments isolated historically from European contact are commonly described, even in secular writings, as having once been an "Eden" or a "paradise" on earth—similar to the creation before the fall.[5]

Creationist language has invaded mainstream environmental politics as well. During his tenure as vice president, Al Gore said that we must cease "heaping contempt on God's creation."[6] Writing in the *New Yorker*, David Remnick describes Gore's more recent warnings concerning the earth's climate as those of a "global Jeremiah" preaching a new "secular evangelism."[7] In a 1995 speech remarkable for its religious candor, interior secretary Bruce Babbitt said that "our covenant" requires that we "protect the whole of Creation."

Sounding much like John Muir, and many Puritan theologians who preceded him, Babbitt argued that wild areas are a source of our core values because they are "a manifestation of the presence of our Creator." It was necessary to protect every animal and plant species, the secretary said, because "the earth is a sacred precinct, designed by and for the purposes of the Creator," and we can thus learn about God by encountering and experiencing His creation.[8]

While Babbitt in this case made specific reference to God, many others do not, even as they employ language explicitly invoking the need to defend "the creation." Some might find this way of speaking objectionable: prominent ecologists, biologists, and other scientists are harshly critical of Christian creationism as false and irrational even as they then turn around and actively proselytize an environmental creationism that comes surprisingly close to the original. The American environmental movement in fact has deep roots in, and still in the end depends heavily on, the conviction that a person finds a reflection of God's thinking in an encounter with wild nature—in biblical terms, that a person is inspired in the presence of God's original handiwork "at the creation." In the absence of some such conviction of this kind, many of the basic beliefs and important parts of the policy agenda of the American environmental movement would be difficult to explain and defend.*

The growing use of creationist language also reflects the increased role that institutional churches of Christianity have recently begun to play in the environmental movement. This has worked to narrow the previous large gap between traditional Christian creationism and secular environmental creationism. In 2005, the Interfaith Climate and Energy Campaign issued a statement on "God's Mandate: Care for Creation." In 2004 the National Council of Churches issued its first ecumenical theological statement on the environment, and in 2006 it distributed a report advocating "creation care" for the Chesapeake Bay.[9] Cassandra Carmichael declares that the Council's "Eco-Justice

---

* The contemporary environmental movement often dates its beginnings to the publication in 1962 of Rachel Carson's *Silent Spring*. Carson does not use explicit creationist language in her writing but conveys the same powerful sense of awe and reverence of encountering nature as being in the presence of God's artwork, a sense that is implicitly creationist in character. As she writes:

> What is the value of preserving and strengthening this sense of awe and wonder, this recognition of something beyond the boundaries of human existence: Is the exploration of the natural world just a pleasant way to pass the golden hours of childhood or is there something deeper?
> I am sure there is something much deeper, something lasting and significant. Those who dwell, as scientists or laymen, among the beauties and mysteries of the earth are never alone or weary of life. Whatever the vexations or concerns of their personal lives, their thoughts can find paths that lead to inner contentment and to renewed excitement in living. Those who contemplate the beauty of the earth find reserves of strength that will endure as long as life lasts. (Rachel Carson, "The Sense of Wonder" [1956], in *This Sacred Earth: Religion, Nature, Environment*, ed. Roger S. Gottlieb [New York: Routledge, 1996], 24)

Program" (which she directs) is "about justice for all of God's creation. Animals, plants and people are all connected and you have to make sure you are having right relationships with all of them." Invoking the classical Christian formulation, as it was especially prominent in the history of Calvinism, Carmichael now explains that "some people compare it to how they can get to know an artist by studying his painting"—and God, as one might say, painted the natural world at the beginning. By studying God's artwork, she adds that "you come to know God both by God's written word and by walking in what God has created and being in relationship with it" in nature.[10]

As a journalistic observer of such developments, Laura Lutz comments that the idea of "environmental stewardship" of the creation is beginning to "resonate across different religious communities." Nevertheless, current Christian groups "are careful to distinguish themselves from secular organizations" that also engage in environmental advocacy. For a valid form of Christianity, Lutz notes, care for "the creation" must involve actions that "are ultimately in reverence to God, and not to nature itself."[11] Or, as Carmichael puts it, and again similar to warnings long heard in Calvinist writings, it is important to keep in mind that "God is the creator, not the creation."[12] The latter would be the heresy of pantheism, in which God is actually present in nature. The dangers are all the greater because the distinction between finding God's artwork in nature and literally finding God in nature can become a fine one.

For most people, there is not much religious inspiration in contemplating the astrophysics of the big bang theory (in fact largely incomprehensible to the average person), the chemical interactions by which life might have first evolved on earth, or even the myriad evolutionary paths by which the current plant and animal world might have developed over a billion years of evolutionary struggle for survival. When current environmentalists, either in outwardly secular organizations or in explicitly religious groups such as the National Council of Churches, speak of their sense of religious awe and reverence in the presence of nature, they do not usually have four-billion-year time frames in mind. As David Lodge and Christopher Hamlin observe, "Our conversations over the years convinced us . . . that the portrayal of the scientific understanding of nature among environmental ethicists . . . bears little relation to the conception that practicing scientists hold."[13] Even when they do not explicitly mention the many antecedents in Christian theology, many members of the environmental movement are implicitly appealing to something much closer to the biblical than to the traditional Darwinist understanding of the origins of the natural world.

Luther and Calvin both wrote at great length on theological subjects, but there has always been a strain within Protestantism holding that formal theology is unnecessary and in some cases can even be a danger. If you think too much, if you spend too much time analyzing, you risk losing your faith. Current environmentalism often shows a similarly disdainful outlook with respect to formal theorizing and other efforts to organize its ideas in a theologically rigorous fashion.* As a result, however, the environmental faithful may easily end up subscribing to a set of jumbled, or even contradictory, tenets of faith. Indeed, recognizing the deep tensions embedded in much environmental thinking, the distinguished environmental historian William Cronon recommends that he and other fellow environmentalists need to rethink the "unexamined, sometimes contradictory, assumptions at the core of our own beliefs."14 This will mean, among other things, that "the time has come to rethink wilderness" areas as the places that represent the highest values—the cathedrals—of environmental religion.15

This is also good advice with respect to the role of "the creation" in environmental thinking today. Leading environmental spokespersons both employ a secular version of Christian creationist language with great enthusiasm and then turn around and attack literal Christian creationism as religious know-nothingism—seemingly not aware that the two are closely connected, often differentiated more by the linguistic metaphors employed than by any great substantive differences.

In our day, the term creationism has taken on a political meaning ever since the 1925 Scopes trial (and later legal disputes in the 1960s and 1980s), and can be used to refer to the conservative Protestant political movement that tries to expel the teaching of evolution from public schools or mandate that the literal Genesis account also be taught.† Although this book will indeed touch

---

* Consider the following passage from Henry David Thoreau:

> I did not regret my not having seen this before, since I now saw it under circumstances so favourable. I was in just the frame of mind to see something wonderful . . . I let science slide, and rejoiced in that light as if it had been a fellow-creature. I saw that it was excellent, and was very glad to know that it was so cheap [to see]. A scientific explanation, as it is called, would have been altogether out of place there. That is for pale daylight. Science with its retorts would have put me to sleep; it was with the opportunity to be ignorant that I improved. It suggested to me that there was something to be seen if one had eyes. . . . It made a believer of me more than before. I believed that the woods were not tenantless, but choke-full of honest spirits as good as myself any day,—not an empty chamber, in which chemistry was left to work alone, but an inhabited house,—and for a few moments I enjoyed fellowship with them. Your so-called wise man goes trying to persuade himself that there is no entity there but himself and his traps, but it is a great deal easier to believe the truth. It suggested, too, that the same experience always gives birth to the same sort of belief or religion. (Henry David Thoreau, *The Maine Woods*, in *A Week on the Concord and Merrimack Rivers; Walden; The Maine Woods; Cape Cod* [New York: Library of America, 1985], 731–32)

† Within the world of Christian creationism, it should be noted, there are in fact several different strands of thought. In the best-known view, those who hold that the earth is six thousand (or possibly up to ten thousand) years old are "young earth" creationists. There are also traditional Bible groups

on the church-state implications of creationism, I will use the term mainly in its historical sense: creationism is the classic belief that the world we see today is roughly as the creator made it in the beginning. Hence, creationism is the belief that the natural world is roughly a "fixed" landscape of an original Eden. This makes creationism exactly opposite to the Darwinian idea that the natural world, at any given time, is simply the chaotic flow of processes over millions of years. Therefore, both literal Bible believers and environmentalists can be "creationists" by virtue of believing in a fixed, ideal state of nature. Indeed, the very idea of North American environmentalism began before Darwin's theory of evolution had been published and still today frequently exhibits powerful creationist elements.

Part III explores such tensions in environmental religion. On the one hand, historically Christian ideas of "the creation" underlie many core environmental worldviews; on the other hand, any explicit ties to Christian creationism are typically rejected. Chapter 8 explores how such tensions have been prominent historically in the thinking of leading ecologists—how the "science" of ecology itself tells an implicit creation story. Chapter 9 examines the attempts of some environmentalists to reconcile the outwardly secular character of environmental creationism with its actual underlying Christian creationist contents. Chapter 10 analyzes the large theological problems that arise in seeking to restore wild nature—that is, to "re-create the creation." And chapter 11 shows how the thinking of environmental creationism in some cases has led to ill-conceived and unjust environmental policies, as when many black Africans were evicted from their native lands in the twentieth century to protect "the creation," as it was said to have existed until recent times in African national parks and other so-called wild areas.

---

that hold to an ancient earth (millions and even billions of years) but a recent human creation (in the past ten thousand years). Also, while seldom described in popular writings as "creationists," it is true that much modernist Protestant and Catholic theology accepts an ancient universe and evolution, but makes it "theistic evolution" and still speaks of the doctrine of creation: that God started it all, God sustains the process moment to moment, that the universe was created "out of nothing," and that the world is contingent, or reliant, on the creator from beginning to end. This view may take the big bang as "creation," but otherwise uses the term in a more theological sense rather than as a "physical" description of a first location that God created. See Larry Witham, *Where Darwin Meets the Bible: Creationists and Evolution in America* (New York: Oxford University Press, 2005).

8

ECOLOGICAL SCIENCE AS A CREATION STORY

MANY ENVIRONMENTALISTS face a substantial tension between their way of thinking about protecting "the creation" and their simultaneous Darwinist understanding of the evolution—now considered to have been taking place for at least a billion years—of the plant and animal world. As modern science tells us, it was not God who created the present-day natural world but rather the workings of Darwinian evolution—reaching a result that is not divinely inspired but a random outcome of many billions of chance events. Even if God may have made the rules for evolution at the beginning, the experience of a product of random natural processes is less likely to inspire feelings of awe and reverence. Poets may have long written about the beauty of natural landscapes but, seen from an evolutionary perspective, as environmental historian Thomas Dunlap comments, "Darwin made it difficult to find God's goodness in the smiling meadow."[1]

For many environmentalists, the simplest course is to ignore this disconcerting turn of events—to partake of strong feelings of religious inspiration in the direct presence of "God's creation," and then to go about their daily lives. Environmental creationism has not come under the same intense public scrutiny and criticism as Christian creationism. There have been fewer social and intellectual pressures for an environmental creationist to work out his or her own precise thinking in this area. It may be best simply not to think about the matter—as sometimes in life it is sometimes necessary to avoid "paralysis by analysis."

Yet for many environmentalists blissful ignorance is not an option. They feel a sense of awe and inspiration in the presence of wild nature yet also believe in Darwinian evolution and its way of studying and understanding the natural world. They are determined, therefore, to incorporate their own powerful religious experiences into a Darwinist framework. This should not be some vague sense that Darwin and environmental religion can be compatible; rather, it should be a well-developed and—at least to their mind—defensible theory in rigorous scientific terms. In the modern age, science has had the greatest authority in understanding the natural world, and environmentalism should be able to draw on a legitimate scientific understanding of nature as well.

The field of "ecological science," or "ecology," is a response to these conflicting pressures. Its beginnings roughly coincide with the rise of Darwinist thinking in the mid- to late nineteenth century. In the twentieth century, interest in ecological subjects increased gradually until the 1960s. Since then, and with the rise of environmentalism, ecology has become a main field of study in American universities, attracting large numbers of students and major funding from public and private sources.

The field of ecology has not, however, been as successful scientifically as it has been in terms of popular interest.[2] In a review of the historical development of the field of ecology in the United States, Eugene Cittadino observes that "ecology, then, is a highly derivative science, one that by its nature relies on language fraught with meaning beyond the science," and thus may lend itself—like economics, and for similar reasons—to religious and other disguised expressions of values.* Although ecologists have often made strong claims to a scientific status—and ecology may be a "science" in some broad classificatory sense—it certainly does not fall in the same category of the "hard" sciences such as physics, chemistry, or molecular biology.[3] Looking back on the history of American ecological science, Cittadino comments that "discussions of ecology and its history always emphasize the great diversity of its subject matter, the extreme differences in methods and approaches depending on the type of environment one is studying or the level of organization (from single-species populations to communities, ecosystems, and the biosphere itself), the lack of consensus on the meanings of terms, the proliferation of empirical generalizations of limited applicability, the paucity of broad general principles, and the prevalence of national and regional styles owing to both environmental and cultural differences."[4]

As this chapter will examine, the outward scientific appearance of ecology, as with economics, masks a powerful underlying religious content. The

---

* The terms ecology and economics have common linguistic origins, both derived from the Greek word *oikos* for home. Both offer grand theories of the world that reflect a vision of the actual relationship of human beings and nature. The largest "ecology" and the largest "economy" are in each case the whole world, including all its creatures, human and nonhuman. There are then many subecologies and subeconomies that ecological theory and economic theory both seek to integrate within their respective overall systems of thought. It has proven difficult, however, to apply mathematical and other rigorous scientific methods to understand the workings of the largest economic and ecological systems, thus often encouraging in both cases those who do undertake such efforts to interject their own strongly held values and beliefs in implicit ways—that is, to turn economics and ecology into metaphors of religious thought.

presence of this religious element is not necessarily a problem in itself, but, in the case of ecology at least, the presentation of religion in the guise of a value-neutral science results in major tensions and even contradictions. Ecological science develops a new creation story that differs in some respects from the original biblical version but also exhibits basic continuities. The result is often both poor science and poor theology—judged from a rigorously analytical viewpoint based in either field.

From Species to Landscapes

Darwin's theory of evolution is about a competitive struggle among individual plant and animal species—or any competitive group in nature, sometimes smaller than a species, that shares common genes. In considering any given species, it is possible to marvel at the ways that it has adapted to its surrounding environment. The giraffe gains a survival advantage through its ability to reach high into African trees, where other, shorter animals cannot go. The internal workings of plants and animals—for animals, their digestive systems, their sensory organs, their bone structures, and so forth—also make up an astonishingly intricate network of interrelated parts. To study the human body is to marvel that such a large and diverse set of organs can come together to form such a complex and well-functioning whole.

Until the modern age, all these things were attributed to the omnipresence and the omnipotence of God in the world. After Darwin, for many people God was pushed out of the picture (He might have started the ball rolling, but there had been a billion or more years of evolution since then). Even without God, however, the internal physical workings of many species are capable of evoking awe and wonder. In this realm of the individual species, it is possible for one person to revere the evolutionary record of history almost in the manner of another person revering the biblical story. Secular and traditional religions often are surprisingly similar in their messages and in their powerful religious effects on true believers. Marx, for example, substituted the evolutionary laws of economic history for God, and the Marxist faithful exhibited attitudes no less enthusiastic and reverential, showing themselves even willing in some cases to be martyrs for the communist cause, much like Christian predecessors in Rome and elsewhere. Indeed, the modern age would be filled with examples of secular gospels that had a powerful religious effect, much as the Jewish and Christian faiths grounded in the Bible had inspired their followers.

When John Muir went to the high Sierras, he was thus enthralled in the presence of an individual sequoia tree and other individual members of various plant and animal species. But there was another and equally, or perhaps even more powerful, source of religious inspiration: Muir was seeing a divine harmony of all parts of the natural world as they served their appointed and interrelated purposes. Everything about the Sierra Nevada—the fact that it existed, the fact that it supported sequoia trees and other plant and animal species, the marvelous ways in which one part of nature seemed interrelated and coordinated with every other part—seemed evidence for Muir of God's handiwork. As John Calvin would have said—and Muir would not have disagreed in any basic sense—the complete spectacle of the Sierras reflected a divine inspiration, a landscape painted by none other than the hand of God, providing a mirror into the workings of God's mind, second only to the Bible in religious importance (for Muir it was first).

Darwinist theory had a great deal to say about the evolution of species and the marvelous results that could be seen in nature at the individual species level. It had much less to say, however, about any powerful ordering forces involving the full set of interactions among a large number of plant and animal species—interactions that we would now call those of an "ecosystem." And it had almost nothing to say about any lasting harmony of nature at the landscape scale that would in itself be a product of the workings of evolution. Darwin's theory was about the evolutionary survival of the fittest individual species, not the fittest landscapes. Indeed, in a Darwinist framework of thought, the overall results in terms of which particular species survive might well be a random accident.

Or, as one might say, Darwinism was a concept of enormous power at the level of the evolution of individual species, so powerful in fact that it transformed thinking about the entire natural order, but it was not a theory of competition among ecological systems. Darwin did posit any mechanism by which one ecosystem would emerge triumphant over another ecosystem. Darwin did not know precisely about genes, but his evolutionary theory, as is now known, has a genetic basis. This raises the question of how, even in concept, one ecosystem, lacking any genes, might be said to compete in evolutionary terms with another. What would the evolutionary triumph of an ecosystem represent and how would it be known? How might some ecosystems be said to show order, logic, and permanence while others might lack these qualities?

Clements, Succession, and the Climax State

The scientific field of ecology was established to address such issues. Its first great American theorist was Frederic Clements. In his comprehensive history of the field of ecology, environmental historian Donald Worster says of

Clements (who died in 1945) that in the first four decades of the twentieth century "no individual had a more profound impact on the course of American as well as British ecological thought."[5] Clements's great contribution to ecology was his view that natural systems are constantly moving toward, and often attain, a "climax state." This might also be described as their assured evolution toward a natural "equilibrium" state. Clements thus offered a theory of the evolution of ecosystems, something missing in standard Darwinist thinking.

Disturbances did frequently occur in nature, and thus no climax state could be expected to endure for long without some changes. In the aftermath of a disruption, however, Clements said that there would be a natural tendency for the ecological system to move back toward the original equilibrium—or climax—condition. As Worster explains, in Clements's view "nature's course . . . is not an aimless wandering to and fro but a steady flow toward stability that can be exactly plotted by the scientist."[6] It was in fact quite similar to the idea of a market equilibrium as advanced by the discipline of economics—and which was also rapidly gaining influence through the writings of neoclassical economists at about the same time that Clements was converting fellow ecologists. In economic equilibrium as well, unexpected disruptive events may occur, but the workings of supply and demand will soon move the market back to its natural equilibrium. God had seemingly made the world, ecologists and economists were saying, to exhibit a happy natural harmony of all its parts. Thomas Aquinas and other Christian theologians had also long ago said as much, if somewhat more complicated by the fact of original sin.

For Clements, the initial physical parameters that set the stage for subsequent evolution of the natural system toward the "climax community" included such matters as temperature, rainfall, wind, elevation, and soil type. Once such environmental factors were in place, the evolution of the natural system "begins with a primitive, inherently unbalanced plant assemblage and ends with a complex formation in relatively permanent equilibrium with the surrounding conditions, capable of perpetuating itself forever."[7] Clements was particularly interested in the North American plains, with their wide grassland expanses in Nebraska, Kansas, and other midwestern states. He believed that this "prairie climax has been in existence for several millions of years at least and with most of the dominant species of today," even though it had occasionally been even massively disturbed by ice ages and other large climatic disruptions.[8]

Thus, rather than focusing on the individual species that had occupied Darwin's attentions, as Clements wrote in 1916, he was himself a pioneer in the scientific study of natural systems in which each system "is a unified mechanism in which the whole is greater than a sum of its parts and hence it constitutes a new kind of organic being with novel properties"—and it was these scientific properties of the ecological "organism" that were to be ecology's object of study.[9] In 1939, Clements would argue that the climax state is in fact a "superorganism created through [the processes of] developmental succession," part of the workings of a natural world in which "all living organisms are united in one communal bond" throughout an ecosystem.[10]

Clements was vague, however, about why his fundamental laws of natural succession should exist. There was no clear basis in evolutionary theory—in fact, as noted above, the very concept of a "natural system" plays little role in Darwinist thinking, other than perhaps as a descriptive term referring to a setting in which the evolutionary struggles among individual plant and animal species take place. Indeed, it was difficult to say what constituted a "natural system." Unlike a species, it has no common genes or other clear basis for uniting a part of nature under a common identity. Where, for example, do the boundaries between one natural system and another fall? Other than the fact that natural systems tended toward a climax state—at least as Clements vigorously asserted and most other ecologists of the time largely agreed—what are the internal forces (or external for that matter) driving the evolution of natural systems? Why should there be any assurance of one "natural" outcome to the workings of ecosystem processes?

In truth, there were no good answers. Rather, as Worster comments, Clements had an "underlying, almost metaphysical faith that the development of vegetation must resemble the growth process of an individual plant or animal organism."[11] In retrospect, his thinking was closer to religion than to science. If natural landscapes exhibited a marvelous order that inspired a powerful sense of admiration for the workings of larger forces in the world, these forces were not those of Darwinist evolution or of anything else that was scientifically well-grounded. There was only one place that this design could have come from. Indeed, there had to be a god who had sculpted the natural landscapes of the earth in such a wonderfully intricate and harmonious fashion.

Despite Clements's preeminent status within the field of ecology at the time, it has since become apparent that there was in fact surprisingly little that was scientific in the whole enterprise. If on a far grander scale of world impact, Marx and Freud were also showing around that time that new, pseudo-scientific religions could substitute for the Jewish, Christian, and other faiths of old. Eventually, however, there would be more careful scrutiny in all three cases. Reflecting the scientific problems, by the mid-twentieth century Clements's climax theory was coming under severe criticism among fellow ecologists and would soon be disavowed—at least in the language used by Clements—by the professional mainstream. By the last few decades of the twentieth century, the standard view among ecologists would be that there is no equilibrium tendency that is automatically manifested in natural systems. Indeed, their normal movement is simply the product of one isolated disturbance outcome followed by another isolated disturbance outcome in a somewhat unpredictable and even random fashion.

Leopold's Religion

The environmental philosopher Max Oelschlaeger regards Henry David Thoreau, John Muir, and Aldo Leopold as the three "giants" of American wilderness philosophy.[12] Thoreau and Muir were products of the nineteenth century, but Leopold was shaped by the events of the first half of the twentieth.[13] His signature work—he wrote less for wider audiences than did Thoreau or Muir—was A Sand County Almanac, published in 1949 (shortly after his death in 1948).[14] Leopold here recast Thoreau's and Muir's environmental religion in the language of ecology, borrowing heavily from Clements. Whereas Thoreau and Muir had said little of Jesus but much more about "God," in Leopold even any explicit mention of God was largely removed.

This was misleading, however, because Leopold's writings and his message reflected a religious understanding of the world through and through. Indeed, much in the manner of Clements, many of Leopold's arguments would make little sense if the existence of a divine authorship of the natural world were not being implicitly invoked. If one appropriately interjects "god" as a newly explicit factor, however, the result is to transform what might otherwise be vague and incomplete—virtual scientific mumbo jumbo in many cases—into something both historically familiar and theologically coherent. If not a rigorous science, Leopold does offer a well-crafted theology, developing an environmental creation story newly adapted to early twentieth-century ecological metaphors.

Over the course of his life, Leopold made the passage from a true believer in economic religion to a true believer in environmental religion, the most famous such secular religious conversion in American history. Much of Leopold's working life—from 1909 to 1928—was spent with the U.S. Forest Service, largely in the southwestern United States. As it had been famously applied by Gifford Pinchot to shape agency culture in the formative years, the religion of the Forest Service was the American progressive "gospel of efficiency," one of the main branches of economic religion.[15] Later in life, however, Leopold would lament the sins against nature that he had once committed in the name of this false gospel. He had once, for example, regarded wolves as predators to be eliminated to improve the prospects for other more desirable species, but he now saw how terribly mistaken he had been.

For Leopold in his mature thinking, communism, capitalism, socialism, and all the other "competitive apostles of a single creed: *salvation by machine*" were alike in their destructive consequences for the natural world.[16] He criticized the "high priests of progress [who] knew nothing of cranes and cared less. What is a species more or less among [economists and] engineers? What good is an undrained marsh anyhow" for an economist?[17] As Oelschlaeger comments, Leopold increasingly concluded over the course of his life that "the human animal was no longer absolute ruler above the web of life but a biotic citizen who recognized that the very endeavour to perpetuate material progress—that shrine [of American life]—was an illusory and self-defeating goal."[18]

Leopold's mission in the last part of his life, culminating in the series of essays assembled in *A Sand County Almanac*, was to spread an environmental alternative to the reigning orthodoxies of economic religion. In this effort, he drew on the accepted thinking of the time among ecologists that there was a single climax state that could be taken as the natural, long-term end result of the workings of an ecological system. It would thus be possible to identify a particular state of nature—this "climax state"—that could be regarded as the one original and valid natural state. As Cittadino comments, "Leopold, never a sophisticated ecological theorist, offered readers the promise of a 'land ethic,' grounded in a belief in the integrity of natural systems."[19] Over time, a host of other synonyms, such as "healthy," "stable," "integrated," "balanced," and "sustainable," would be applied to describe what in essence was still the natural climax state of early twentieth-century ecology.

Even after human beings arrived on the earth, their numbers and their physical capacities were at first limited, and there was no significant threat immediately posed to the natural order. As Leopold, like many others before him (Jean-Jacques Rousseau perhaps most famously of all), came to see matters, however, this had all begun to change with the arrival of organized agriculture, then of built cities, and finally with the rise of modern industry. It reached a crescendo in the nineteenth and twentieth centuries when human beings had commenced to massively alter the workings of the earth's ecological systems. Previously unchanged for tens of thousands, or in some cases even millions, of years, the physical and biological circumstances that had worked to produce a climax state were being transformed by human beings. In the future, there might no longer be anything "natural," "healthy," or "sustainable" left anywhere in the world. Human beings had now commenced to remake nature; they were substituting their own humanly created works for nature's—really for God's—original creation. Rather than being a part of nature, the human presence on earth had come in the modern era to transcend nature, imposing a human dominance over the natural order that no other species on earth had ever possessed before for all the previous billions of years.

Owing to the "value-neutral" cannons of science, Clements and many other ecologists were reluctant to condemn all this new human power in explicitly moral language. Ecologists did, however, assert the unhappy separation of human beings from nature in a less direct way. Ecological models normally left human beings out of the natural systems being studied, which was an indirect way of saying that human beings—at least in the present time—are no longer natural. Because the goal of most ecologists is to sustain and restore the workings of natural systems, it was also an indirect way of saying that human impacts are harmful—that the very presence of humans tends to destroy the natural order of things. In seeking to play God, and thus to substitute themselves in His place, modern human beings are committing the ultimate biblical sin—but now this message is delivered through the technical language of ecological models that leave "unnatural" humans out of the picture.

As Leopold's thinking evolved, however, he departed more and more from the formalities of ecological science, feeling fewer limitations in stating explicitly his strong moral convictions. By the time that *A Sand County Almanac* was published, he would proclaim it necessary to achieve a "land ethic [that] changes the role of homo sapiens from conqueror of the land-community to plain member and citizen of it." Each person must come to realize that he or she "is a member of a community of interdependent parts. . . . The land ethic simply enlarges the boundaries of the community to include soils, waters, plants, and animals; or collectively, the land."[20] Like the residents of any well-functioning community, its members must live according to high ethical standards in mutual respect, including the human members in their interactions with the nonhuman living members and even the nonliving parts of the land community.

Unfortunately, as Leopold now lamented, human beings very frequently violated their proper ethical place in the world. Events in the twentieth century had shown that "our tools are better than we are, and grow better faster than we do. They suffice to crack the atom, to command the tides. But they do not suffice for the oldest task in human history: to live on a piece of land without spoiling it."[21] When he speaks of "spoiling," Leopold shows his debt to Clements. To "spoil" here means in effect to become "unnatural" or "unhealthy"—to permanently disrupt the climax state, or something very much like it, by human action. Oelschlaeger, a self-professed disciple of Leopold, comments that Leopold's land ethic demanded one to see "things steadily, and whole, particularly as this related to viewing the human species and nature as dynamically interrelated, and recognizing that society and land constitute a community of ongoing life—bound into one natural history."[22] As Clements had said, even a natural system could have an organic identity, almost as though it were itself a living thing, and there was one correct ecological condition for each such system—the one state of nature unaltered by human hands.

Many contemporary environmentalists find in Leopold's writings the leading inspirational source for their own ethical thinking—as close as there is to a "bible" of their environmental religion. Oelschlaeger, for example, describes the gospel of *Sand County Almanac*, which now attracts him and so many other ardent admirers, in the following terms. The essays collected there:

> are remarkable statements—Thoreauvian in their literary quality and much of their underlying philosophy. "Thinking Like a Mountain" (1944) is representative of the changes in Leopold's outlook: a confession (in some ways almost Augustinian) that through his own short sightedness and human centeredness he had sinned against nature. As in "Marshland Elegy," nature was animated through Leopold's unique prose. "A deep chesty bawl echoes from rimrock to rimrock, rolls down the mountain, and fades into the far blackness of the night. It is an outburst of wild defiant sorrow, and of contempt for all adversities of the world." Leopold's intuition was grounded in a personal relation to the mountain itself . . . a mountain which recognized in the cry of the wolf a "deeper meaning, known only to the mountain itself. Only the mountain has lived long enough to listen objectively to the howl of a wolf." This statement metaphorically endows the mountain with sentience—the basis of an interconnectedness between the massif and the timber and animals that inhabit its slopes. What in imperial ecology would be a mechanical equilibrium of the ecosystem had been animated and metaphorically personified, but not anthropomorphized. Crucially, the mountain has lived through the longueurs of geological and biological time: long enough to be free of the prejudice that taints human perception of the wolf.
>
> Leopold here verged on recapturing a Paleolithic consciousness of *nature in its order of operation*—escaping the prison of conventional categories and finding his way back to the green world from which his kind had come, becoming one with the mountain.[23]

When Oelschlaeger—reflecting a reading of Leopold that he shares with many other fellow environmentalists—says that nature is "animated," that the mountain has "sentience," that the cry of the wolf "speaks of a deeper meaning," he obviously is not saying that the natural world is literally speaking words that a person can listen to. What, then, does he mean? From a strictly scientific perspective, it would be difficult to know; perhaps the words mean nothing at all; they may simply be empty phrases that sound good to many people. Or they may be seen as metaphors of an environmental poetry that symbolically captures the beauty of the mountains and of nature in general. The mountains are inspirational just as a painting by Michelangelo or Rembrandt is inspirational.

Leopold, however, seems to have a deeper purpose than preaching the aesthetic attractions of mountain or other scenery. Indeed, seen in the historical light of Christian religion, Leopold's message is more familiar. The workings of nature provide a mirror of the mind of God, as put there at the creation, which has now been transposed to a much earlier time than suggested by the biblical story. To encounter natural systems as they existed prior to human impacts—as found in the climax state—is to see into the deepest meanings of the universe, to discover a divine order, to come to know God. The creation might have not occurred six thousand years ago, but there was a new moment of the creation, the point in natural history when the climax state was first achieved. Stated in an old-fashioned Christian way, a person must still read the Book of Nature to discover there essential truths of God, and Leopold was the new reading instructor; he understood that Darwin and other geological and biological discoveries of the nineteenth century must be entered into the picture, as was being done through the ecological thinking of the first half of the twentieth century.

In another ancient Christian theme that Leopold translated to an ecological vocabulary, being a member in good standing of the land community means putting individual concerns and even human welfare in a secondary status, and thus in effect submitting fully to the authority of God. That is, human beings must give up their arrogant pridefulness and the presumption that they can do as they wish with God's creation. They must respect the divine authorship of all the plants and animals, who are God's creatures as well. God may have said that humans should have dominion over the earth, but this did not mean that human beings should wantonly and sinfully disrespect and alter His works. In the nineteenth and twentieth centuries, the human rebellion against God had gone well beyond anything previously known in the earth's history. Indeed, the powers of modern science and industry were being used by human beings literally to transform significant parts of the natural world to serve their own selfish and prideful purposes—altering the one "natural" state that was originally put there by the divine author Himself.

In the Old Testament, such grave transgressions against God's authority would inevitably draw His wrath and bring on a severe punishment, usually of an environmental kind (an element admittedly less emphasized in Leopold's writings than those of many other environmentalists). As is common in environmental writings, the moment of the fall for Leopold is the beginning of organized agriculture about ten thousand years ago (not that far, interestingly enough, from the estimated biblical timing of the fall in the Garden). This development let loose a new form of ecological "original sin" in the world that has resulted in many terrible things that are only worsening in the present time—in fact, the sinfulness of the human presence in the world may be growing by the day.

In Leopold's rendition of the fall, admittedly, the state of human existence is perhaps somewhat less depraved than in some other environmental writings. Leopold, unlike many leading environmentalists of the twentieth century, did not grow up in a devout Calvinist family (rather, his background was Lutheran and much less fervent). It was even possible for Leopold in his early days to have fallen under the spell of the great heresy of economic religion, and to have been a prominent scientific expert for his time in the technical aspects of "game management" for hunting and other human-centered purposes.[24]

But these are points of emphasis. In *A Sand County Almanac* and other of Leopold's later writings, he is relating once again a story of the creation and its corruption by human beings, who have succumbed to the temptation to know and do what only God should know and do.* An American historian of environmental thought, Thomas Dunlap, thus commented recently that Leopold "did not use explicitly religious language, probably would have been skeptical of an environmental 'religion,' and surely would have been horrified at the suggestion that he was helping to establish one. Yet, his work spoke to the religious dimension of life and to ultimate questions and needs, and the public made him, deservedly, an environmental nature saint." It was part of a broad historical phenomenon, Dunlap observes, whereby "ever since Emerson, Americans who failed to find God in church took terms and perspectives from Christian theology into their search for ecstatic experiences in nature"—in the process establishing a secular environmental religion to justify and sustain the rise of the American environmental movement in the last few decades of the twentieth century.[25]

---

* Leopold seldom spoke directly about religion. On at least one occasion near the end of his life, however, he discussed his beliefs with his daughter Estella. According to Leopold's biographer, Curt Meine:

> As they talked, Estella saw her chance finally to find out what was going on inside her father's mind. She veered the conversation toward religion, a subject about which he still never talked. Estella asked him point blank whether he believed in God. "He replied that he believed there was a mystical supreme power that guided the Universe," Estella recalled. "But to him this power was not a personalized God. It was more akin to the laws of nature. He thought organized religion was all right for many people, but he did not partake of it himself, having left that behind him a long time ago. His religion came from nature, he said." [His son] Luna gave a similar assessment of his father's beliefs. . . . "The organization of the universe was enough to take the place of God, if you will. He certainly didn't believe in a personal God, as far as I can tell. But the wonders of nature were, of course, objects of admiration and satisfaction to him." (Curt Meine, *Aldo Leopold: His Life and Work* [Madison: University of Wisconsin Press, 1988], 506–7)

In the late nineteenth century, the prominent American social gospeler and economist Richard Ely could describe the tenets of economic religion within a broadly Christian setting and vocabulary, much as John Muir was doing at the same time for environmental religion. By the early twentieth century, however, Ely knew that this was no longer scientifically respectable within the mainstream of American economics and intellectual life. In the future Ely would cease speaking of God in professional settings, confining his economic writings to a more strictly "scientific" terminology of economic equilibria and other technical phenomena, thereby masking his deeper religious meaning.[26] The leading voices of the American economics profession would in the future proselytize a powerful religion, drawing heavily on original Christian sources, but with ever denser overlays of scientific camouflage. Much the same could be said of professional ecology and environmental religion over the course of the twentieth century, and Leopold was the leading figure in interpreting the results for the American public.*

Ecology as Physics

When the terrible wars and other experiences of the first half of the twentieth century showed that some very dangerous forces had been set loose in human affairs, one response was a new determination that the utmost care should be exercised to objectively verify any truth claims being made by the partisans of one or another worldview. In the late nineteenth and early twentieth centuries, there had been too many grandiose ideas—ideologies, secular religions, or whatever one chooses to call them—that had made great claims to scientific validity and yet in retrospect now appeared to lack this feature almost completely. Indeed, the record of Marxism, National Socialism, and

---

* Environmental philosopher Roger Gottlieb sees a main question for human beings in the twenty-first century as regarding "the central goals of human existence. If life's main purposes are not ceaseless 'progress' and more stuff all around, what are they?" In addressing such matters, "religion has a distinct role to play." Religion must be understood broadly in the sense that "God" is not some father figure in the sky but is synonymous with "Ultimate Truth." One of these ultimate truths is that "the universe as a whole and human existence within it are more beautiful and profound than we can ever fully realize." Aldo Leopold preached a similar message, although he was less explicit about the theological element of his efforts. If Leopold's writings are ultimately more about religion than about ecology or any other science, that should not be considered a criticism in and of itself; in fact that was precisely the reason for his celebrated status as perhaps the leading environmental prophet of the twentieth century. As Gottlieb writes: "Why do we need ecotheology? Simply because before we can act, we must think, and before religion can act in response to the environmental crisis, it must learn to think religiously about it. Thus, the task of the new ecotheology is to think about the environmental crisis, and our human response to it, in religious terms." See Roger S. Gottlieb, *A Greener Faith: Religious Environmentalism and Our Planet's Future* (New York: Oxford University Press, 2006), 12–13, viii, 9.

still other all-encompassing worldviews seemed to show that many human beings were still remarkably susceptible to half-baked ideas and schemes that falsely claimed to know and explain everything important about the world. As it has been said, rather than believe in nothing, most people will believe in anything.

In this intellectual climate, the methods and the historical successes of physics—also having recently experienced a great wave of fundamental discoveries in the first half of the twentieth century—looked especially appealing. In economics, MIT economist Paul Samuelson (winner of the 1970 Nobel Prize in Economics for his efforts) became the most admired economist of the second half of the twentieth century by leading the charge to convert the practice of economics to the quantitative methods of physics.[27] Many other economists would soon be following in his path, a movement toward formal model building and mathematical modes of economic reasoning—buttressed by rigorous empirical work employing advanced statistical methods—that continues little altered to the present day. Rather than a rigorous science analogous to physics, professional economics today may be mostly religious poetry in algebraic symbols and numbers, but the American public is often unable to recognize the difference.[28]

Similar methodological pressures were being felt in the field of ecology around the same time. The climax state and other ecological theories of Clements were increasingly criticized as portraying an organic and even metaphysical and mystical element in nature that lacked any operational scientific content. It was really a variant on Christian religion, as described above, expressed in an unorthodox ecological vocabulary. In the future, to ensure greater objectivity, more rigorous methods needed to be put to work in ecology as well as economics. In this new view, ecological systems should be precisely characterized in terms of the behavior of their individual component parts, and then the functioning of the whole systems should be explained by mathematically working out the model details. As Donald Worster notes, beginning in the 1940s "words like 'energy flow' and 'trophic levels' and 'ecosystem' appeared in the leading journals, and they indicated a view of nature shaped more by physics than [the] botany" of the past.[29]

The formal concept of an "ecosystem" in particular began to play a growing role in environmental thought. It had been first defined in 1935 by ecologist A. G. Tansley, who adapted the concept from the work of Frederic Clements: "[Ecosystems] are of the most various kinds and sizes. They form one category of the multitudinous physical systems of the universe, which range from the universe as a whole down to the atom. The whole method of science . . . is to isolate systems mentally for purposes of study. . . . The systems we isolate mentally are not only included as parts of larger ones, but they also overlap, interlock and interact with one another. The isolation is partly artificial, but is the only possible way in which we can proceed."[30]

Many ecologists would soon be working to model and simulate ecosystem functioning with mathematical methods. Large sets of complicated equations could be developed, later making extensive use of high-speed computing capacities and other "scientific" apparatuses, seemingly resembling the methods of physics. The ecosystem as an organizing theme for ecological study eventually proved so popular that, by the 1990s, the federal government would officially adopt "ecosystem management" as the guiding philosophy for public lands and other natural resources.[31]

After World War II, the leading proponent of the ecosystem concept was Eugene Odum, who in 1953 published *The Fundamentals of Ecology*—the equivalent for ecology, one might say, of Paul Samuelson's 1947 book *Foundations of Economic Analysis*.[32] In both cases, admittedly, the transition in professional methodology was considerably greater than the novelty of the disciplinary conclusions reached. Samuelson largely advocated Keynesian policies to support a managed market economy—meaning in practice mainly a free market but with macroeconomic oversight to ensure greater stability, occasional government regulation as needed in certain areas of the economy, and large-scale redistribution of income that would be collected from tax sources. Odum's ecosystems were in fact not greatly different from the natural systems previously described by Clements, also inevitably and naturally gravitating toward a final equilibrium state, if no longer described as a "climax" outcome.

Ecosystems, according to Odum and other mathematical ecologists of the time, still exhibited clear patterns of succession. This movement was "directed toward achieving as large and diverse an organic structure as is possible within the limits set by the available energy input and the prevailing physical conditions of existence." The whole process was a manifestation of "nature's strategy," which tends toward "a world of mutualism and cooperation among the organisms inhabiting an area."[33] As Worster comments, "Odum may have used different terms than Clements, may even have had a radically different vision of nature at times; but he did not repudiate Clements's notion that nature moves toward order and harmony. In the place of the theory of the 'climax' stage he put the theory of the 'mature ecosystem.'"[34]

To achieve such a point of "homeostasis," it would be necessary that "the living components of an ecosystem . . . evolve a structure of interrelatedness and cooperation that can, to some extent, manage the physical world—manage it for maximum efficiency and mutual benefit." At the point at which the ecosystem achieves its resting equilibrium, "it expends less energy on increasing production and more on furnishing protection from external vicissitudes:

that is, the biomass in an area reaches a steady level, neither increasing nor decreasing, and the emphasis in the system is on keeping it that way." Critically, a key feature of this end point is that there will be "more diversity in the community—i.e., a greater diversity of species."[35] Odum did not, admittedly, answer the key question of how all this ecological order and structure came to be in the first place. Certainly, there was no genetic or other Darwinist basis for such an ordered landscape. As before in the field of ecology, there was really only one good answer. Although Odum did not put it this way, he was implicitly describing the "natural" workings of the world as put there by some outside power or force. In Christianity, there is no confusion about this matter: it is God who has ordered the universe and its ecosystems.

Odum preached that the functioning of ecosystems, tending toward a desirable end state, does and should work independently of a human presence within the ecosystem. Indeed, as Clements before them, ecologists such as Odum saw human beings as representing a potential threat to the natural order and stability of all the well-functioning ecosystems of the world. Although seldom explicit about it, post–World War II ecologists here continued to assert a powerful value judgment. As Worster states, "Odum's view of nature as a series of balanced ecosystems, achieved or in the making, led him to take a strong stand in favor of preserving the landscape in as nearly natural a condition as possible," a condition free of human alteration.[36] Then, in effect, the emergence of the human power to remake the natural workings of the earth reflected an ecological moment of original sin. Human beings must renounce their sinful imperial impulses to dominate nature; instead, they must learn once again to live humbly, in "unity" with nature.

Odum specifically warned that the attempt to obtain "as much 'production' from the landscape as possible," using monocultures and other man-made systems, was shortsighted and harmful both to the long-run human prospect and to nature itself. The outputs of unnatural human efforts to "use" nature were measured in conventional economic terms, such as the physical volume and dollar value of the wood harvested from the forest or the water withdrawn from the river. There were other additional valuable services from nature, however, that had never conventionally entered the market system or otherwise been assigned a dollar value and that might in fact be equally important to both human welfare and the ecological "health" of the natural order. As Odum wrote, "Many essential life cycle resources, not to mention recreational and aesthetic needs, are best provided man by the less 'productive' landscapes. In other words, the landscape is not just a supply depot but is also the *oikos*—the home—in which we must live."[37]

Aldo Leopold in *A Sand County Almanac* had said much the same thing in the metaphors of ecological poetry; Odum was now repeating Leopold's message of environmental creationism in the metaphors of physics (with some of the interpretation in ordinary words, as seen above). The two efforts were in fact complementary. Leopold's writings inspired large numbers of ordinary Americans to experience religiously the natural world and to make a commitment to work for the environmental cause; Odum—and many other ecologists who followed after him—provided scientific credentials and authority. A scientific status was particularly important when issues of government policy and management arose. The actions of the government, as Americans believed in the twentieth century, should not be based on inspirational religious literature but rather should have a valid professional and scientific basis—and most Americans had not considered the possibility that "expert" fields such as economics and ecology could write inspirational "scientific poetry" that nevertheless fell in essentially the same category as Leopold's efforts.

In retrospect, however, the ecologists of Odum's generation, and continuing into the 1970s and in some cases to the present, were also writing inspirational religious literature of a new form. By modeling and otherwise applying a scientific apparatus to the study of ecosystems, a powerful religious message was being sent: that the workings of ecosystems had a higher order, and that they reflected a greater design than simply the cumulative outcome of many independent actions of each ecosystem's component parts. An ecosystem equilibrium might not be hundreds of millions of years old, but in most cases it involved a creation well before human actions began to transform the world of nature. The natural order thus existed first according to a well-crafted natural design; humans came later and were now sinning against the original created universe by destroying its original harmonious workings. If there was to be any hope that the original paradise might be restored, human beings would have to renounce their abusive ways. They would have to give up their arrogant view that the earth was meant for their own use alone. As such, unlike the biblical dating of six thousand years—and the Bible's authority in any case was by now widely suspect—the field of ecology was revealing a creation story that was seemingly compatible with modern biology and yet could still validly develop a religious understanding in which nature, understood as the handiwork of God, must be respected and protected.

While ecological science won many new followers in its religious capacity, the scientific success of the ecological models was another matter. For the most part, as a retrospective judgment has now been rendered, Odum and other ecologists of the period did not produce much that was substantially new or of major intellectual interest concerning the workings of the natural order. Indeed, much that Odum said is now considered to have been misleading or even outright false. As Worster explains the present ecological consensus, "There is no such thing . . . as balance or equilibrium or steady-state [or climax state]. Each and every plant association is nothing but a temporary gathering of strangers, a clustering of species unrelated to one another, here for a brief while today, on their way somewhere else tomorrow."[38]

Robert O'Neill, the first president of the U.S. Society for Ecological Economics, suggested ironically in 1996 that ecologists "must give up their favorite fiction: the 'natural' world."[39] Yet this fiction refuses to die; it is too important to abandon; without it, much of contemporary environmentalism would face a severe crisis of faith. Hoping to find greater meaning in the world, even many ostensibly tough-minded ecologists routinely revert back to such ideas as the "health," "balance," "equilibrium," "integrity," and "sustainability" of nature in their policy and other public discussions (even as it may sometimes be otherwise in their official scientific papers). As Cittadino comments, the science of ecology through most of its history:

> has rested, sometimes uneasily and never without internal critics, on the notion of an ideal, stable, self-rejuvenating, primal nature, existing outside human influence, whose inner workings it is the ultimate goal of the science to reveal. This is a notion that has been difficult to discard for scientists and nonscientists alike, since it fits in so well with the earlier belief in a fundamentally beneficent and self-sustaining nature, with the aspirations and the hopes of utopian regional planners, with the evangelical Protestant idealism of many environmentalists, and even with the hopes and dreams of more pragmatic, and secular, rational planners and managers.[40]

A Plant and Animal "Holocaust"

In terms both of the substantive content and the high literary quality of his writings (he has won two Pulitzer prizes), the Harvard biologist E. O. Wilson is a follower in the path of Henry David Thoreau and Aldo Leopold. In certain respects, however, Wilson is an exception; a devout Christian as a teenager, Wilson is one of the few environmental figures of note to have a Southern Baptist background, even though the Southern Baptists are the largest U.S. Protestant denomination.[41] In publications such as *Sociobiology*, Wilson has shown an admirable fearlessness in taking controversial positions that sometimes brought him withering criticism from other leading intellectuals in American public life.[42] He has also mainly limited his environmental advocacy to his articles and books, refraining from the frequent stump speaking and political activism characteristic of many environmental moralists in the Calvinist tradition.

Substantively in terms of environmental religion, Wilson's greatest departure has been to shift the focus of ecological study and interest in the natural world away from landscapes and toward biological systems.[43] The part of the creation of greatest interest to him is specifically the plant and animal world—now known to encompass many millions of species. By the later part of the twentieth century, as described above, the earlier ecological language that portrayed a physical landscape as virtually a living organism was increasingly criticized, and had become perhaps even scientifically untenable and embarrassing. Even if they did not put it quite this way, the implicit creationist content was becoming too obvious. By contrast, a biological plant or animal species had common genes and otherwise a clearer scientific basis for defining its existence (although there could be complex issues of the precise boundaries between species). Ecologists could study the character of individual biological species in more validly scientific ways than had been possible in addressing the workings of wider ecological systems on a landscape scale.

Reflecting such developments, there was growing scientific concern by the 1980s and 1990s that the "wilderness" concept, despite its continuing appeal to the broader public, was no longer scientifically justifiable. Given the pervasiveness of human impacts on the earth, there might not actually be any areas genuinely "untrammelled by man" (the language of the Wilderness Act as enacted by the U.S. Congress in 1964). Moreover, as noted above, the very existence of natural states of ecological equilibrium at a landscape scale, as long described by ecologists, was increasingly being called into question; nature was apparently more chaotic. Hence, professional ecologists were turning to "biodiversity" as their leading subject of interest, giving less attention to the nonliving elements of the "land community." The field of "conservation biology" was established in 1985 to build the requisite knowledge base and to educate students. Wilson was perhaps the most visible spokesperson of the late twentieth century in communicating these developments to the broader public. As his Harvard colleague Stephen Jay Gould wrote in 1993, "He is the finest Franciscan journalist of our time," whose efforts to communicate the wonders of nature to the American public are characterized by "wonderful writing."[44]

Earlier in his career, Wilson made important scientific contributions to the biology of ants, and with Robert MacArthur he famously explored in the 1960s the relationship between island area and species diversity (studying how the smaller an isolated area of habitat, the fewer species will be found). Wilson is thus a distinguished scientist in his own right. Relying on his own and other biologists' research, a Wilson book or article is usually crammed with lengthy biological details concerning the precise workings of nature, as illustrated in the following representative passage:

Fast-growing, small in stature, and short-lived, they form a single canopy that matures far below the upper crowns of the older trees all around. Their tissue is soft and vulnerable to herbivores. The palmate-leaved trees of the genus *Cecropia*, one of the gap-filling specialists of Central and South America, harbor vicious ants in hollow internodes of the trunk. . . .

All around the second-growth vegetation, the fallen trees and branches rot and crumble, offering hiding places and food to a vast array of basidiomycete fungi, slime molds, ponerine ants, scolytid beetles, bark lice, earwigs, embiopteran web spinners, zorapterans, entomobryomorph springtails, japygid diplurans, schizomid arachnids, pseudoscorpions, real scorpions, and other forms that live mostly or exclusively in this habitat. They add thousands of species to the diversity of the primary forest.[45]

Yet, while the vocabulary is more technical and detailed, and Wilson can appeal to his own high scientific standing for authority, Wilson's message in the end follows a familiar path. Like Aldo Leopold regarding natural systems as whole, Wilson now speaks of a "community of species," of which human beings must understand that they are only one of the parts and have an obligation to respect all the others. Still showing debts to ecological ideas going as far back as Frederic Clements, Wilson sees the workings of the natural world as involving a series of "successional stages" that yield, as Wilson writes, a biological process by which "every habitat, from Brazilian rain forest to Antarctic bay to thermal vent, harbors a unique combination of plants and animals." This natural "dynamic equilibrium" in plant and animal habitats can be disrupted, even severely, but then there will be a process of "succession that circles back to something resembling the original state of the environment." The workings of biological systems reflect an "assembly of life that took a billion years to evolve. It has eaten the storms—folded them into its genes—and created the world that created us. It holds the world steady."[46] There is, in other words, a biological equilibrium in nature to which plant and animal communities of species will continually return—in essence, a biological climax state.

Again in the vein of earlier ecological writers, Wilson sees one great exception to the stability and adaptability of the earth's biological systems. Like Clements, Leopold, and most twentieth-century ecologists, Wilson thinks of and studies biological systems as independent of a human presence. Human beings in this respect are not a part of but are strictly outside nature—unnatural beings with godlike powers. Or, as Wilson writes, they are latecomers to the earth who "walked upright onto the stage, bearing Promethean fire—self-awareness and knowledge taken from the gods—and everything changed."

Eventually coming to think they were virtual gods themselves, human beings have now challenged the authority of the original divine author, seeking to impose their own designs on even God's original creation.

Thus the biological extinction of species is now being "pressed with a [new] vengeance by modern generations" against even insects, bacteria, and other tiny and less visible members of earth's natural community. For example, "the fungi of western Europe appear to be in the midst of a mass extinction on at least a local scale." Wilson labels current biodiversity declines as the sixth "great extinction spasm" over the earth, this time caused directly by human beings rather than by giant meteorites, volcanoes, climate change, or other natural forces for the previous five extinction episodes. Perversely, scientific knowledge has now empowered human beings in unprecedented ways, but "in the instant of achieving self-understanding through the mind of man, life has doomed its most beautiful creations. And thus humanity closes the door to its past."[47] Arrogantly abusing their new powers, human beings are bringing about a "holocaust," as Wilson labels it, for the other species of the earth. Human sinfulness is being directed not only against fellow human beings as in Nazi Germany but also against the plant and animal creatures of the natural world.

Wilson thus has no doubts about an appropriate moral judgment with respect to current human actions affecting the other members of the earth's biological communities. Wilson laments that so many people today are so narrow in their vision that they are unable to "weep for the past, [instead thinking that] humanity is a new order of life." They are willing to "let species die if they block progress, [assuming that] scientific and technological genius will find another way" to serve human welfare without the presence of any particular species.[48] In other words, and very much as Aldo Leopold thought, a false economic religion still too often triumphs over the higher truths of environmental religion. Besides his pure scientific enterprises, Wilson's life crusade is to change all that.

Wilson's vision in fact amounts to a full-fledged environmental religion, dressed in yet another new vocabulary that is Wilson's special contribution to late twentieth-century environmentalism. Wilson's actual writings do in fact evoke a powerful sense that nature testifies to the glory of God's creation. He achieves this result through the development of extensive biological metaphors in place of the landscape and other wider ecosystem imagery of Leopold and many other environmental writers. But the effect is much the same. Oxford University professor Alister McGrath, who holds doctorates in both molecular biology and divinity, thus comments of Wilson that, "though showing no signs of being [himself] aware of the fact, Wilson has simply smuggled in a belief system under the cover of legitimate scientific explanations." Wilson, however, denies the existence of God or other transcendent values outside the natural world, leaving him "vulnerable to the charge of asserting moral values that are purely arbitrary or temporary human conventions that are dependent upon culture and historical location. How can morality have credibility in a world of mere fact, from which God, religion, and any form of transcendent values have been eliminated?"[49] Even as sympathetic a commentator as Stephen Jay Gould finds that important elements of Wilson's thinking amount to little more than "romantic nonsense."[50]

Environmental historian Mark Stoll comments of Wilson that, reflecting his Southern Baptist origins, his "is the voice of the evangelist, not of the priest or pope, because while scientists will identify the biological origins of [an environmental] ethics, they will not operate like bishops or priests," who instruct the people in the convictions they must hold. In Wilson's plan for the world, the new "universal code of ethics will be worked out in good Baptist fashion: democratically."[51] If Leopold sought to spread the ethic of a "land community," Wilson's large body of popular writings are designed to teach the ethical imperative of biological species preservation. It all amounts, however, to much the same thing—to respect, to feel awe and inspiration in the presence of, and to protect the future of God's creation here on earth.

The Book of Ecology

For people who regard ecology as a branch of science, the large role of such religious and other subjective elements often comes as a surprise. The University of California ecologist Daniel Botkin thus explains that he wrote his 1990 book *Discordant Harmonies* because of the wide neglect in public decision making of valid scientific results, even among many working ecologists themselves. As Botkin explains his original mystification, "In the mid-1970s, I confronted several curious contradictions that I attempted to explain: decisions about managing nature were based on ideas that were clearly contradicted by [the] facts" of ecology. What was most surprising was that the neglect of the facts was common even among his fellow ecologists themselves: "In my own field of ecology, those same ideas dominated, yet the facts that contradicted them were gathered by ecologists. We repeatedly failed to deal successfully with our environment, and [as ecologists] we seemed to ignore the very facts that could most help us."[52]

Even when ecologists were not directly responsible themselves for making policy and management decisions based on misleading or even erroneous ecological understandings, they often either encouraged—or at a minimum, refrained from criticizing in public—the responsible government policy makers who did. As Botkin observed, for example, many of his fellow ecologists advocated further wilderness designations, even though it was no great mystery that "there is no longer any part of the Earth that is untouched by our actions in some way, either directly or indirectly." As a result, objectively speaking, "there are no wildernesses in the sense of places completely unaffected by people," despite wide assertions to the contrary in the rhetoric of environmental policy making.[53]

As a result of such disconcerting experiences, Botkin undertook a "search for an explanation [that] led down many paths and required peeling back layer after layer of impression and observation. At the surface were the activities of our society: scientists doing research; legislators signing bills; government officials dealing with policies." There was more to the absence of a valid scientific foundation, however, than the practical limitations of existing governing institutions. Botkin found that, in the development of environmental policy, "underneath there was a layer of belief, myth and assumption, of symbol and metaphor. . . . [At issue was] the character of nature undisturbed" as ecologists were presenting this image to the wider public. Ecologists were being asked and giving answers to questions as old as Adam and Eve: "What is the proper role for human beings in nature?" As Botkin came to believe, the religious stakes had been so large that previous ecologists had too often acquiesced to public demands for an appealing imagery of "metaphor, myth, and assumption," transcending simple knowledge of the actual physical workings of ecological systems alone.[54] Ecologists were simply accommodating the overwhelming public desire to find a deep meaning in the workings of the natural world—to encounter the handiwork of God there, although Botkin does not say it quite this way himself.*

---

* Botkin was writing in 1990, but not much has changed. A funding solicitation letter sent out by the Sierra Club in 2008 was still echoing the familiar environment themes of protecting true nature from human violation carried out in the service of greed and other selfish motives. The Sierra Club declared that "you and I are being robbed of thousands of acres of irreplaceable wild and ancient forests"—areas threatened by many " 'sweetheart' deals" to build "logging roads to make the land more attractive to potential buyers." In Idaho, for example, the Forest Service was seeking to "open up at least 80% of Idaho's last wild forests to commercial development." In Oregon and California, new timber sales threatened "one of the last, great wild places in the United States." It was a reminder of the words of Theodore Roosevelt, who had been "sadly prophetic with regard to those today who wish to sacrifice public wildlands across the nation, for the sake of a profit." But the members of the Sierra Club stood for much higher values as they sought to "stand up to those who will literally sell off our nation's natural heritage for the sake of a buck." The idea of an "ancient forest" in an original natural condition may be fictional by the standards of Botkin and many other ecological scientists, but the Sierra Club is appealing to a story as old as the Bible—a contemporary version of the money changers invading the temple combined with a call for a new day when God's creation will be saved. See funding solicitation letter from the Sierra Club, undated, received by the author, May 28, 2008.

As a scientist, Botkin is unhappily aware of the large extent to which ecology is playing a religious role in American government and society. But he also acknowledges the psychological disorientation that many people would feel in the face of an accurate understanding of the disorderly and chaotic realities of the natural world—what Botkin knew to be the actual scientific conclusions of the technical literature in ecology, if not the popular interpretations of this literature, even by many ecologists. As Botkin explained: "To abandon a belief in the constancy of undisturbed nature is psychologically uncomfortable. As long as we could believe that nature undisturbed was constant, we were provided with a simple standard against which to judge our actions . . . providing us with a sense of continuity and permanence that was comforting. Abandoning those beliefs leaves us in an extreme existential position: we are like small boats without anchors in a sea of time; how we long for safe harbor on a shore."[55]

In the face of such an "extreme existential position," many people will seek comfort in ecological stories, fictional or not. A Darwinian universe, whatever its scientific merits, seems to many people a universe without a larger purpose to human existence. That is to say, it is a world without God or creation. It may therefore be necessary to reject more scientifically accurate depictions of the natural world; for example, some Christian creationists deny the reality of dinosaurs.[*] As Botkin has shown, although perhaps not as extreme, many environmental creationists masquerading as scientific ecologists have their own set of denied facts, thereby giving greater meaning to their universe as well.[56]

Ecological Politics

The creation stories told by ecologists have had a significant impact in many areas of government policy and management. Indeed, "ecosystem management" is today the guiding management principle in many areas of federal policy affecting the environment. As public land agencies turned to ecosystem management, timber harvesters, livestock ranchers, mining companies, and other traditional user groups saw their access to public lands and resources

---

[*] It should be noted that they may not actually dispute that dinosaur bones have been discovered; rather, they may say that dinosaurs lived thousand of years ago beside humans (à la *The Flintstones*). Their main argument would then be that the earth is young (six to ten thousand years old), so dinosaur fossils must be recent as well. Some such creationists may look in the book of Job and read about Behemoth and Leviathan, and say that they are dinosaurs. Some fundamentalists use dinosaurs as the main attraction to interest young people in young earth, literal Genesis "creationism." See Larry A. Witham, *Where Darwin Meets the Bible: Creationists and Evolutionists in America* (New York: Oxford University Press, 2002).

often significantly curtailed. By comparison, backcountry hikers, cross-country skiers, bird-watchers, rock climbers, and other open space recreationists have seen their access significantly increased. The substituting of "ecosystem management" in the 1990s for the old "multiple-use management" resulted in many political winners and losers.*

Some of the losers were bitter when their long-favored uses of the land were eliminated or curtailed in the name of what they regarded as a set of ecological fictions. In a 1999 book, *Defending Illusions*, they found a strong advocate in Allan Fitzsimmons, who put environmental religion under a critical lens.[57] Even when they have been aware of the very intellectual and scientific difficulties discussed above, the interest-group beneficiaries of ecosystem management policies have often been unwilling to address such problems publicly. Fitzsimmons, however, represented the losing side and had no reason to pull his punches.

He thus bluntly declares that the idea of an ecosystem is a social construction that does not correspond to any objective reality in nature: "People, not nature, delimit ecosystem boundaries because ecosystems are mental constructs, and so are their boundaries. Humans, selecting components of the physical environment or using subjective classifications of climate, vegetation, and the like, create ecosystem boundaries." As a result, there are "as many different ecosystems as there are individuals out there using different approaches, variables, scales, and so on to define ecosystems." For example, a given geographic area may "be in the drainage of the East Fork of Tiny Creek, which lies within the drainage of Tiny Creek, which lies within the drainage of Not-Quite-So-Tiny Creek, and so on." Moreover, given the vagueness of the ecosystem concept, and the potential for ecosystems to be defined in multiple ways, the reality is that there can be "an indefinitely large number of ecosystems in the United States," ranging from "a dung pile, [to] a watershed, a forest, or the entire planet."[58]

Fitzsimmons criticized the continuing tendency in pursuing ecosystem management to treat natural systems as though they were themselves alive—in effect as "superorganisms," in the manner of Frederic Clements. In many cases, environmental advocates and policy makers today still speak of seeking to advance or protect the "health" of an ecosystem, as though it were an actual living thing that could be given a medical diagnosis. Still more common, and

---

* Indeed, from the viewpoint of some branches of economic religion that explain the rise and fall of ideas in economic terms (Marxism was particularly notable in this regard), the historical role of ecology and environmental religion might be interpreted as providing a new "false consciousness" that rationalizes—provides new ideological and religious justifications for—the growing political and economic power of recreational and other new user groups in society.

to similar effect, is to speak of an ecosystem as being in a "natural" condition, as if one ecosystem state could be so identified as corresponding to an ideal natural state of affairs, despite much scientific evidence to the contrary. Another powerfully value-laden term is to speak of the "sustainability" of an ecosystem, again referring to a particular condition of nature as though such an ideal existed and could therefore be protected and preserved. Fitzsimmons considered all this to involve an "enormous amount of confusion" and a "muddleheadedness" that was commonly advanced by ecological "scientists (who should know better) and nonscientists alike."[59]

As Fitzsimmons saw matters, ecosystem management in practice had come to mean recovering "the landscape [as it] would look like if Europeans had never landed in North America, that is . . . what an uninhibited Nature would have done to the land if left alone since 1492." Ecosystem management in practice, therefore, meant "undisturbed by Europeans," the human sinners who had somehow acquired a vast and unprecedented power to play God in the world.[60] The pursuit of natural conditions on the land, as so defined, would be endorsed in the 1990s by top government officials, including interior secretary Bruce Babbitt, who declared at a 1997 Idaho conference that the forests and other lands under his direction must be managed to restore them "to presettlement equilibrium"—meaning European settlement, not the Native American kind.[61] Federal government decisions were being made in the 1990s according to a specific vision of the ideal natural workings of ecological systems, which were conceived, as in the Garden of Eden before the fall, to have an innate harmony and otherwise ideally to work independently of human control and manipulation.

Humans might be present, but their impacts—as before the moment of original sin—should be negligible and thus should not disturb the happy harmony of God's creation. The arrival of agriculture about ten thousand years ago, and subsequent developments in Europe and Asia, had meant the end of this original natural condition over much of the earth. In North and South America, however, the human influence was small (or so it was widely believed, although mounting evidence now increasingly suggests otherwise), and ecosystems still functioned in a truly natural way until Europeans arrived.[62] That is to say, God's creation in North and South America had not been greatly marred by the effects of original sin prior to the arrival of Christopher Columbus.[63]

It was difficult to do much about privately owned lands, but the federally owned lands, as Babbitt and many others believed, offered a prime setting for reversing the past impacts of human sinfulness. It would also mean, perhaps not coincidentally, empowering Babbitt's environmental supporters, enabling them to pursue more public recreation and to set aside more environmental "churches" while disempowering the ranchers, mining companies, timber har-vesters, and others who for most of the twentieth century had exercised tight political control—in their case often given legitimacy in the name of economic religion—over the federal management decisions for the public lands.[64]

Conclusion

Ed Marston was for many years the editor of the biweekly *High Country News*, then the leading news source on environmental matters across the western United States. As Marston wrote in 1989, "Environmentalism is still and never more than today, a moral movement: It is telling humanity, with a thousand voices, that we are destroying what we should be cherishing, that we must change our ways, and that unless we change, we will make of the earth a hell for all living things." If human beings would simply reform their sinful ways, however, there could be hope for the future because, "like any moral move-ment, environmentalism holds out a paradise. In our paradise, the air is clear, the water pure, and the wildlife plentiful"—and nature could still be found unaltered by human beings, revealing God's original creation.[65]

Whatever the scientific validity, ecologists told and retold this new creation story over the course of the twentieth century. Despite the large differences in language, it was surprisingly similar to the older biblical version, which was also growing in popularity among traditional Christian creationists over much the same period of time. The wide reach of so much creationist think-ing in such diverse forms suggests the unease that the Darwinist worldview was provoking for many people. Darwin might easily be taken to say that the human presence on earth, the protection of the natural world, the ob-servance of ethical standards by human beings, and many other traditional beliefs of Western civilization were all objectively meaningless. If that was the case, there was growing evidence that in the end, Darwinian science ironically would itself be an evolutionary loser, if it ever came down to that.

9

ENVIRONMENTAL CREATIONISM AND CHRISTIAN CREATIONISM

IN THE 1970S, IOWA DEMOCRATIC SENATOR John Culver was a leading supporter of the Endangered Species Act. Speaking on the floor of the U.S. Senate during the 1978 debate over the renewal of the Act, Senator Culver stated that "we have the ethical and moral responsibility to pass on to future generations, in as pristine a state as possible, what we in turn have inherited."[1] He told his fellow senators that they were addressing a question of basic religious significance: "Those questions, Mr. President, are very fundamental ones. They go to the nature of our universe. They go to the nature of our ecosystems, and our biosphere. They go to basic questions of 'What does it all mean' and whether one is intellectually and spiritually persuaded that what we experience in life is the result of some divine creation and guiding hand."[2]

Even for those who might have disagreed with his specific policy views in the Endangered Species Act debate, Senator Culver's invocation of the language of environmental creationism in American public debate was not controversial. Indeed, if asked to comment, most Americans probably would have regarded it favorably, showing him to be a political leader of high character and ideals. The same would not have been true, however, if another senator had made a similar appeal in the language of Christian creationism. Indeed, Christian creationists have often been subject to harsh public criticism. Strenuous efforts have been made—and widely approved among the scientific elite of American society, including many who strongly support environmental causes—to drive Christian creationism from the public arena.

This much different treatment of environmental creationism and Christian creationism might reflect basic differences in their scientific and religious content. Environmental creationism, for example, might be based in the "hard" findings of ecological science, whereas Christian creationism might require a rejection of Darwinist and other valid scientific methods of inquiry. The previous chapter, however, found that the scientific foundations for the creation story as provided by the field of ecology are not nearly as strong as many people might assume. Indeed, at heart the ecological creation story is a rewriting of the Christian creation story in a new vocabulary. Like the Christian version, the message is ultimately moral and religious. As one American secular environmentalist states, "Those who willfully ignore limits are ecologically wicked. Accommodating wickedness is sinful."[3]

In American life today, science is the reigning orthodoxy. Christianity may still celebrate its historical forms at Christmas, Easter, and other special occasions, but the most important public decisions in American society are guided by scientific knowledge—in most domains of life the actual source of religious authority and legitimacy for our age. When confronted by Christian creationism, present-day scientific censors have been no less vigilant than the Roman Catholic Church was in forcing earlier scientists such as Galileo to recant of their heretical teachings. It is ironic, however, that many of the same scientific censors today enthusiastically endorse environmental creationism. It is possible that they are simply being hypocritical; it more likely, however, that they have never examined closely the theological roots and basis for their own environmental thinking, and have never seen any need to reconcile the close kinship of environmental creationism and Christian creationism.

This chapter explores further the relationship between environmental creationism and Christian creationism. Most observers seem altogether oblivious to the close ties, although a few others see—and in some cases even celebrate— the connections. Indeed, the number of the latter may grow more rapidly in the future. John Micklethwait, writing in the *Economist*, predicted in 2007 that "the culture wars" seen in the United States in recent years—often involving God and religion—will increasingly engage the attention of "politicians on a global scale." One likely subject of especially intense future cultural debate, as Micklethwait predicted, would be "the environment—or 'creation care,' as religious people like to call it. The idea that man is ruining God's dominion could yet become the biggest cultural war of all."[4] If the fiercest religious conflicts of the twentieth century were mostly fought among different branches of economic religion, the new holy wars are more likely to be fought between economic and environmental religion.

Given the growing following of environmental creationism, few people, however, have addressed a fundamental question: How is it that, if environmental creationism and Christian creationism are essentially two sides of the same religious coin, one is now widely celebrated in American public life, and the other is relegated to the margins, considered legitimate only in the private spheres of church teachings and individual belief? Environmental creationism is actively taught in the public schools, while a closely parallel set of beliefs as found in Christian creationism is aggressively excluded.[5] How might this be regarded, and can it be—if at all—reasonably defended? Or might it in fact be an aggressive act of religious imperialism by secular religion in the United States, excluding older institutional Christian faiths—theologically similar but nevertheless religious competitors—from the public arena?[6]

"The Creation" in Popular Thought

In 1995, Willett Kempton, James Boster, and Jennifer Hartley (an environmental policy expert and two anthropologists, respectively) published *Environmental Values in American Culture.* In that volume they sought to explore the core beliefs not only of a sample of environmental activists but also of the wider American public, whose largely secular views in this area they characterized as a "lay environmentalism."[7] As part of their research, they conducted forty-three in-depth, "semi-structured" personal interviews with twenty "laypeople," and twenty-one in-depth interviews with "specialists" in areas related to environmental advocacy and policy. This was followed up by the collection of 142 responses to a written survey questionnaire distributed to members belonging to five groups: (1) the "radical" environmental organization Earth First!; (2) the Sierra Club (representing a more mainstream set of environmental opinions); (3) the general public; (4) small businesspeople in the dry cleaning industry; and (5) workers in sawmills. The intent was to include a wide spectrum, ranging from those expected to be especially sympathetic to the environmental cause to those expected to be hostile.

Yet, after their research was concluded, the authors were surprised to find how small the differences in basic values were among the five groups—that "most Americans share a common set of environmental beliefs and values" that guide their thinking about "the relationship between humanity and nature." They found, for example, that a "purely utilitarian view" of the purposes of environmental protection was "held by only a small minority" of Americans. Instead, there was a wide commitment among Americans of differing backgrounds to environmental protection as both an expression of a moral "obligation to descendents" and a new way of expressing the messages of "traditional religious teachings." There was also a strong sense widely expressed among all those interviewed of "valuing nature for its own sake."[8]

Perhaps most surprising to the authors, even the members of the ostensibly radical environmental organization Earth First! "agreed on many statements [about environmental values] with all other groups, including the sawmill workers." The greatest difference was that the Earth First! members were "willing to make greater personal sacrifices for their environmental values" (e.g., engaging in political activism). The authors concluded that "since our analysis of patterns of variation did find substantial sharing [among all Americans] of models, beliefs and values, we would agree that it is reasonable to call American environmentalism a paradigm" that is widely accepted across the United States.[9]

What Kempton, Boster, and Hartley call a "paradigm," especially when it involves such basic beliefs and values, others might well call a "religion." Indeed, their skittishness in using the term religion reflects long-standing difficulties of American social science in dealing with religious subjects. The social sciences typically do not provide a helpful vocabulary in this area; when they speak of religion at all, it tends to be in terms of "explaining" the existence and character of a religion, or else the practical "purposes" served by religion. Questions of the ultimate validity of a religion, or of the fundamental sources of its core values, have little or no place in contemporary social science discourse. Yet the actual detailed analysis of environmental values developed by Kempton, Boster, and Hartley revealed a much different picture, even as these academic researchers showed considerable confusion in deciding how to present their findings in a standard social science framework.

The authors found, for example, that among Americans broadly, "70 to 80 percent say it is wrong to abuse the natural world because God created it." Curiously enough, even 50 percent of self-declared "nonbelievers" in their survey agreed with this creationist statement.[10] The authors did not explore, however, what it means for a "nonbeliever" to explicitly invoke God and creation as a basis for his or her environmental values. Perhaps they are not really nonbelievers but instead are uncomfortable with many elements of a Christian or other traditional religious vocabulary. Hence, they express powerful religious convictions rooted in the Christian history of Western civilization even as they deny having a religion at all (although they are often more comfortable with being described as "spiritual" as opposed to "religious"—as if there is any difference). Alternatively, when speaking of "the creation," it may be simply a metaphorical use of a convenient descriptive term and not meant in any literal sense.

It is thus not only social scientists and ecologists but also many other Americans who may be having difficulty in finding an appropriate vocabulary in this area. Another survey item asked whether respondents agreed with the statement that "we don't have the right to play God by manipulating nature." Eighty-six percent of Earth First! respondents agreed but so did 53 percent from the sample of dry cleaners and 67 percent of the sawmill workers. Only 42 percent of Sierra Club members, curiously enough, agreed, perhaps reflecting a greater secularization among a more highly educated group and a lesser degree of comfort in explicitly invoking "God" to defend their own environmental values. Thus, when a reference to God was taken out and a similar question was asked, 82 percent of Sierra Club members agreed that "all species have a right to evolve without human interference" (which comes close to the idea that they are all God's creatures).[11]

Reflecting the large role of religious considerations in shaping environmental views, 93 percent of the average Americans surveyed agreed that "being out in nature can revitalize everything in you."[12] In one of the personal interviews, the authors heard from a former member of the Catholic Church about such an inspirational encounter she had had with nature:

> I've experienced something bigger than what my own self contains. I think that people and living things somehow are united by some sort of force, or some sort of awareness or consciousness. And [a] very few times in my life I feel like I've sort of tapped into that, and it's given me a glimpse of why life has any meaning at all. . . . Once, alone in the jungle of Mexico, I felt a unity with the natural world. I felt a presence of other intelligences, not mine. Something outside of myself that was not necessarily human, it was just some sort of consciousness. And I felt united and tapped into that. And sort of complacent about my physical surroundings.[13]

For centuries in Western civilization, such thoughts and feelings would have been expressed in terms of feeling God's presence. Today, many people have much the same experiences, but they have improvised a new language of "lay environmentalism" that often makes little reference to any historical Christian vocabulary. References to "the creation," however, have become increasingly common, even among those who are reluctant to specify who or what has been doing the creating. As Kempton, Boster, and Hartley comment, across American life "there is widespread agreement with creation as a reason for environmental protection." These views were held not only by members of organized religions: "Of those who did not belong to any organized religion, 69 percent agree with statement 58 about [justifying environmental protection in terms of] creation. Of those who stated that they did not even believe there was a spiritual force in the universe, 46 percent agreed with this."[14]

Kempton, Boster, and Hartley express some bewilderment at their own research findings. They ask, "What is going on here? Why should so many nonbelievers argue on the basis of God's creation" to defend their environmental values?[15] Indeed, they acknowledge that they would not have even placed any statements about God and creation in their final written survey questionnaire had they not discovered the great importance of such thinking in the personal interview stage of their research. If a social science researcher were to take the explicit secular statements of environmental religion at face value, he or she would never recognize the large underlying domain of implicit environmental religion. Indeed, any understanding of the environmental movement that leaves out the (mainly) implicit religious elements would be seriously incomplete, if not altogether misleading.

As a result of both the personal interviews and the written survey, however, Kempton, Boster, and Hartley could only conclude that in U.S. lay environmentalism "divine creation is the closest concept American culture provides to express the sacredness of nature. Regardless of whether one actually believes in biblical Creation, it is the best vehicle we have to express this value." Many Americans thus use the language of Christian creation even when they profess not to believe in God. One possible explanation is that they do in fact believe in God, although they lack a vocabulary to express this belief in terms that they would regard as acceptable in an age of Darwinist and other scientific skepticism. Thus the authors frequently encountered the expression of strong "feelings of spirituality in nature" among people who in most respects rejected "explicit church teachings." Instead, they considered it simply a matter of "experiencing this spiritual feeling directly from contact with nature" alone, outside the less comfortable setting of any Christian church or other institutional religion.[16]

The common American way of thinking about nature, as Kempton, Boster, and Hartley discovered, nevertheless sees a basic moral obligation of human beings to protect nature—and correspondingly sees human existence as outside the Darwinist struggle for survival that engages every other plant and animal species throughout its lifetime. Hence, fully 83 percent of the average Americans in their survey agreed that "other species have as much right to be on this earth as we do. Just because we are smarter than other animals doesn't make us better." Ninety percent of Americans agreed with the very un-Darwinist notion that "justice is not just for human beings. We need to be as fair to plants and animals as we are towards people." The total rejection of a Darwinist framework of thought becomes most striking when 20 percent of the survey respondents from the subsample of average Americans agreed that "if any species has to become extinct as a result of human activities, it should be the human species."[17]

Given the pervasiveness of "nonutilitarian values" in the thinking of most Americans about the environment, Kempton, Boster, and Hartley suggest that environmental advocates should make greater efforts to appeal to more explicitly religious—or "spiritual," as might be the preferred term—values in protecting nature. When environmentalists argue in practical terms that we should "protect the rain forest because it has potential medicines," they miss the point for most Americans. The rain forest is to be protected because it is the rain forest. The authors found, however, that when they offered this advice to environmental activists, those "who work in the political arena tell us that utility is still a more convincing argument for politicians—it may be hard for a [political] representative to argue for the right of other species when his or her constituents are threatened by unemployment."[18] Even as environmental religion gains influence in American society, it is still apparently difficult to challenge directly the historical dominance of economic religion in public life.

Kempton, Boster, and Hartley never say so explicitly, but their research results point to the following conclusion. The Christian creation story is one of the central ideas in the history of Western civilization. Chapter 7 described how for many centuries followers in the Christian religion—and particularly Calvinists—saw their encounters with nature as an act of reading the Book of Nature, second in importance only to the Book of the Bible in revealing the mind and thinking of God. Today, many Americans are still reading the Book of Nature in this same light, and still experiencing powerful feelings of religious awe and reverence in the presence of what they perceive to be wild nature. But many of these people, ironically, no longer regard themselves as Christians; they are uncomfortable with the use of any explicit Christian idiom to describe their religious feelings, even as these feelings often correspond closely to traditional Christian categories.

Beneath all the muddled language and other confusions, however, it is still in essence the Christian creation story to which—as Kempton, Boster, and Hartley discovered to their own great surprise—a large majority of Americans today subscribe. Some devout Christians are happy to use a traditional creationist or biblical vocabulary to express this religious conviction. Many other Americans are willing to speak of "God" and "the creation" in describing their own thinking but otherwise wish to exclude traditional Christian language—especially any mention of original sin or the role of Jesus Christ in releasing human beings from a depraved and corrupted state. Still others prefer to exclude altogether any language that recalls a traditional Christian message. Beneath all the rhetorical confusion and obfuscation, however, many environmentalists and other Americans are saying much the same thing. Whether in a vocabulary of environmental creationism or of Christian creationism, encounters with nature powerfully inspire feelings of religious awe in contemplating the handiwork of God.

Caring for Creation

In a 1994 book titled *Caring for Creation*, the environmental philosopher Max Oelschlaeger—unusually for a member of the American environmental movement—attempts to address some of these issues. One of his main purposes is to rebut a common view of "environmentalists generally" that "religion is the cause or part of the cause of [the] ecocrisis" seen in the world today. This negative view of religion derives partly from the concern of some environmentalists that "Judeo-Christians believe that they have dominion over the earth and do not believe that they are an integral part of biotic communities."[19] Lynn White was one of the first to make this claim in 1967 and many other environmentalists still hold similar views to this day.

Oelschlaeger argues that, to the contrary, traditional religions have an "irreplaceable function" in the attempt to "resolve the environmental crisis" of our times. Indeed, in his view "religious discourse . . . is potentially more important than secular environmentalism" in mobilizing American society to address its environmental problems.[20] This will involve, moreover, drawing on traditional Jewish and Christian understandings of the meaning and importance of "the creation." By appealing to the status of the natural world as a part of God's creation, Oelschlaeger hopes that the institutional churches of the United States can be persuaded to lend their potentially powerful political support to the environmental cause.[21] Because Christian creationism in any case has a close affinity with environmental creationism, the two should be natural allies in working together in a common political endeavor.*

Oelschlaeger traces the "beginnings of an epochal transformation in western culture" to the 1860s, the moment at which Darwin's theory of evolution began to have a large intellectual impact. Since then, there has been a growing separation of science and religion. The separation is seen in "the religious conservative, who believes that Genesis is infallible and therefore irreconcilable with Darwin." But it also exists for many religious moderates and liberals for whom "the looming possibility of ecocatastrophe undercuts faith in the notion that God designed the earth for Man."[22] It seems that there is a widespread belief in the central importance of divine action in the world, even

---

*Similar views are expressed by a growing number of environmental writers today, including Roger Gottlieb. In a recent work, he states that a "spiritual processing of our moral errors" is necessary today to address environmental concerns, requiring a "real moral transformation" in society. In pursuing this goal, "it is particularly important to turn to religious environmentalists on this issue, for they offer a comprehensive vision in which care for the earth and care for people go hand in hand. This vision is not simply about what is wrong but about what can be right, not just about 'living with less' but about living an authentic and ultimately much more satisfying form of life." For those who seek an environmental reformation in American life, it is a matter of not just changing their personal lives but also participating in the "environmental politics" by which collective decisions relating to the treatment of the environment will be made. Here the support of traditional religion, including Christian creationists, will be essential. Even secular environmentalists face the burden of working out their precise religious thinking through the development of an "ecotheology" to inform their policy advocacy. See Roger S. Gottlieb, *A Greener Faith, Religious Environmentalism, and Our Planet's Future* (New York: Oxford University Press, 2006), 12–13, 21.

among many people who are uncomfortable with the traditional biblical vocabulary with which such beliefs have been expressed in the past.

Through his writings, Oelschlaeger hopes to help to bring science and religion closer together by developing "a new metaphor—caring for Creation."[23]
Traditional Christian religions ranging from conservative to liberal, he suggests, all can agree with secular environmentalists on the importance of protecting "the creation." The combined weight of U.S institutional religions, if
they can be newly enlisted to the environmental cause, may in fact substantially exceed that of the followers of the more secular creeds of environmental
creationism, who have tended to dominate in the environmental movement
up to now:

> I claim that across the spectrum of faith, almost without exception,
> the faithful are given ample reason to care for the Creation and that
> through that caring we can come together on an environmental agenda.
> Religious discourse offers the best chance that ecology might influence
> public policy. By assuming its role in a time of ecocrisis, religion might
> establish its place in public discourse, its vital place in the maintenance
> of our world. Indeed, from my perspective, religious discourse neces-
> sarily has a place.
>
> By caring for creation we can begin to re-establish ourselves as a
> moral community, as a nation with some collective sense of who we
> are and where we are going, even though this community grows out of
> diverse traditions of faith. . . . Any movement toward sustainability re-
> quires a political consensus, the will to act, that does not now exist. The
> prevailing definition of the public good is stuck inside the conversation
> of utilitarian individualism. Religious narrative is our best chance to
> break free of this as a democratic people.[24]

In *Caring for Creation* Oelschlaeger reviews the understandings of "the
creation" as found in various American religions.[25] He notes that Protestant
"religious conservatives argue that the Bible explicitly mandates that humankind is to care for creation." This includes the understanding that, rejecting
the traditional methods of economic analysis, "nature must not be treated
by Christians as having use-value only: the imperative of the bottom line is a
false god." Conservative Roman Catholics similarly believe that "the creation
of God is good. Original sin, however, ruptured the relation between man
and nature. Ecological crisis is the consequence [in our time]. Only obedience to God's law can restore what sin has put asunder." Pope John Paul II, as
Oelschlaeger comments, described "the ecological crisis [as a 'moral issue'
and argues that a socially just, religiously inspired ecological ethic is required"

to solve our environmental problems. In the Old Testament, Oelschlaeger recalls, both the Jewish and Christian faithful learn in Psalm 104 that "O Lord, how manifold are thy works! In wisdom hast thou made them all; the earth is full of thy creatures. Yonder is the sea, great and wide, which teems with things innumerable, living things both small and great." Moreover, "the Creation is not only an Old Testament but a constant biblical theme, from Genesis to Revelation," providing ample theological justification for the development of a "Christian mission of environmental stewardship of the earth."[26]

Among more moderate and liberal branches of Protestant Christianity—who mostly do accept the Darwinist account of evolution—Oelschlaeger finds similar views that the Bible requires an ethic of stewardship with respect to God's creation. One well-known Methodist theologian, for example, preaches a "doctrine of creation" in which he finds that "the Bible makes it clear that the entire creation, flora and fauna, is endowed with an intrinsic moral significance."[27] Some Protestant churches have focused almost entirely on matters relating to personal salvation and a heavenly destination, but, as James Nash sees the matter, "that interpretation . . . is too narrow, too restrictive, too anthropocentric, since the entirety of creation is an expression of grace, that is, God's free and faithful loving kindness that characterizes God's nature and acts. . . . The creative process, therefore, is an act of love, and its creatures are products of love and recipients of ongoing love."[28] The Bible, as Oelschlaeger concludes, teaches that "the Creation itself has a redemptive purpose; this places an ultimate obligation on Christians to become stewards of earth."[29] Minus the specifically Christian references, the secular branches of the contemporary environmental movement are saying much the same thing.

Oelschlaeger, however, says little about the secular forms of environmental creationism described in previous chapters. Indeed, when he speaks of religion and creation throughout the book, it is mostly in terms of a creation lens as supplied by traditional Jewish and Christian faiths. In suggesting that the influence of religion should be newly drawn to the environmental struggle, he thus neglects the fact that the mainstream environmental movement has long had its own secular creation story. Indeed, environmental creationism has been all the more powerful because it has been presented under the authority and legitimizing influence of "ecological science." Although the fundamental reality may be otherwise, environmental creationism at least outwardly takes Darwinism as a starting point, thus avoiding the tensions that often arise between the theory of evolution and literalist Christian interpretations of the creation.

Besides seeking to bring together the various creationist perspectives in a common environmental cause, Oelschlaeger also directs his fire at a common enemy: the many modern secular religions of economic progress that have encouraged and promoted widespread unconcern for environmental damages. Unlike Lynn White, he finds that newer ideas, essentially derived from the Enlightenment, are the real culprit in destroying the natural world. Oelschlaeger explicitly labels the most important of these post-Enlightenment secular gospels as "the religion of economics." As he writes, the "high priests of the American civil religion" are the "economists who staff the Council of Economic Advisors, tend the National Income Accounts, and more generally attempt to manage the economy." It is this "elite cadre" of professional economists who "now rules our society with the legitimating narratives of economic discourse," all the while falsely claiming that the methods of economics are "objective and impartial (value free)." In economic religion, the ultimate measure of value is the "efficiency" of an action as it contributes to the "maximization of the production and consumption cycle, . . . the criterion used to judge the political and corporate elite" of American life.[30]

Perhaps underestimating the power of environmental ideas among the general American public, Oelschlaeger thinks that economic religion's large influence is important because, for "the present generation of Americans, the managerial elite and the voting public, insofar as they even entertain questions of environmental policy, reduce them to questions of economics." And regrettably, this "almost exclusively and narrowly defined economic decision-making matrix has led America into ecocrisis." More broadly, and reflecting the influence of a pervasive "modern paradigm," the outcome "in the twentieth century [has been] . . . the emergence of an increasingly rationalized, planned society controlled by experts" such as economists, along with the planners, engineers, and other professional contributors to "progress." Yet Oelschlaeger has no faith in these or any other kind of modern professional experts. Indeed, "the experts . . . are more part of the problem than the solution." As they exerted their professional and technical influence over the key instruments of public policy and management over the course of the twentieth century, the result has been that "we are destroying the environment."[31]

Hence, only a new and superior set of prevailing religious values can supplant the harmful consequences of the old worship of economic religion. Oelschlaeger is thus explicit that he is working to spread a new "religion [that] offers a powerful language for dealing with ecological crisis, especially through ethical narrative that turns on the metaphor of caring for creation." This will entail a recognition that the natural world is valuable in and of itself, independent of any economic or other material outputs produced for the direct benefit of human beings. The churches of the United States must be enlisted in this process of "religious discourse [that] offers the most accessible alternative to the [economic] language of utilitarian individualism, which holds the [contemporary] state, the corporation and the university in its sway. . . . The church then, is a necessary part of the politics of community, for it can sustain a dialog that can take us beyond ecocrisis" through a reverence for the creation that was largely lost in the modern headlong pursuit of economic growth and development.[32] If they are shown the real stakes in the conflict, Oelschlaeger is saying, the Christian churches can be persuaded to join the new holy wars on the environmental side.[33]

The Creation According to E. O. Wilson

A surprisingly similar position is taken by E. O. Wilson in a 2006 book, *The Creation: An Appeal to Save Life on Earth*.[34] Wilson here goes beyond his previous writings in exploring the religious side of environmentalism. His book is framed as a letter to an anonymous "Dear Pastor" in the Southern Baptist denomination, the same faith in which Wilson was a devout follower as a youth. As Wilson sets the stage, his imaginary correspondent is a person who is "a literalist interpreter of Christian Holy Scripture," rejects "the conclusion of science that mankind evolved from lower forms," and is sure that those who are redeemed in Christ will attain to a "second, eternal life." As an adult, however, Wilson himself rejected these beliefs to become a "secular humanist," convinced that "our ancestors were apelike animals" and that "heaven and hell are what we create for ourselves, on this planet," not a matter of any divine reward or punishment. For Wilson, the basic truths of the universe are to be discovered by science, replacing the prior role of Christian scripture and other traditional teachings. Since the Enlightenment, the methods of science have generated "knowledge in the most productive and unifying manner [ever] contrived in history."[35]

Wilson thus makes no concessions in rejecting some of the main tenets of the Southern Baptist faith, even as he proposes to his parson correspondent that "we set aside our differences in order to save the Creation." Indeed, now in an even more forcefully argued fashion than Oelschlaeger, Wilson finds that the Christian message and his own secular environmentalism have much in common. If an alliance can be formed, it will bring together "religion and science [which] are the two most powerful forces in the world today, including especially the United States." If they combine their efforts in the public arena, it will hold out the promise of protecting a "beautiful, rich, and healthful environment." There is no reason that Southern Baptists and secular humanists should not agree that human beings must act quickly and forcefully "to prevent the extinction of species and, with it, the pauperization of Earth's ecosystems—hence of the Creation."[36]

Wilson's frequent references to "the creation" are merely one example of his common use of a traditional Christian vocabulary, even as he himself rejects the essential truthfulness of main elements of the Christian message. Indeed, Wilson's book is filled with moralistic language with which he would have been comfortable in his Southern Baptist youth. The earth, he says, must be saved from its current "plundering," a conviction based on the power of a "universal moral imperative of saving the Creation." For those of us living today, success or failure will mean that we "will earn either everlasting honor or everlasting contempt." In considering the possibility of applying future technical knowledge to "create artificial organisms and species" through bioengineering of new plants and animals, Wilson says that "there are words appropriate for [such] artifactual biodiversity: . . . desecration, corruption, abomination." Protecting wild areas today is so important because "only in what remains of Eden, teeming with life forms independent of us, is it possible to experience the kind of wonder that shaped the human psyche at its birth."[37]

Wilson also relates his own story of the fall of man. He is in full agreement with his anonymous pastor correspondent that "somewhere back in history humanity lost its way."[38] Indeed, the dating of Wilson's moment of the fall is surprisingly similar to the pastor's—within the past ten thousand years. Similar to other environmental writings described in previous chapters, Wilson tells this story of the fall:

> According to archaeological evidence, we strayed from Nature with the beginning of civilization roughly ten thousand years ago. That quantum leap beguiled us with an illusion of freedom from the world that had given us birth. It nourished the belief that the human spirit can be molded into something new to fit changes in the environment and culture, and as a result the timetables of history desynchronized. A wiser intelligence might now truthfully say of us at this point: here is a chimera, a new and very odd species come shambling into our universe, a mix of Stone age emotion, medieval self-image, and godlike technology.[39]

Since "we strayed from Nature" within the past ten thousand years, human beings thus have increasingly followed false principles; they have been led into ever greater sin by their rapidly growing scientific and economic knowledge that enabled them to remake the world—to literally play God. Indeed, matters are getting worse by the day: "The human impact on the natural environment is accelerating and makes a frightening picture." In destroying the earth, we are doing terrible damage to "our home, our wellspring, our physical and much of our spiritual sustenance." It is a failure of biblical proportions, as human beings "have ignored the command of the Abrahamic God on the fourth day of the world's birth to 'let the waters teem with countless living creatures, and let birds fly over the land across the vault of heaven.'" As God commanded of Noah in Genesis, Wilson proclaims that it will now again be necessary to protect every living species of the earth, no matter how minor or trivial its practical importance may seem to us: "Each species is a small universe in itself . . . and a self-perpetuating system created during an almost unimaginably complicated evolutionary history. Each species merits careers of scientific study and celebration by historians and poets."[40] As Wilson exhorts his fellow human beings, Christian and non-Christian alike, sounding more and more like a prophet of old:

> Save the Creation, save all of it! No lesser goal is defensible. However biodiversity arose, it was not put on this planet to be erased by any one species. . . . All that human beings can imagine, . . . all our games, simulations, epics, myths, and histories, and yes, all our science dwindle to little beside the full productions of the biosphere. . . .
>
> It is true that nonhuman life preceded us on this planet. . . . The biosphere into which humanity was born had its Nature-born crises, but it was overall a beautifully balanced and functioning ecosystem. It would have continued to be so in the absence of Homo sapiens. . . .
>
> Think of it. With the smaller population that can be reached within a century, and a higher and sustainable per capita consumption spread more evenly around the world, this planet can be paradise. But only if we also take the rest of life with us.[41]

Human beings have turned away from God, Wilson is telling us, and they must now repent and mend their fallen ways. If they do, there can still be hope that a new earthly paradise lies in store. This will require, however, abandoning the false pride that has afflicted human beings since modern industry and technology came into their possession. If the vocabulary is his own, Wilson's message is hardly new. Wilson concludes his book with an appeal to his parson correspondent that "you and I are about equally ethical, patriotic, and altruistic. . . . We would gladly serve on the same jury, fight the same wars, sanctify human life with the same intensity. And surely we also share a love of the Creation." In the end, while "science and religion wax and wane in the minds of men, there remains the earthborn, yet transcendental, obligation we are both morally bound to share"—to protect the earth and all its plant and animal species.[42]

Wilson's secular environmentalism thus closely parallels the traditional Christian concern for "the creation." The affinity may reflect more than a set of metaphorical similarities that just happen to exist between two otherwise distinct worldviews. Rather, although Wilson insists that he speaks only in the voice of science, it is more plausible to think that his early Southern Baptist faith has a stronger hold on him than he realizes. All his disavowals to the contrary, Wilson may in fact still be a Christian believer who, like many others in our time, finds it impossible to express his Christian understandings in the traditional biblical language.* Whatever the intellectual—really theological—confusions it may involve, Wilson in his voluminous writings of the past thirty years may have been retelling a biblical creation story in the outwardly scientific language of biology. Karl Marx once substituted the laws of economics for the Christian God and otherwise transposed large elements of the Christian message to economics; Wilson has now taken the same tack with an alternative—and for him superior—form of scientific omniscience: the laws of biology.†

* Jared Diamond is another leading contemporary writer who, like Wilson, comes from a scientific background and has invoked his considerable scientific authority to give legitimacy to his wider efforts in environmental advocacy. In his 2005 book *Collapse*, as Ted Nordhaus and Michael Schellenberger find, Diamond makes "an argument against human attempts to control, ignore, or live out of balance with Nature. The stories that Diamond tells . . . are tales of human hubris, of societies that neglected the laws of Nature in pursuit of human follies and were punished accordingly." As Nordhaus and Schellenberger remark, however, and despite Diamond's scientific pedigree, the vision of a nature of balanced equilibrium is not tenable scientifically. Instead, nature is a world of constant disruption and disequilibrium. Diamond's vision, they find, is not really scientific but at heart Christian: "In so doing, Diamond is unaware that [in his book *Collapse*] he has told a biblical rather than a scientific story, a theological cautionary tale wrapped in the white laboratory coat of Science." See Ted Nordhaus and Michael Schellenberger, *Break Through: From the Death of Environmentalism to the Politics of Possibility* (New York: Houghton Mifflin, 2007), 136, 138.

† Outwardly at least, Wilson professes to believe in a scientific materialism that is no less fully encompassing than that of Marx. As Wilson asserts in *The Creation*, the study of biology is not only a way of understanding the workings of the natural world but is also "the discipline most immediately relevant to human concerns." Thus, before modern "science there had to be [traditional] religion, in order to explain man's place in the universe"; commencing three hundred years ago in the Enlightenment, however, "step by step, often opposed by the followers of Holy Scripture, science constructed an alternative worldview based on a testable and self-reliant human image." As a result, biology has become the principal discipline today capable of showing the path "to explain the nature of mind and reality and the meaning of life." This is because, ultimately, "all the known properties of life," including even elements of human culture and ideas, "are obedient to the laws of physics and chemistry."

The final fulfilment of a complete biological understanding of the world, however, still lies well in the future. As Wilson explains, "Most of biology consists of emergent properties and for the time being therefore can be only loosely connected in causal explanation to physics and chemistry." The long-run goal, nevertheless, and Wilson is fully confident that it will be realized, is to ground biology—including all of life, the thinking of human beings not excepted—in the methods of physics and chemistry. At one point in *The Creation*, Wilson describes the final outcome that he expects for biological research. In his estimation, it will provide a God-like knowledge to "create life"—for example, to "complete the mapping of a species of simple bacterium at the molecular level, simulate its processes by computers, then construct individual bacteria from the constituent molecules."

Once this can be done for bacteria, biology will then move on to higher orders of species. Biology for Wilson will replace Genesis by providing a much more detailed knowledge of how to "construct the steps that led to the origin of life" billions of years ago. As only God knows our thoughts today, in the future even human mental processes will be understandable in biological terms; the discoveries of biological research will "explain the mind with models of chemical and electrical transmission and the

For many Christians, to be sure, and despite the roots of his thinking in Christianity, Wilson will remain a misguided heretic.[43] In a review of *The Creation*, S. M. Hutchens acknowledges that the book is "an evangelistic tract" that reveals Wilson to be "a passionately religious man." It shows "Wilson's love of the abundance and intricacy of the creation," reflecting a deep "appreciation of the Mind of the Creator" as it is encountered there. Nonetheless, Hutchens finds in Wilson only a "vestigial element of traditional [Christian] faith." The commonalities cannot cover over a vast "chasm that exists between [true] biblical religion and [the] earth piety" of Wilson. For a good Christian, unlike Wilson, the earth must not be "a final thing" but rather a "*first* creation" to be followed by a future kingdom of God. In God's plan, the "principle reason for the earth's existence is to serve the cause of human redemption" in the future. For Wilson, by contrast, Hutchens finds that the ultimate "ethical end humanity . . . is bound to seek, is the maximum health, abundance, and diversity of living things"—the central environmental goal of "biodiversity." For Wilson, the human responsibility for the earth's "use is not principally to God, in accordance with an eschatology assumed in divine directives, or to the human race, in accordance with the philosophical concept of human good, but to the biosphere itself"—a false message by any Christian standard.[44]

Yet Hutchens may take Wilson too literally. "The biosphere" and the language of biodiversity for Wilson may be a new way by which he is able to speak metaphorically of God. Seen in this way, responding to "the dictates of the biosphere," as Wilson might put it, is really just another way of saying that humans should obey the commands of God. For example, as God commanded Noah, humans are still required in Wilson's religion to save every species. Within Christianity as well, some writers have argued that the new heaven to come will include the plant and animal creatures of the earth along

---

molecular basis of nerve-cell growth and network formation, [making it possible to] simulate the mind with the combination of artificial intelligence and artificial emotion." In the future it will therefore be possible to perform miracles using biological "information with increasing effectiveness to cure disease and repair injuries," cures every bit as extraordinary as the miracles performed by Jesus in the Bible.

Finally, achieving a total scientific omniscience, when biological knowledge is altogether complete (admittedly at some rather distant point in the future), this will provide an integrating synthesis to "bridge, if not outright unify, the natural sciences, social sciences, and humanities by exploration of the biological foundation of mind and human nature." As the author in 1975 of *Sociobiology*, Wilson has held a lifelong conviction that the "coevolution of genes and culture" is the driving factor in all of human society and history, and that genetic factors ultimately determine cultural outcomes according to the workings of a Darwinian evolutionary process. At some point, this evolutionary interaction of genetic and cultural forces will be perfectly understood biologically, thus enabling human beings to know completely their reasons for existence and their ultimate destination. Wilson thus joins with those who reject the economic god; for Wilson, the true god actually works his ways in the world through biological processes. See E. O. Wilson, *The Creation: An Appeal to Save Life on Earth* (New York: Norton, 2006), 105–7, 111.

with human beings. In terms of the stories told, Wilson's religion is admittedly far from the literal language of the Bible, but some might still choose to place it within the very large tent that Christianity has historically encompassed.

Modern secular religion in general has allowed many people such as Wilson to profess historically Christian messages without having to rely for their ultimate legitimacy and authority on the Bible, formal Christian theology, or the institutional Christian churches. In the end, Wilson's environmental efforts over his long career have perhaps involved more linguistic obfuscation—including his own self-deception—than fundamental departures from the Southern Baptist faith of his youth.

God the Mathematician

Alister McGrath is a professor of theology at Oxford University, following an early research career in molecular biophysics. Unlike Wilson and other writers discussed above, he is less concerned with Darwin and biology and more concerned with the religious significance of Newton and physics. McGrath sees little tension between Christianity and physics—the two intellectual loves of his life—in their manner of understanding the creation. In his youth, he had many experiences of "nature [which] has a splendid way of impressing us. There are few who have not been overwhelmed, time after time, by a sense of awe at the beauty of a glorious sunset, the sight of distant mountains shrouded in a soft blue haze of mist, or the brilliance of a starlit night." Such powerful feelings led to his initially pursuing a career of "studying the natural sciences," allowing McGrath to "feed my relentless appetite to understand nature and appreciate its majesty. It seemed to me that the universe was something that teemed with significance and purpose. What greater privilege and excitement could there be than to engage with its wonders and mysteries" through the advancement of its scientific understanding?[45]

In the early 1970s McGrath became a devout Christian, and a few years later he decided to leave the physical sciences for the formal study of religion. In his 2002 book *The Reenchantment of Nature*, and similar to Oelschlaeger and Wilson, McGrath makes the case that the environmental movement and Christianity are natural allies who have too often been separated. They are frequently saying much the same thing, McGrath argues, despite the large outward differences. Thus, explaining the "Christian doctrine of creation," he now understands that his long-standing powerful feelings in the presence of nature reflected "our sense of wonder at the beauty of nature [which] is thus an *indirect* appreciation for the beauty of God. Rightly perceived, nature points beyond itself. . . . The doctrine of creation introduces a new dimension to nature—as a means by which the glory and radiance of God can be reflected toward humanity."[46]

McGrath examines how Christian theology since its earliest days has seen nature as a mirror of the mind of God. For Augustine, as McGrath explains, "the beautiful things of the world point to God as their creator."[47] Bonaventura in the thirteenth century wrote that "all the creatures of this sensible world lead the soul of the wise and contemplative person to the eternal God."[48] Thomas Aquinas explained that:

> meditation on God's works enables us, at least to some extent to admire and reflect on God's wisdom. . . . We are thus able to infer God's wisdom from reflection upon God's works. . . . This consideration of God's works leads to an admiration of God's sublime power, and consequently inspires reverence for God in human hearts. . . . This consideration also incites human souls to the love of God's goodness. . . . If the goodness, beauty and wonder of creatures are so delightful to the human mind, the fountainhead of God's own goodness (compared with the trickles of goodness found in creatures) will draw excited human minds entirely to itself.[49]

When John Calvin later put his own stamp of religious authority even more strongly behind such a way of thinking about nature, as McGrath notes, it helped to provide "a new religious motivation to the scientific investigation of nature." The resulting improvements in scientific method offered newly powerful ways of learning about nature, and thus about God. Shortly after Newton published his *Principia Mathematica*, a contemporary stated that the well-ordered physical structure of the universe revealed therein provided clear evidence of "the wisdom of God." Newton himself understood the significance of his own discoveries in such terms. Even to the present day, as McGrath learned from his own personal encounters, many physical scientists have "basic religious motivations for [their] scientific research—the passionate belief that to gain an enhanced appreciation of the beauty of the world is to glimpse something of the glory of God."[50]

McGrath notes that "the human mind could easily have been shaped in such a way that it did *not* regard the world as beautiful." That a sense of the wonderful qualities of nature is so powerfully felt by so many people—acknowledged Christian believers and self-proclaimed nonbelievers alike—suggests that "we have [all] been programmed or hardwired to recognize and respond to the beauty of the world." It is as though there is "a congruence or fundamental resonance between our sense of beauty and the beauty that is actually embodied in the natural world."[51] Absent a Christian doctrine of the creation, this would be difficult to understand. It is more readily explained, however, in terms of the Christian understanding of human beings created in the image of God. That is to say, there is already within each human being a spark of the divine. In encountering nature, itself a reflection of the divine, human beings also experience the presence and are reminded of some God-like elements that can be found within themselves—if far short of God's full powers and qualities. As McGrath thus explains:

> Why is it that the human mind is able to discern the patterning of the world? We have already seen that this understanding of creation allows us to posit a fundamental resonance between the rationality of God, the ordering of creation, and the ability of the human mind to comprehend at least something of the rationality of the world. Why is it that there appears to be some correspondence between the rationality of the cosmos and our own rationality? If there were not, the universe would remain a mystery to us.
>
> The answers . . . converge in this great truth: we have been created with the ability to peer into the mind of God. If our reasoning has its source in God, it has the potential to lead us to its fountainhead. Even though it may be attenuated through our weakness and frailty, our created reason retains its God-given ability to point us toward its creator. The stream can point us to its source. The resonance between reason, the world, and God is no accident; it is an integral aspect of the Christian doctrine of creation.[52]

As McGrath explains, Galileo considered that his successes in applying mathematics to understand the natural world were attributable to "mathematics being grounded in the being of God"—and thus the created world exhibited a mathematical structure put there by God and comprehensible to humans, who uniquely among all plant and animal creatures shared with God the capacity to think mathematically.[53] As such, the scientific endeavor consisted of efforts to discover the correspondences between mathematical ideas preexisting in human minds (or at least the preexisting capacity to explore and further refine detailed mathematical concepts over time) and the created world of a God who imposed a mathematical order on the universe at the beginning.[54] This idea was expressed not long ago by the Cambridge University theoretical physicist and theologian John Polkinghorne as follows: "If the deep-seated convergence of the rationality present in our minds with the rationality present in the world is to find a true explanation, it must surely lie in some more profound reason which is the ground of both. Such a reason would be provided by the Rationality of the Creator."[55]

In the Enlightenment, however, for many people a large separation developed between science and religion. Many leading thinkers of the age became deists, adopting a mechanical view of nature, following the analogy of a clock. God may have created and set the natural world in motion, establishing the mathematical laws of physics and chemistry for its subsequent operation, but otherwise He had withdrawn from active involvement. Perhaps still more religiously significant was the increasing application of the discoveries of the physical sciences to use and manipulate the natural world for human purposes. The growing human powers to put nature to practical uses led, as McGrath writes, to the "disenchantment" of human beings from the natural world. In a newer, modern way of thinking, "no longer does humanity have to respect nature; it can dominate and direct it through the rise of technology."[56] This development was not a result of any Christian teachings, according to McGrath, but the product of a modern, secular outlook—a post-Christian outlook—that substituted human knowledge and human purposes for the former place of God in the world. Although McGrath does not use precisely this language, the modern world, as one might say, has sought its salvation through an economic god here on earth rather than the traditional Christian God in heaven.

With the rise of the environmental movement at the end of the twentieth century, however, McGrath finds a new appreciation—or an old appreciation revived—for the divine authorship of nature. Yet contemporary environmentalism has also often been critical of Christianity. McGrath argues that this reflects a basic theological confusion and maybe even ignorance. In truth, Christianity makes a powerful religious case—for McGrath the strongest case possible—for the protection of the natural environment. Today, as much as at any time in the past, it is still true that "nature . . . bears witness to God's wisdom, just as a great building bears witness to the genius of its designer."[57] Christians and environmentalists should be able to easily agree that the earthly cathedrals built by God Himself should not now be wantonly destroyed by worshippers of false economic gods.

There is, nevertheless, a central missing element in McGrath's argument. When he speaks of experiencing a powerful reverential feeling in the presence of nature, his favorite example is the stars in the heavens. Unlike the plant and animal species of the earth, the stars are little changed on the time scale that complex living creatures have existed on earth. The scientific understanding of the big bang adds some complications, but it is possible to think of the stars as really being present today as they were "at the creation"—or as they have certainly existed for at least a few hundred million years. When it comes to observing the natural world on earth, however, there has been constant flux on the time frame of even a few hundred years. Even leaving aside the pervasive human impacts on nature, we now know that the "creation" as observed to-day on earth may be significantly altered by natural forces within a short time frame on the order of a few hundred years or less.

As suggested previously, Darwinism posed a more formidable challenge to Christianity than did Newtonian physics and the other physical sciences.* The physical laws of the natural world, mathematically expressed, can reason-ably be taken as permanent manifestations of God's thinking, unchanged now and in the past (e.g., the law of gravity does not evolve). In studying the cre-ation as it is seen in present-day plants and animals, however, this principle does not hold true. The meaning of "the creation" then becomes more elusive. Darwin's evolutionary understanding of the history of the world, along with other discoveries in geology, also posed a more direct conflict with the bib-lical story of the creation and the subsequent six-thousand-year history of the world. The most powerful of the "atheistic" ideologies, such as Marxism and Freudianism, as criticized by McGrath, were conceived and developed in an allegedly superior Darwinist framework for understanding the world—a main reason that they had such an extraordinary impact on the world, at least for a time.

For the strict Darwinist, the created world today is a random accident of a billion or more years of natural evolution. This is ironic and paradoxical because many secular environmental creationists are also among the leading defenders of the Darwinist message. They thus end up revering nature in the

---

* It should also be said that, perhaps more than McGrath would agree, the mathematical character underlying the workings of the natural world, as newly revealed by modern science, did itself raise difficult theological problems for Christianity. This meant that the mind of God—as given a physical representation at the creation through the structures of the natural world—must be at least in signifi-cant part that of a mathematician. God seemingly had been applying his perfect knowledge of algebra, calculus, differential equations, and many other mathematical subjects when he created the natural world. Why, then, had Jesus not taught or even suggested the central importance of mathematics in God's design for the creation? The biblical messages were more seriously incomplete than had been believed. Was it even possible that Newton might actually have known more about the ways of God—been closer to God in his thinking—than Jesus was?

The extraordinary power of the scientific method was also difficult to understand from a Protes-tant perspective, in particular because the Reformation message was that each individual must come to know God directly by his or her own efforts. Yet the technical difficulties of doing higher-level mathematics substantially exceeded the mental abilities of most people. Indeed, most ordinary people could never hope to understand well the physics and the chemistry that underlay the mathematical workings of God's creation. They would have to rely on a new scientific priesthood of mathemati-cians and physical scientists for their religious instruction, a group of experts similar in its exclusive religious understanding of the world to the Roman Catholic priesthood, who claimed to have special knowledge of religious truths. The Protestant conception of a "priesthood of all believers" might in fact be theologically untenable in a mathematically governed universe. At a minimum, owing espe-cially to the large importance of nature in Protestant theology, and now the discovery of the math-ematical character of the physical universe, the role of the Bible and the ordinary Protestant ministry in comprehending God's full design at the creation had been significantly reduced.

manner of worshipping a place designed by God, even as they see little place for God in the actual creation of the natural world as we experience it today. It is possible to be inspired by the miraculous outputs of the workings of Darwinist evolution, but those workings themselves—a competitive struggle often leaving a trail of blood and promising the eventual extinction of every current plant and animal species—hardly seem cathedral-like in character. It is a source of intellectual and theological confusion today, one that many environmentalists seemingly have not been able to sort out in their own minds, and in many cases may not have even confronted directly in their own thinking. McGrath is also of little help in addressing such issues.

Conclusion

Many Americans reject the scientific and economic idea that nature is simply a "natural resource" to be used for greater production and, in the long run, the maximization of human consumption (even recognizing that "consumption" can include matters such as aesthetic enjoyments). Instead, Americans frequently apply other religious criteria in thinking about nature. In the Christian tradition, the main resource for understanding the proper relationship of man and nature is the biblical creation story. Even when they no longer consider themselves believing Jews or Christians, it seems that many Americans still implicitly apply a biblical creationist account in their thinking about environmental issues. To alter the creation, as found in those areas on earth little touched by human hand, is in effect to deface a visible manifestation of the original artwork of God.[58]

To recognize the close connections between Christian and environmental creationism, however, is to enter into some difficult theological—and also political and legal—territory.* Among the problems, none of the authors ex-

* The potential constitutional complications of recognizing environmentalism formally as a religion are explored—perhaps for the first time ever by serious legal scholars—in a 2009 article in the journal *Environmental Law*. Andrew Morriss and Benjamin Cramer begin by noting that "the United States Supreme Court's Religion Clauses jurisprudence is charitably described as confused." For the purposes of addressing issues of the separation of church and state, it is necessary to have a working definition of a religion. Yet, as Morriss and Cramer find, "there is no definitive answer in either the historical record or the Court's jurisprudence as to exactly what constitutes a religion in the constitutional sense." The presence of a god in the hereafter, it would appear, is not necessary for the Supreme Court to find a religion. They go on to argue that environmentalism thus meets many of the criteria that would properly put it in the constitutional category of a religion. They then suggest that some, although not all, parts of the practice of environmental policy making amount to government efforts to establish a particular religion, thereby coming into conflict with the "disestablishment" provisions of the U.S. Constitution prohibiting official government support of particular religions. New wilderness "churches," for example, might have to be privately created and maintained, and existing wilderness

amined thus far, nor any others of whom I am aware, has a good answer to the question initially posed at the beginning of this chapter. Given the large similarity of religious content, how might one justify the strict exclusion of Christian creationism from official settings such as the public schools, while a surprisingly similar set of creationist religious beliefs, as found in a secular environmental religion, are welcomed and indeed actively proselytized in those very same public settings?[59]

areas transferred to private ownership. As they write: "Our approach to disestablishment does not presume that every belief relating to environmental protection is somehow religious. And we also do not believe that being labeled as 'religious' is somehow bad. . . . But we would not want an official state body to resolve matters of faith, whether sectarian within Christianity such as transubstantiation or the ordination of women, or cross-creedally among Buddhism, Christianity, Hinduism, Islam, and Judaism. We suggest that disestablishment [of environmental religion] will not crush environmental . . . thought or practice; it will instead give environmentalism the freedom it needs to thrive." See Andrew P. Morriss and Benjamin D. Cramer, "Disestablishing Environmentalism," *Environmental Law* 39 (Spring 2009). See also Robert H. Nelson, "Wilderness, Church, and State," *Liberty*, September 1992.

10

***

IN 1999, CONNIE BARLOW, an advocate for environmental causes, declared that the "rewilding [of nature] must be undertaken because, next to outright species extinctions, the most abhorrent outcome—the greatest crime against creation—humankind might effect would be for surviving lineages [of plant and animal species] to skew their future evolution substantially in response to us." She acknowledged that the human species in this case would not be acting according to Darwin's model of competitive struggle. Rather, it was based on a "strong ethical, even religious appeal." Like many secular environmentalists, she was notably vague about the basis for her strong religious convictions. Perhaps the theological sources did not need to be spelled out formally—a view consistent with Pietist and some other branches of Protestantism that historically have been skeptical of any "Scholastic" tendencies toward an overly intellectual statement of their beliefs. In essence, for her it was self-evident that "we shudder because we know in our souls that this behavior [of human hegemony over nature] is not right. This is not the way we wish to be human. This is not our ideal for participation in the Earth Community."[1] Indeed, it was a simple truth too obvious to require elaborate justification: human beings must not play God with the world.

The idea of "rewilding" large parts of the North American landscape was the most radical form of what in fact had become a general theme of mainstream American environmentalism—the urgent necessity of "restoring" significant parts of the natural world.[2] This was not meant to be merely a general statement of philosophical principles but rather a specific guide for government policy and management.[3] Restoration of ecological systems, environmentalists increasingly declared, should be the operational goal of the U.S. Forest Service, the National Park Service, the Bureau of Land Management (BLM), and the many other government agencies whose activities had in the past and could in the future still significantly affect the natural world.

But "restoration" to what natural order? The answer of a literalist Christian conservative might be to restore nature to the condition of the world as found at the beginning—some six thousand years ago. But even such a Christian would have to admit that it would be difficult to know now what this original state of nature might have been, either in a general way for the earth as a whole or for any given landscape. The answer would have seemed much clearer before the nineteenth century because the world then was seen in static terms, and the restoration of "the creation" could be interpreted as simply reversing any recent modifications of nature (the only ones likely to be known) that had resulted from human actions. Since the nineteenth century, however, there has been a much greater awareness of both the very long history of the earth and the continuing dynamic and evolutionary character of the natural world, operating in some cases to transform natural conditions significantly even within a time frame of six thousand years or less (e.g., through rapid climatic shifts). Until around 3,500 B.C.E., for example, much of the current area of the Sahara desert received much more rainfall than it does today.

As Barlow suggested, one solution to this problem would be to restore nature to the condition that existed at the specific point in the past where human actions began to alter the character of evolution. Even if this did not result in the restoration of the one "creation state" (an impossibility in any case), it would mean that the outcome of evolution might itself be described as "natural." Many environmentalists, moreover, have assumed that North and South America were largely unaltered by human actions until the arrival of Europeans. For them, restoring a natural evolutionary order has meant a return to the biological world of the Americas as they existed before European settlement.[4]

Barlow saw the Eurocentric fallacy of this thinking. As she had to acknowledge, there is "strong scientific evidence that we humans are centrally implicated" in the large-scale loss of mammoths, mastodons, saber-toothed cats, American lions, and many other megafauna that lived in North and South America at that time. The arrival of modern humans from Asia had seemingly led to the extinction of many species. Barlow considers that it will therefore be necessary to redress this earlier "crime against creation" in the Americas.[5] It is difficult to see how this could be accomplished, however, given the absence of any surviving megafauna. As a substitute, Barlow proposes the restoration of African elephants in North America today as wild animals.

Although hardly a perfect solution, and certainly a politically unlikely prospect, it would be in concept—along with introducing wild lions, tigers, and other appropriate large species now found only in Africa and Asia—the closest approximation possible to the goal of restoring some of the great

American megafauna of the past.* If we do not "bring elephants back and offer them a chance for an evolving, deepening citizenship" in the current natural world, she says, "then Order Proboscidea will never again produce American endemics; the evolution of Order Proboscidea in the New World will be over."[6] For Barlow, that would be unconscionable and unimaginable— a terrible evil. Instead, elephants should be brought back and allowed to evolve in whatever directions nature might take them, perhaps eventually resulting in new species of "wild" American elephants altogether.

Barlow has of course ended up in a tangle of contradictions. She wants natural evolution to occur without human impact and control, and then goes ahead to propose that current human actions should set the stage for future evolution in the Americas. She sees a natural evolution as the highest policy goal and yet is asking human beings to behave in the most unnatural of ways by the standards of any other species. She does not speak directly of human acts of "playing God" but would no doubt disavow any such objective. Yet the idea of "restoring the creation" is about as God-like an action as can be imagined, tantamount to "re-creating the Creation." It presumes that human beings not only should replicate the plan for the world that God had at the beginning, but also that human beings have the same capacity as God to take a divine design and transform it into a physical reality. In other words, human beings would virtually have to be God, the very antithesis of the goal supposedly being sought by Barlow and others with similar views.

Barlow is not alone in her confusions. Leaving aside any talk of God and the creation, the goal of restoring nature is widely advocated among environmentalists, even as they also advocate less human "manipulation" of the natural world. But it cannot be both ways. The technical and engineering skills that would have to be applied to restore past natural conditions would be substantial. Large financial and other resources would have to be committed to scientific study of the workings of ecological systems. Large numbers of ecological "engineers" would have to be put in the field. It would be a new comprehensive "scientific management" of nature—achieving what might be called a new form of "environmental progress." Yet a main theme

---

* Others with stronger scientific credentials would later take up this idea. In 2005, Josh Donlan of the Cornell University Department of Ecology and Evolutionary Biology, together with eleven coauthors, proposed in the scientific journal *Nature* "a bold plan for preserving some of our global megafaunal heritage—one that aims to restore some of the evolutionary and ecological potential that was lost 13,000 years ago, and which offers an alternative vision for 21st century conservation biology." In pursuit of a goal of "Pleistocene re-wilding," there would be a reintroduction "of large wild vertebrates into North America," including elephants, lions, camels, and many others. If it was desirable to restore the creation as it had existed before its evolutionary path was significantly changed by human actions, it would be necessary to go back to a natural order much older than the moment of the arrival of Europeans a mere five hundred years ago. See Josh Donlan and others, "Re-wilding North America," *Nature* 346 (August 18, 2005): 913.

of contemporary environmentalism is the past failures of scientific management of nature, its frequent infeasibility and inappropriateness for the future. Environmentalism routinely criticizes the misguided worship of a false god of scientific and economic "progress."

Some environmentalists are aware of these tensions in thinking about restoration and have sought to address them.[7] Probably the majority of environmentalists have not thought the matter through in any careful way; shunting aside critical examination, American environmentalism has had the character of a moral crusade.* As with Barlow above, it is enough to feel and assert powerful new (or old) religious convictions in the treatment of the natural environment. There has been little urgency given to developing a well-crafted and carefully reasoned body of environmental theology that would reconcile messages that might otherwise seem contradictory. This anti-intellectual strategy has thus far been workable at the level of enunciating broad environmental values and declaring their central ethical importance for the future protection of the earth. But more careful analysis and thought will eventually be necessary in making specific policy recommendations to government agencies, which will then be responsible for the regulation and management of American lands and other parts of the natural world in the future.

Restoring the Public Lands

Robert Keiter is the Wallace Stegner professor of law at the University of Utah and director of its Center for Land, Resources, and the Environment. He is certainly no environmental radical; rather, many would describe him as a

---

* This is not a matter simply of intellectual—or theological—interest. American environmentalism has actively sought to implement its moral visions through public policy. Environmentalists, for example, have often regarded any pollution as a moral offense against nature and thus as something to be prohibited. This moralistic view was reflected in the Clean Water Act of 1972, which officially set a goal for the Environmental Protection Agency to eliminate all discharges of pollution into U.S. waters by 1985. Some people might regard this as a utopian goal—and thus as a metaphorical or symbolic statement, not meant to be taken seriously in practice. In 1993, however, three staff members of the Natural Resources Defense Council (NRDC) authored a stinging attack on the EPA's administration of the Clean Water Act, blaming it for a failure to move rapidly enough toward the 1985 zero-discharge target. As Robert Adler, Jessica Landman, and Diane Cameron declared, in the enactment of the Clean Water Act "'the use of any river, lake, stream or ocean as a waste treatment system' was deemed to be unacceptable." It might be temporarily necessary to authorize some degree of pollution under EPA "water quality standards . . . but only as a rest stop on the road to zero discharge." All releases of unnatural pollutants into the rivers, lakes, and other waters of the United States were to stop as soon as practically feasible. The nation, these NRDC staffers were saying, should be willing to make the economic and other sacrifices necessary to return its water bodies to a pristine condition, as untouched by human hands as any mountain wilderness area (a goal, admittedly, about as practically feasible as Barlow's plan to restore wild elephants to the American plains). See Robert W. Adler, Jessica C. Landman, and Diane M. Cameron, *The Clean Water Act 20 Years Later* (Washington, D.C.: Island Press, 1993), 137, 138.

responsible and practical advocate for environmental causes who seeks in his numerous writings to give due and fair consideration to every viewpoint. In a 2003 book, *Keeping Faith with Nature: Ecosystems, Democracy, and America's Public Lands,* Keiter reviews the policy and management history since the 1980s for the public lands, which encompass about 30 percent of the land area of the United States (the great majority in the West, where 50 percent of all land is public).[8] Keiter documents the shift during this time frame from the old utilitarian and conservationist philosophy of "multiple-use management" to a new environmental and preservationist philosophy of "ecosystem management."[9] At the heart of ecosystem management is the restoration of the public lands "to sustain vital natural systems" and thereby "to emulate nature, not to subdue or discount it." He observes that there has been a much "heralded advent of ecological management and restoration policies within all of the principal federal agencies responsible for the public lands."[10]

The new concern for ecosystem management and restoration, Keiter thinks, reflects the rise of "new social values." In the old days, the presence of wolves, forest fires, floods, and other "destructive" natural events was seen as a virtual symbol, as he says, of "evil incarnate."[11] One purpose of government land management was to abolish any such perceived threats to human welfare, seeking through the Smokey Bear campaign, for example, to eliminate forest fires completely from the national forests, or for many years in the early twentieth century to exterminate the wolves in Yellowstone National Park. In 1908, an advocate for the conservation movement wrote that the essence of the use of "the public land and the public water" in the West could be defined in terms of the various forms that their economic productivity took—that is, the "fuel, power, timber, navigable streams, irrigable plains, and valuable minerals" that they provided for the nation. These precious "resources" were being wantonly wasted under the existing private "policy of alienation and waste"; it would therefore be necessary to achieve their "utmost conservation" in the future through government scientific management to "assure a modicum of prosperity for our old age."[12]

This point of view was an extension of the tenets of economic religion, which had long sought maximum efficiency in achieving the most productive use of the nation's resources, including the public lands (and also requiring that "sustained yields" of outputs be maintained over the long run).[13] In economic religion, providing a steady supply of wood to build the homes needed by the American people was a more important use of the national forests than any biological goal such as species diversity. The efficient use of the public lands would help—along with many other similarly efficient government policies and actions in all areas—to move the nation along the road to a new earthly paradise. It was an era in which, as Harvard historian Jill

Lepore writes, it seemed self-evident that "technology was changing every-thing for the better, saving the Union, making us who we are. . . . Technology seemed to be driving, and even redeeming, the course of human events." For the whole world, salvation now meant that "every society, once on board a train called Progress, makes station stops at Literacy, Urbanization, Capital-ism, and Democracy before reaching the end of the line at [full] Prosperity"—the moment of the arrival at a new heaven on earth.[14]

But in the future under ecosystem management, as Keiter writes, there will be new goals with a new kind of "spiritual" purpose, in many cases seek-ing to reverse the sinful actions of the past that had been undertaken in the name of progress and economic efficiency. Public land managers must newly provide habitat and otherwise seek to sustain "creatures and natural phenomena that have no apparent economic value" (other than "existence value"—see chap. 3). A main policy goal will be "that degraded ecological conditions must be restored." There will be a new emphasis on "wildlife and wilderness protection [that] have been linked under the rubric of biodiver-sity conservation, . . . the next battleground in the politics of preservation." Using the existing public lands as a key biodiversity building block (similar in concept if less radical in application to Barlow's "rewilding" goals), fur-ther steps should be taken to restore "a network of large, interconnected re-serves consisting of protected core areas, carefully regulated adjacent lands, and strategic linkage corridors to ensure secure habitat and opportunities for genetic interchange."[15] In other words, the reigning gospel of public land management must shift from the economic religion of the past to the new messages of environmental religion.

Keiter is a sober and cautious analyst of public land management who, like most of his colleagues in the academic world, is wary of entering directly into the complexities and strong emotions of explicit religious controversy. Hence, while he is prepared to acknowledge directly the newly important "spiritual" elements in public land management—even this measured language would not have appeared in similar public land treatises as recently as two decades ago—he makes little effort to investigate the specific theological basis for these new spiritual dimensions (which might be multiple). Like most mainstream policy analysts, Keiter is not inclined to employ the language of "the creation" in his discussions of public land policy and history. If there is to be any role for creationist considerations, it will have to be implicit in his way of thinking about and seeking to change public land policy and management.

The philosopher of environmental ethics Paul Taylor states that "the idea of a natural ecosystem . . . means any collection of ecological interrelated living things that, without human intrusion or control, maintain their exis-tence as species-populations over time, each population occupying its own

environmental niche and each shaped by the evolutionary processes of genetic variation and natural selection."[16] Keiter describes the American West
before European settlement as meeting this standard of naturalness, consisting of "a largely untouched and still primitive landscape." Its "native ecosystems, having evolved over the millennia, were shaped primarily by natural
disturbance regimes" outside human influence. All this was changed from
the mid-nineteenth century onward, however, by the "persistent onslaught
of modern civilization," which has "eliminated entire species and disrupted
natural processes on a hitherto unprecedented scale." This pervasive human
impact, as Keiter thinks, must now be reversed: "Emerging ecological management concepts are designed to reverse this pattern and to restore extir-
pated species as well as historic disturbance regimes." On the public lands, as
"restoration initiatives expand in size and scope, they are . . . redefining the
human relationship with nature."[17]

Thus, even if he does not label it explicitly as such, Keiter does have a creation story in mind. In this version of history, the American West—where
the great majority of the public lands are located—was originally a natural
paradise that as recently as 150 years ago had not been significantly disrupted
by unnatural human influences. Indeed, it was much like the Garden of Eden
before Adam and Eve succumbed to the temptations of the pursuit of forbidden knowledge. But then fallen European human beings entered the picture,
increasingly possessing the God-like powers of modern science and economics, and began to commit many terrible evils. These first Europeans, and
those many others who followed after, were often motivated by greed, lust for
power, hatreds and jealousies, and the many other forms of sinfulness that
entered the world after the fall. Their capacity to do harm to the land, moreover, was now greatly magnified by the instruments of modern scientific and
economic "progress" available to them. The time has now come, however, for
human beings to acknowledge their past wayward (sinful) behavior and to
commit their lives to higher purposes—or as a believing Christian would say
(and many environmentalists implicitly are also saying), to newly recognize
God's authority and to obey His commands. When human beings have done
so, there will be at least the hope that an Edenic paradise can be restored to
the public lands of the American West.*

---

* It is not only the members of environmental groups who are attracted to the language of wild
nature protected and restored. Such themes continue to resonate powerfully with the American public and thus, not surprisingly, dominate much of the current American mainstream media portrayal
of environmental matters. In June 2008, for example, *Washington Post* environmental writer Juliet
Eilperin wrote on the paper's front page about proposed wilderness legislation by which Congress
would act to "keep [the] land untamed"—that is, little if at all touched by human hands. More than
a dozen "pristine areas" covering more than two million remaining acres "of the country's most

Keiter mostly writes dryly, in the language of mainstream law, economics, ecology, and other elements of the policy sciences. Toward the end of his long book, however, he lets his guard down somewhat to describe some features of the future Edenic existence he is hoping to recover. Unlike the visions of some more radical environmentalists, his is not a place where the human presence has been altogether eliminated. Keiter does not see humans as the "cancer of the earth." Short of a massive and unlikely depopulation of the planet, people will have to live somewhere and will have to have a job to make a living. But they should make greater sacrifices than in the past to ensure the preservation and the restoration of a genuinely natural order. There should also be some places, such as wilderness areas, where any permanent human presence should be excluded altogether:

> Given the pervasive nature of change in the modern world, it is clear that public lands will look quite different in a few short decades. If we can merge the new ecosystem management and devolution strategies, we may actually see a more diverse landscape and harmonious populace. Picture the possibilities: Substantial numbers of grizzly bears and wolves roam well beyond the isolated enclaves they now inhabit. . . . The logging and ranching industries continue to operate on the public domain, but in a more restrained and sustainable manner. Recreation and tourism continue to flourish, but without any new legal entitlements; the worst excesses of industrial-scale recreation have been curbed. . . . Ecological preservation has taken hold with interconnected nature reserves stretching across the map, designed to both sustain our biological heritage and afford compatible economic opportunities to nearby communities. New jobs are more about restoring the landscape than stripping it bare. . . . Operating under a new set of ecologically sensitive statutory priorities, the responsible agencies are actively coordinating their planning activities. . . . Private landowners have begun to assume biodiversity conservation responsibilities. . . . By consensus, a biodiversity conservation ethic prevails on the public lands and a new civility has taken hold within the adjacent communities.[18]

---

unspoiled land" would be set aside in this protected category. One area would be designated the "Wild Sky Wilderness." By this means, Congress would be acting "to preserve them as they are, as they have been for generations, and preserve them for future generations." The remaining parts of God's creation, as Eilperin was effectively saying to her readers, must not be lost to the short-run motives of private profit. Some of the lands were also "ecologically critical," representing parts of "the most vulnerable areas" in the federal land domain. See Juliet Eilperin, "Congress Pushes to Keep Land Untamed: Bills Could Add Millions of Acres of Wilderness," *Washington Post*, June 16, 2008, A1.

Although Keiter recognizes full well that this happy vision of the future may be seen by some people as "utopian" (his term), he still has faith. He is in fact optimistic that the West and the management of the public lands are already moving steadily along "the road to a more enlightened policy regime."[19] Yet, even while offering this grand restoration vision for the public lands, Keiter is sophisticated enough to recognize that there are a number of complex and even philosophically (or theologically, although Keiter himself would probably not use this word) confusing policy issues to be addressed.

Indeed, he comments that "translating ecological restoration concepts into comprehensive policy prescriptions for the public domain raises several vexing and divisive issues." There is, for example, the issue that concerned Barlow: the increasing awareness of the past substantial "ecological impacts of Native Americans, who most environmental historians [now] agree played a considerable role in shaping the landscape the early [European] settlers encountered."[20] The nineteenth-century explorer of the West John Wesley Powell in fact found that "Native Americans ignited fires regularly [which] destroyed larger or smaller districts of timber . . . and this destruction is on a scale so vast that the amount taken from the lands for industrial purposes sinks by comparison into insignificance."[21] Native American burning of grasses and other rangeland vegetation was also widespread.[22]

One option, as noted above, would be to set a benchmark for restoration of "nature" that precedes the arrival of Native Americans. As a practical guide for public policy and management, however, this is virtually hopeless. For one thing, the knowledge of the workings of natural systems prior to the arrival of Native Americans—at a minimum more than ten thousand years ago—would be altogether inadequate. Moreover, those ecological systems were adapted to climatic and other natural conditions that do not exist today. Yet, like most environmentalists, Keiter is strongly committed to the restoration of the natural world to a state when it (or its evolution) had been little, if at all, altered by human actions.

How might this be possible? It would clearly be racist and obnoxious to suggest that Native Americans do not count as members of the human race. Keiter is left to suggest somewhat lamely that the issue perhaps can simply be set aside because Native American impacts, while substantial, still pale before the impacts following the arrival of European civilization. If the truth is otherwise, as many researchers are increasingly concluding, he is left with theological conundrums that he simply cannot resolve.[23] Most fellow environmentalists have dealt with the issue by ignoring it altogether (perhaps recognizing implicitly that no solution is forthcoming).

There are other basic tensions in Keiter's restoration agenda. In the American West, European settlement did not arrive until the second half of the nineteenth century. Hence, ecological restoration there typically aims to re-cover natural conditions of 100 to 150 years ago. Identifying those conditions with the precision necessary to implement a real-world restoration agenda is often difficult and sometimes impossible. The Forest Service has been search-ing actively for old photographs of forests prior to 1900, but such evidence inevitably is in short supply. Things become even more difficult in the eastern United States and other areas where European settlement arrived several hun-dred years earlier (to say nothing of Europe itself).

Let us nevertheless say for the purposes of discussion that it would be pos-sible to restore precisely pre-European conditions. Assume further, for ex-ample, that Europeans arrived in an area two hundred years ago and that the original natural conditions of that time have in fact now been restored. This does not mean, however, that the next two hundred years of evolutionary change will corresponded closely to what might have happened in the past two hundred (even assuming "natural" conditions over that period). Many broader climatic and other factors (drought, for example) can affect the evolu-tionary dynamic—often occurring at a rapid pace—of a particular ecosystem. These factors will differ significantly in the next two hundred (or however many) years from the previous two hundred (or however many) years, even if both processes had been "natural." In short, even if some original past condi-tion could be exactly restored today, the subsequent path of ecological evolu-tion from today forward would no longer correspond to anything that would have "naturally" occurred before. If the future can therefore never actually re-create the past—can never be natural in the sense of an evolutionary result outside any past human influence (such as a two-hundred-year delay while natural evolution effectively was suspended)—then what is the real point of going to such expensive restoration efforts? It is still a human-controlled and -managed result. Neither Keiter nor other environmentalists have an answer.

Yet another vexing issue is that it will often be necessary to take heroic human actions today to restore, however accurately or inaccurately, past natural ecological conditions. Keiter criticizes the old utilitarian conserva-tion policies on the grounds that "nature manipulation was the province of the resource disciplines. It was the agriculture, range, forestry, hydrology, and wildlife scientists who were energetically engineering nature to increase crop, forage, timber, water, and big game productivity." He has to concede, however, that "scientists now regularly manipulate ecosystems to study dis-turbance processes." By applying the knowledge gained, "they generally agree that ecological systems can be re-created" through purposeful human activity. Indeed, it is evident that "restoration frequently entails active management 'to accelerate recovery of degraded ecosystems by complementing or reinforcing natural processes.'"[24] A large restored ecosystem, in short, may be no less an engineered human artifact, a product of the scientific management of nature, than the past damming of a great river.

In some cases, such as the handling of U.S. condor populations, all the birds had to be trapped and then released, and they are still actively monitored and managed. It is difficult to say in what sense, if any, this population might still be described as "wild." Perhaps it is more accurate to consider the circumstances of American condors as a special kind of large outdoor "zoo." Similarly, as Keiter notes, prescribed burning, mechanical removal of trees, and other active human engineering will be necessary to restore many forests in the American West to a pre-European condition. In some cases, the degree of degradation of an existing forest ecosystem is already so severe that an act of restoration will be tantamount to creating a brand new ecology as a replica of the old one. Can one say that this newly engineered human reproduction of a past state of nature is in any meaningful sense "natural"?

Keiter is scrupulously fair in raising all these issues.[25] Frequently, however, he has no good answers, even as he strongly advocates large expenditures of public funds and major redirections of government land policies based on such restoration goals and values. It is as though his desire to "restore" nature is so powerful that he cannot abide the thought that in reality it may be impossible. In practice, the actual results of Keiter's policy agenda are likely to be closer to a Disneyland fantasy of nature restored. To be sure, it is an attractive fantasy and, like other Disney efforts, may well be popular with the American public. It might even be defended in a strictly utilitarian way, as offering net benefits for the American public in the same way that the making and watching of a good movie, whether fictional or not, increases overall social welfare. As long as large numbers of Americans believe that the public lands are being restored, and many of them visit these lands thinking that they are seeing an "undisturbed" or "untamed" natural landscape, large national welfare gains (economic benefits) may in principle be realized, independent of any actual degree of restoration successes—or even any good understanding of what restoration to eliminate human influences would mean.

If one applies a nonutilitarian standard, however—that the restoration should in fact be an actual or "true" restoration—the prospects are bleak. Indeed, the two-hundred-year historical record of public land management since the founding of the nation is filled with many such failed policies and management plans. In many cases there was wide confusion at the time as to the actual purposes of public land management and the best manner of pursuing them. Politicians in Washington and in the West played to popular misconceptions and emotions, rather than seeking a sounder base of knowledge and a deeper understanding of both the practical realities of land management and the workings of natural systems.[26] The current goal to restore the public lands may simply be the latest episode in a long history of public land policy and management failure.[27]

Spotted Owls and Barred Owls

There is no more visible project for ecological restoration on the public lands than the federal effort to protect and revive populations of the northern spotted owl—and the "old growth" (or "ancient" in environmental writings) forests in which spotted owls live. Indeed, in the late 1980s and early 1990s the political and legal struggle over the fate of the spotted owl set the stage for the emergence of ecosystem management as the guiding philosophy of public land management. Partly based on court interpretations of the federal Endangered Species Act, timber harvesting was drastically reduced on public lands in Oregon, Washington, and northern California to set aside large areas for spotted owl habitat. Biodiversity objectives of species preservation for the first time had trumped a high-value economic use of the public lands across an entire region of the United States.

It is thus ironic that the spotted owl has now become a prominent symbol of the tensions, confusions, and even contradictions endemic to environmental religion. Despite all the heroic federal and other government efforts of the past twenty years, as reported in 2008 in the *High Country News* (the unofficial environmental journal for the mountain West), the spotted owl "is now in a steep, unanticipated tailspin." There was no sure scientific consensus, but "one of the most likely contributors to the bird's decline is a newcomer to the Pacific Northwest. The barred owl, which has been moving in from the East, is bigger than the spotted owl and more aggressive. And it has been thriving as the spotted owl falters." In terms of a Darwinian struggle, although similar in many respects, the barred owl had significant advantages. "Compared to spotted owls, barred owls . . . are as much as 15 percent bigger. Their young emerge earlier, and there are more of them"—broods that averaged three barred-owl young, versus one or two for spotted owls. Also, "barred owls are not picky about what they eat, picking up insects, frogs, shrews, and moles," while "the spotted owl is much more dependent on rodents" alone.[28]

Historically common in the East, until seventy-five years ago there were no reports of barred owls in the Pacific Northwest. Then, "in British Columbia, signs [of barred owls] had appeared in the 1940s" and in the 1970s in Oregon and Washington. Even as the protections for the spotted owl were being set in place in the late 1980s and early 1990s, there were emerging reports of "giant, ghostly owls [that] . . . had yellow-green beaks like spotted owls and tails like barred owls." They were, in fact, "hybrids," usually the product of a male spotted owl mating with a female barred owl (even though separate species, they are capable of jointly producing sterile offspring). In one Oregon forest, even though barred owls were seldom seen as recently as ten years ago, in 2008 they outnumbered spotted owls by three to two. Despite the absence of definitive scientific proof, as one northern California biologist states, "biologists in the field know without a doubt that the barred owls are having an effect on spotted owls." Indeed, he knew of no cases in which "a spotted owl has managed to retain its territory when a barred owl shows up."[29]

Given the emblematic status of the spotted owl as the poster child of the Endangered Species Act, all this was disconcerting if not embarrassing for the Act's defenders. A bitter political war had raged for years across the Pacific Northwest, and many small rural economies had been thrown into turmoil under the auspices of the Endangered Species Act, perhaps now to no avail. Darwinian laws were more powerful than human hopes and expectations. The protections of the Endangered Species Act in their own way were another attempt by human beings to play God, but the God in heaven (or "nature") was not cooperating. Perhaps again He had not been pleased, despite the novel form of this particular challenge to his authority, which now claimed to scientifically "restore" rather than "use" God's own creation.

Perhaps because of the emblematic importance of the spotted owl crusade, the owl's advocates were not prepared to give up. They suggested that perhaps the barred owl was really a nonnative or exotic species to the Pacific Northwest. The barred owl had in fact probably moved from its historic habitats in the East by travelling through forests that had been significantly altered by past human actions—"perhaps making their way through forests that grew as humans suppressed fire, perhaps taking advantage of higher summer temperatures in altered habitat, perhaps using trees along [humanly altered] creeks and rivers as pathways across the Plains."[30] But it was impossible to really say with scientific certainty whether the arrival of the barred owl in the Pacific Northwest was "natural" or "unnatural" (or even precisely what this distinction might mean). Perhaps the new competitive success of the barred owl was just another evolutionary episode following after many millions of other such Darwinian events over a billion years of natural evolution of the earth's plant and animal species.

In any case, the possibility of the wide killing of barred owls to save the spotted owl is now being actively considered. In 2007 a new federal draft recovery plan for the spotted owl included an appendix on a "Barred Owl Removal Strategy." According to another proposal, "One person, well-versed in barred owl strategies, could shoot two to four pair a night. . . . Getting adults in the spring before they breed would keep populations low enough to give the spotted owl a chance." The government is already moving to keep barred owls from moving further south in national forests of California as part of an Endangered Species Act strategy to protect the genetically different Mexican spotted owl. If any barred owls show up in these more southerly national forests, the policy now is that they should all be killed as soon as possible. Further north in Oregon and Washington, however, the goal might be to manage them to sustain surviving populations of both northern spotted owls and barred owls. A complicating factor here is that this action would probably induce new evolutionary changes in spotted owls—"the resulting bird would probably be smaller, to exploit niches unavailable to the larger barred owl. In south-central Mexico, the diminutive Mexican spotted owl coexists with a subspecies of barred owl that is larger than those moving in to the north."[31]

As discussed above, the basic objectives of ecosystem management and restoration of the public lands are that wild nature should be kept "untouched by human hand" to the maximum extent possible and, when nature has already been altered by human influences, should be restored to an unaltered condition to the extent practically feasible. As is now being contemplated, however, the Darwinian workings of recent possibly "natural" forces might actually result in the extinction of the northern spotted owl. If that threat exists, it is also being suggested that perhaps human beings must now actively manage the forests to protect the original (or at least pre-European) status of "the creation"—a natural condition that included large numbers of spotted owls and no barred owls in the Pacific Northwest. As the conservation director for the Audubon Society of Portland states, and however uncomfortable the choice, it may be necessary to kill barred owls because, if they are not removed, "you may be making a decision to allow another species to go extinct"—for him an even more morally offensive outcome.[32]

If the choice is between protecting the original creation (however this is understood) and allowing new evolutionary forces to do their thing, the former objective seemingly must prevail. Once again, secular environmental creationism implicitly comes close to its Christian fundamentalist cousin. If the goal is to protect "the creation," and the creation has not been altered from the original six days in Genesis, then Darwin be damned. And it is not only the northern and the Mexican spotted owls: "Natural" sea lions and Caspian terns have been removed from the mouth of the Columbia River to protect endangered salmon runs. In the Channel Islands off California, growing numbers of federally protected golden eagles threatened the survival of an endangered subspecies of the gray fox. In response, a 2003 article in *Science* proposed "lethal removal" as a means of "removing protected populations [of eagles] to save [other] endangered species." The National Park Service backed off from directly killing the golden eagles but did succeed (with the use of helicopters) in capturing and removing them (at very high public expense). As Kim Todd

reports, "It's only recently that agencies have begun trying to control one animal for the sake of another that is more endangered. But it's happening now
with increasing frequency."[33]

The result is a contradiction of the goal to maintain a true "natural" condition. Nature is being actively managed in pursuit of human theological understandings, however confused they sometimes are. The spotted owl habitat of
the Pacific Northwest is on the verge of becoming a vast permanent zoological
garden. The spotted owls will have to be protected from all potential threats,
"natural" and "unnatural" alike. The inherent contradictions of environmental religion at this point become glaring. It is simply not logically possible to
actively manage something to achieve the goal of an unmanaged result. And
such theological confusion inevitably will lead the federal natural resource
agencies to a corresponding policy confusion—to be sure, a typical outcome
in practice over the two hundred years of public land history.[34]

Wolves and Coyotes

Yet another example of the theological complexities of trying to restore elements of "nature" is found in the emergence of wolf-coyote "hybrids" in the
eastern United States. In the East, wolf populations were generally decimated
in the nineteenth and twentieth centuries, although a few wolves survived.
Coyotes, which were more able to coexist with humans, moved into the ecological niches formerly occupied by wolves. They then interbred with the
small number of remaining wolves, producing a new animal creature that was
on average twenty pounds heavier than a typical coyote and also had a reddish
shaggy coat, rather than the typical coyote short gray-brown fur. These larger
hybrid "wolf-coyotes" were capable of hunting deer, unlike ordinary coyotes,
and spread in significant numbers (they were also capable, unlike many hybrids of two species, of reproducing). As Douglas Fox reports, "These curious
coyotes amaze outsiders, and they have prompted a quiet debate [among conservation biologists] about their true identity."[35]

They also pose a major obstacle to any attempted restoration of wild wolf
populations in the East. If wolves are reintroduced now, many would soon mate
with the new hybrids. In one case, the federal government is trying to protect
a uniquely eastern species, the red wolf. Most of the red wolves in the wild
had already mated with coyotes, but the federal government rounded up four
hundred wild red wolves and somehow determined that fourteen of them were
genetically "pure" red wolf. It then captive bred these fourteen wolves while
wildlife managers also often sought to exterminate the "nonpure" red wolves
remaining in the wild (a small-scale animal kingdom "holocaust," as one might

call it, also based on theories of genetic purification). As Fox reports, "To avoid hybridization with coyotes, wildlife managers then reintroduced the [captive-bred] pure red wolf population on a single peninsula along the North Carolina coast in the late 1980s, and have since enforced a coyote-free buffer zone along the trunk of the peninsula." Seeking to protect and restore genetic purity, "they monitor canids in the buffer zone by genetically testing pups and analyzing fecal DNA. Coyotes and coyote-red wolf hybrids are sterilized or removed." As Fox notes the irony in this effort to restore "natural" red wolf populations, "The growth of healthy [red] wolf packs with a stable social fabric may eventually reduce the tendency of wolves to settle for coyote mates, but for now the task falls to humans."[36]

The theological dilemma of wolf restoration is thus the following. In the eastern United States, the human presence has dramatically altered the "natural" conditions of forests and other lands almost everywhere. Unless wolves are specifically protected from human depredations, the real Darwinian survivors are coyotes and wolf-coyote hybrids. The spread of such populations represented a natural evolution in the Darwinian sense—coyotes and wolf-coyotes proved better adapted to the eastern environmental circumstances of the nineteenth and twentieth centuries (circumstances that included large numbers of farmers and many humans with guns). Eastern wolves, by contrast, have been evolutionary failures since the early nineteenth century. If "natural" is understood in a strict Darwinian sense, coyotes and coyote-wolf hybrids are the evolutionary winners, so they are the "natural" outcome. If, however, "natural" is understood as an unchanging state of nature since the "the creation," interpreted for practical purposes to be the eastern state of nature that preceded European settlement, then coyotes and coyote-wolf hybrids are "unnatural," and it is the red wolf and other historical populations of eastern wolves that are the "natural" species. In the real world of government policy making, the U.S. Fish and Wildlife Service has opted for the creationist understanding of "natural," rejecting the Darwinian understanding. In this respect, the Fish and Wildlife Service has been faithful to the tenets of the pervasive environmental creationism underlying so much of U.S. restoration and other environmental policy making.

Faking Nature

Philosophers often take particular pleasure in sharpening the edges of debate, as has been the case with respect to the goal of restoring wild nature. The Australian philosopher Robert Elliot suggested in a 1982 article that a restoration of wild nature might simply be an act of "faking nature." It might thus have no greater value, relative to the original, than a fake work of art.[37] A genuine Rembrandt would typically be worth many millions of dollars, but no one, certainly, would compare it in value to a copy. Even if a heroic effort was made to reproduce the original Rembrandt in every detail and very few people could tell the difference, the original would still be worth far more, monetarily and artistically.

Elliot was drawn into this discussion as a rebuttal to arguments being made by mining companies and others proposing to develop natural sites intensively. The mining companies acknowledged that they might erase the natural features but promised later to restore them fully and accurately. They would be temporary occupants and, following their departure (probably in a few decades), they were claiming that everything would be put back as it otherwise would have been in their absence. Elliot's rebuttal was that, even if one assumed for the purposes of discussion the achievement of a perfect ecological restoration in every natural detail, a sin would still have been be committed against nature—and the company therefore should be denied access to the site for mining. The restored ecology would be a "fake" form of nature in the same manner and with the same limited value as a new reproduction of an original work of art (no matter how well executed).

If taken seriously, however, Elliot's argument would also pose a threat to the restoration agenda of Keiter and many other environmentalists. If restoration efforts could only succeed in producing a fake version of nature, why go to great expense and otherwise make heroic efforts to restore many public land and other sites? Elliot attempted to address this and other criticisms in a 1997 book, *Faking Nature*.[38] By this time he had realized that his argument might have much broader applicability than just preventing the evils of mining. He therefore now took pains to state that he approved of environmental restoration in cases where the damage had already been done (unlike a prospective mine). Even in such cases, however, it was necessary to recognize that restoration was a palliative measure; it would never be possible to achieve an outcome fully identical to the original natural condition.

Another environmental philosopher, Eric Katz, stated the case even more boldly, declaring that the "human restoration of nature," even in cases where the environment had already been degraded, amounted to a "big lie."[39] Although Katz did support restoration in such circumstances, he was saying that no one should have any illusions about the actual ability to reverse the human misdeeds of the past. Elliot and Katz, not surprisingly, encountered a barrage of criticism. Even if they did in the end actively encourage the restoration of existing degraded landscapes, their arguments suggested that less urgency and fewer resources might be attached to restoration efforts. The world has many practical needs and there are many other important values—lifting many of the world's poorest people out of their suffering condition, for one—that compete with restoration objectives. Perhaps much less should be spent on restoring degraded landscapes if the results could only be a fake version of nature? Having adopted ecosystem management in the 1990s as a new guiding philosophy, these arguments raised the possibility that the U.S. Forest Service, the BLM, and other government agencies might be engaged in a large taxpayer deception, involving a considerable misallocation of American taxpayers' money.

Elliot's position depends crucially on his view that the actual "origin is important as an integral part of the evaluation process" in considering an object in nature. For Elliot, if the origin of an object (such as the evolutionary path that produced it) is "natural," the object will be much more valuable than an otherwise identical outcome in the world that has arrived by an "unnatural" route. Or, as he says, the origin "is important because our beliefs about it determine the evaluations we make. It is also important in that the discovery that something has an origin quite different from the one we initially believe it to have can literally alter the way we perceive that thing."[40] As Elliot reminds us, this is certainly true for a piece of art that I might admire; if I genuinely think that it is an original work of art but then discover later that it is a replica or forgery, my perception and valuation will be drastically altered.

But why should this be so for nature? On aesthetic grounds alone, and still assuming for purposes of discussion a perfect restoration, the natural object being perceived will be identical in either case. Applying strictly scientific criteria, it is difficult to see why a different origin of two otherwise identical objects in nature makes a great deal of difference. Moreover, Elliot seems to assume that any unnatural origins will be revealed to the world, but that does not have to be the case. The restorers of the public lands, for example, might simply allow the public to believe that restored ecosystems have always been present. Not knowing otherwise, much of the public would react as though it is in the presence of an unaltered original version of nature—a place never touched by human hands, as wilderness areas are often advertised.

In addition, almost any restoration will involve significant natural elements itself. The act of restoration does not simply set the final restored ecosystem in place as an accomplished fact—and without any reliance on natural evolutionary processes within an ecosystem. Rather, the restoration procedure will typically consist of doing some initial ecosystem engineering to set the initial conditions in place and then allow an actual natural ecological evolution to proceed from there toward the desired goal. By the time the restoration is completed, there may have been a substantial natural process of evolutionary change that has occurred within the ecosystem.

Elliot's fixation on the origin of an outcome in nature might thus be regarded as a personal idiosyncrasy; because it is widely shared, however, it would seem that some other factor must be at work. Indeed, there is another possible and more persuasive basis for his argument. This is suggested by the many analogies he draws with art and with the limited value of a replica of an original artwork. As examined in previous chapters, there is a powerful sense in which nature may also be seen as a work of art. Indeed, a main tenet of Christian theology has long been that nature is the handiwork, or the artwork, of God. As a person might today go to an art museum for educational purposes as well as aesthetic enjoyments, good Christians for centuries have been taught to read the "Book of Nature" to learn about the mind of God.

Indeed, the analogy with art will hold here with particular force. In this case, the artist is not just another human being but God himself. As compared with encountering a state of nature literally created by God, it will be a much less powerful and a much inferior experience encountering even an identical reproduction of such a state of nature—an ecological condition not actually created by God at the beginning but rather a mere human replica engineered much more recently. As the greatest artist of all, any replicas of God's works, even those devised by the cleverest of current restoration engineers, will have a limited value, just as a replica of the Rembrandt would not be worth much.

Evoking the language of Christian theology, and in support of this interpretation, Elliot speaks frequently about the great importance of "original nature." At one point, for example, he states that "it is . . . clear that the judgement that faked nature has less value than original nature has a rational and plausible basis." At another point he alludes to the first book of the Bible, saying that the appreciation of a natural area depends crucially on "the manner of an area's genesis."[41] This and previous chapters have shown that creationist thinking is pervasive in the way that many Americans view the natural world, having a much wider scope than is typically recognized. Andrew Curry reported in 2009 in *Science* magazine that "surveys consistently show that less than half of Americans accept the theory of evolution."[42] But the influence of creationist thinking extends more broadly because there are many secular creationists as well—true believers in secular understandings of an environmental original nature.

It seems that Elliot is a follower in this ostensibly non-believing and thus only implicit side of environmental creationism. Indeed, such secular creationists often deny that there are any deep religious roots to their thinking and may well be offended by the suggestion that they have anything significantly in common with Christian creationists. Elliot seems mostly to think this way, although at one point he concedes that "there may even be some connection with the idea of blasphemy" in the strong sense of disgust that fake nature evokes in him. But then he hastens to add that, even if there is something to be said for the metaphor of blasphemy, this thought would have to be "somehow secularized" for him to take it seriously as a matter for his rigorous philosophical analysis.[43]

In a few places, nevertheless, Elliot lets his guard down to the extent of introducing a surprisingly Christian moral vocabulary, saying that the "destruction of natural value motivated by greed" may be worse than precisely the same degree of destruction when there is some other, more acceptable motive. Elliot is reminding us that, after the fall in the Garden, the sin of greed (along with many others) was set loose in the world, a main source of the resulting human corruption of the original natural state at the creation. At another point, Elliot also acknowledges a "duty of restitution."[44] It would seem that efforts to restore already degraded landscapes may also serve as compensation for the past sins of human beings, another strong ethical imperative that would be difficult to justify in any strictly secular statement of Elliot's thinking.

Admittedly, Elliot does occasionally speak vaguely of a creation. At one point, commenting on the powerful responses evoked in the presence of a wilderness or other truly natural place, he says that such responses are derived from the "knowledge of the particular circumstances and determinants of the creation of a natural area." It is "knowledge of this kind" of the original manner of creation that "is capable of transforming a hitherto uninteresting landscape into one that is compelling." It is particularly important that we can be confident in encountering a natural area that we really know that its origins reach "back into the past prior to the development of human cultures and technologies"—or as one might reinterpret this, that we are actually encountering the creation as God made it at the beginning, and not a "fake" replica.[45] All this of course must be left unsaid in any explicit way. Indeed, if such creationist themes were put to Elliot directly as the most logical explanation of his own powerful spiritual feelings in the presence of "wild" nature, and if Elliot did not simply reject the argument, he would be confronted by a probably painful choice—accept the creationism implicit in his own thinking, or disavow his own past criticisms of "fake" nature.

Without the explicit religious vocabulary, Elliot thus is raising in a disguised form the following important theological questions: When elements of God's original creation are found today on earth (assuming that there are any still to be found), then when, if ever, is it permissible to destroy them by human action? If an act of destruction of some part of the original creation is permitted, will it ever be possible thereafter to restore this part of the creation to its former religious significance? For parts of the creation that have already been degraded and no longer represent the original condition at the creation, is it possible to restore these areas to their original natural state in any meaningful and religiously important way? That is, should human beings seek to replicate the past actions of God—or as it might seem to many, should human beings seek today to "play God" by "re-creating the creation," restoring the natural world according to God's original design?

Does "Nature" Exist?

When environmentalists are asked to specify the goal of restoration, the usual declared objective is to restore "nature." As suggested above, however, the term "nature" may carry as much baggage and be subject to as many interpretations—some of them in virtual direct contradiction to one another—as any word in the English language.[46] In *What Is Nature?* the philosopher Kate Soper formally addressed some of these matters. As Soper comments, "Nature carries an immensely complex and contradictory symbolic load; it is the subject of very contrary ideologies; and it has been represented in an enormous variety of differing ways." Soper recognizes that, in one of the most important recent uses, the idea of "nature" has come "to occupy a central place on the political agenda as a result of ecological crisis, where it figures as a general concept through which we are asked to re-think our current use of resources, our relations to other forms of life, and our place within, and responsibilities towards the eco-system."[47] In other words, "nature" provides a lens for framing the evolving environmental understanding of the proper place of human beings in the world.*

Unlike many of the authors reviewed in this book, Soper is not an environmentalist. Indeed, she has many critical things to say, often finding environmental thinking to be confused or even outright contradictory. As she says, "The ecology movement, when viewed as a whole, draws its force from a range of arguments whose ethical underpinnings are really quite divergent and difficult to reconcile."[48] Soper is concerned, moreover, that ideas of the "natural" have been used in the past for many ideological and political purposes, some of which she finds objectionable. The sexual orientation of homosexuals has been condemned as "unnatural"; women have been discriminated against historically and excluded from public life as a matter of assigning them a supposed "natural" place in society; and in recent years the use of stem cells

---

* The great normative power that can be assigned to the term "natural" (and "unnatural") is illustrated by the 2007 example of Knut, a baby polar bear born in the Zoo Berlin but rejected by its mother. When zookeepers adopted the baby bear, feeding and otherwise caring for it in place of the mother, some critics instead called for putting the baby polar bear to death—"rather than be raised 'unnaturally.'" In escaping this fate, however, Knut has since instead become much loved and world famous as a symbol of the "unnatural" threat to polar bears posed by global warming of the Arctic regions. See Anne Applebaum, "A Global Warm and Fuzzy Escape," *Washington Post*, April 10, 2007.

for medical research has been rejected as an "unnatural" violation of the human potential that comes into existence from the moment an embryonic cell comes into the world.

Many of the moral teachings of the Roman Catholic Church are grounded in a conformance—or lack of such—to an assumed "natural" essence of things. In his 1995 encyclical on "The Gospel of Life," Pope John Paul II thus justified the Catholic position on birth control as limiting individuals to use of "natural methods of regulating fertility." Rejection of euthanasia was a matter of opposing anything that was not a "natural death." Abortion was condemned as the violation of "an innocent person's natural right to life."[49] In encouraging the Catholic faithful to continue to fight against contrary laws, even when they have been legally enacted by democratic legislatures, Pope John Paul II invoked the words of Saint Thomas Aquinas: "Every law made by man can be called a law insofar as it derives from the natural law. But if it is somehow opposed to natural law, then it is not really a law but a corruption of the law"—and therefore should be opposed by the Roman Catholic Church, no matter how large the popular majority that might be in favor of it.[50]

Environmental religion thus is hardly alone in making extensive use of the language of the "natural" to define and justify its deepest moral stances. Outside environmental and Catholic circles (this being one of the few areas where environmentalism has more in common religiously with Catholicism, compared with Protestantism), however, there is often greater skepticism. Soper thus says of the meaning of "nature" in such contemporary discourse that "postmodernist cultural theory and criticism looks with suspicion on any appeal to the idea [of a single authentic nature] as an attempt to 'eternize' what in reality is merely conventional, and has invited us to view the order of nature as entirely linguistically constructed." She comments ironically that "the only thing that is not 'natural' is nature herself."[51]

Consider, for example, some alternative ways of perceiving the evolutionary state of the tiger as a species today.* In India and elsewhere, tigers have

---

* Another good example is found in the world of sport. Baseball has been consumed by controversy relating to the alleged past use of steroids by such stars as Barry Bonds, Roger Clemens, Rafael Palmeiro, Alex Rodriguez, and other presumed—at least before their steroid use came to light—great heroes of the sport. But baseball players and other athletes routinely draw on pain killers, anti-inflammatories, and indeed a whole host of acceptable drugs. So what is the problem with steroids? For reasons that are less than philosophically clear, and much like human interference with the "natural" order in environmental matters, steroids have somehow been deemed "unnatural." As *Washington Post* sportswriter Tom Boswell anguished, Barry Bonds had "cheated" himself, the fans, and the sport of baseball in using steroids to "unnaturally" boost his athletic performance, illegitimately helping him to surpass Hank Aaron's career home runs record. The *Economist* magazine, however, notes that a Finnish cross-country skier and double Olympic gold medalist, Eero Mäntyranta, benefits greatly from a mutation that significantly "stimulates the production of red blood cells. A synthetic version

declined to a few thousand in the wild, and their future status is in doubt. As a species, however, tigers are not in danger. There are now more total tigers in the United States than in the wild, kept in zoos and in large numbers as private pets and in other captive domestic circumstances. It turns out that the tiger has an important evolutionary survival advantage for the current stage of natural history: tigers do unusually well and, unlike many other wild animal species, breed easily in captivity. Given their exotic quality, and as long as government laws do not prohibit their ownership, there will be a substantial (and probably growing) demand for the foreseeable future for tigers as private pets. In China, again assuming that laws do not prohibit it, tigers could be farm bred and raised, supplying the large Chinese demand for tiger parts. All these many domesticated tigers may be as genetically diverse as those now in the wild, especially if the owners—as they would have good practical reasons to do—take care to maintain an active program of crossbreeding.

Nobody planned this new evolutionary survival mechanism for tigers. Like most other variations in nature, it is a Darwinian accident. Tigers thus may "naturally" survive well in a domesticated status, even as they could well go extinct in wild "nature." Most environmentalists, of course, would find this outcome disturbing, if not abhorrent—a grave moral offense against "nature." Some might even suggest that it would be better to have no tigers at all, as compared with a substantial population of domestic tigers privately and thus "unnaturally" owned as pets and farmed animals. (Even while kept in captivity, these tigers would of course still be wild in the sense that they would be perfectly capable of killing their owners if given the chance.)

Many environmentalists have such a strong visceral antagonism to the idea of tiger domestication and other such "unnatural" acts that they may have never stopped to ponder the socially constructed—really religiously

of it is the (banned) drug of choice for endurance athletes." But Mäntyranta was allowed to compete "because his advantage was held to be a 'natural' gift" while his competitors were denied the same—"unnatural" in their case—advantage. One might equally have argued that Mäntyranta should have been banned because he was a "genetic freak" with whom "normal" human beings had no fair chance of competing (as some alleged "women" have been banned from female sports events because they had too many male features). Such issues, as the *Economist* notes, bring to the fore "the question of what is natural?" which is "no less vexed than of what is fair" in sports. "What is natural about electric muscle stimulants," which are allowed? In the end, as environmentalism may have to abandon the "natural"/"unnatural" distinction, the *Economist* finds that the only logically coherent stance may be to ban drugs that can be shown to be literally dangerous to the health of competitors (itself a less than clear standard) and to emphasize instead full disclosure. Although this would result in much wider freedom to use drugs of their choice, "athletes should disclose all the pills they take, just as they register the other forms of equipment they use, so that others can catch up." Under this new approach, "the sole concern when it comes to [allowable use of an] enhancing athletic performance [drug] should be: is it safe for the athletes" and not whether it is a "natural" or "unnatural" method of enhancing sports performance. See "Fairly Safe," *Economist*, August 2, 2008, 16.

constructed—basis for their reactions. Judged by strictly Darwinist scientific criteria, any process of ecological evolution will be "natural," just as the operation of gravity according to Newtonian laws must always be a "natural" force in the universe. In Darwinist terms, there can never be an "unnatural" evolutionary moment—a time when the laws of evolution are somehow suspended or inoperable. It is true that human actions can redirect or alter the evolutionary course in nature, just as engineers can manipulate gravity and other laws of physics to achieve planned physical objectives in the world (sending human beings to the moon, for example). The fact of the human manipulation of the outcome does not mean, however, that the workings of either Newtonian gravity or Darwinist evolution then become any more or less "natural."

Hence, judging one course of evolution versus another—as in the case of tigers—requires the imposition of ethical views outside any strictly scientific framework of understanding the natural world. The application of the terms "natural" and "unnatural" really signifies "ethical" and "unethical," or "good" and "evil," in a Western civilization where a Christian moral framework long dominated all thought. In this respect, as a trained philosopher, Soper finds many problems with environmental ethical reasoning. Environmentalists commonly say, for example, that the human species must abandon its false—unethical—"anthropocentric" way of thinking and learn instead to be "a part of nature." As Soper notes, however, this is an impossibility because "it is inevitable [that] our attitudes to nature will be 'anthropocentric' in certain respects since there is no way of conceiving our relations to it other than through the mediation of [human] ideas about ourselves. To suggest that it could be otherwise is to be insensitive to those ways in which the rest of nature is different, and should be respected as being so."[52] Indeed, the real need is just the opposite; the assertion of a responsible environmental ethic will depend on a clear anthropocentric separation of human beings from nature. As Soper spells all this out:

> I have consistently argued that there can be no ecological prescription that does not presuppose a demarcation between humanity and nature. Unless human beings are differentiated from other organic and inorganic forms of being, they can be made no more liable for the effects of their occupancy of the ecosystem than can any other species, and it would make no more sense to call upon them to desist from "destroying" nature than to call upon cats to stop killing birds. Since any ecopolitics, however dismissive of the superiority of *homo sapiens* over other species, accords humanity responsibilities for nature, it presumes the possession by human beings of attributes that set them apart from all other forms of life.[53]

Environmentalism also speaks frequently of the "intrinsic worth" of nature, which can be distinguished from the "anthropocentric" use of nature for human purposes. Soper, however, finds that even the more radical environmentalists show a "pervasive inclination to point to humanly admired qualities [of nature]—its diversity, richness, autonomy and beauty, for example—as those that [actually] endow it with 'intrinsic' value." It is quite apparent that environmentalists "want the beauties of nature saved for the sake of the pleasure and solace that human beings find in them. . . . Even ecocentric arguments tacitly rely in their defense of the 'intrinsic' value of nature on the appeal to human aesthetic and moral sensibilities."[54]

What environmentalism is really saying, properly understood, is that in many cases "nature is (or should be) valued for other than instrumental purposes," even when this may have to proceed "at the cost of other projects they [human beings] also value, and even (such is the perspective of an extreme eco-centrism) if it means sacrificing their own species well-being or survival." In itself, this is all very much a human-centered way of thinking. Even as environmentalism rejects instrumental uses, nature is still judged in a human framework, even if not a conventional utilitarian one. All in all, as Soper argues, there is no other way of thinking about nature except by a complex set of distinctly human ideas and trade-offs that will combine "reference to human utilitarian, moral, or aesthetic interests and predispositions."[55]

Admittedly, Soper speaks from a humanistic philosophical perspective. Her negative verdict on the coherence of environmental thought might be less severe, however, if a greater religious element were introduced. If God is brought into the equation, the environmental rejection of anthropocentric thinking and the appeal to intrinsic worth can be given a much clearer and more philosophically (or theologically) coherent justification. When environmentalists appeal to the intrinsic worth of nature, and thereby suggest that human needs and plans should not be controlling, it may be one way of saying indirectly and implicitly that God's plans for the natural world must be respected and followed—whatever human beings may think, feel, dislike, believe, enjoy, or otherwise perceive in their relationship to nature. That is, a logically coherent meaning of "intrinsic value" is that God Himself has decreed that His creation must be preserved and protected. Any human feelings, benefits, values, or actions must be subordinate to God's command, thus transcending any "anthropocentric" considerations.

Mainstream environmentalism, however, has been unwilling to make this argument explicitly—even as the commanding presence of a Christian God is a powerful and probably essential implicit element of any logically well-developed body of environmental thought. Appealing more truthfully to God—making the Christianity explicit instead of implicit—to reestablish the coherence of environmental ethical arguments, admittedly, would introduce other major problems for the environmental movement. These problems are suggested, for example, in considering the prospect of a government policy goal to restore the natural world—to "re-create the creation"—as God has made it. Aside from any technical questions, how is this restoration goal to be reconciled with the supposed religious neutrality of the American state? Yet the alternative, seeking to ground environmental ethics in a strictly human-istic set of arguments, as Soper makes clear from a humanistic philosophical perspective, also raises large and probably insurmountable obstacles. When the Forest Service, National Park Service, BLM, and many other government agencies are told to pursue policies such as natural restoration that rest on such uncertain and philosophically—really religiously—incoherent premises and logical foundations, it should be no surprise when the policy makers of-ten appear in practice to be hesitant, confused, contradictory, hypocritical, blustering, and otherwise unsuccessful in their assignments.[56]

The Gospel According to Conservation Biology

The Society for Conservation Biology was founded in 1985 and its influential journal, *Conservation Biology*, was established soon thereafter. Subsequently, programs for the study of conservation biology were created at a number of leading American universities. The task of conservation biology has been to rework the goals and language of American environmentalism—at least with respect to endangered species, ecosystems, and other parts of "nature"—to a more scientific basis. The goal should now be the preservation and restoration of "biodiversity," a term coined by conservation biologists in the mid-1980s. If the American environment is to be restored, the field of conservation biology will be among the main sources of expert knowledge and trained personnel.[57]

In 1992, David Takacs—who describes himself as a "lifelong environmen-talist"—interviewed twenty-three leading figures in conservation biology, including Michael Soule, Reed Noss, E. O. Wilson, Thomas Lovejoy, Paul Ehrlich, and Jerry Franklin. His purpose was to explore their reasons for be-coming involved in the field, the methods of conservation biology, the values reflected in those efforts, the prospects for the future, and many other mat-ters. Takacs assembled the materials from these interviews, conducted ad-ditional interviews specifically concerned with environmental issues in Costa Rica, and in 1996 published an insightful book, *The Idea of Biodiversity: Phi-losophies of Paradise*.[58] The book includes Takacs's broader reflections on the thinking of the conservation biologists he interviewed, as well as extensive direct quotes from his interviewees.

Takacs sees the rise of conservation biology, and the new focus on a goal of biodiversity, as a reflection of perceived problems—many of them described in this book—with earlier environmental goals, especially the wilderness ideal of protecting wild nature. By the 1980s, for instance, there was a growing awareness that pre-European human impacts on the natural world in the Americas might have been much greater than previously suspected. In Costa Rica, for example, Takacs noted that "researchers are turning up pottery shards and crop residues that point to past civilizations where until recently we had imagined only wilderness." More broadly, an environmental goal of "wilderness preservation . . . is redolent of class privilege, culturally rooted, and ontologically precarious." In light of these and other concerns, by the 1980s there was a developing perception among the more scientifically rigorous thinkers in the environmental movement that "plotting conservation around wilderness is a dubious strategy."[59] It also had the practical liabilities that by then many of the wildest U.S. areas were already included in the national wilderness system, and such a strategy offered little justification or guidance for environmental protection of the large majority of places that would never qualify as wild.

As Takacs explains, the questioning of a wilderness strategy was one element in a broader concern among biologists and other scientists with respect to "the negative connotations the word *nature* holds."[60] Nature was the subject of romantic poetry, transcendental philosophical speculations, and many other approaches that fell well short of the "scientific." Yet science is the greatest source of authority and legitimacy in American life. If environmental goals were to gain wider public acceptance, it might be desirable to put them on a firmer scientific grounding.[61] Indeed, this was a main purpose of elevating the goal of "biodiversity" in place of the older and now seemingly less compelling environmental language of "nature, wilderness, natural variety, endangered species, and biological diversity."[62]

One of the issues explored by Takacs in his interviews with conservation biologists was the definition of "biodiversity." Don Falk considered that biodiversity takes in "ecosystem functions, community processes, and genetic diversity within species, and so on." Reed Noss stated that "it is life and all that sustains life." When asked to give "biodiversity" a more precise definition, as a specific goal that might be achieved or not, even leading authorities in the field had difficulty. As Takacs reported, "Little is concrete about most definitions of *biodiversity*." One of those interviewed, David Ehrenfeld, was skeptical of the very term itself, considering that biodiversity "has a broad appeal, like motherhood."[63]

Given such a broad scope, Takacs sought to examine how the idea of biodiversity might differ from the idea of nature. He concluded that for most conservation biologists there was in fact not much difference. The language of biodiversity mostly amounted to a rhetorical act of "scientizing the concept of nature." Whether conservation biologists consciously intended this or not, their goals were actually political and social. As Takacs finds, "The word *biodiversity* is part of a convincing strategy—that is, it is designed to convince [the American public and political leadership] and has been quite convincing thus far" in advancing traditional environmental purposes in a new language.[64] Takacs summarizes the forces at play in the establishment of the new field of conservation biology:

> Conservation biologists do not often go to bat for nature per se; they do not often describe nature in their writing. According to Neil Evernden, "The environmental advocate sits on the horns of a dilemma: the time honoured technique of invoking the authority of nature has been essential to the presentation of a persuasive argument, and yet that technique is now vulnerable to charges of fraud." The term *nature* not only carries a multiplicity of confusing, often self-serving meanings; it also carries the taint of association with bleeding-heart liberal tree huggers. To be considered a "nature-lover" is not a compliment in many quarters. So rather than running to nature, biologists flee from it. Instead, they describe and defend biodiversity. It maintains an aura of scientific respectability while still meaning so many different things to so many different people, without having yet acquired the notorious etymological reputation of the word *nature.*[65]

The leadership of the field of conservation biology has come predominately from biological scientists. Unlike many scientists who are content to work in their laboratories and leave politics and policy making to others, however, most conservation biologists have been determined to make a difference in the world. That has been one of the distinct features of conservation biology and has required its members to think about many subjects that fall outside the scope of their own professional expertise (or even outside science as a whole). Conservation biologists have had to enter into political and economic realms and to try to understand—and influence—the workings of policy-making processes in government. It has all involved, as Takacs notes, paying attention to a host of "multi-disciplinary concerns" that were brought together "under the rubric of biodiversity, . . . repackaged to unite amorphous, diverse endeavors in a streamlined, do-or-die conservation effort with biologists at the helm."[66]

Takacs also explores the roots of this crusading spirit that animates the efforts of so many conservation biologists. Not surprisingly, the sources lie mainly outside the scientific method and the biological expertise possessed by members in the field. Indeed, despite its efforts to distinguish itself, Takacs finds that conservation biology is sustained by powerful ethical ideas and spiritual values similar to those of the older conservation and environmental movements that sought to protect "nature." Most conservation biologists, however, have not been particularly self-reflective about all this; they have not applied a scientific and analytical lens to explore the contents of their own powerful value feelings associated with biodiversity (and nature). This probably reflects in part the ambivalent feelings that such an analysis might arouse. Conservation biology advertises itself as belonging to the scientific community and as adhering to strict cannons of scientific objectivity and value-neutrality. As Takacs notes, however, conservation biologists in actual fact "attempt to speak for values that go far beyond what one might think of as falling within their realm of expertise." They engage in "public advocacy" in support of a powerful "ethical imperative," one that encompasses many "extrascientific values." Michael Soule, for example, espouses an "ecosophy" according to which "biological diversity, ecological complexity, and evolution are 'good,' . . . and biological diversity has value exclusive of any potential use to humans."[67]

Some of Takacs's conservation biology interviewees were more self-aware than others in recognizing the tensions between their public advocacy and their strictly scientific roles. This tension showed up in the advice given to some young biologists without tenure that they might need to "wait before they engage in conservation activities as part of their professional lives."[68] Walter Rosen stated his concern that "science is supposed to be objective, yet I, who am a scientist, nevertheless feel very strongly in this and that value." Moreover, there could even be an element of misrepresentation, Rosen acknowledged, because "if I'm going to be listened to, it's probably because I'm a scientist, even though I'm making a non-scientific assertion."[69] Takacs suggests that one solution might be for conservation biologists to distinguish clearly in their public roles between their statements as scientists and their statements as citizens of the world who are advocating particular values and biodiversity policies. But then he acknowledges that in practice any such attempt to separate these two roles is probably unworkable.

Substantial portions of Takacs's book are devoted to exploring the contents of the powerful value systems that he finds underlying the public advocacy of conservation biologists. A number of conservation biologists agreed that biodiversity is important to the world because of its "transformative value," a concept first developed by the environmental philosopher Bryan Norton.[70] When a person is "surrounded by diversity," there is an identification "with the natural world; one is inextricably part of it. The transformation of values occurs partly because if you are inextricable from the grand process of nature, by consuming it or altering it, you irrevocably hurt yourself."[71]

Analogies to religion came readily to mind when conservation biologists spoke of the transformative power of experiencing biodiversity. Takacs comments that they "seek to encourage this 'conversion effect' by putting people in direct contact with biodiversity. Biologists may feel such conversion is possible because they themselves went through precisely this kind of transformation, usually in childhood." Indeed, there are parallels here to being born again in Christianity. E. O. Wilson relates that for him "natural history came like salvation at a very early age." Thomas Eisner describes a youth in which he was "exposed to the smell of the woods, to looking under rocks and looking under logs. And there was just an overwhelming feeling." Reed Noss expresses his sense that "many people do have that feeling, that there is a larger self. And when they're defending nature, they're defending that larger self."[72]

Takacs also examines the importance of "intrinsic value" in the thinking of many conservation biologists. Given that intrinsic value by definition exists "apart from any human valuer," it is not an observable and measurable thing; further, as Takacs notes, it goes "well beyond the realm of what we might expect scientists to acknowledge and defend." Indeed, Takacs agrees that, as suggested above, intrinsic value may have to be justified from "certain religious standpoints. If God or some other deity or sacred process created the natural world alongside humans, then all creatures are imbued with sacredness: all have intrinsic value" independent of any human thoughts or actions. Paul Ehrlich, one of the conservation biologists committed to the idea of intrinsic value, does not ground his arguments in Genesis or other biblical texts, but he does go so far as to recognize explicitly that "this is fundamentally a religious argument. There is no scientific way to 'prove' that nonhuman organisms . . . have a right to exist." Takacs notes the irony of many conservation biologists proclaiming beliefs dependent on the existence of a god or other deity, yet "most biologists have no such religious views" that they can articulate in any detail.[73]

At one point in his interview process, Takacs raised the subject of religion more explicitly, asking specifically about the role of "spiritual values" in the thinking of conservation biologists. This is a difficult area for many conservation biologists because "if it seems a priori odd that some scientists believe and preach a concept like intrinsic value that cannot be proven scientifically—indeed, it can barely be expressed at all—it may seem totally bizarre that scientists talk about biodiversity's spiritual value." Yet the majority of the conservation biologists interviewed spoke in terms of having deep spiritual convictions relating to biodiversity. S. J McNaughton described his powerful "spiritual experience" in once being surrounded by wildebeests and other forms of nature on an African plain. Reed Noss described his strong sense of "a kind of spiritual or at least a nonrational connection to nature." Noss hastened to add, however, that "I wouldn't call it religious." Takacs comments that many conservation biologists make similar distinctions, reflecting the fact that, among his interviewees, almost all "these biologists reject organized Western religion, sometimes quite forcefully."[74] Thus, they are willing to admit to having a strong sense of "spirituality" in the presence of nature while rejecting the idea of following any institutional forms of "religion."

While they may not have a systematic theology, it was nevertheless evident to Takacs that ideas and reactions of a deeply religious character were central to the whole enterprise of conservation biology:

> Such feelings run deep, infusing their bearers with sentiment. At a loss for language adequate to express this sentiment, they resort to the word one resorts to when one can't explain something: *spiritual*. For these biologists and for many others, being in nature—surrounding oneself with biodiversity—can almost not help but bring about experiences to leave the senses reeling, the mouth agape. The incomprehensible complexity of it all: we can't handle it. Our brains go numb when faced with such richness out there, so much bigger than ourselves. How can we help but feel awed? And biologists spend their lives digging deeper into the intricacies, developing profound awareness of both the mindblowing intricacies they have unearthed and the complicated skein they haven't begun to entangle.[75]

Although such religious experiences are widespread among conservation biologists, Takacs notes that many are reluctant to "speak out publicly because they feel they must preserve the boundaries between rational and intuitive, mind and body, science and emotion." Crudely put, putting their intense religious feelings about biodiversity into the public view might blow their scientific cover. A few conservation biologists, admittedly, do think that this reluctance is a mistake; for one thing, the cause of conservation biology probably cannot succeed unless its core values are more widely accepted among Americans, and this process of conversion will require a more explicit statement of the religious significance of biodiversity. Since "the values are there already," Takacs says, "why not be honest, making conservation biologists' work more accurate and holistic? Simultaneously, they'd be laying their values bare for others to emulate."[76]

Thus, there was no mistaking the fact that, among the conservation biologists Takacs interviewed, they "attach the label *spiritual* to deep, driving feelings they can't understand, but that give their lives meaning, impel their professional activities, and make them ardent conservationists. Getting to know biodiversity better takes the place of getting to know God better."

Indeed, despite the reluctance of most conservation biologists to use the term "religion" in describing their own beliefs, this was mainly an act of linguistic camouflage. It was quite evident to Takacs that "some biologists have found their own brand of religion, and it's based on biodiversity." Although it might pose a threat of some outside critics speaking harshly of conservation biologists as the new "eco-ayatollahs," Takacs suggests that conservation biology should more courageously and honestly put its true religious face forward.[77]

Takacs does not explore, and few conservation biologists have sought to delve into, the specific religious sources of the powerful religious feelings of awe and reverence that these biologists experience in the presence of nature—or, as they have now relabeled it, in the presence of "biodiversity." When it comes to their "spiritual" side, conservation biologists have shown little interest in systematically investigating and analyzing the underlying sources—the very opposite, it might be noted, of their approach to the biological workings of the natural world that they study so intently. Such a formal analysis of their spiritual views would come within the realm of theology, a subject in which most conservation biologists have shown little interest and to which they have had little exposure.

Most conservation biologists have been brought up in a world in which the Western religious tradition still resonates strongly, even when many of its institutional representatives in the temples and churches have been in decline. As this book has argued, however, a Christian (and also Jewish) understanding of the world has survived in many areas in new forms (including economic as well as environmental religion)—often in total unawareness of the original source. It would seem that the field of conservation biology is yet another example of this modern phenomenon of powerfully felt and expressed religions without the traditional language of religion. While conservation biologists almost all reject Christian creationism, they may not have travelled as far as they think. The descriptions they give of experiencing biodiversity are little different from the classic Christian feelings of religious awe and reverence in experiencing the presence of "God's creation."

Restoration Penance

The environmental goal of restoring a state of the natural world as it existed before significant human alteration has been widely adopted by federal, state, and other government agencies. It lies at the core of the ideas of "ecosystem management," the official management philosophy since the 1990s of the U.S. Forest Service, National Park Service, and other government agencies that regulate and manage the human impacts on the natural world. In the western

United States, where heavy settlement mostly did not occur until after 1850, the restoration of nature has often been defined operationally to mean the recovery of the "pre-European" condition of the lands and other features of the environment from around 1850 to 1900.

The popularity of the restoration agenda has reflected its underlying creationism. It has been publicly espoused for the most part by environmental creationists who speak in a secular vocabulary, but the restoration goal is now growing in appeal to many traditional Christian creationists as well. Indeed, there are few Americans who would be opposed to restoring "the creation"— at least selectively in areas where the disruptions to normal patterns of human living would not be too great. The problem is that, from a scientific viewpoint, the result of any objective to restore the creation will inevitably be a mere fiction. In a Darwinist evolutionary framework of thought, it is impossible to single out any one past moment of the evolutionary process to declare that the state of nature at that moment represented "the creation." Whatever it is called—and the terms are numerous, including "natural," "healthy," "sustainable," "equilibrium," "biologically diverse," and so forth—it will be an illusion of the creation. And even if it were somehow miraculously possible to restore the creation, the value of this "fake" human version might not be very great.

It is not only that the current state of the natural world is the product of many millions of years of evolution. In many cases, the workings of evolution (aside from any human impacts) have caused rapid changes in the state of nature within the framework of much shorter periods of time—sometimes a few thousand or even a few hundred years. As early as the 1950s, as Eugene Cittadino notes, ecological research "was beginning to call into question some of its earlier cherished notions about balance, harmony, and stability in nature"—and thus states of nature that could easily be seen as God's creation.[78] Environmental religion—much like its cousin, economic religion—was not to be deterred, however, by a few scientific problems.[79] Its leading advocates made passing reference to ecology as the scientific source of environmental truths, even while ignoring any inconvenient ecological discoveries.[80] As Cittadino observes, "A simple, uncomplicated ecological vision began to gain momentum outside of scientific ecology at a time when ecology, as science, was becoming anything but simple and uncomplicated."[81] By the 1970s:

> ecology had become more than a science. For those who turned to communal living, homesteading, organic food cooperatives, and other ecologically correct alternative life styles, ecology provided guidelines for living and conferred a sort of moral purity on their actions. There were parallels here with a longstanding American tradition of utopian communities, such as the Shakers, New Harmony, the Oneida community,

and the original Mormons, including similarities in underlying philosophy, with elements of the older utopian societies—abandonment of private property, alternatives to traditional marital and family practices, a new work ethic—now given a scientific sanction. Historian and cultural critic Theodore Rozak, writing two years after the first Earth Day, made clear the debt of this countercultural vision to ecology with cryptic statements like the following: "The science we call ecology is the nearest approach that objective consciousness makes to the sacramental vision of nature which underlies the vision of Oneness." The adoption of ecology as philosophy for living, with a strongly implied, if not always stated, spiritual dimension, has echoed through various movements over the past three decades—deep ecology, varieties of green politics, ecofeminism, and so on.[82]

In 1907, Harvard University acquired nearly three thousand acres of forestland in central Massachusetts for research purposes. This forest is among the most intensively studied in the United States. About five thousand years ago, as revealed by the research performed there, an insect pest virtually wiped out the hemlock trees of the northeastern United States, leaving a forest condition that lasted for about one thousand years. Even when hemlock recovery occurred, it was "with considerable geographic variation in the rate and extent of recovery." Another major change was "the arrival of chestnut [trees] around 1,500 to 2,000 years ago," significantly altering the successional patterns that followed after large disturbances. It was also evident that "powerful hurricanes" and other tropical storms "episodically disrupt and shape New England forests," along with "less intense disturbance resulting from northeasterlies, downbursts, ice storms, and late-season snowstorms."[83] Impacts of American Indians were also substantial and changed considerably over time, owing to such developments as the widespread New England Indian "adoption of corn, or maize, a Central American plant," beginning one thousand years go. Indians also made common use of fire as "the major mechanism through which they could affect forests on a broad scale."[84] The Harvard forest researchers summarized the overall results of their research as follows:

> Interpretations based primarily on records of pollen and other fossils preserved in the sediments of lakes and wetlands confirm that the environment and vegetation of New England have changed continually through time. Although the rate and extent of change have varied since the last Ice Age, precipitation, temperature, storminess, and growing season length have all been dynamic as a consequence of long-term

changes in solar, orbital, global, and atmospheric processes. The changing environment has initiated shifts, some subtle and others quite substantial, in the range and relative abundance of plant and animal species and in the composition, structure, and function of forest ecosystems. . . .

. . . we now recognize that environmental changes are multifaceted and complex and often lack any modern equivalents. Not only the amount but also the seasonal and daily distributions of rainfall or temperature change through time, and these may vary as factors, such as storminess, atmospheric CO_2 concentrations, or animal and human populations, also change. As a consequence, the environmental conditions that have occurred in the past, and will develop in the future, may have no close parallels in any current landscape. In fact, the continual development of novel environmental settings through time is a major reason that fossils and other historical records attest to a long and changing sequence of unique and "nonanalog" plant and animal assemblages and ecosystem dynamics.[85]

In order words, the idea of "restoring" a single uniquely "natural" environment of the past—typically defined operationally as a "pre-European" natural order—is a myth, however central it has been to the thinking of environmental religion. This fiction survives, despite frequent scientific refutation in recent decades, because it has such immense religious appeal, offering a seeming pathway to experiencing the creation and thus to learning more about the thinking of God. In a secular age, even "nonbelievers" apparently require a source of meaning to their lives and, if forced, will choose illusion over purposeless nihilism. Contemporary environmentalism, to be sure, is far from the first instance in the modern era of an idea grounded in illusions having major political and economic consequences for human affairs. Indeed, in pessimistic moments it might easily seem that, historically, this has been more the norm than the exception.

Whatever the problematic conceptual foundations of environmental religion, and its restoration objectives to be realized by means of ecosystem management, large amounts of U.S. federal and state government money are already being spent to "restore" the natural environment—and these levels of funding could well increase substantially in the future. It is unclear, to be sure, what is being "restored"—although we can say for sure that it is not the creation. In practice, restoration money will probably be spent to remove dams, canals, trails, bridges, power lines, and many other symbols of the past scientific management of nature for economic purposes. Formerly drained wetlands will be re-flooded, rivers will be returned to their former channels, and many other similar steps will be taken. Symbolically, it will be a repudiation of our past false worship of the god of economic religion, the deity in whose name many of these physical manipulations of nature were undertaken. As far as the eventual environment outcome on the ground, it is likely to be something brand-new. Even leaving aside the fact of the rapid transitions from one state of nature to another at most sites, the heroic "restoration" efforts now being made will not result in any natural condition that has ever previously existed before.

Despite the negative restoration outcome, there will be another practical side to all the spending. Owing to our worship of false gods, there is a strong contemporary sense that human beings have previously sinned against nature—and also against the God above, who is the author of the creation. Those who sin, as we know from the Bible and other traditional sources of religious knowledge, should make amends. The penance in this case will include American society spending large amounts of money on restoration efforts. Even if the restoration does not succeed literally, the large financial sacrifices required will be a form of restitution for the many evils committed in the twentieth-century progressive economic campaign to subdue nature for human purposes, which resulted in the destruction of large parts of God's creation. Human beings in the twentieth century turned away from God; "restoration" may now be good for our souls even if it does little—or nothing—for "the earth."

Conclusion

Christian creationists have a logically developed an internally consistent way of understanding the creation. The problem for them is that Darwinism and other products of modern geological and biological investigations contradict the biblical story. Secular environmental creationists experience virtually the same sense of religious awe and inspiration in the presence of nature—"the creation"—as their Christian counterparts. Yet they also profess to accept Darwin and other modern science. The result would seem to be a significant confusion in their thinking about the natural world. They experience it religiously, on the one hand, as "the creation," and yet also write as professional experts and speak about it in biological terms as the product of hundreds of millions of years of random mutation and other Darwinist evolutionary workings. As noted above in the introduction, the ecological economist Herman Daly characterizes this as the "lurking inconsistency" in the thinking of the contemporary environmental movement.[86]

These tensions within secular environmental creationism come to the fore when it is necessary to consider the meaning of ecosystem management and its central goal of environmental restoration. What is it that is being restored?

In practice, it cannot be "the creation." Moreover, it is not necessary to restore a process of Darwinian evolution, because the workings of evolution never stopped—nor in principle could evolution ever be halted by human action. The goal might be to reset the evolutionary clock to a time frame preceding human impacts on the evolutionary result, but it now appears that this would have to be many tens of thousands, or perhaps even a few hundred thousand or more, years ago. Given the theological tenets of environmental creationism, in short, the goal of restoring the natural world would seem to be incoherent.

Nevertheless, heroic human activities are taking place with a justification of "restoring" nature. If the results are likely to be problematic, it will be due to intellectual—really theological—confusions as much as any technical difficulties in reengineering past natural systems. Theology is not just a matter of living a private moral life, or finding the personal path to a salvation in the hereafter. Religion, contrary to a widespread current impression, is not limited to matters of faith and emotion. A theology can be grounded in well-established facts and otherwise be well constructed, or it can exhibit an irrational logic, ignore valid scientific understandings, and otherwise be intellectually deficient. A misguided environmental theology is then likely to also produce wide policy and management confusions among the many government agencies that today must attempt to work out issues of the true and proper relationship of human beings and nature.[87]

11

ENVIRONMENTAL COLONIALISM:
"SAVING" AFRICA FROM AFRICANS

IN THE UNITED STATES, air pollution is down substantially in many cities—in Los Angeles, for example, nearby hills are now visible that would have been shrouded in smog forty years ago. The extent of releases of toxic substances into the air, waters, and lands of the nation has been sharply reduced. Old toxic sites left from past eras of uncontrolled dumping have been cleaned up under the Superfund program. Unsightly and environmentally damaging forestry, mining, and other resource extraction activities are now more closely monitored and regulated. There were, however, many excesses associated with all these developments; the environmental movement, for example, often exaggerated the health dangers of inaction.[1] The costs of environmental cleanups were also much higher in many cases than they needed to be. Nonetheless, on balance the United States is clearly much better off as a result of the efforts of the environmental movement over the past four decades.[2]

The greatest successes, to be sure, have been in matters of public health, such as cleaner air and water. The objective has been better defined in these areas, the public support stronger, and the level of technical understanding higher. Yet improving public health has not been the defining feature of the contemporary environmental movement. Public health has long been on the governmental agenda, and the greatest American successes in this field came in the nineteenth century.[3] Rather, it is the goal of protecting and restoring wild nature that has given contemporary environmentalism its distinctive character. When it comes to achieving that goal, however, the environmental record is less impressive.

A significant part of the problem, as previous chapters have explored, is the difficulty of saying what "wild nature" is. When the goal cannot be adequately specified, and indeed often reflects muddled thinking, it is difficult to pursue effective government policies. Policy making easily becomes more a matter of looking good—creating appealing images in the minds of many Americans—than of concrete environmental accomplishments. Policy and management may also be easily manipulated for private gain or limited ideological and religious purposes. Even when the nature protection goal becomes clearer, as in the case of protecting a plant or animal species from extinction, American environmental policies have not been very successful. Some species have probably avoided extinction due to government policy actions, but few have been restored to viable populations—and when a species did come back, as in the case of bald and golden eagles, it was seldom due to the Endangered Species Act (in the case of eagles, it was the banning of DDT).

Seeking to protect "wild nature" can also involve large social costs. Such a policy has typically meant excluding human impacts from an area. Over the past fifty years, timber harvesting, mining, livestock grazing, and many other forms of resource use have been excluded from many places in the United States (sometimes even requiring that the existing activities be eliminated). If the larger costs for the nation have often been minimal, there has been a significant economic burden for the residents of many rural areas that previously had been dependent economically on resource utilization. Moreover, because the United States has not curbed its total resource use, declining domestic availability has required new imports of lumber, minerals, petroleum, and other products for a modern economy, potentially transferring harmful environmental effects to other nations (often with fewer environmental protections).

Aside from the conceptual confusions discussed above, efforts to protect and restore wild nature potentially have large negative practical impacts that for the most part have been ignored or dismissed by the environmental movement. Such concerns come to a head when the negatively affected group consists of Native Americans (and other native populations in other parts of the world). Because Native Americans had no concept of protecting wild nature, and there were no Indian protected areas, most of the North American continent was occupied, if often sparsely, by Indian tribes. Since the arrival of European civilization, excluding a human presence from a "wild" area therefore meant either removing the Native Americans or preventing their return (when they had previously been removed for some other reason).

Given the strong public enthusiasm for environmental causes, this less savory side of environmental history has not received much attention. It has not, however, gone altogether unnoticed.[4] In his mostly sympathetic history of the American wilderness movement, Paul Sutter comments that there was at least one large unhappy element: "Scholars have shown that Euro-Americans used the wilderness idea to dispossess Native Americans who had competing and prior claims to the landscape."[5] As happened too many times, "by implying that certain areas were empty of human settlement, and thus of legitimate claims to landownership, those who wielded the wilderness idea justified theft" of land from Native American populations. It was thus not only the original European settlers who forcibly took the land from the Indians for agricultural and other productive uses; this was also a result of the "more recent advocacy for the protection of national parks and other natural areas. Moreover, by calling an area wilderness and preserving it as such, . . . preservationists had aided and abetted a pristine myth that continues to obscure a deep history of Native American land use."[6] This could be ecologically consequential as well, since Native Americans had often been an important part of the workings of "nature" prior to European settlement. The current Yellowstone National Park, for example, is missing a critical element of its ecological evolution over thousands of years—the presence of Native Americans who helped (with wolves) to keep down elk and other large mammal populations (whose presence today in very large numbers can be harmful to other species).[7]

In all this there is an implicit racism; in treating the North American continent as an untouched Eden, the original Native American occupants are put in a different category than the later Europeans. It is as though the former did not really belong to the human species.* Sutter also notes that other studies have reached similar conclusions concerning the application of wilderness ideals in other less developed parts of the world. There is "a growing body of [critical] scholarship on the relationship between colonialism, the developing world, and the appropriateness of exporting wilderness as a guiding ideal for international preservation efforts."[8] International efforts to protect wild nature have been particularly problematic in Africa. Exploring this issue can shed light not

---

* As Utah State University professors Charles Kay and Randy Simmons comment, "Most environmental laws and regulations, such as the Wilderness Act, the Park Service Organic Act, and the Endangered Species Act, *assume* a certain fundamental state of nature, as does all environmental philosophy, at least in the United States." But this assumption, among other problems, ignores the large impact of Native Americans—through deliberate setting of fires, hunting, and other activities— over many thousands of years. As Kay and Simmons thus argue, the typical neglect in environmental thinking of the ecological role of native Americans:

> is not scientifically correct. Moreover, we suggest that it is also racist. In fact . . . the original concept of America as wilderness was invented, in part, by our forefathers to justify the theft of the aboriginal lands and the genocide that befell America's original owners. Even those who regard native people as conservationists are guilty of what historian Richard White describes as "an act of immense condescension. For in a modern world defined by change, whites are portrayed as the only beings who make a difference. [Environmentalists may be] . . . pious toward Indian peoples, but [they] don't take them seriously [for they] don't credit [native people] with the capacity to make changes. (Charles E. Kay and Randy T. Simmons, "Preface," in *Wilderness and Political Ecology: Aboriginal Influences and the Original State of Nature*, ed. Kay and Simmons [Salt Lake City: University of Utah Press, 2002], xi–xii)

only on the particular policy episodes under discussion but also on the wider thinking and other characteristics of the environmental movement.

Excluding Africans

Ideas have consequences, and the ideas of environmental creationism are no exception. Some of the most important applications have been in sub-Saharan Africa, and the results have not always been happy. In the name of protecting wild nature as found at "the creation" (if not always put quite so explicitly), colonial governments set aside large areas of land in Africa as parks and other protected "natural" areas. The native Africans living there were usually evicted because the purpose, reflecting Western thinking about saving "wild nature," was to maintain areas minimally affected by human hands. It was not all that different from the confiscation of agricultural lands and other more familiar forms of European colonialism. The practical consequence amounted, as one might say, to an environmental policy to "'save' Africa from Africans."

The theological tenets of environmental creationism were particularly important for Africa because, other than Antarctica, this continent was the last significant part of the earth's land mass to experience major impacts of modern European civilization. Indeed, European exploration of the interior of Africa did not begin on a large scale until the mid-nineteenth century. Except for the ocean coasts and South Africa, significant European settlement of sub-Saharan Africa mostly began in the second half of the nineteenth century and often not did not occur until well into the twentieth century.[9] There are still many places today in Africa that have been little affected by Western economic influences. In the minds of many people, therefore, it has not been necessary to "restore the creation" in Africa. Rather, because human actions had so small an impact in the first place—or so it was widely believed—the goal of environmentalism in Africa could instead be to "protect the creation." This provided a powerful motivation and gave a particular urgency to natural area protection in a number of African colonies and later in independent African countries.

Other observers have also noted the "neocolonial" character of nature protection in Africa. Raymond Bonner is a *New York Times* reporter who came to the African scene in the early 1990s after a long career in investigative journalism. He found that most of his preconceptions about African wildlife management were erroneous. Indeed, Bonner would write that "the longer I stayed in Africa . . . the more I realized that the issues weren't so simple. . . . I realized that the way I, a Westerner, looked at wildlife wasn't necessarily the way Africans did." As Africans achieved greater political maturity, Bonner thought, they would no longer "allow themselves to be dominated by Europe and the United States." "They threw off colonialism" once, and Bonner predicted that "one day they will throw off eco-colonialism" in the management of their wildlife and other aspects of the natural environment.[10]

In further exploring the policy and management impact of environmental creationism in African, this chapter draws on a significant body of recent scholarly research. Indeed, a surprising amount of this literature involves Tanzania. Even though this nation is often considered to be among the most enlightened of African countries—a place where the corruption of government, the exploitation of ordinary people, the divisions of tribalism, and other African ills have been less severe—in Tanzania the creation of national parks and other game preserves has been and is still often being pursued to the detriment of ordinary Tanzanians. The result has all too often been the displacement of native tribal groups from their historic homelands, leaving them worse off economically—and in some cases in dire poverty.[11]

People who would be placed on the traditional "left" of the political spectrum write many of these studies of environmental policies in Tanzania. As seen from their perspective, it is no longer businesspeople who are today most likely to be "exploiting" Africans for their own gain (most current "capitalists" are actually indifferent to Africa, preferring to put their money elsewhere, where the returns are higher and more predictable). The disregard of the welfare of ordinary Africans is now more frequently associated with the activities of the international environmental movement, following the tenets of environmental creationism.*

Hollywood Africa

In *The Myth of Wild Africa*, Jonathan Adams and Thomas McShane in 1996 described how images of nature in Africa have long been crafted to appeal to European sensitivities.[12] The image of the "noble savage" has had an enduring attraction for many Western minds. Even though he knew better, David

---

*This is not to suggest that the problems of environmental colonialism have gone entirely unnoticed, including within some important parts of the environmental community. Indeed, for at least two decades there has been a strong movement for "community based natural resource management" (CBNRM), which has been led by environmentalists based mostly in eastern and southern Africa. The advocates of CBNRM have argued that the assistance of local African populations is required for successful wildlife conservation. They have emphasized the importance of local economic benefits to create positive incentives for the protection of wildlife and other parts of the African environment. The efforts of such Africa-based environmentalists, however, have often been undertaken without much support by their European and American counterparts. See David Western, *In the Dust of Kilimanjaro* (Washington, D.C.: Island Press, 1997).

Livingstone wrote for the English public in the mid-nineteenth century that "to one who has observed the hard toil of the poor in civilized countries, the state in which the inhabitants [of Africa] live is one of glorious ease. . . . Food abounds and very little effort is needed for its cultivation; the soil is so rich that no manure is required."[13] This characterization was part of a common depiction of Africa as a virtual Garden of Eden, innocent of the ills of modern civilization. Roderick Neumann thus writes that "the identity myth of a colonizing society returning to or discovering an earthly Eden is deeply implicated in the establishment of national parks [in Africa]."[14] (This romantic image, to be sure, was often in conflict with another common view of Africa as a land of wild savages who must be rescued by Christian religion and more modern ways of living.)

To the present day, Africa is still being presented in such Edenic terms. The Eden myth with Africans present, however, would soon be supplanted by images of an Edenic wilderness in which a permanent presence of current Africans, as well as Europeans, had to be excluded. As Neumann comments, "National parks in Tanzania could accommodate the presence of the noble savage for only a brief time."[15] In Western eyes, the original innocence of nature would now be found in places where modern Africans themselves had to be kept out, since they had also been acquiring the technological capacities to subject nature to human domination. The African Eden thus now required protected places, such as the systems of national parks that have been created throughout the continent.

These parks are marketed to Western tourists as places where they can come to see nature in its "true" form. A promotional brochure of a South African safari operator, for example, explains that:

> Tanzania, the land of Kilimanjaro and undoubtedly one of the most beautiful countries of Africa, boasts some of the most sensational wildlife refuges in the world. Tanzania has long been considered the finest safari destination in all of Africa and within its borders lie legendary game reserves and game areas that combine incredible concentrations of wildlife. The Ngorongoro crater and the Serengeti National Park contain almost two million animals. The Selous Game Reserve [in southeastern Tanzania] is the largest wildlife reserve in all of Africa, much of it totally unexplored. Here the lion remains "king of beasts" over large populations of buffalo. It is remote and peaceful, but more importantly, it is the true Africa, undamaged and unspoilt.[16]

Such imagery boosts tourist interest in the Selous Game Reserve and serves both the interests of safari operators and the revenue goals of the Tanzanian national government. It has almost nothing to do, however, with the reality of Selous history. Until the end of World War I, the colony of Tanganyika was under German control. In 1905, the native African populations living in the Selous area revolted against their colonial masters. The Germans found it difficult to defeat the Africans—who were operating in small guerrilla groups—by direct military means. Instead, they adopted a strategy of deliberately starving the local populations. As John Reader explains in his magisterial history of the African continent, "Three columns advanced through the region, pursuing a scorched earth policy—creating famine. People were forced from their homes, villages were burned to the ground; food crops that could not be taken way or given to loyal groups were destroyed."[17] By some estimates, as many as three hundred thousand Africans died, perhaps a third of the total population in the area.

In this fashion, the groundwork was laid for the eventual creation of the "natural" Selous Game Reserve. The Western popular desire to experience the presence of the creation is so strong that, if it cannot be accomplished in reality, it will be made available though fantasy. Reader can hardly contain his sarcasm in describing the ironies of the situation:

> Paraphrasing Tacitus' verdict on the Roman warfare in Germany, a commentator wrote that "the Germans in East Africa made a solitude and called it a peace." The *Maji-Maji* districts were at peace again, but it was the peace of the wilderness. Survivors attempting to re-establish themselves in the region found it transformed, with forest encroaching on village sites and game reoccupying previously cultivated land. More ominously, the tsetse fly was there too. . . . For agriculturalists in the southern regions of German East Africa, . . . vast areas of their homeland were uninhabitable; from its midst the British colonial administration [which had replaced the Germans after World War I] carved out the world's largest game park—the Selous.[18]

Given its large size, here were, to be sure, some populations of Africans that survived to live in the Selous. This remnant population of forty thousand people scattered through the Liwale District had to be removed to create the Selous reserve. In his 1977 classic *Ecology Control and Economic Development in East African History*, Helge Kjekshus (past lecturer at the University of Dar es Salaam) reports that "the man in charge of the operations, Rooke Johnston . . . held that development [of the Selous] depended on the eradication of all human rights and interests in the areas."[19] Johnston would write that in this pursuit, "I went all out to achieve what I had conceived in 1931 to be the betterment of Liwale District and its people, namely its elimination."[20] If the Selous appears today to be "wild Africa," it is the product of the extermination and removal of its peoples by deliberate European strategy in the early twentieth century. Before that, there were large populations of Africans who were actively engaged in the manipulation of the Selous natural environment for their food supply, habitation, and other human benefits.

The Rinderpest Plague

Most of the future national park areas of Africa were not depopulated, however, by military means and administrative actions. As in North and South America a few centuries earlier, diseases introduced by Europeans served to wipe out native populations. Many Africans died from smallpox, which was introduced from Europe and to which Africans had no natural immunity. Unlike in the Americas, the greatest impacts of the new diseases in Africa were felt by its animal populations. Reader describes the rinderpest epidemic of the late nineteenth century as "the greatest natural calamity ever to befall the African continent, a calamity which has no natural parallel elsewhere." Between 1889 and the early 1900s, the rinderpest plague killed off between 90 and 95 percent of all the cattle in Africa (goats and sheep were affected too). The rinderpest first appeared in Somaliland and rapidly spread to engulf the entire continent, reaching as far as Cape Town in South Africa. For the many African tribes that depended on livestock, their economic means of support was decimated. Whole areas where livestock raising had traditionally taken place were depopulated. By one estimate, two-thirds of the Maasai population in Tanzania died as a result of the rinderpest plague.[21]

The rinderpest affected wildlife as well. Over wide areas of Africa, the existing populations of buffalo, giraffe, and eland, along with most small antelopes and warthogs, were virtually wiped out. Ordinary Africans were thus deprived of this source of traditional sustenance as well. The ecological balance that had kept the tsetse fly under control was also disrupted. Cattle grazing had traditionally kept the grasslands from growing into dense fields and thickets. With cattle removed and much of the wildlife also gone, these grasslands were free to grow without any check from the clipping and thinning of traditional animal foraging. The new habitat that grew up was much better suited to the tsetse fly. In Uganda, an estimated two hundred thousand people died between 1902 and 1906 from sleeping sickness spread by new hordes of tsetse flies now spreading across the landscape.

The native wildlife populations of Africa had long been exposed to tsetse flies and were immune to the sleeping sickness spread by their bite. Domestic cattle were a more recent arrival in the continent, however, and were susceptible, along with humans, to the disease. With most of the cattle of Africa now dead, large areas were newly available for wildlife habitat without the traditional competition from livestock; even though the rinderpest had decimated wildlife as well, they rebounded rapidly. Thus, in the early twentieth century, and free of traditional cattle grazing and other human impacts, large parts of Africa had newly abundant wildlife populations. For European conservationists, typically ignorant of the recent ecological history of the continent, this appeared to be the "true Africa" of abundant wild game and other natural features—among the few last remaining places on earth where "the creation" could still be found.

The lack of basic biological and other scientific knowledge among African conservationists and game park managers is an observation of long standing. In 1973, A. D. Graham would declare, based on his long experience in Kenya and other parts of Africa, that "to the scientist it was their abysmal professional ignorance that was so disappointing. Simple facts about the animals and the wilderness were evidently quite unknown to the conservationists. Yet, almost without exception, the preservationists themselves claimed a profound knowledge of those very facts; claimed them in fact with such authority that the uninitiated accepted their distinction without demur."[22]

The conservationists actively sought to set aside preserves in natural parks to prevent the reintroduction of human impacts. Reader again describes the terrible ironies of these events, which were the source of much of the national parkland of current eastern and southern Africa:

> The overall effect of the rinderpest plague, compounded by initial depopulation and the subsequent migration of people away from the bite of the tsetse fly, was to shift the ecological balance of the trypanosome [sleeping sickness] cycle heavily in favour of wild-animal populations. In East Africa in particular, areas which had once supported large and relatively prosperous populations of herders and farmers were transformed into tsetse-infested bush and woodland inhabited only by wild animals. Influential colonists during the colonial period assumed that these regions were precious examples of African environments which had existed since time began. Believing that the plains and woodlands packed with animals were a manifestation of "natural" perfection, untouched by humanity, they declared that they should be preserved from human depredation for evermore. Most are now tsetse-infected game parks: Serengeti, the Masai Mara, Tsavo, Selous, Ruaha, Luangwa, Kafue, Wankie, Okayango, Kruger . . .[23]

Kjekshus similarly reports that, long before Europeans arrived in the late nineteenth century, ordinary Africans had established "a relationship between man and his environment which had grown out of centuries of clearing the ground, introducing managed vegetations, and controlling the fauna." A main goal of this active management of the environment was to limit the harmful influence of the tsetse fly; indeed, for centuries it had succeeded in making the tsetse fly "a largely irrelevant consideration for economic prosperity" of native Africans. This happy world was destroyed at the beginning of the twentieth century when an "eruption of tsetse-borne sleeping sickness epidemics" produced a "sudden human and cattle depopulation and the attendant loss of control over the environment." In the larger scope of East African history, Kjekshus considers that the social impacts of these ecological developments exceeded even "earlier events like slave-raiding and intertribal warfare, to which historians have given so much attention."[24]

The creation of national parks in eastern and southern Africa thus typically served to prevent ordinary Africans from reoccupying areas from with they had been expelled by European military force and disease within the previous half century. The "true Africa" seen by tourists visiting the parks—popularly imagined to be unchanged since the creation—was in fact the product of the decimation of traditional African life as experienced in the aftermath of European settlement.

Ironically, the creation of a park area would also serve to change the behavior of the animals. Lions had never previously allowed humans to approach within a few feet, as is now possible in vehicles in park areas. The national parks of Africa increasingly are taking on the character of large open-air zoos. The tourists love the experience because they can see animals that in earlier times would have taken care to stay far removed from any human presence. If someone today wants to see the behavior of a "natural" lion, the closest approximations will be found precisely in areas outside park boundaries—where Africans continue to hunt lions, and lions consequently remain alert to avoid humans.

The "Paradise" of Serengeti

Kruger National Park in South Africa was created in 1926. In 1933, the Convention for the Protection of African Flora and Fauna met in London. Adams and McShane say of this meeting that "the age of Africa's national parks truly began with the international agreement of 1933."[25] The events of World War II intervened, but after the war national parks were soon being created by colonial administrations across Africa.[26] In 1951 the British administrators of Tanganyika created the Serengeti National Park (which had already been protected under a less formal status), today perhaps the most famous national park in the world, widely regarded as a surviving remnant of "original Africa." The park is 5,600 square miles, about the size of Connecticut.

The Serengeti area had in fact been occupied for several centuries by the Maasai people, themselves earlier invaders from the north. In the mid-nineteenth century, before the arrival of Europeans, there were about fifty thousand Maasai occupying large areas of what is now Kenya and north-central Tanzania. The Maasai nomadic lifestyle was based on the raising of cattle, and thus the Maasai were among those tribes decimated by the rinderpest. The Maasai also lost large parts of their land to colonial policies that evicted them to make way for European agricultural settlement. Yet another large part of the Maasai land was taken away for the creation of national parks—not only Serengeti but also Tarangire and Lake Manyara national parks in Tanzania, and Nairobi, Amboseli, and Tsavo national parks in Kenya (along with the Masai Mara National Reserve, also in Kenya).

As a result of the ecological consequences of the rinderpest, as described above, in 1951 "woodlands covered the northern reaches of the Serengeti, though less than half a century earlier the area had been open, grassy plains, inhabited by people and their animals."[27] Although leading conservationists persisted in calling Serengeti "a glimpse into Africa as it was before the white man ever crossed its shores," that was far from the truth.[28] The consequences of the European arrival in the late nineteenth century had already massively altered both the human and the wildlife circumstances of the Serengeti. The Europeans who saw wild nature in the Serengeti were actually seeing the product of their own recent human manipulations. The Serengeti was already a large "garden," some parts the equivalent of (unintended) wild weeds, other parts more like (intended) domestic plants.

Thus, before these manipulations of the past 125 years, as Adams and McShane report of the Serengeti area:

> Tsetse had long inhabited the no-man's-land between African settlements, such as the ungrazed areas that separated one Maasai settlement from another in and around the Serengeti Plain. Africans knew of these focal points of infection and avoided them, while Maasai cattle ate young sprouts, preventing them from maturing into tough, thorny scrub, and thus kept the tsetse in check. The hunting practices of tribes other than the Maasai also helped deter the spread of tsetse by regulating wildlife populations that could provide hosts for the flies. Africans . . . had thus established "a mobile ecological equilibrium" with wildlife and their associated diseases.
>
> The equilibrium collapsed when Africans and their cattle began dying in large numbers from diseases brought by Europeans. On the

Serengeti and elsewhere, a vicious cycle began: the bush returned because cattle no longer kept the bush down, the flies multiplied, further lowering both human and cattle populations, leading to more habitat for tsetse, and so on.[29]

Yet, in areas outside the protected national parks, new forces in the 1950s and 1960s would again significantly alter the ecological order. The new availability of modern medicines led to the recovery and significant increase of Maasai populations. In the late 1950s, a new campaign was waged against the tsetse fly using insecticides and traps. As the Maasai experienced greater health and vitality, they returned to older burning practices on the plains, which further reduced the habitat suited to tsetse flies. Maasai cattle numbers again grew rapidly, pressing against the capacity of the grazing resources, especially in light of the large areas of traditional Maasai lands now converted to agriculture and set aside in national parks and other reserves (and thus unavailable for traditional grazing use).

With the limited lands available, the Maasai looked to return to their former grazing lands in the national parks. In the mid-1950s, the Tanganyika legislature moved to cut the size of Serengeti Park in half to allow the Maasai to reoccupy the central plain. This would have provided the Maasai with much needed flexibility as they moved their cattle from area to area according to traditional grazing practices. It would also have posed little hazard to wildlife; populations of livestock and wildlife had previously coexisted in these areas for centuries. Moreover, the Maasai—unusual among African tribes—have religious prohibitions against the routine killing and eating of wild animals in normal times.

Led by the famed international conservationist Bernhard Grzimek (the president of the Frankford Zoological Society), and motivated by creationist ways of thinking about nature that demanded the exclusion of any human—sinful—presence, the world conservation movement mobilized to block any such Maasai aspirations. With the British still making the final decisions in colonial Tanganyika, the plan to reduce Serengeti was soon shelved. The center of controversy then shifted to the Ngorongoro Crater, where Maasai had begun grazing as a result of the loss of their traditional grazing areas in Serengeti and elsewhere. Grzimek led a campaign there as well to evict the Maasai and to make it yet another area "free of human impact." The Ngorongoro Conservation Area (NCA) was in fact set aside in 1959 and Maasai cattle grazing was banned within the area of the crater.

In a compromise reflecting a greater recognition of the needs of native Africans, grazing was allowed in the 1960s in some areas outside the Ngorongoro Crater but within the NCA. Agriculture was also allowed within these areas, making it possible for the Maasai to support cattle populations in part through raising grain. In 1975, however, the Tanzanian government banned agriculture altogether in the NCA, thus essentially eliminating any feasibility of sustainable livestock raising there by the Maasai.

The modern environmental movement is no gentle society of aristocrats. Hardball practitioners of politics and media relations have won the many triumphs of environmentalism over the past half century. As memorably described by John McPhee in *Conversations with the Archdruid*, the leader of the Sierra Club, David Brower, pioneered these methods in the United States in the 1950s and 1960s in battles over Dinosaur National Monument, the Grand Canyon, and other park areas.[30] For Brower and many other environmental activists to come, factual accuracy would have to take a back seat to practical results when the fate of the earth—the creation—was at stake.

Grzimek was applying the same kinds of hardball tactics on the African environmental scene. He produced an internationally acclaimed book and film of the same name, *Serengeti Must Not Die*. Although enormously influential, as Adams and McShane report in hindsight, "it also was another of Grzimek's propaganda tools, filled with misleading, often falsified data." The overall image, immensely appealing in its own way to European and American audiences, was "that Africa is dying and . . . what little remains must be saved from mankind"—that is to say, saved from the Maasai use of the land as it had been taking place for several centuries.[31] Summarizing this infamous episode in conservation history, Adams and McShane report that:

> in 1959, Tanganyika seemed poised to take the crucial step of allowing local people to share their land with wild animals in and around a protected area. Bernhard Grzimek, however, was horrified at the thought of people wandering around in "his" national park, so he fought the NCA as he fought all the battles over wildlife conservation, with any weapon at his disposal; "First by soft line, then by hard line, next by bribery, and if necessary by outright blackmail," according to one journalist. . . . Grzimek once described himself as "a showman of pity." Indeed, his campaigns to save wild animals were based on manipulating the emotions and expectations of both the general public in Europe and politicians in Africa.
>
> The NCA is today just another park or preserve, and a poorly managed one at that. The goals set for the NCA in 1959 . . . have never been realized. The harmonious existence of people, livestock, and wild animals has not been achieved, and the rights and needs of the local Maasai community are often ignored.[32]

Reflecting similar outcomes across many parts of Africa, a contemporary conservationist, Barnabas Dickson, comments that "when the effect of past conservation policies on indigenous people is properly recognized, the record is a shameful one." He describes the "colonial approach to conservation"— which has often been carried forward by new African governments in the aftermath of the colonial era—as both a practical failure and "unjust":

> [This] approach involved the state assuming ownership of wildlife and instigating widespread restrictions on the use of wildlife. . . . [But] it did not work because the rural people living closest to wildlife had little incentive to conserve wildlife. Since they had no legal claim on that wildlife they saw little long-term gain from it. On the contrary, it was often a threat to their livelihoods (when wild animals destroyed their crops) and sometimes to their lives. They had no reason not to acquiesce in poaching and positive reason to engage in the practice themselves. In these circumstances, it should not have been surprising that state attempts to protect wildlife often ended in failure. The colonial approach was condemned as unjust because the colonial authorities had deprived indigenous people of a valuable resource that, prior to colonialization, they had regarded as their own. In addition, the state typically sought to protect wildlife under its nominal ownership by the use of extremely harsh methods, including the extra-judicial execution of suspected poachers.[33]

Restoration in Mkomazi Game Reserve, 1988

It might be thought that the end of the colonial era in Africa would also have meant the end of environmental colonialism. Native African religions had no similar reverence for "protecting the creation." The forms of European influence on environmental policy did indeed shift; it was no longer possible simply to issue an administrative edict from London or Paris. African nations and governments, however, survived in a condition of great dependence on outside donor agencies. For those Africans who were fortunate enough to be able to live a Western lifestyle, the money to sustain it typically came from these agencies, foreign tourists, and other foreign sources. The main commercial industry was mining, also controlled by outside forces, and little native industry developed. Hence, continuation of the flow of money depended in significant part on a deep respect for the wishes of Europeans and Americans, including prominently international environmental organizations and their supporters.

The European conquest of Africa was often assisted by the deep divisions among Africans themselves. Much earlier, the practice of slavery had depended on the willingness of Africans to capture, transport, and sell slaves to European (and Arab) slave traders. There have always been Africans who found that serving outside needs and demands was the easiest route to their own prosperity and well-being. Their advantage, admittedly, was frequently derived from the suffering of other Africans. The unifying bonds among different tribes and different regions of Africa have never been strong. In a more recent illustration of this phenomenon, African government administrators of protected park and wildlife areas have sought actively to please European and American donors and clients, even as ordinary Africans suffered from their actions. The 2002 Constitution of Kenya Review Commission, created by the government, listened to local people throughout the country and reported back that "one of the most common areas of complaint related to the use of land for game parks but to the exclusion of the local people." The Commission heard of "a sense experienced very widely: that local control of resources, and therefore of their lives, had been wrested away" by outsiders who insisted that nature and humans had to be kept separate in protected areas.

Sharing a long border, Kenya and Tanzania were similar in this respect. In 1988, the local inhabitants of Mkomazi Game Reserve in northeast Tanzania were expelled from the area by action of the Tanzanian national government. The circumstances that led to this "restoration" action, and the consequences for the people there, were described by Dan Brockington in *Fortress Conservation: The Preservation of the Mkomazi Game Reserve, Tanzania*.[34] It is yet another story of environmental colonialism as motivated and justified by the religious tenets of environmental creationism. The new twist is that native Tanzanians had now stepped into the shoes of the old colonial overseers. In fact, similar developments can be widely found over the African continent. In nation after nation, the old colonial instruments of state control were captured by new African governing elites for their own private purposes.[35]

As Brockington explains, "The rural poor in Africa tend to be weak and marginal to their countries' affairs." In Mkomazi and many other places, "they can be, and often are, ignored by their rulers." By contrast, "conservation receives continual and valuable support from a number of non-governmental organizations (NGOs), which lobby and raise money for conservation causes. They provide valuable funds to African governments." Foreign tourism also brings in large revenues that can be used to support the Africans who staff national government agencies. The NGOs are important not only for the direct infusions of money they contribute but also for the political legitimacy they provide. As Brockington comments, "The resources provided by conservation interests, as well as the powerful rhetoric of providing for future generations, may serve to justify the existence of protected areas to government officials" who themselves benefit significantly from the existence of these areas.[36]

The Mkomazi Game Reserve is located in northeastern Tanzania, adjacent to the border with Kenya. The reserve was formally established in 1951 to protect an area with significant numbers of elephants and other wild animals (the area is part of the broader ecosystem that includes Tsavo National Park in Kenya). Reflecting long-standing use, the grazing of cattle was allowed to continue in the eastern part of the reserve; the western part was opened to livestock grazing as well in 1969. In the following years, the numbers of cattle in the reserve increased rapidly, reaching ninety thousand cattle and thirty-three thousand sheep and goats in 1984. As part of this grazing use, some settlement occurred as well.

Arguing that this livestock use was degrading the resource and reducing its value for wildlife preservation, the Tanzanian national government and international conservation organizations pressed for the restoration of the area through the expulsion of the livestock from the reserve. They argued that the heaviest-grazing users were not indigenous to the area and thus had less moral claim—they were not a part of the "original nature" there—to continued use. Initial efforts to remove the livestock had limited success in the face of local resistance, but in 1986 the Tanzanian Wildlife Division finally issued an order to remove all livestock and associated settlement. The actual removal took place largely in 1988. Although some illegal use continued, it is estimated that the number of cattle in the reserve decreased by 75 percent. The people evicted often suffered large and uncompensated losses in their economic circumstances. Aided by international human rights groups, Maasai and Parakuyo tribespeople would eventually bring court cases seeking compensation for their losses.

In reviewing this history, Brockington finds that "the truth" is illusive amid numerous claims and counterclaims. In a complex ecological system—both in human, and plant and animal terms—it would require large resources to undertake the scientific studies to disentangle all the various factors. One of the major uncertainties concerns the impact of grazing. According to one scientific view: "The disturbance caused by grazing and burning does not necessarily cause damage; it is more likely to result in disturbances that foster biodiversity. Livestock do not necessarily exclude wildlife, rather the greatest concentrations of wildlife in East Africa depend on pastures grazed with livestock."[37] Indeed, livestock grazing is not a recent innovation; it has been a part of the African ecological dynamic for thousands of years. The absence of livestock does not protect any such thing as "original nature"; in fact, the act of removing the cattle creates something brand-new.

It may also, ironically, reduce biodiversity. All in all, as Brockington finds, "there is no clear evidence about the effect of people and their stock on the biodiversity of the Reserve. It remains possible that they enhanced it."[38] Brockington also refutes the claims about the absence of a long-term presence of the grazing users in the reserve. He portrays systematic misuse of information by world conservation organizations in their enthusiasm to "save" a part of wild Africa. These organizations and their allies in the Tanzanian government frequently claimed that the Mkomazi Reserve was "one of the richest savannas in Africa and possibly the world in terms of rare and endemic fauna and flora."[39] The reality is that, "as regards biodiversity, Mkomazi is species-rich for plants and birds, but not outstanding in global or regional terms." There is nothing extraordinary about the mammal populations, although "invertebrates are numerous." Overall, any grand claims for the rare quality of biodiversity in Mkomazi are misleading; the "evaluation of its conservation value awaits better research in similar ecosystems" that may in fact be biologically richer.[40] Yet international conservation organizations engaged in a powerful campaign in Europe and the United States to portray Mkomazi as a unique biological resource in Africa, thus justifying the removal of the local African populations from the area.

As Brockington writes, "The international representation of Mkomaze ends up being an almost Orwellian rewriting of the Reserves, and its people's, histories."[41] The advocates of exclusion were driven by the familiar myths of a "wild Africa" that must be maintained in an original "wilderness" condition— the creation protected. The emotional power of these images for European and American audiences is not in doubt, nor is their usefulness for fund-raising purposes. From a crassly cynical point of view, one might suggest that the spreading of "creation fictions" can promote the maximum "utility" in society—the fictions do in fact make many people feel good. In this sense, although the international conservation organizations belong more in the category of Hollywood producers of illusion, the propagation of their myths may in fact enhance the total economic "product" of the world.*

---

* It is not only in Africa of course that such illusions of "true" nature have been perpetuated with Madison Avenue methods and skills. Bottled water, as scientific testing shows, is usually not cleaner or healthier than tap water—and in some cases is dirtier. But the sellers of bottled water are not concerned with the results of scientific health tests. They are actually selling images and illusions that appeal widely to the American public. Remarkably enough, a main image propagated by the sellers of bottled water is that it is more truly "natural." As the *Washington Post* reported, "The latest [bottled] waters are [depicted on the labels as coming] from Antarctica and Iceland; there is glacier water and iceberg water and water that is a million years old and water from 3,000 feet down off Hawaii. All of these things promise an untouched nature far from human beings." The Fiji Water Company ships about 1 percent of the bottled water in the United States, which has to travel all the way across the Pacific to reach its buyers. According to the *Post*, "The company's Web site prominently says that its water is 'untouched by man.'" Thus, the wide contemporary sense of modern civilization as a corruption of an original and truer nature—a story as old as the temptation of Adam and Eve in the Garden—is now being effectively put to many commercial and other uses, ranging from the marketing of national parks in Africa to the selling of bottled water in the United States. As in Africa, such environmental sales pitches, ironically, have often had environmentally harmful results; bottled water is sold in plastic containers and often has to be transported long distances, all of which consumes significant amounts of energy,

Indeed, if social science is truly to be "value-neutral," as it often claims to be, there may be no grounds to object to the use of falsehoods that make people feel better. It is obvious that Brockington personally is offended by the outcomes he observed in the course of his Mkomazi research. Feeding the emotional needs of Europeans and Americans on the backs of the rural African poor is not a pretty sight. Brockington also recognizes an obligation to the cannons of the academy, however, that supposedly limits "subjective" judgments, which may be based on strong personal convictions of a moral nature. At some points in *Fortress Conservation*, he thus feels an obligation to adopt an "objective" posture with respect to the obvious illusions and deceptions employed by the international environmental organizations involved: "The case of Mkomazi suggests two reasons for the strength of fortress conservation [that requires the exclusion of people]. The first is that myths work. The Mkomazi myths can bring in much revenue. They result in the enforcement of exclusion and the creation of wilderness in the image desired by the creators. Myths may be wrong, but that is not the point. Myths are powerful. They motivate people; they help them to organize and understand their worlds; they provide structure and meaning; they are the source of beliefs, hopes and plans."[42]

Beliefs that help people "organize and understand their worlds" are often called religions. In the Western developed world, environmental creationism has exerted an extraordinarily strong attraction for many people over the past forty years. In a world of rapid change, where new scientific discoveries are seemingly announced every day, many people feel disoriented. The citizens of the developed world seem willing to cling to any rock available, and the environmental movement has offered them hope that some vestiges of the real and permanent "original nature" of the creation can still be found—and even visited occasionally in person. These last remaining places where human impacts have not already transformed the natural world must be preserved as parks and "wilderness." If there is little historically or ecologically accurate in all this, environmental religion would not be the first religion to maintain a hold over masses of believers in the face of strong contrary scientific evidence.

Conclusion

Yet another rendition of "the myth of wild Africa" in Tanzania involves Arusha National Park, set aside as a reserve in 1953 and made into a national park in 1960. It is yet another story, as Roderick Neumann characterizes it, in which

---

and many of the bottles end up littering the landscape. See Shankar Vedantam, "What's Colorless and Tasteless And Smells Like . . . Money?" *Washington Post*, June 30, 2008, A1.

"the portrayal of the national park as pristine nature symbolically and materially appropriates the landscape of Mount Meru for the consumptive pleasures of foreign tourists while denying its human history." The more recent "European appropriation of the African landscape for aesthetic consumption" follows directly in the path of an earlier colonial tradition of "appropriation of African land for material production."[43]

Neumann recognizes that the many allusions to wild Africa as a new Eden are more than a metaphor alone. Western conservation efforts in Africa are infused with a missionary spirit; at the famous Arusha conference in 1961, "conservationists were encouraged to 'work among the masses with missionary zeal' and 'to awaken African public opinion to the economic and cultural values of their unique heritage of wildlife.'"[44] Religious ideals have in fact always been a central element in the interaction of the Western world with African society. In fact, religion was a main motivation for the original Portuguese explorations in the fifteenth century to discover the coast of Africa. Henry the Navigator was seeking to reunite European Christianity with the legendary Christian kingdom of "Prester John"—believed to have survived in isolation for around a thousand years at the location of present-day Ethiopia. In the nineteenth century, David Livingstone opened up the interior of Africa in hopes of bringing Christianity to these domains. Yet the results of these religious missions have not always been very "Christian." Indeed, the spread of slavery and other forms of exploitation of ordinary Africans frequently followed in their wake.

Some of the greatest current efforts to "save" Africa are associated with contemporary environmentalism. And once again, Westerners have often used religion to justify actions taken to serve their own purposes in Africa to the neglect of the native populations. The national parks of Tanzania (and other African countries) have today become grist for the scriptwriters of environmental Hollywood fantasies. A cynic might say that this "Disneyland management" of Africa's park areas is their actual highest and best use. Fantasy sells and there are many millions of people in Europe and the United States, living in London, New York, and other congested urban centers, who enjoy images of the Garden of Eden, whether in Africa or elsewhere in the world. By contrast, the rural people in these areas, who are directly affected by the setting aside of surrounding parkland, constitute a politically weak (and less moneyed) minority with little influence within their own national governments or in international political arenas.

Yet a critical problem with the use of rural Africa as a playland for romantic fantasies is the potential for disillusionment to set in, for contrary images to arise. If the current Hollywood imagery and management practices are exposed for what they are, the viewer pleasures will be much reduced. Large

European and American commitments of funds—and other large costs borne by the local people who live in close proximity to the African park areas—will have gone for naught. Rather than being seen as heroes, many American and European environmentalists on the African scene may yet come to be regarded as having succumbed to false temptations. They could be the new Elmer Gantrys of our time.

The fact that environmental religion has justified objectionable outcomes—in Africa in this case—does not distinguish it from other historic religions. Some kind of religion in the sense of providing a framework for understanding and making judgments about the world seems to be essential for human existence. Thus, virtually everyone has a religion, whether they call it one or not. But history has shown that religions can have a large negative impact as well, sometimes giving legitimacy to events such as terrorism, crusades, inquisitions and other persecutions. Religion often works to divide the world into us and them, sinners and saved, good people and evil people. In assessing the theological merits of a religion, the negative uses to which a religion might have been put offer only one part of the full picture. But it is a factor to be weighed, as in the efforts of some followers in environmental religion to "'save' Africa from Africans."

PART IV

ENVIRONMENTALISM AND LIBERTARIANISM

INTRODUCTION

As Part I of this book described, the American economics profession in the twentieth century was the priesthood of a religion of economic progress. It was in concept possible that an American economist could play his or her assigned priestly role without having any strong beliefs in the actual redeeming benefits of progress. There have probably always been a few such economists—just as some Roman Catholic priests and nuns have no doubt harbored doubts about aspects of the Christian faith (apparently including Mother Teresa, even as she committed her life to helping the poor of Calcutta).[1] Indeed, the number of economic agnostics or atheists may well have risen substantially toward the end of the twentieth century. For most of the twentieth century, however, the great majority of economists were themselves not only the technical experts but also true believers in the cause of economic progress.

There were, nevertheless, a few well-known apostates. Among the best known was Frank Knight, a leading figure in the 1930s founding of the Chicago school of economics. Early in his career, Knight made important technical contributions that were the main reason for his being honored with the presidency of the American Economic Association in 1950. For most of his professional life, however, Knight abandoned mainstream economics and became in essence a political philosopher. In this role he was a skeptic within the American economic priesthood, doubting both its claims to comprehensive scientific knowledge and its expectations that economic progress would save the world. Although he was hostile to formal religion, and especially the Roman Catholic Church, Knight was much influenced by a Calvinist upbringing in which he learned that human beings were corrupted by original sin and that God alone could abolish the resulting pervasive sinfulness of the human condition.

Knight, in short, would have had much in common with the many contemporary environmentalists who believe, as explored in chapter 7 of this book, in a new "Calvinism minus God." Besides a questioning attitude toward the religion of economic progress, Knight would have agreed with many such environmentalists that the scientific management of society is both technically infeasible and ethically suspect. He rejected the idea that lasting happiness is attained through higher and higher levels of consumption. Knight would have shared a conviction that the central challenge—however difficult and uncertain any hopes for lasting gains might be—lies in the ethical realms of society. The modern hope that technical solutions can be found to every important problem in the world is antithetical both to Knight and to much of contemporary environmentalism.

Of course, Knight did not write and speak in a vocabulary of ecosystem health, sustainability, or other terms of contemporary environmental discourse. His thinking was not focused on issues of the proper human treatment of the natural world. He probably would not have agreed with the goal to restore the natural environment to a condition that preceded human impacts. Yet Knight was preoccupied with broader questions of the relationship of man and nature, and of the significance of the human presence in the world. Unlike most fellow economists, he had a deep interest in religion, once cowriting a book titled *The Economic Order and Religion*.[2] He self-consciously labeled his presidential address to the American Economic Association his professional "sermon."[3]

The affinities between Knight and contemporary environmentalism are important because they may offer important hints about the religious future in the twenty-first century. As this book has explored, the two most important American religions today (at least in the public arena) are an economic and an environmental faith. The history of religion shows that its evolution often proceeds through a process of synthesis. Knight was a brilliant economist in the narrowly technical sense, even though he abandoned such efforts at a fairly early stage in his career. Recognizing that there are many areas of agreement in terms of basic values, environmentalists may find that they have much to learn from the writings of a sympathetic economist of such high technical abilities and wide economic knowledge.*

---

* Matters have somewhat changed in recent years, but for much of its history the environmental movement was almost innocent of a knowledge of economics. The University of Maryland economist Wallace Oates reports that in the 1970s and 1980s there was "virtually no one" in the Washington "environmental policy-making community . . . who could express a clear understanding of the basic

However central it has been in the past, the idea of separating human be-ings from nature as a central goal of environmental policy has now become a hindrance to environmental thinking. Environmental creationism is not much more intellectually (or theologically) credible than Christian creation-ism. Yet if this idea is abandoned, the world becomes more complex. Future environmentalists will have to consider issues of the treatment of a natural world that is not distinct from but rather filled with living and breathing hu-man beings. Rather than the mechanically simple (if theologically confused) goal of excluding human beings, they will have to find ways to reconcile their concerns for nature protection and biodiversity with the very real needs of such human beings—some of them in less developed parts of the world, where they are still severely deprived economically—for jobs and income that will enable them to obtain basics such as food, shelter, and clothing. This is a broader social, economic, and specifically environmental concern; addressing it will require the integration of many fields of study. Whatever their religious differences of the past, therefore, environmentalists will have to collaborate with economists, and vice versa. Here again, Knight may have important things to say because his own writings and teaching were characterized by a disdain for disciplinary boundaries.

Knight has had only a few followers among present-day economists. The best known is James Buchanan, a student of Knight's at the University of Chi-cago, who went on to become a founder of the "public choice" school of eco-nomics, winning the Nobel Prize in Economics in 1986 for his work in this

---

rationale for incentive-based policy measures." It was almost as though environmentalists believed that the actions of human beings could be understood and policy measures devised outside any real un-derstanding of the private incentives that these human beings would face. As a result, "the economic perspective on environmental management played essentially no role in the determination of the major legislation of the early 1970s," which set the basic framework for environmental law and regulation to this day. Oates was surprised by this obvious impracticality and sought to understand it better:

> Why was the economic approach to environmental management so uninfluential in this early legislation? . . . First, there was no constituency or interest group for whom the economists' policy prescriptions had much appeal. [Second,] environmentalists were decidedly suspi-cious, if not outrightly hostile to, reliance on a system of "environmental prices." For many, the market system was the culprit: it was the source of environmental damage. The implication to many environmentalists was that polluting activities needed to be prohibited or, at least, strictly controlled [by direct government commands and controls]. [And third,] some saw the economic approach to environmental management as basically immoral because it involved placing a price on invaluable environmental assets.

While economics has many significant limitations, and often makes unwarranted imperial claims, any attempt to devise a social framework of government management outside an understanding of basic economic forces and workings will inevitably be flawed, as were the environmental laws of the 1970s. See Wallace E. Oates, "From Research to Policy: The Case of Environmental Economics," *University of Illinois Law Review* 2000, no. 1 (2000): 141, 137, 138.

area. It is significant that in addition to their economic work, both Knight and Buchanan are also among the intellectual leaders of libertarian thought of the twentieth century. Milton Friedman is another important contemporary economist and libertarian who was influenced by and often spoke well of Knight, a fellow faculty member for many years in the University of Chicago economics department. Friedman largely shared Knight's skepticism with respect to the prospects for the progressive scientific management of American society, although (unlike Knight) he is a true believer in the salvation of the world by economic progress.

Knight, Buchanan, and Friedman, along with a few other economists typically connected in some fashion with the University of Chicago, were among the small number of libertarian members of the American economics profession of the twentieth century (although by the end of the century that number was growing). American economists were mainly progressive believers in the government scientifically managing economic progress to save the world. There were other important libertarian writers on economic subjects, however, outside the economics profession. As noted in the introduction to this book, moreover, environmentalism and libertarianism have important common elements.

Both outlooks are fearful of the uses to which human beings will put the enormous new powers made available by the modern products of science and economics. Environmentalists are most concerned about the impacts on the natural world and libertarians about the impacts on human freedom. This reflects a common recognition that the expansion of human technical and economic capabilities has greatly exceeded the improvement in human political institutions—the workings of "politics"—to use and manage these capabilities. Both environmentalism and libertarianism doubt that the social sciences are capable of revealing any complete understanding of the "laws of society" (which might then provide a basis for a comprehensive management of the social order). Even if this were possible, an all-encompassing scientific management of every area of human existence would be ethically undesirable. Each human being would then amount to little more than a "parameter" to be assigned his or her "optimal" place in a grand scientific and economic system to perfect the world.

One significant difference is that libertarians do not share the environmentalist aversion—as a matter of basic principle—to human manipulations of the natural world. But even here one finds some surprising areas of agreement. It is a core principle of libertarianism that one individual's actions should do no harm to the body or possessions of another person. Yet significant levels of pollution can have just such impacts—your toxic substance, if not properly controlled, could do me great personal harm. Indeed, in an ideal libertarian world all (uncompensated) emissions of pollutants would be banned altogether. (In practice, admittedly, some pollution will have to be allowed for society to function.) Environmentalists have a surprisingly similar view—that even though all pollution ideally should be eliminated, in practice it is necessary to have a more limited target of pollution reduction. In making the practical compromises required, moreover, many libertarians also are just as skeptical as many environmentalists that the formal economic methods of benefit-cost analysis will be of much help—or that the economics profession should be assigned the task of socially engineering the appropriate reductions in pollution levels.

The roots of libertarian thinking date back at least to Adam Smith and John Locke, who both reflected the strong influence of Calvinism in both Scotland and England. As Brooks Holifield comments, "the covenant language" of the Puritans "had a broad scope. It encompassed not only the intricacies of salvation but also the institutional arrangements of colonial society." Society should consist of "a covenanted community of visible saints." All covenants (or contracts) should be entered into, as Thomas Hooker said, as "natural free engagements." As Holifield comments, the principle of the covenant should "govern the relationships between prince and people, husband and wives, masters and servants, all confederations and all corporations," even God and his faithful on earth. Indeed, anticipating libertarian goals in the late twentieth century, among the Puritans "every social relationship grounded in mutual free consent presupposed a covenant, whether implicit or explicit."[4]

There is thus an "economic Calvinism" to match the "environmental Calvinism" described in Part II. Admittedly, economic Calvinism was a small part of the overall American economics profession and had a limited impact on American government policies in the twentieth century (and Calvinist churches were also capable in some times and places of limiting the freedoms of others). The influence of a broadly Calvinist outlook may grow, however, in the twenty-first century, partly as a result of the waning faith of many people in the redeeming benefits of economic progress. It no longer seems plausible to large numbers of people that the end of material scarcity will eliminate evil and otherwise cure the problems of the world. An economic religion reworked to include a greater recognition of the wide scope for human sinfulness—an understanding central to Calvinist theology—may now be necessary.

Part IV raises the possibility of an emerging partial religious synthesis that would incorporate elements of both environmental and economic Calvinism—a new "libertarian environmentalism," as it might be called. Chapter 12 describes the Calvinist economic religion of Frank Knight, so different from that of most of his contemporaries. Chapter 13 sketches briefly a possible design for blending the thinking of economic libertarians such as Knight with the views of many environmental Calvinists.

12

FRANK KNIGHT AND ECONOMIC CALVINISM

FRANK KNIGHT REJECTED THE PROGRESSIVE OPTIMISM that dominated the American economics profession in the twentieth century, holding out little hope of any looming heaven on earth. For Knight, human beings were deeply flawed and improvements in their material conditions could not fundamentally alter this condition. The strongest human motive in any case was not greater riches but increased power. Maintaining the peace in society among power-hungry men and women was at least an equally difficult and urgent task as raising the standard of living—and Knight was preaching this message even before the existence of nuclear weapons. Knight also considered that ethical factors significantly influenced the course of events in society. He altogether rejected the economic determinism of so much thought of his day. In these and other respects, Knight (who lived from 1885 to 1972) was closer to the temper of our own times. Looking back on many events of modern history, few can dispute that the religion of economic progress offered a misleading portrayal of the human experience. Both economists and environmentalists today can benefit from renewed study of the political and economic philosophy—the economic Calvinism, as one might label it—of Frank Knight.

Knight and Economics

Many people would say that John Maynard Keynes had more of an impact on the history of the twentieth century than any other economist; it would not be farfetched to suggest, however, that Frank Knight could be ranked alongside Keynes in this regard. The manner of their influence, to be sure, was altogether different. Besides writing the landmark *General Theory of Employment,*

Interest, and Money in 1936,[1] Keynes circulated his policy advice at the highest levels of the British government and had a great ability to influence public opinion through his popular writings; Knight, on the other hand, entirely lacked these qualities. Knight's great impact on the world was, remarkably enough, as a teacher. Indeed, the history of the Chicago school of economics begins with Frank Knight; it is quite possible that its influential economic outlook would never have existed if Frank Knight had never taught at the University of Chicago. Given the subsequent extraordinary impact of Chicago economics on the world (as has been recognized in the nineteen Nobel prizes in economics awarded since 1975 to current and former Chicago faculty and doctoral students), it is fair to say that the source can in some real sense be traced back to Frank Knight.*

Knight's greatness as a teacher was not as an inspirational lecturer or in instilling any specific body of doctrine or knowledge in the students and younger faculty who passed through the University of Chicago economics department. Indeed, beyond the common antagonism of most leading members of the Chicago school to the scientific management of society through government planning and implementation, much of what Knight believed would later be rejected by his followers in the Chicago school. Knight's greatest source of influence was in the spirit of radical questioning that he inculcated in his students and colleagues. Almost in the manner of Socrates, Knight was a doubter of every orthodoxy, often even extending this attitude to his own past arguments.[2] As George Stigler has commented, Knight was the original source of the Chicago tradition that "great reputation and high office deserve little respect." At Chicago, students were taught a "studied irreverence toward authority," which had a "special slant: contemporary ideas were to be treated even more skeptically than those of earlier periods."[3] Following after Knight, Chicago economists like Milton Friedman, George Stigler, Ronald Coase, Gary Becker, and others would all show great independence of mind. Chicago economists have consistently exhibited a courage to advance ideas that at least initially might be offensive if not outrageous according to conventional wisdom and the economic mainstream of American society.

* According to Melvin Reder, "The personal affection and mutual esteem in which Knight and his protégés held one another facilitated the collaborative efforts of the latter. The informal but very effective promotional aspect of the Chicago School sprang from the affinity group of Knight's students and protégés that formed in the middle 1930s. The principal members of this group were Milton and Rose Director Friedman, George Stigler, Allen Wallis, and Henry Simons." As a result, "the 'baton passer' of the initial Chicago group . . . was Knight." See Melvin W. Reder, "Chicago Economics: Permanence and Change," *Journal of Economic Literature* 20 (March 1982): 6–7.

Knight and Religion

Knight did not consider himself a Christian—indeed, he was famous for his antagonism to traditional religion.[4] Yet in teaching his economics courses, as Don Patinkin observed, Knight was prone to engage in "long digressions on the nature of man and society—and God."[5] The core social and economic problem in Knight's view was one of "discovery and definition of values—a moral, not to say a religious, problem," which stood in great contrast to the progressive aspirations for "value-free" scientific management of society.[6]

Most professional economists today know Knight best for his influential 1921 book *Risk, Uncertainty, and Profit.*[7] Knight would soon move on, however, to become more of a moral philosopher than a microeconomist.[8] If the ethics of self-interest is the core moral/religious problem for economics, Knight's way of thinking about the place of self-interest in society stood in contrast to that of most of his fellow economists. Knight doubted that there could be any possibility of the scientific management of society, through the manipulation of self-interest in the market or otherwise. Human reason, he believed, was a frail instrument, often corrupted by the baser elements in human nature. He thought, in contrast to the great majority of economists of his time, that the economic problem in society was in the end a religious problem. The defense of freedom—including the opportunity to express self-interest in the market—must rest not on a scientific demonstration but rather on an adequate moral/philosophical foundation.

For Knight that foundation lay in the central moral importance he ascribed to individual freedom. Knight had a strong libertarian strain, which represented the beginnings of the powerful libertarian influence that continues at Chicago to the present time. Yet he did not believe that individuals could exist independent of a grounding in some culture or society—human beings, he thought, were social by nature. Everyone had to be situated in some cultural system, which includes religion as a main source of group identity throughout history. Nevertheless, given the inevitable wide range of religious views and the potential for strong disagreements, the market provided a place where people from different creeds could come together for voluntary exchange and mutual benefit, an alternative much preferable to the wars and other terrible conflicts of past human history—often the most destructive when fought in the name of religion.

If Knight's views were unusual for an economist of his time, they were less novel than they appeared to many of his professional contemporaries. Indeed, if now taking a secular form, Knight was expressing a classic Christian view of fallen man, beset by original sin. In a long-standing Christian tradition (not the only such tradition), the existence of private property and the marketplace has been seen as an unfortunate but necessary concession to the pervasive presence of evil in the world. In the past (in the Garden of Eden) and in the future (in heaven) there will be no private property (or government). In the current world infected by sin, it is simply that private property and the pursuit of profit are the best way to maintain a semblance of order in society. As Richard Schlatter explains, there has been a long-standing view in Christianity that "since the Fall [in the Garden] the natures of men, all of them depraved, make necessary instruments of social domination. The division of property, which gives some men a power over the lives of others, is one such instrument."[9]

For Knight, even a priesthood—of economists or otherwise—could not be exempt from the general human condition; like their earlier Roman Catholic counterparts (Knight was especially critical of the historical Roman Catholic Church), the professional experts in the economic priesthood will be sinners as well. Knight stands as the beginning of the Chicago school's fundamental break with the economic mainstream of the time; in this new outlook, self-interest will be expressed not only in the marketplace but also in the actions of government and indeed perhaps in every area of society. It is a secular form of an old view, characteristic of Calvin and other Protestant Reformers, that sin has fundamentally invaded every aspect of human existence. Although Roman Catholic theologians also recognized the centrality of sin in the world, they tended to show considerably greater faith in human reason and in the possibilities for rational striving toward improvement in the human condition.

Deluded Progressives

The key economist in the founding of the American Economic Association, Richard Ely, argued early in his career (he later would be more cautious in his rhetoric, although his core values would not change much) that the organizing principle of social behavior should be the biblical commandment that "thou shalt love thy neighbor as thyself" (Lev. 19:18). Thus, it was impossible to both "serve God and mammon; for the ruling motive of the one service—egotism, selfishness—is the opposite of the ruling motive of the other—altruism, devotion to others, consecration of heart, soul and intellect to the service of others." For Ely in the social gospel phase of his life (in the 1880s and 1890s), the chief motivating force in the world—even in labor and business—must be "love" of fellow human beings, rather than the "self-interest" long favored by most economists.[10]

Ely's attitudes in this respect were in fact representative of many leading intellectuals of the American progressive movement (commonly dated from 1890 to 1920), often associated with the social gospel movement.[11] For Knight, this was just one example of how progressive intellectuals had substituted "romantic" thinking for a realistic approach to the human condition.* It is impossible, he says, to conceive of the application of "the 'love' doctrine" as a guiding economic principle "over, say, the population of a modern nation—and, of course, it must ultimately be over the world since, for a world religion [like Christianity], national boundaries have no moral significance."[12]

Similarly, Knight strongly rejected the economic determinism of American progressive thought and the resulting hopes for a radical improvement in the condition of the world if the economic problem could ever be finally solved (perhaps attaining a state of affairs where "love" would in fact rule). As he stated, "There is no reason to believe that if all properly economic problems were solved once for all through a fairy gift to every individual of the power to work physical miracles, the social struggle and strife would either be reduced in amount or intensity, or essentially changed in form, to say nothing of improvement—in the absence of some moral revolution which could by no means be assumed to follow in consequence of the change itself."[13] Thus, as Knight sees matters, a core assumption of the progressive gospel—that economic circumstances shape human actions and that economic events are the driving forces in history—is a serious misreading of the human condition. The presence of sin in the world cannot be abolished so easily as by the mere achievement of a state of great material abundance. As Knight once put the matter:

> The idea that the social problem is essentially or primarily economic, in the sense that social action may be concentrated on the economic aspect and other aspects left to take care of themselves, is a fallacy, and to outgrow this fallacy is one of the conditions of progress toward a real solution of the social problem as a whole, including the economic aspect itself. Examination will show that while many conflicts which seem to have a non-economic character are "really" economic, it is just as true that what is called "economic" conflict is "really" rooted in other interests and other forms of rivalry, and that these would remain unabated after any conceivable change in the sphere of economics alone.[14]

In the grand scheme of things, rather than "love," and if one motive had to be emphasized, this motive for Knight would be "power." The "solemn fact is

---

* This kind of thinking was still widespread in Christian social reform circles even in the late twentieth century. Max Stackhouse and Dennis McCann comment that "all too many religious leaders still cling to the belief that capitalism is greedy, individualistic, exploitative and failing; that socialism is generous, community-affirming, equitable and coming; and that the transition from the one to the other is what God is doing in the world." See Max L. Stackhouse and Dennis P. McCann, "A Postcommunist Manifesto: Public Theology After the Collapse of Socialism," *Christian Century*, January 16, 1991, 44.

that what people most commonly want for themselves is their 'own way,' as such, or especially *power*."[15] Knight sometimes chastised free-market economists, including his own Chicago colleagues, for putting too much emphasis on standard economic motives. In their thinking, "the main argument for *laissez-faire* was instrumental . . . it was intended to increase efficiency"—not so very different in this respect from the progressive "gospel of efficiency." For Knight, freedom instead means a maximum of power for an individual to control his or her own actions, and this must be "an end or value in itself," not something merely "instrumental to efficiency."[16] Knight's was closer to a libertarian than to a mainstream economic way of thinking.

Indeed, separating himself clearly from the economic mainstream of his time, Knight believes that "men actually prefer freedom to efficiency, within limits; and both our highest ideals and our laws and institutions recognize that they ought to do so if they do not." Knight is even prepared to argue that people "may even rightly be forced to be free."[17] To submit to power is for Knight to succumb to the temptations of a modern devil—to chose sin over salvation. No one can be allowed, any more in modern times than in days of old, to make this choice.

For Knight—somewhat paradoxically, in light of the obviously powerful influence of Christianity on his own thinking—one of the main threats to freedom was found in the Christian religion.[18] Indeed, the "history of Christianity" shows that the role of its teachings "has been to sanction established morality, law, and authority, not reform, at least in any constructive or progressive sense." In the Middle Ages, the Roman Catholic "church became a theocracy" and demonstrated as much concern for preserving its own power as any kings or other secular authorities.[19] Once in power, Christianity forgot all its core messages of love of fellow human beings and became a "violently intolerant" religion, given to episodes of fierce persecution of heresy and oppression of perceived enemies. Knight noted the "familiar fact" that over many centuries "the Church never condemned or officially opposed slavery."[20]

If mainstream economics' progressive views followed in the natural law tradition of emphasizing a rational world, Knight was particularly hostile to the ideas of natural law that have been central to much of the development of Catholic theology over the centuries. Knight never made any secret of his special dislike for the Catholic Church. Natural law concepts, he argued, had been "bandied about since the earliest beginnings of the European intellectual tradition," but they had mainly served "to beg the question in favor of any position which a particular writer or school happened to wish to defend or promote." At one time or another, leading theologians had declared rigid social castes, rule by absolute authority, and various other forms of oppression to be in conformance with the laws of nature. As Knight thus considered, "Natural law has served as a defense for any existing order against any change and as an argument for change in any direction."[21] The whole concept of natural law, in short, was for Knight nothing short of a religious scandal—the perversion of reason rather than its reaching to the greatest heights.

Scientific Oppression

If the Christian religion had often been false to its own founding principles, in the modern age the Christian churches were no longer the greatest threat to human freedom. As Knight explained, even as Christianity was much weakened, we now confronted a new "milieu in which science as such is a religion."[22] Knight would write in 1947 that the newer forms of religion promoted a "gospel" that involved a kind of "salvation by science," following in the path of the old natural law theories that promised a path to salvation by following God's laws.[23] The progressive follies of his day thus followed in a long tradition of religious pandering to power and oppression in the name of reason.[24]

The "plea of communism," Knight thus argues, with its claims to scientific authority, is much "like that of Christianity": both worldviews assert unique access to final truth, and in this way justify "absolute authority, ignoring freedom."[25] Communism is only one of the species of modern totalitarianisms, each of which offers "a priesthood as the custodian of [scientific] Truth, 'conditioning' each generation in helpless infancy to unquestioning belief." These new modern forms of scientific authoritarianism drew on "an inheritance" from earlier Christian traditions of "conformity to a sacred law and obedience to consecrated authority, Holy Mother Church and Holy Father King."[26]

Knight saw great danger in the tendency of most social scientists to believe that human behavior is rationally explainable in terms of behavioral laws and principles analogous to the laws discovered by the physical sciences.[27] It would serve merely to open the way to the expression of less exalted motives: "Any attempt at use of the unqualified procedures of natural science in solving problems of human relations is just another name for a struggle for power, ultimately a completely lawless one."[28] If the construction of a dam to control a raging river depended on knowledge of physical science, the advocates of the "scientific management" of society sought to employ social science to bring human actions under similar control.[29] Given the frailties of the political arrangements by which human beings governed themselves, and the unruly character of human nature, the end of human freedom was likely to be among the consequences. The grand schemes of American progressive economists—increasingly dominant in the mainstream of the profession in the years after World War II—were based on an assumption that the world is a rational place; nonetheless, they were bound to fail in the face of "human nature being as irrational as it is."[30]

Knight directed his barbs, for example, at a leading work of sociology published in 1947, the same year as Paul Samuelson's *Foundations of Economic Analysis* (and one year before his introductory textbook *Economics*), and reflecting a similar value system.[31] Much as Samuelson throughout his career would seek to convert economics to the methods of physics, the author of this best-selling work of popular sociology, George Lundberg, believed that "the problems of personal life, social relations, and political and economic organization are of the same kind as the prediction and control of events in (non-human) nature and so will similarly yield gradually to the same mode of attack." To solve social problems, as Knight characterized Lundberg's views, all that is needed "is that intellectual leaders . . . be converted to the scientific point of view" so that "the social problem will be solved by the application of scientific method."[32]

Such thinking, however, as Knight labels it, is mere rationalist and "scientistic propaganda."[33] Indeed, the "fetish of 'scientific method' in the study of society is one of the two most pernicious forms of romantic folly that are current among the educated"—as bad as the natural law follies of earlier Christian eras. The plain fact is that a fully rational "science of human behavior, in the literal sense, is impossible." Or again, as Knight writes, a "natural or positive science of human conduct" is "an absurdity."[34] One reason that a science of society is impossible is that the scientific analysis is not independent of the object under scrutiny. The very ideas of social scientists such as Samuelson and Milton Friedman can themselves change the conception of society and thus alter the very character of the object being studied.

Moreover, even if a true science of society were possible, it would not be desirable.[35] An individual whose behavior is perfectly and scientifically predictable is not a real human being. It is the element of self-consciousness and the ability to choose—the existence of "free will" in the classic Christian formulation—that distinguishes us from the animal world. If all is as determinate as in biology, what is to separate a man or woman in moral terms from a dog or an insect?* It may well be, Knight comments, "the idiot" who has the greatest amount of "happiness" among human beings, but the pursuit of this

---

*Among contemporary economists one finds the clearest echo of Knight's thinking in the writings of his former student James Buchanan. Indeed, on many subjects Buchanan sounds remarkably similar. For example, Buchanan considers that a person who behaves strictly according to scientific laws "could not be concerned with choice at all." Indeed, it is "internally contradictory" to speak of individual "choice making under [scientific] certainty." If human dignity and freedom require the power to choose, if the ability to do good or evil must be within the scope of individual decision making, then Buchanan believes that human behavior cannot be strictly determined by scientific rules. The

kind of pleasurable set of sensations "is not what makes human life worth while."[36] Many centuries earlier Martin Luther had similarly complained that the Roman Catholic Church had diminished its followers and endangered human freedom by encouraging the faithful to believe that life—even in such fundamental matters as the attainment of salvation in the hereafter—could follow mechanical rules as set by the church hierarchy.

Rather, even if there is considerable truth to the idea that a human being is a biological entity governed by laws of physical nature, "we must [finally] understand ourselves and each other and act intelligently in relation to both, in other terms altogether." Hence, the rational methods of science—yielding the legalistic decrees of any church (Roman, scientific, or otherwise)—can hold "no clue to the answer to the essential problems of free society" and living lives of genuine "spiritual freedom."[37] In opposition to Roman Catholic theology, the Protestant Reformation made its watchword that salvation is "by faith alone," and faith is ultimately a mystery fathomable only to God. Even in the modern age, a "free society" must act to "find norms somewhere outside the factual space-time world" with which the rational scientific method is concerned.

In these regards Knight thus was following in the tradition of the old-fashioned Protestant thinking—so contrary to the rationalism of contemporary economics—that original sin would inevitably undermine any human efforts to achieve a systematic order in the world. One of Luther's favorite sayings was the message of Saint Paul that "the flesh lusteth against the spirit and the spirit contrary to the flesh," and therefore "so that ye cannot do the things that ye would do."[38] Knight's thinking thus adapts a characteristic Protestant skepticism of a world of beneficial human "works." He is opposed to the core ideas of American progressive thought—found in such influential works as Samuelson's textbook *Economics*—and the optimistic faith that the scientific management of society (a particular form of "works") is the path to a future perfection of human existence. Contrary to the rationalist theology of natural law, and now the mechanical prescriptions of science, no given set of rules will ever show the way to heaven, on earth or otherwise.* As seen by Ross

---

scientific view of a human being as mechanical instrument denies a person his or her basic humanity. See James M. Buchanan, *What Should Economists Do?* (Indianapolis: Liberty Press, 1979), 281.

* In my 1991 book *Reaching for Heaven on Earth*, I argued that modern economics has derived much of its basic worldview from earlier Jewish and Christian sources. Moreover, within Christianity there had been two broad and often conflicting basic trends of thought, a "Roman tradition" (more closely associated with Thomas Aquinas and the theology of the Roman Catholic Church) and a "Protestant tradition" (more closely associated with Martin Luther, John Calvin, and the theology of the Protestant Reformation). I did not say much about Knight in that book, but he would clearly fall in the Protestant tradition. By contrast, the great majority of mainstream economists of the twentieth century, as I argued, fell in the "Roman tradition." See Robert H. Nelson, *Reaching for Heaven on Earth: The Theological Meaning of Economics* (Lanham, Md.: Rowman and Littlefield, 1991).

Emmett, a leading contemporary interpreter of Knight's moral philosophy, his thinking reflects an underlying theological view of the basic economic choices facing any society:

> In a society which has no recourse to the providential nature of a God who is present in human history, the provision of a justification for the way society works is a "theological" undertaking. Despite the fact that modern economists often forget it, their investigation of the universal problem of scarcity and its consequences for human behavior and social organization is a form of theological inquiry: in a world where there is no God, scarcity replaces moral evil as the central problem of theodicy, and the process of assigning value becomes the central problem of morality. Knight's (implicit) recognition of the theological nature of economic inquiry in this regard is one of the reasons for his rejection of positivism in economics and his insistence on the fundamentally normative and apologetic character of economics. In some sense, therefore, it is appropriate to say that Knight understood that his role in a society which did not or could not recognize the presence of God was similar to the role of a theologian in a society which explicitly acknowledged God's presence. As a student of society, he was obliged to contribute to society's discussion of the appropriate mechanisms for the coordination of individuals' actions, and to remind the members of society that their discussion could never be divorced from consideration of the type of society they wanted to create and the kind of people they wanted to become.[39]

Rediscovering Original Sin

In the modern era there have been three main competing visions in the Western world of the origins of human nature. First, there is the traditional Judeo-Christian view of human nature as shaped by—corrupted by—original sin since the fall in the Garden of Eden, leading most men and women to lead lives of frequent falsity, hatred, theft, lying, and other forms of corruption of their original, truer, and better natures. Second, there is the Darwinian view in which human nature is determined by a genetic inheritance that is the product of many thousands (or millions) of years of biological evolution—and in which human nature is a form of behavior that has evolved to promote the long-run survival of the human species. (In this view, any concepts of good and evil have no ultimate moral content but rather represent instruments of the workings of the evolutionary process.) In the third main view, human nature is shaped by the current surrounding environment, predominantly the economic environment—and thus creating the possibility of human beings acting on their own to abolish poverty and other causes of evil behavior, and in this fashion eventually to perfect the conditions of human existence on earth.

A great iconoclast (might we say a modern "protester" in the spirit of Luther and Calvin), Knight seemingly rejects all these explanations for the existence of evil, yet he does not offer any explicit alternative of his own. One must read between the lines to find Knight's views of the human condition. Indeed, despite all his outward hostility to Christianity, Knight's own theology—mainly expressed in an implicit fashion—follows surprisingly closely after the Calvinist understanding of the Christian Bible.* Although any notion of an actual fall in the Garden of Eden might be a myth, human beings in Knight's view are in fact corrupt creatures whose actual behavior in the world corresponds closely to the biblical understanding of the consequences of original sin.†

Knight's system of thought is so far outside the assumptions of the economics mainstream that most economists have simply chosen to ignore his moral philosophy, concentrating (when they paid any attention at all) on his technical arguments. His preaching is for many economists virtually incomprehensible, at times a seeming muddle of confused or even contradictory ideas, made all the more puzzling by the obvious fact of Knight's central role in the history of the Chicago school of economics. This failure of so many economists to understand better the direction of Knight's thought is powerful evidence—if any more should be needed—of the secularization of American society and the lack of knowledge among economists of old-fashioned Protestant theology. Once it is recognized that Knight's supposed antagonism to Christianity exists only on the surface, Knight's thinking is easily seen as a secular version of Calvinist Christianity, grounded in a conception of the ever-present and powerful workings of sin in the world. Knight himself perhaps did not fully recognize the Christian sources of his thinking, in

---

* John Calvin was born in 1509 and followed soon after Martin Luther as a leading figure of the Protestant Reformation. Calvinists adopted a yet more radical version of Luther's indictment of the Roman Catholic Church. A pivotal figure in the history of Western religion, Calvin died in 1564. The Puritans in England were among the leading branches of Calvinism in Europe—many of whom then settled in Massachusetts in the seventeenth century. See William Bouwsma, *John Calvin: A Sixteenth-Century Portrait* (New York: Oxford University Press, 1988).

† While the unhappy consequences of the fall are central to every historical branch of Christianity, the Protestantism of the Reformation saw human nature as having been especially corrupted by original sin—thus precluding any prospect of rationally directed action to achieve future salvation. A typical Protestant expression was found in the writings of Richard Hooker (1553–1600), who wrote of "the shame of our defiled natures," which would surely "shut us out from the kingdom of heaven," if not for the great mercy of God. See John Kent, "Christianity: Protestantism," in *Encyclopedia of the World's Religions*, ed. R. C. Zaehner (New York: Barnes and Noble, 1997), 102.

this respect resembling many of the environmentalists discussed in previous chapters. It has been a characteristic of the modern age that many people outwardly antagonistic to Christian religion in fact owe a much greater debt to it than they have ever understood.

His student and disciple James Buchanan asks: "Why was Knight so different from his peers? My hypothesis is that he can be explained, phenomenologically, only through recalling his roots in evangelical Christianity." Knight was "a product of middle America, of the agricultural economy of Illinois, of the late nineteenth century, of evangelical Christianity." Buchanan attributes Knight's "intense critical spirit" to his having been forced to wrestle with conflicts and doubts about Christianity in his youth.[40] Here I think Buchanan goes wrong. A better explanation is that this critical spirit was a direct manifestation—if now taking a secular form—of a characteristic Protestant outlook on the world. The Calvinist and Puritan mentality in particular has been characterized by deep introspection and a harshly critical attitude toward all claims to authority, worldly or otherwise. Few individuals are capable of understanding even themselves well. It is an outgrowth of the Calvinist conviction that all human beings, infected by original sin, are deeply flawed and that our best efforts are not likely to be worth much—and especially among those who make the grandest of claims.[41]

Thus, one might say that Knight's real religion was a secular Calvinism—his own distinctive economic brand of "Calvinism minus God." For example, like Calvin—and the English and American Puritans who later followed in the tradition of Calvinist theology—Knight saw a "positive moral value of pain and suffering. . . . The need for this emphasis is indubitable; human nature proverbially appears finer in adversity than in prosperity."[42] Much as Puritan theology had preached that excessive wealth was a temptation to sin and thus a danger to one's eternal soul, Knight would remark on another occasion that "it is human nature to be more dissatisfied the better off one is." The motive for providing one's labor was often as much a pride of "workmanship" as any desire for more income to obtain greater consumption. Knight found that mankind was in general a "contrary critter" prone to present a "false exterior."[43]

Knight was developing in a secular fashion a set of attitudes that were in fact common in American life in his formative years.[44] A study of rural life in upstate New York near the end of the nineteenth century finds a common belief that "virtue inhered in hard work." Work was not a burden but rather a source of "contentment," as Paula Baker writes. In this perspective there were large "moral and economic benefits" to the very act of labor itself. Indeed, it was no overstatement that hard labor "provided the basis for virtue in the producer's republic."[45] These attitudes, although far removed from—virtually incompatible with—the narrow utilitarianism of mainstream economic thought, did manifest themselves in Knight's thinking. As Knight had argued as early as 1923, it was necessary to reject "the assumption that human wants are objective and measurable magnitudes and that the satisfaction of such wants is the essence and criterion of value, and . . . on the basis of this assumption to reduce ethics to a sort of glorified economics."[46]

An American student of the Puritan influence on American history, Paul Conkin, finds that the Puritan view of the human condition, as derived from Calvinist thinking, has had a great staying power in American life. As he explains:

> Briefly characterized, the typical Puritan, in 1630 or 1930, reflected ideological assurance but was, at least in most areas and when at his best, open to new ideas. He was very much a moralist, a political activist. . . . He venerated the rule of objective laws or principles, but he just as insistently believed in congregation and local democracy. He usually reflected a sense of mission, even of a peculiar destiny, and an atmosphere of seriousness and self-importance. Yet he was, or wanted to be, pious, ever mindful of his dependence upon an overarching but never quite fathomable reality, which he loved even without full understanding. Although he sought redemption above all else, he had a wholesome respect for the instrumentality of both material goods and scientific knowledge, trying always to keep either from becoming usurping ends. He demanded a conscientious stewardship of all men and wanted all to have a useful and fulfilling calling or vocation.[47]

While Knight does not fit every aspect of this description, on the whole it is close. According to Knight, few people are likely to achieve a goal of happiness. The utilitarian philosophy of life is empirically in error and metaphysically shallow. The modern Calvinist must as always recognize the inevitability of pain and suffering, an outcome that perversely is likely to be aggravated by an excessive emphasis on the pursuit of happiness as the central goal in life. Indeed, an excess of utilitarianism is one of the many snares of the devil. Since the fall in the Garden of Eden, the rational faculties of human beings have been undermined by their unruly emotions and their easy susceptibility to various hatreds, jealousies, biases, and other psychological maladies.*

---

* George Stigler comments with respect to Knight that:

> economic theory prescribes the efficient ways of achieving given ends: this to Knight was a pathetically small part of human activity. The effects of acts often diverge grotesquely from the desires which led to them. Wants themselves are highly unstable, and it is their essential nature to change and grow. "The Chief thing which the common-sense individual wants is

Hence, as Luther and Calvin both preached, and Knight also believes, owing to the frailties of the human condition, projects for self-improvement are
often likely to achieve consequences that are the very opposite of the intended
effect. Ascetic discipline rather than pursuit of happiness should guide human
conduct. Patinkin recalled from his classroom lectures "Knight's commenting
that from the long-run viewpoint . . . denial of wants was the only way that a
definitive adjustment of wants to resources could be achieved; for history had
shown that Western society created new wants just as fast (if not faster than!)
it expanded the means of satisfying them."[48] It was a view that would find few
listeners among Knight's fellow economists but is echoed now in the teachings of environmental religion, reflecting shared Calvinist roots.

In a recent commentary on Knight's economic philosophy, Richard Boyd
notes that Knight's thinking has "much more in common with Augustine
Christianity than it does with the [rationalism and utilitarianism of the] Enlightenment."[49] Martin Luther had originally been an Augustinian monk who
despised Thomas Aquinas's rational and mechanical (as he saw it) medieval
theology of natural law, instead looking—and followed in this respect by many
other Protestant Reformers—to the earlier and more pessimistic (with respect
to a sinful life in this fallen world) theology of Augustine.[50] As Boyd adds,
Knight thus exhibits a fundamentally different world view than Adam Smith,
Friedrich Hayek, and Milton Friedman, all of whom believed more optimisti-
cally in the "benefits of progress, development and economic efficiency."[51]

The Augustinian and Calvinist view stands in great contrast to the economic mainstream's progressive view of a rational utilitarian choosing how to
maximize his or her own happiness, or the view of a society acting by a rational process of scientific management to perfect the human condition here on
earth. In coming down on the Calvinist rather than the progressive and rationalist side, Knight was a modern kind of Protestant fundamentalist, reacting
against the thinking of virtually the entire economics profession of his time.

Knight makes his Calvinist proclivities clear in his unique manner of justifying a classical liberal outlook on the world.[52] Knight painted the following
picture, so different from other economists' aspirations to the scientific management of society: "While effort is justified by good results, these are not expected ever to be satisfying. The experienced reward is more the joy of pursuit
than of possession. It is recognized that the solution of any problem will raise

---

not satisfactions for the wants he had, but more, and *better* wants." So man is an explorer and
experimenter, a seeker for unknown and perhaps unknowable truths, a creature better understood through the study of literature than by the scientific method. (George J. Stigler, "Frank
Knight," in *The New Palgrave: A Dictionary of Economics*, ed. John Eatwell, Murray Milgate,
and Peter Newman [New York: Stockton Press, 1987], 58)

more questions than it answers, so that man is committed—'doomed' . . . —to strive toward goals which recede more rapidly than he as an individual, or even society, advances towards them. Thus life is finally, if one chooses, or if one's temperament so dictates, a sort of labor of Sisyphus."[53]

In the broadest view, one might say that, intellectually and theologically speaking, much of American history has reflected a struggle between the pessimistic Puritan view of fallen, sinful man and the optimistic Enlightenment view of rational, utilitarian man. If the great majority of American economists have fallen on the Enlightenment and progressive side of this divide, Knight was one of the rare exceptions.

If economics were truly a value-neutral undertaking, one would expect that members of the economics profession would have developed a full body of economic thought—and with a significant investment of resources and depth of technical analysis—based on Calvinist and Puritan assumptions. If economists had wanted to avoid taking any sides on fundamental value questions, they should have explored thoroughly the workings of Calvinist economic models of the world. An economics that conformed to Calvinist assumptions would have to be very different from mainstream economic models of individual behavior. Efficiency could not be the highest value because wealth would have to be treated as not a benefit but a temptation to sin—and thus to depravity on this earth and a danger to one's eternal soul. The benefits of work would not lie in the goods and services obtained for consumptive purposes; rather, in a true Calvinist economics, a person would labor not for the benefit of the consumption obtained but for the disciplining by hard work of unruly minds and souls that are always in danger of succumbing to the temptations of the devil.

Technically speaking, "utility" would be derived from the labor and the other inputs. A potential excess of consumption resulting from such labor would be a constraint (a threat to one's eternal soul, potentially with disastrous consequences, if constant vigilance were not maintained) rather than a desired outcome in itself. The real economic problem would be to serve a calling, to work long and hard, without producing so much wealth in the process as to fall inevitably into temptation and sin. Furthermore, pain and suffering in Calvinist theology (and a valid accompanying Calvinist economics), as Knight commented of his own thinking, can often be a benefit rather than a cost.

All this would amount to almost a complete inversion of the foundational assumptions of mainstream economics. That is to say, progressive benefits would systematically be Calvinist costs, and vice versa. To be sure, economics is not a value-neutral field of study, and few microeconomists have ever shown any interest in developing the technical details of a "counter economics" grounded in Calvinist and Puritan value assumptions. With respect specifically to American society, where the value grounds have always been fiercely contested, economists have never sought to conduct an empirical examination of the predictive capacities (or other usefulness) of economic models grounded in Calvinist and Knightian assumptions about the basic character of human motivation, as compared with the predictive powers of conventional economic models grounded in individualistic, rational, and utilitarian assumptions about human nature.

Scientifically, all this is indefensible; instead of being value-neutral, the economics profession has actually been defending a strong value position. In building from only one view of human nature, mainstream economists have in effect been asserting that this is the one true and correct view. By their own teaching of economics, moreover, they have hoped to contribute to the further development and spread of a rational world, grounded in economic truths.

Communities of Believers

For most mainstream economists the issue of preference formation has been considered outside the bounds of economic analysis. The structure of preferences—the utility function—is simply assumed to exist, wherever it may have come from (and it could have come directly from God—it matters little). In economics, individuals come first, and then any collective actions are assumed to be organized through processes of individuals joining together in common efforts but still directed at maximizing their own benefits (giving rise to "free rider," "prisoner's dilemma," and many other logical quandaries in explaining how collective actions come to occur in the first place). Knight, however, argues that it is a "fundamental error" to regard "the individual as given, and . . . the social problem as one of right relations between given individuals."[54] Rather, the problem of ordering society should be conceived in the following terms: "The social problem in the strict sense . . . is purely intellectual-moral. All physical activity involved in social-legal process is carried out by individuals who act as the agents of society, in so far as they are true to the trust confided to them. Social action, which is social decision, uses as data both facts and cause-and-effect relations, pertaining both to nature and to man. But the social problem is not one of fact—except as values are also facts—nor is it one of means and end. It is a problem of values."[55]

Such views led Knight to embrace a democratic politics of widespread "discussion," a theme found over and over again in his writings. Calvin and other Protestant Reformers had much earlier denounced the top-down attempts of the Roman Catholic priesthood to impose authoritative and binding interpretations of faith on all the members of the church; instead, as the early Protestant Reformers declared, each person must come to his or her own understanding of religious truth, worked out in processes of discussion with fellow parishioners. Calvinism introduced a powerful commitment to local democracy in the church. For Knight as well, the citizenry will simply have to find through internal political processes of deliberation some common value basis for social actions, however lengthy and cumbersome this social process of discussion may be. New communities of believers—perhaps now often believers in secular religions—are no less needed today.

Thus, whether organized on a market basis or any other, "society depends upon—we may almost say that it *is*—moral like-mindedness."[56] It is essential for Knight that this like-mindedness must not be dictated by any modern equivalent of the Roman bureaucracy of old, which in the current era would most likely come from acting in the name of the authoritative decrees of the social sciences. The truths of modern religion as well must be reached from the bottom-up, from the interactions of free citizens in a democratic polity.[57]

To be sure, a process of democratic discussion requires a whole host of intermediate institutions between the individual and the wider society. The process of discussion must yield "superindividual norms." It is no help in finding agreement on these norms to hear from each person the "mere expression of individual desires." Indeed, the carrying over of the individualism of the free market into the realm of democratic discussion would "intensify the problem" of bringing about any fruitful outcome.[58] The tension in seeking to limit tightly the scope of individualistic motives in many areas of society, even as they are strongly encouraged in commercial market domains, might be characterized as "the market paradox."[59]

With a few rare exceptions, Knight finds, the individual never exists independent of some surrounding institutional and cultural context from which he or she derives basic values and an identity. For Knight the term "individual" as used in economic theory should in fact be regarded as a shorthand for "family."* Mainstream economics has misconceived the social problem for American society because it has taken its individualistic and utilitarian models of human behavior too literally. We are all products of our own time and place, Knight says. The idea of the lone individual creating (or obtaining in some manner) his or her own tastes and wants as an independent act of self-definition is truly a heroic fiction. Instead, we all live within a specific "culture" that teaches common "taste and appreciation," which is "more im-

---

* Gary Becker follows closely in the tradition of Knight and the Chicago school in many respects, including his directing of an attitude of radical questioning toward all the conventional values of society. If Knight still held to his many statements in his writings, however, he would have to be severely critical of Becker's recent economic approach to the study of the workings of family life, in which he portrays it as an arrangement among autonomous individuals acting within the family group in pursuit of their own individual maximum gain. For Becker's views, see Gary S. Becker, *A Treatise on the Family* (Cambridge: Harvard University Press, 1991).

portant than means of gratification" in determining our sense of ourselves as a person and of our individual well-being.[60]

Hence, for Knight, discussion in society is not about bargaining from fixed individual preference positions to enlarge and divide up the economic pie. Rather, the whole point of political discussion is to change minds; as a result of democratic deliberation, individual preferences should be constantly revised, leading to the necessary convergence ("like-mindedness") of values in the community. If much of the theoretical apparatus of economics is of little use in a world of constantly shifting preference structures, so much for mainstream economics.

As a strong defender of market freedoms, Knight partly blamed the current advocates of the free market, including some of his own Chicago colleagues, for the erosion of market freedoms and the wholesale turn to European socialism and American progressive principles that he saw taking place in his time. In the nineteenth century there had been a "religion of liberalism [which] had a positive social-moral content," but the necessary value-foundations for sustaining free markets had somewhere and somehow been lost: "One of the main factors in the present crisis is that the public has lost faith, such faith as it ever had, in the moral validity of market values."[61] Or as Knight similarly stated in another context, "The real breakdown of *bourgeois* society is only superficially economic . . . it is rather political, since indisputably it is the business of the political system to make the economic system function; fundamentally, however, the breakdown is not structural at all, but moral." Classical liberalism had made a basic "intellectual mistake" in that it "failed to see that the social problem is not at bottom intellectual, but moral."[62] And no adequate moral defense of the free market had been forthcoming either at Chicago or among any other group of prominent economists in the twentieth century.

Again departing radically from the mainstream, Knight argues that the typical economist's description of the market as a "competitive" system has been "calamitous for understanding" of the true merits of a market system.* For Knight, the market is ultimately desirable not because competition drives

---

* According to Stigler, one of his closest colleagues at Chicago, Knight had an explicitly normative vision of the case for the market, in contrast to most of his fellow economists:

> For most present-day economists, the primary purpose of their study is to increase our knowledge of the workings of the enterprise and other economic systems. For Knight, the primary role of economic theory is rather different: it is to contribute to the understanding of how by consensus based upon rational discussion we can fashion liberal society in which individual freedom is preserved and a satisfactory economic performance achieved. This vast social undertaking allows only a small role for the economist, and that role requires only a correct understanding of the central core of value theory. (George J. Stigler, "Frank Knight," in *The New Palgrave: A Dictionary of Economics*, ed. John Eatwell, Murray Milgate, and Peter Newman [New York: Stockton Press, 1987], 58)

down costs and prices—thus putting the case for the free market in conventional progressive and instrumental terms of efficiency—but because the market provides the one practical mechanism for resolving in a more satisfactory way (one that preserves individual freedom) the value tensions that will permeate any large and diverse society. Rather than competition, Knight argues that the advantages of the market should be understood in terms of promoting a "pattern of cooperation" among people who come together on a noncoercive basis for mutual advantage.[63] In this way, exchanging goods and services impersonally in a market, even people in a pluralist society who have fundamentally different belief systems—different religions—are able to work together without first having to reconcile their values to some common set of norms.

Hence, as Knight puts it, the market minimizes the role of power in human interactions because in a market "there are no power relations."* The market enables each person "to be the judge of his own values and of the use of his own means to achieve them." In grounding actions on mutual consent, the market leaves out any judgments of "selfishness" or other factors of "moral quality or artistic taste" in determining social interactions. A Christian can as easily trade in a market with a Buddhist as with a fellow Christian; if they had first been required to agree on normative subjects such as religion, no exchanges might ever have taken place.

Here again, Knight's views hark back to Christian origins. In Christian theology, the existence of private property—and the necessity of markets as well—is a product of original sin. In an ideal world, neither would exist. In the current fallen world, property and markets give the most acceptable outlets available—certainly much preferable to warfare and other forms of group violence—to human strivings for power and advantage. It may be an imperfect solution, but it is better than the alternatives.

If Knight strongly favored the market over central state control, here again he was manifesting a Calvinist quality of thought. As compared with the Roman Catholic Church, Protestantism—in making each of the Protestant faithful responsible for his or her relationship with God, where salvation was a matter of individual "faith alone"—was fundamentally an individualistic religion. This strong individualism eventually had profound social consequences outside the realm of Protestant theology. The Calvinist religious beliefs of the English Puritans laid the basis for modern freedoms in the realms of both government (the democratic system) and the economy (the free market). As one authority on Puritan thought comments, "The preponderance of modern

---

*It does not undermine his fundamental point, but Knight might be criticized here for conveniently ignoring the role of the state in coercively enforcing the initial assignment, and subsequent holdings, of property rights, which are essential to the workings of the market.

libertarian theory—from French Huguenots, the Netherlands, Scotland and England—came from Calvinists."[64]

The distinguished German theologian Ernst Troeltsch would similarly explain the great impact of the Puritans in shaping the basic values and social institutions of the modern age:

> The great ideas of the separation of Church and State, toleration of different Church societies alongside of one another, the principle of Voluntaryism in the formation of these Church-bodies, the (at first, no doubt, only relative) liberty of conviction and opinion in all matters of world-view and religion. Here are the roots of the old liberal theory of the inviolability of the inner personal life by the State, which was subsequently extended to more outward things; here is brought about the end of the medieval idea of civilisation, and coercive Church-and-State civilisation gives place to individual civilisation free of Church direction. The idea is at first religious. Later, it becomes secularized. . . . But its real foundations are laid in the English Puritan Revolution. The momentum of its religious impulse opened the way for modern freedom.[65]

Conclusion

Despite these advances, the Boston Puritans were also capable of hanging Quakers on the village square for religious heresy. Even as Protestants were oppressed elsewhere in Europe, Calvin's Geneva put tight limits on the tolerance for diversity of religious opinion. Protestantism encouraged each small sect to believe fervently that it had found the one true faith and that dissenters were not only threats to civic harmony but virtual (or perhaps actual) agents of the devil. Persecution of sinners proved easy to justify among the Protestant elect. The Protestant Reformation plunged Europe into many disastrous wars that continued for 150 years, and individual freedom was often a casualty. If Knight was ultimately unable to resolve the tension between individual rights and freedoms (including the pursuit of self-interest) and the claims to the common good of the community, it must be said that he has had a great deal of company in Protestant theology over the past five centuries.

Gradually, the Calvinist elements in Knight's economic thought would be recast by later members of the Chicago school in a more unambiguously libertarian direction. Libertarianism may not have all the answers—libertarians also experience a tension in resolving the claims of individualism versus the demands of community—but in clearly and explicitly rejecting the orthodoxies of the American progressive gospel and its prescription for the scientific management of society, contemporary libertarian thought opens the way to discussion of whole new governing philosophies. Contemporary environmentalism might want to join in this discussion as well. Much of Knight's critique of American economics would be shared by the environmental movement; Knight's search for an appropriate form of social organization might therefore also be of particular interest for the future development of environmental thought. Although holding similar religious values in many areas, few environmentalists have been able to bring to the table the full extent of detailed knowledge of the workings of the American economy that Knight possessed—an essential part of any discussion of the future economic and environmental character of the North American continent and the world.

13

LIBERTARIAN ENVIRONMENTALISM

BY THE END OF THE TWENTIETH CENTURY, economic religion—along with mainstream Protestantism, which had incorporated large elements of economic religion into its dogmas and church practices—was fading. Within the institutional Christian churches, however, evangelical and Pentecostal faiths were growing rapidly. Environmentalism, a type of secular (if partially disguised) fundamentalism, was also rapidly winning new converts. Economic religion was in some ways the last holdout in still seeing a rational world in which an authoritative priesthood could provide a body of universally valid knowledge, thus showing the way to the salvation of the world. The mainstream members of the economics profession, whose beliefs derived originally from the Enlightenment faith in reason and natural law, continued in the tradition of the universal Roman Catholic Church—in contrast to the many feuding denominations of Protestantism that had encouraged a legitimate pluralism of multiple religious perspectives.

By the standards of religious prophesy, the economic priesthood had proven in one respect more accurate than many predecessors. Extraordinary economic growth and development had in fact occurred over the course of the twentieth century, in the last decades extending even well outside the West to nations such as China and India. In another respect, however, the modern economic prophets were no more accurate than the many others before them who had predicted the final days and the looming arrival of a new earth. Contrary to the expectations of the economic true believers, it had become apparent over the course of the century that the vastly expanded human powers of the modern age could all too easily be used for malevolent as well as beneficial human purposes.

Despite the fading of economic religion, the great majority of Americans do very much want to keep their comfortable lives—now taken for granted—in which they are well fed, housed, and clothed. They want jobs that are not physically taxing and are often interesting and provide enough income and vacation time to travel widely, retire in good health, and otherwise enjoy the benefits of modern affluence. Environmentalism sometimes seems to oppose these desires, but the environmental movement is susceptible to charges of hypocrisy in this regard. Too many environmentalists who publicly profess the desirability of an ascetic or monastic lifestyle also demand in practice all the benefits of modern economic progress.[1] They live in large houses on large private lots; listen to music, send e-mails, watch plasma televisions, and otherwise use electronic equipment that requires large energy inputs; and often fly thousands of miles in jet airplanes to comfortable resorts in remote places, ostensibly to show their commitment to living in harmony with "nature."

In any case, few Americans are likely to adopt a vow of poverty. Thus, outside wilderness areas and a few other symbolic places where it may be possible to limit tightly the human presence, it will be necessary to find methods of reconciling the presence of large numbers of human beings and their pursuit of human welfare with the goal of protecting the natural environment.[2] An economically uninformed and administratively clumsy environmentalism—as was too often the case in the past—is not likely to have great successes in this regard. The implicit secular creationism that still commonly underlies environmental religion is likely to be more of a hindrance than a help in addressing such issues. Environmental religion makes many valid points in its strong disagreements with economic religion, but it too falls short in critical respects.[3] The environmental movement should now look to new ideas and resources as it seeks to redefine its future.[4]

Frank Knight was an excellent technical economist and, unlike most mainstream economists, also a Calvinist in his basic outlook on life (even as he was, admittedly, a nonbeliever). Like most current libertarians, Knight emphasized the central importance of human freedom in organizing society. In this chapter, I will suggest that environmentalists should look to libertarian thinkers such as Knight as a source of new ideas. In general, there is a greater affinity between libertarianism and environmentalism—or at least between the perspectives of economic and environmental Calvinism—than most people realize. Georgetown University law professor Richard Lazarus states, for example, that "many environmentalists equate environmental risks with assaults on their persons. . . . They begin with the premise that such assaults should be unlawful per se because no one has the right to subject another to health risks."[5] This is in essence the principle that also lies at the heart of libertarian thinking—that one person's use of his or her property should not harm another person. According to David Schoenbrod, a former staff member at the Natural Resources Defense Council in the 1970s, the members of this organization saw their mission as protecting the "environment [which] is society's home and the law is society's official way of stopping harmful conduct. 'Environmental law' was not something that would be done to society but rather what society, acting through its government, would do to protect its home from harm."[6] For this to be a libertarian statement, one would hardly need to change a word.

Unlike the original Calvinism, admittedly, a libertarian environmentalism would not be a faith that proclaimed any one sure religious truth. But it would be like the old Calvinism in asserting a complete freedom of individual religious conscience. Much as in Knight's thinking, a main goal of a new Calvinism might be to find a way for human beings to survive and thrive in a future of religious pluralism. Even as the world might not be perfected anytime soon, individuals and communities could pursue their own visions of their own ideal society. Or, for some, their goal might simply be a good life— according to whatever model of human happiness they happened to follow.[7]

Whatever the precise outcome, any search for libertarian and environmental areas of agreement begins with their common rejection since the 1960s of the core tenets of American progressive religion—as it took shape one hundred years ago (the Progressive Era is typically dated from 1890 to 1920) and then significantly influenced the development of the American welfare and regulatory state over the course of the twentieth century. If progressivism promoted an ever-growing concentration of government power at the national level in the United States, the fading of the progressive faith is likely to operate in a reverse direction. Thus some of the leading spokespersons for both libertarian and environmental causes today agree on the need for a major decentralization in the organizational arrangements for American society. The nation-state as an institution may be increasingly challenged; Washington may be a new Rome that has usurped the legitimate authority of the people. Indeed, a few bold libertarian and environmentalist theorists alike have even gone so far as to raise the option of a future American right of free secession—a provision of the proposed European Union constitution (which was rejected for other reasons), although a subject largely excluded from even the possibility of active public discussion in the United States since the Civil War.[8]

The Progressive Gospel

In the twentieth century, the progressive gospel of efficiency dominated thinking about the organization of American government.[9] The basic premise of progressivism was that there must be a central coordinating intelligence for all of American society, and that it would fall to the federal government to fulfill this role. Farmers left to the vagaries of the market, for example, faced boom and bust, so government must act to stabilize agricultural supplies and prices. Owners of private forests cut the timber too rapidly and devastated the land, requiring the U.S. Forest Service (created in 1905) and other government agencies to oversee the management of the nation's forest lands. Moreover, the competitive marketplace creates many losers as well as winners; therefore, in a civilized society, a central government must provide a social welfare network to assure a minimum living standard for every person.

All such efforts of government, the progressives taught, are to be administered with expert efficiency based on scientific knowledge.[10] If science was transforming the physical conditions of human existence in the late nineteenth and early twentieth centuries, many people believed it could do likewise for the social conditions. Due in part to the efforts of enthusiasts such as Frederick Taylor, the methods of scientific management spread rapidly throughout the world of American business. Progressives such as Gifford Pinchot argued that similar methods could and should be applied to the world of government. If American industries were increasingly concentrated in a few large corporations of nationwide scope, the federal government in Washington, D.C., should similarly oversee a nationally coordinated planning and management for American government. It fit well within the Western religious tradition because science is, after all, an enterprise in which one truth—now replacing the one Christian truth in the public arena—is established for all times and places. The support of scientific research, and then the dissemination of the resulting scientific laws and knowledge throughout the United States, would be a task best undertaken, in short, at a central level by national authorities.

Writing in the leading U.S. journal of administrative practice, Eliza Lee thus says of this progressive gospel that "scientific management redefines what had hitherto been political problems as management problems, the solution of which is governed by the logic of science." The Progressive Era proponents sought "the establishment of science as the institution of governance and the centralization of power in the hands of scientists." Professional groups, the bodies responsible for applying scientific knowledge to the practical affairs of society, became the new priesthoods in American life. Professional claims to legitimacy were not based on private power or any other narrow objectives. Rather, the professional experts were to direct the actions of the American government because the very processes of government administration were conceived to be "objective, universal, natural, altogether devoid of historical and cultural contexts, and dictated only by scientific laws," to which the experts had a special access.[11]

A new political order would arise and American government would genuinely serve the "common good"—or, as this traditional Christian language had been rechristened in the Progressive Era, "the public interest." Like other forms of economic religion, the ultimate purpose of the progressive gospel was the end of scarcity through economic progress—it was, after all, the "progressive" era in which this gospel came to prominence in American life. Continuing rapid economic growth and development would mean the abolition of all significant material scarcities (in as short a time as perhaps a few generations) and, as a result, a new heaven on earth.

A Crisis of Faith

Although American government in the twentieth century was shaped by the tenets of progressive economic religion, as one critic recently wrote, the progressive gospel is now "under skeptical reconsideration." Even though it offered "the story line for explaining America" and the development of its twentieth-century welfare and regulatory state, progressive ideas were "more than a little frayed at the intellectual edges." Indeed, it is the crisis of progressive faith that is significantly responsible for "the current disarray and uncertainty in our politics."[12] The old religion of the American welfare and regulatory state can no longer defend or sustain it, but no new religion has emerged to take its place. Instead, religious—and thus also governmental and social—confusion and disorder reigns.

Many now doubt that the social and administrative sciences achieved in practice—or are even capable of achieving in principle—the levels of knowledge required to manage centrally the affairs of a nation as large as the United States. Even if the scientific management of American society might be technically possible, the implications are troublesome. Would scientific management also mean the control of society by a technical elite? What happens to popular democracy in such a world? Increasing numbers also doubt the central importance of the highest goal of the progressive faith: rapid economic growth and development, which will abolish material shortages altogether everywhere on earth. Economic progress in the twentieth century has meant the loss of wilderness, the eradication of many plant and animal species, and indeed the wholesale alteration of the natural conditions over much of the earth. All this has been profoundly disorienting for many people.

Material progress for the progressives had a much higher purpose than the mere attainment of higher levels of private consumption of goods and services. Indeed, progress was supposed to bring an end to killing, stealing, lying, and other sinful actions on earth. The history of the twentieth century, however, mostly dashed such hopes. Two world wars, the Holocaust, Siberian prison camps, and many other dismal events showed how technical efficiency all too often seemed to heighten the magnitude of the disasters. An answer to our current problems of American government thus is not a matter simply of better administration, a change in political practices, new court rulings, a revised constitutional arrangement, or any other mechanical or technical adjustments—it is a matter of finding a new political religion.

In the twentieth century, Americans were brought together by a progressive collective commitment to the achievement, through economic progress, of the good life on earth for all. As William Schambra writes, the American progressive economic religion of the early twentieth century offered a vision of "a genuine national community which could evoke from the American people a self-denying devotion to the public good, a community in which citizens would be linked tightly by bonds of compassion and neighborliness. Americans would be asked to transcend their traditional laissez-faire individualism (which had been aggravated by the forces of modern industrialism) in order to bond themselves as one to the 'national idea.'"[13] This national political faith in progress, however, is no longer capable of providing the unifying force to hold together the far-flung and diverse American community.

Rethinking Progressivism

The libertarian outlook is much broader than the official Libertarian Party and its sometimes-doctrinaire positions. Understood in a broad sense, libertarian ideas have achieved a substantial influence in the United States since the 1970s, closely paralleling the rise of the environmental movement.[14] The libertarian viewpoint seeks a sharp reduction in, if not the outright dismantling of, much of the welfare and regulatory state in Washington. The federal regulatory commissions, federal land management agencies, and other national institutions created in the name of the scientific management of American society have too often failed their purposes. Instead of realizing progressive ideals, private interests and narrow ideological and religious causes have converted the far-ranging powers of the federal government into instruments of their own limited goals. The progressive faith in the governmental ability to achieve a unified national "public interest" has been lost. Lacking the necessary moral cement, government effectiveness and efficiency have also declined correspondingly.

Both the environmental and libertarian movements comprise people of diverse views. Within environmentalism, there are those who are in effect new economic progressives; they seek an improved scientific management of society that will take greater account of the environment. Some of these progressive environmentalists are members of the economics profession who consider protecting the environment simply a matter of doing economics better, now factoring in all the social (including nonmarket) benefits and taking proper account of all those private actions that have impacts not fully reflected in market prices (the "externalities," in economic jargon). The Clean Air Act of 1970 and the Clean Water Act of 1972 created large federal bureaucracies in Washington and extended federal power into many new areas of American life.

Yet to dwell on such progressive elements of environmentalism is to miss the larger picture. The political meaning of the environmental movement is also manifested significantly in the "not-in-my-backyard" (NIMBY) opposition that has spread throughout American life.[15] Environmentalists have led powerful movements of grassroots opposition to power plants, apartments buildings, shopping centers, dams, mines, highways, and all kinds of developments and facilities. Environmental NIMBYism is in effect a statement that the professional experts do not know best, that the national government (or any other central authority) should not direct the ordinary lives of the citizenry, and that power in American society must be significantly devolved. It is an expression of an understanding, however cloudy in the minds of many environmental activists, that those with expert claims to scientific authority should no longer have the controlling say in the management of American society.

In the past, even when highways, power plants, and other obtrusive facilities had a negative impact on them personally, many citizens would have virtuously accepted these facilities as part of their "civic duty to progress." Today, however, they often reject this religious obligation. The real message is that local groups no longer believe in the claims of economic progress: the argument that economic growth will save the whole nation (or even all the world), a progressive cause that should therefore properly command local deference and sacrifice among all citizens of good will. Moreover, it is a message that, however great the differences in formal reasoning in arriving at it, is compatible with many elements of libertarian thinking. As environmental philosopher Mark Sagoff declares, "I agree with middle-of-the-road Libertarians that public policy should seek primarily to improve the institutional arrangements" that can sustain a newly decentralized American political and economic system. Criticizing reliance on benefit-cost valuation and other familiar progressive economic methods in environmental policy, he argues that "the fundamental choice . . . lies between the institutions of a free society and the [progressive] pretensions of social science. That is the big trade-off."[16] Sagoff is among those seeking today to work out the messages of a new libertarian environmentalism.[17]

The Case of James Buchanan

The winner of the Nobel Prize in Economics in 1986, James Buchanan is a former doctoral student of Frank Knight and a leading U.S. advocate for libertarian ideas. Buchanan finds that, both in its practical results and in its intellectual foundations, the American welfare and regulatory state is bankrupt. Progressive doctrines have imbued government, Buchanan finds, with a pervasive "social engineering" mentality. In pursuing a vision of the scientific management of society, the welfare and regulatory state has come to play the role of a "potentially benevolent despot" in American life. Following the precepts of progressive religion, it is the role of economists and other social scientists to "counsel this despot" on the best methods for the management of American society.[18]

In the welfare and regulatory state, according to the progressive gospel, the needs of the national community should be paramount. Speaking with the voice of authority for all the nation, a scientific priesthood is the deliverer of ultimate truths, the modern heir to Rome. The commands of science must therefore be obeyed. Buchanan's great mission, however, is to inspire a rebellion against this modern oppressive collectivism—this new claimant to universal religious truth. Humanity must shift its fundamental allegiances "from the organizational entity as the unit to the individual-in-the-organization." If men and women will not stand up to the false claims of scientific authority, if they are so weak and craven as to fail to assert their individual freedom and dignity against the imperial claims of scientific expertise, then "we do not deserve to survive."[19]

The contemporary economics profession is, for Buchanan, one of the chief offenders. The economists of our time assert that human beings should behave rationally to maximize their well-being ("utility," in economic jargon), a standard that economic science is said to show how to rationally achieve through its scientific investigations. Yet, as Buchanan laments, a scientifically directed life for such a person "could not be concerned with choice at all." For there to be choice, there must be a multiplicity of "imagined 'possibles.'" It is "internally contradictory" to speak of individual "choice making under [scientific] certainty."[20] As a result, the progressive teachings of the American state would reduce individuals to automatons who follow with unfailing loyalty the decrees of economics and other social sciences. Religiously speaking, it would be the end of free will, as an omnipotent economic authority controlled every individual action in pursuit of a maximum total production of goods and services. If Martin Luther once argued that the Roman Catholic Church had undermined the role of individual faith, Buchanan is a contemporary protester who now calls for an American reformation directed against a new Roman theocracy of economic and other social sciences.[21]

Current economists not only spread false teachings but also have themselves fallen into evil ways. They have squandered the resources that American society has so generously provided them, wasting their time and efforts on the "escapist puzzles of modern mathematics." Instead of scientific advance, there has been retrogression. Buchanan writes that "most modern economists have no idea of what they are doing or even of what they are ideally supposed to be doing. . . . The king really has no clothes." Not only do economists deal only with "piddling trivialities," but the "empirical work in economics" mostly confirms the obvious and is no more profound than "proving water runs down hill."[22] The economics profession, in short, is yet another of the many priesthoods of history to fall into a condition of cynicism, corruption, internal decay, and loss of purpose. Economists are the new Scholastics of our time.[23] Absorbed with minutiae, they are unable to see the main trends and events of the day (until those trends become obvious to everyone else as well).

The fate of the American welfare and regulatory state and the acceptance of progressive ideas are for Buchanan closely linked. Abandon one and the other is no longer tenable. If few of his colleagues are willing to venture into such uncharted waters, Buchanan does not shrink from exploring the full consequences of his line of reasoning. Absent a progressive religious consensus, a unified national community on the scale of the American state is simply not, in Buchanan's view, sustainable over the long run.

As the federal government has taken control over more and more areas of American life, the inevitable result has been that "the dependence of order on some extended range of moral responsibilities increases."[24] Although common values may exist at a local level, it is less likely in a large nation whose population comprises a diversity of beliefs, values, and backgrounds. Great crises, such as a world war, may temporarily unify the nation, but in normal times national politics will tend to degenerate into the beggar-thy-neighbor undermining of broader purposes that has become so widespread in the United States today: "What can a person be predicted to do when the external institutions force upon him a role in a community that extends beyond his moral-ethical limits? The tension shifts toward the self-interest pole of behavior; moral-ethical principles are necessarily sublimated. The shift is exaggerated when a person realizes that others in the extended community of arbitrary and basically amoral size will find themselves in positions comparable to his own. How can a person act politically in other than his own narrowly defined self-interest in an arbitrarily sized nation of more than 200 million?"[25]

Buchanan thus calls for a radical decentralization of responsibility in the American welfare and regulatory state—the abolition of many of the institutional triumphs of American progressivism in the twentieth century. For him it is worth at least raising the possibility of the "secession" of some regions from the United States. Even if a movement for secession was not successful, at least "such a threat [might] force some devolution of central government power." Buchanan is searching for a "federal alternative to the enveloping Leviathan. . . . Who will join me in offering to make a small contribution to the Texas National Party? Or to the Nantucket Separatists?" In such a large nation as the United States, the very existence of "such things as 'national goals,' [or] 'national priorities,'" must be "absurd."[26] The breakup in the early 1990s of the old Soviet Union thus may not be the isolated event that most American have assumed, but may prove to be prophetic for other large nations as well.

Not surprisingly, Buchanan finds few allies on these issues within the mainstream of the American economics profession. Even among libertarians he is unusual in his emphasis on the failure of the moral underpinnings— the religious inadequacies, one might say—of the progressive gospel. If some of his fellow libertarians recommend turning to the market as a technical mechanism that will more efficiently solve the economic problems of society, Buchanan is at least as concerned to find answers through a radical decentralization of political authority. A sharp reduction in the administrative apparatus of the federal government is for Buchanan a first step in breaking free from the great mischief spread by progressive religion in the twentieth century.

The Message of Deep Ecology

As part of a political movement concerned with achieving practical results, mainstream environmental leaders typically avoid extreme statements that might alienate public opinion. Other members of the environmental movement, however, have made a different choice; they seek to explore the far-reaching political and economic implications of abandoning the progressive economic design of the twentieth century. They are willing to carry an initial set of environmental premises to their full logic, wherever this may lead and however potentially controversial. This second group serves to make explicit ideas that are only half formed or may even be in conflict with other aspects of the thinking of the first group. Yet it is in the writings of the iconoclasts of the environmental movement—the environmental Buchanans—that the most distinctive contributions of environmentalism to contemporary public discussion can be found.

In *Deep Ecology*, Bill Devall and George Sessions's 1985 leading statement of this group's principles, the authors give an overview of such thinking.[27] They direct their ire above all at "the ultimate value judgment upon which [current] technological society rests—progress conceived as the further development and expansion of the artificial environment necessarily at the expense of the natural world." Rather than progress, its headlong pursuit must in practice be viewed as "unequivocal regress." If Buchanan sees the scientific ideal as undermining moral responsibility and reducing life to the mere following of a scientific formula, Devall and Sessions write similarly that in technocratic society humans "come to be looked upon as a resource to be managed in the best interests of the emerging urban-industrial society."[28]

By following the precepts of "modern scientific management," as Devall and Sessions explain, "people" become "personnel," whose role in life is to be manipulated by scientific controllers in the interest of "more efficient production of commodities." The "experts" in the progressive design are "in the business of managing people" according to technocratic plans. The end result is a world in which men and women are alienated not only "from the rest of Nature but also . . . from themselves and each other."[29] It was not due to any original sin in the Garden of Eden, but rather in the never-ending pursuit of material progress and economic efficiency, that human beings have become alienated from their true selves. The progressive design for the scientific management of American society, in short, threatens not only human freedom but also the "freedom" of the plant and animal species of the world and other parts of wild nature.

Buchanan regards the progressive social engineering mentality in the welfare and regulatory state as a main source of legitimacy for the current overbearing national government. Devall and Sessions perceive contemporary society as offering "bureaucratic hierarchies" that stifle the "individuality of persons" and create an environment that encourages people to behave and think "like machines." It is thus necessary to escape current "machine-based societies" in which scientific imperatives have taken over and dominate "the whole life of society." If the instruments of social domination for Devall and Sessions can take the form of the "civil power" of government or the "market," it may be necessary to abandon current understandings of governments and markets.[30]

Buchanan expresses a deep skepticism with respect to the current role of the social sciences. Devall and Sessions also observe that social science is based on a view that "technological and social progress can continue without limit, making all social problems ultimately soluble" by the experts. In practice, however, the methods developed by social scientists often prove inadequate. Devall and Sessions note that in the field of natural resources one finds "'abstract models' which in our estimation have little relevance to site specific situations." Misplaced confidence in the claims of social science often "lulls the manager into thinking he has the relevant variables under control," when the truth is that the world is "more complex than we now know and more complex than we possibly can know."[31]

Indeed, Devall and Sessions assert that "there is no reason to believe that scientific theories and models will ever capture the full intricacy of the natural ecosystem functioning." If Buchanan decries the false "scientism" of the progressive economic vision, Devall and Sessions argue that deep ecologists should "not be constrained by scientism, and by the definition of Nature as just a collection of bits of data to be manipulated by humans." It is imperative to recognize that "science and technology alone are a dangerous substitute for land wisdom." Buchanan decries the moral consequences of a progressive view that mankind must follow the controlling prescriptions of economic and other sciences; along similar lines, deep ecologists argue that "scientists and technologists" do "not have objective, neutral answers." Although the true believers in economic progress do "not discuss ethical issues" in an explicit and honest fashion, their outlook implicitly contains far-ranging and unacceptable ethical implications.[32]

Devall and Sessions, for example, write that, although "resource economists look at wilderness," their outlook makes them incapable of really "seeing it." Even those economists sympathetic to environmental causes regard creating a wilderness as an economic step to maximize benefits minus costs—taking account of the fact that wilderness may have a calculable "existence value" (see chap. 3) in dollar terms and other special types of quantifiable economic benefits. The attempt to impose a utilitarian framework on a moral decision, however, inevitably must fail. It yields, as Buchanan sees in many other efforts of economists, irrelevant and misdirected economic analysis. If Buchanan decries the loss of human freedom implied in the utility-maximizing framework of economics, Devall and Sessions similarly reject "the premise of instrumental rationality—the narrowly utilitarian view" of economics. This outlook must be rejected because it "fails to distinguish vital human needs from mere desires, egotistical arrogance and adventurism in technology."[33]

As discussed above, Buchanan suggests the need to revitalize the sense of community by means of a radical devolution of power in American society—even going so far as to suggest that some regions might have to secede from the nation. Similarly, Devall and Sessions note that a number of deep ecologists call for "the decentralization of society." For example, in the field of education it is necessary "to make the small community the primary environment for educational activity." A description of "an ecotopian vision" consists of a small and self-sustaining island in the South Pacific. An appropriate worldview emphasizes "small communal farms, monastic groups, and continuing attempts to scale down the size of institutions, organizations and industry." The goal should be a "decentralized, non-hierarchical, democratic" society of "small-scale community" that emphasizes "self-responsibility" and respect for "spiritual-religious mentors."[34] If Buchanan sees the large nation-state as lacking the "moral-ethical cement" to hold it together, and smaller institutions as the hope for reasserting a stronger sense of community identity and moral purpose, Devall and Sessions take a similar stance.[35]

In *Ecotopia*, a novel by environmentalist author Ernest Callenbach, a utopian existence is portrayed as consisting of a pastoral life in the Pacific Northwest. This region has seceded from the United States, suspending both market and political relationships with the rest of the country. It has done so to avoid any outside disruptions or dislocations, whether they originate from the market or the government. The fundamental problem, and the reason for seceding, has been the deep offensiveness to Ecotopia's social values of the "underlying national philosophy of America: ever-continuing progress, the fruits of industrialization for all, a rising gross national product"—that is to say, the false god of economic religion.[36]

Opposing Religious Idolatry

As this book has argued, the basic beliefs of economists and environmentalists, to a greater extent than most of them recognize, often follow in the path of earlier Christian teachings and practices. Economic religion promises salvation here on earth; the American welfare and regulatory state is the new church of the progressive gospel; and the headquarters of economic religion is Washington, D.C., the new Rome. The critical views of economic and environmental Calvinists can then be seen as secular ways of attacking the claims to legitimacy and authority of the progressive national church (now united in an American state "secular theocracy"). The economic god, these new Calvinists are saying, is a false god; the church in Washington that operates in the name of economic religion lacks legitimacy; and, as Calvin once said of Rome, a vile economic heresy now being spread from Washington has usurped the legitimate role of other, truer religions.

It is not only in secular statements such as libertarianism and deep ecology that such criticisms of economic religion and the powers of the American state are communicated; they are sometimes expressed in traditional Christian settings and language as well. Stanley Hauerwas is a professor of theology at Duke Divinity School who in 2000–2001 delivered the Gifford Lectures in Scotland, the most prestigious world platform in Christian theology. In 2001, *Time* magazine named him "America's best theologian" (he responded by saying, "Best is not a theological category").[37] Earlier, in 1992's *Against the Nations* and in other writings, Hauerwas argued that too many Christians are active followers of secular religions that sustain the modern nation-state, effectively turning away from a more valid Christian faith. As he writes, "Accounts of the Christian moral life have too long been accommodated to the needs of the nation state, and in particular, to the nation state we call the United States of America." If Christianity is to flourish again, it will require "a recovery of the independence of the church from its subservience to liberal culture and its corresponding agencies of the state."[38] In its most dangerous form in the United States, that state is to be found in the federal government in Washington, a place now seen by skeptical Protestants such as Hauerwas as a new fountain of heresy of our times.[39]

As he laments, too many Christians "have let the Gospel be identified with utopian fantasies" such as the progressive gospel of efficiency and other forms of economic religion. As Hauerwas complains, the underlying "Christian substance is translated into Marxism, into secularized forms of biblical eschatology, existentialism, and psychology; and it develops themes from [Protestant] Reformation anthropology divorced from Reformation theology." Many adherents of secular gospels such as economic and environmental religion have abandoned Christianity altogether, but Hauerwas is equally disturbed by the invasion of secular ideas into the institutional Christian churches themselves. He is critical of the many "attempts to interpret the Kingdom [of God] in terms of liberal presumptions about what constitutes human progress."[40]

American progressives—commonly found both inside and outside the institutional Christian churches—have believed that the world can be perfected by human action alone, when the truth is that "the kingdom [of God] is not to be established by men but by God alone." As Hauerwas explains, it is impossible even for human beings to know precisely the character of any final heavenly destination because "scripturally there seems to be no good grounds to associate the kingdom of God with any form of political organization and/or to assume that it is best characterized by any one set of ethical ideals such as love and justice." Partly because it is impossible to know God's true design for the world, and rejecting the missionary vision that the United States offers an ethical and political model that should be preached and followed throughout the world, Hauerwas declares that as Christians "it is not our task to make the 'world' the kingdom." When a Christian church "thinks and acts as if 'America has a peculiar place in God's promises and purposes,'" it betrays its proper role and loses its "ability to be a 'zone of truth-telling in a world of mendacity.'" A true Christian must remain vigilant to the "ways the democratic state remains a state that continues to wear the head of the beast"—indeed, thereby posing a particularly insidious threat to a valid Christian faith in the United States.[41]

Hauerwas is no libertarian and in fact has critical things to say about the corrosive individualism of the libertarian philosophy. Yet he also argues that "no state will keep itself limited, no constitution or ideology is sufficient to that task, unless there is a body of people separated from the nation that is willing to say 'No' to the state's claims on their loyalties."[42] This is a task that has also been advanced by many NIMBYite environmentalists in resisting the scientific management plans for economic development of the American progressive state. But many other Americans have instead become worshippers in economic religion and have looked to federal power to advance their sure belief in the redeeming character of economic progress. For a devout Christian such as Hauerwas, separation of church and state does not exist in the United States, only separation of traditional Christian (and Jewish) religion from the state.*

For all too many Christians, as Hauerwas thus explains further, American "democracy has in fact become an end in itself that captures our souls in subtle ways we hardly notice." The result is that, rather than independent religious voices, many Christian churches have "in fact become a captive to and in America" of its various secular (and for Hauerwas heretical and thus non-Christian) creeds. Their ostensible Christian religion has been subordinated to economic religion, environmental religion, the American constitutional faith, a national mission to save the world, and other powerful elements of U.S. secular religions of salvation. In the face of the temptations of American patriotism, Hauerwas warns, it is necessary for more devout Christians to keep in mind that "the true history of the world, that history that determines our destiny, is not carried by the nation state. In spite of its powerful moral appeal, this history [of the nation state] is the history of godlessness."[43] Libertarians such as James Buchanan, or environmentalists such as the authors of *Deep Ecology*, say much the same thing, if without the explicit Christian references.

---

* A few mainstream American politicians are now even making such arguments. In seeking to address concerns of the American electorate with respect to his Mormon religion, Mitt Romney (former Massachusetts governor and candidate for the 2008 Republican presidential nomination) gave a widely publicized speech at Texas A&M University in December 2007. He declared that many current attempts to separate church and state were going too far, amounting in practice to discrimination against traditional Jewish and Christian faiths. As Romney put it, "It's as if they're intent on establishing a new religion in America—the religion of secularism." While denying their own religious essence, secular religions often sought to ban more traditional expressions of religious conviction from the public arena. See Dan Balz, "In Speech on Faith, Romney Vows to Serve 'No One Cause,'" *Washington Post*, December 7, 2007, A1.

A Higher Authority Than the State

Paul Watson is a founder of the environmental organization Greenpeace who in 1977 also founded the Sea Shepherd Conservation Society, which he led for many years, employing confrontational methods in seeking to halt international whaling and other ocean environmental offenses. In 2000, *Time* magazine listed him as one of its environmental heroes of the twentieth century. From 2003 to 2006, he served on the national board of the Sierra Club. In 1988, Watson gave a speech to the Western Public Interest Law Conference at the University of Oregon Law School explaining the basic goals and values—the implicit theology—that motivated his environmental efforts.[44] A main purpose was to justify his willingness to violate national laws to protect the plant and animal species of the world's oceans.

As Watson declared, "I respect the laws of a nation-state only to the extent that such laws respect the higher order." Watson instead took his higher-order guidance from "natural law," including, most importantly, "ecological laws [that] govern the interrelationships of all life" and reign "supreme." In Iceland in 1986, for example, Watson destroyed a whaling station and sank two whaling boats because "Iceland was whaling without an [International Whaling Commission, IWC] permit and it stated that it would continue to do so despite the fact that it was a signatory to the [IWC] moratorium agreement." When the national governments of the world failed to rebuke Iceland, Watson felt a higher obligation to take "action to prevent further violations of the regulations and to protect the whales."[45] At Nuremburg, the prosecutors of Nazi war criminals argued that the defendants were guilty even when they were following the laws of the German nation-state, and Watson now asserted a similar allegiance to laws higher than the state relating to the treatment of the natural world.

Christian theology has also long pondered the issue of the relationship of the individual and the state. In matters of religion and ultimate truth, religious authority must stand above state authority. But in regulating the practical affairs of life, the laws of the state must normally be obeyed. Only in circumstances of exceptional injustice is an individual allowed to violate the laws of the state in which he or she lives. Many learned volumes have been devoted to defining a degree of injustice adequate to justify a revolt. Watson is an environmental activist and does not appeal to this past body of theological writings. Instead, he simply asserts that "when people are deprived of their rights, there is a rebellion against the law. The same is true when the planet and her millions of species are denied rights—there will be a reaction."[46]

When human beings defy God's commands in the Bible, they can expect to suffer harsh punishments, including frequently environmental calamities. For Watson, the natural laws of ecosystems have become a substitute for the commands of a Jewish and Christian God. As he states, "When the human species ignores the logical implications of these laws of ecology, we are guilty of crimes against the Earth. We will not be judged by men for these crimes, but with a terrible justice rendered against us by the Earth herself." Human beings are already on "a course which leads toward destruction of the eco-systems of the Earth [and that] is a course which will destroy the human spe-cies."[47] In seeking to enforce higher ecological laws, Watson thus is seeking to save human beings from their own sinfulness and from the resulting terrible wrath of the "Earth" (i.e., God).

In his speech Watson makes no explicit references to God, Jesus Christ, or the Bible, but he nevertheless has a traditional Christian understanding of the origins of human sinfulness: "As a species, we have an understanding of right and wrong and good and evil. We are innately good, but because we drifted from the garden so many centuries ago, we have lost touch with natural real-ity and natural law." To halt our evil actions in destroying the natural world, it will be necessary for the world to be born again environmentally. Echoing the language of Aldo Leopold in *A Sand County Almanac*, Watson pronounces: "We need a new ethic that changes *Homo sapiens* from conquerer of the Earth to be just plain citizen upon it, equal to the other citizen species. Develop-ing this new ethic will require nothing less than a revolution in our spiritual, political and economic values."[48] That is to say, it will require a new religion faithful to the true god.

When many current governments are in the hands of sinful men and women, however, Watson asserts the unilateral "right to take the law into our own hands. . . . It is our right to uphold and to defend the laws of nature." Any environmentalist of real conviction, true to his or her religious conscience, must be willing to secede from the powers of the state. Yet, in so doing, Watson—speaking in 1988—is anxious to explain to his audience that "my field officers and I are not hooligan terrorists" but rather "adhere to a strict set of ethical guidelines," which include an absolute rule against killing or otherwise doing physical violence to another person.[49] Specifically, there are five higher com-mands for those who will act with him outside formal state authority and in the defense of the earth's natural laws of the ecological order: "First, we cannot use weapons. Second, we cannot use explosives. Third, we cannot undertake any action that involves any risk of injury to any living thing. Fourth, we must accept responsibility for our actions. Fifth, we must be prepared and willing to accept the consequences, moral and legal, for our actions."[50]

Standing up for the natural laws of ecology, Watson and his team have ripped rifles out of the hands of sealers in the Scottish Orkney Islands and thrown them into the sea; they have blockaded the sealing fleet in St. John's, Newfoundland, to keep it locked up in the harbor; they have dived in an airplane between a pack of wolves and its hunters flying in helicopters; and they have chased the Japanese drift net fleet from the North Pacific. By means of these and other actions, Watson is proud that "we have saved thousands of whales, tens of thousands of dolphins, and hundreds of thousands of seals. Our work is very satisfying for the soul"—in effect, doing god's good work on earth.[51] Although his moral system resembles Christian ethics in many respects, the laws of Watson's god are not to be found in the Bible but rather in the workings of nature—the "laws of ecology" of the earth. John Muir, Ralph Waldo Emerson, and Henry David Thoreau once looked to nature to discover God's thinking, and before them Jonathan Edwards and other New England Calvinists, who were all following after the teachings of John Calvin himself. Watson may have traveled the farthest distance theologically, and may be unorthodox in other respects, but his 1988 sermon still delivered a message with which Calvin—who had himself invoked a higher authority in daring to rebel against the Church authorities in Rome—might have sympathized. Nation-states are now the central churches of economic religion of our times, and, as Watson declares, "I envision a world where nations have been eliminated, and we all live under natural law within the context of a planetary nation."[52]

The origins of American libertarianism are found in the fierce Calvinist defense of individual religious freedom. In England, no action by the king or other government authority could infringe on a Calvinist's obligation to worship according to the dictates of his or her own beliefs. Indeed, Oliver Cromwell and his followers made Charles II pay the ultimate price for his refusal to accept their Calvinist prerogatives. Today, Paul Watson asserts a similar religious obligation to obey the ethical commands of a higher authority than the state—not a Christian God but in many ways a close substitute, the natural laws of "Earth," as revealed by the science of ecology (see also chap. 8).

The Obsolescence of the Nation-State

Norman Macrae is an economic journalist of libertarian persuasion who served for many years as a writer and editor for the *Economist* magazine. Although he would seem an unlikely ally of Watson, he shares Watson's skeptical view of the powers of the modern nation-state. In the twentieth century, nation-states were not only harmful for the natural world but also provided the organizational basis for the waging of many terrible wars and other destructive acts on a worldwide scale, including in many cases the persecution and even killing of their own people. Seeking a powerful antidote to this toxic global force, Macrae offered in *The 2025 Report* a vision of a world that might be described as a libertarian utopia without large nation-states.

Much like Buchanan, Macrae sees the members of any large nation-state as too diverse in outlook to maintain tight communal bonds. He suggests instead a libertarian world of "genuine pluralism." It would have a few world-wide governing institutions that performed key global tasks, but otherwise would encourage the "free dispersal into small communities where every-one could do her or his own thing." Large nation-states would disappear and instead everyone could "set up their own forms of very local government—communes, monasteries, profit-making local governments run by private-enterprise performance contractors, beach clubs on desert isles. . . . whatever people wanted."[53] Macrae thus offers a version of a modern feudalism. Each person finds his or her own fiefdom, where they are free to pursue their own style and preference in cultural, religious, and other matters.

Unlike the feudalism of the medieval era, however, and departing from deep ecology in this respect, free trade would blossom in Macrae's vision of the future. The spread of a worldwide trading system, including the creation of multinational free trade areas such as the European Union and the North American Free Trade Zone, has undercut the main economic function of na-tion-states in the modern age, providing open market areas large enough to encourage full economic specialization and realization of economies of scale that can now transcend national boundaries. Indeed, Macrae sees the spread of modern technology and the growth of economic interrelationships binding the world together more closely than ever before. Ever-improving telecom-munications technology would play an especially important role, transform-ing not only the ease of personal communication but also job markets, which would become highly decentralized: at this point "brain workers—which in rich countries already meant most workers—no longer needed to live near their work. They could live on the beach of Tahiti if they wanted to, and tele-commute daily to computers and other colleagues in the New York or London or Hamburg or Timbuctoo-tax-haven office through which they worked."[54]

While Macrae's proposal for radical decentralization might have seemed far-fetched and even altogether utopian when he first authored it in 1984, events have since moved with surprising speed in the directions he outlined. In the United States there has been a proliferation of "private community as-sociations" (a category including home owners associations, condominiums, and cooperatives) across the nation. In 1970 fewer than 1 percent of Ameri-cans lived in a private community association, but this figure had risen to 20 percent in 2009. Between 1980 and 2000, fully half the new housing built in the United States was subject to the private governance of a community asso-ciation. As private entities not subject to many of the constitutional rules ap-plicable to public entities, community associations had a wide scope to define their own cultural styles, aesthetic preferences, and other manifestations of the specific collective preferences of their residents. Many private communities, for example, limit their residents to senior citizens (older than fifty-five); a few of them specialize in providing a social environment and otherwise meeting the needs of gay senior citizens. Other private communities have sought to provide environmentally sustainable landscapes that would appeal to ecologically minded residents. I described the full scope and analyzed the larger political and economic significance of this development—one that is consistent with the messages of libertarian environmentalism as described in this chapter—for the United States in *Private Neighborhoods and the Transformation of Local Government*.[55]

Moreover, similar private transformations have been occurring on a global scale, again surprisingly mirroring the governance shifts advocated by Macrae. In a book describing this important worldwide trend towards decentralized private governments, Chris Webster and Georg Glasze explain that:

> private neighborhoods are beyond doubt a highly significant feature of post-modern urbanism. They are a global phenomenon, they signify a distinct shift in the way cities are organized, they represent an extreme decentralization of decision-making, they create new socio-spatial divides, their popularity has spawned a commodified neighbourhood industry, they create micro-territories with their own local constitutions, they represent a new model of collective action in the coordination of demand for public goods, they break down traditional social geographies and create new ones, they provide an alternative model for financing civic goods, they do for home-buyers what the package tour industry has done for individual holiday buyers, they enhance the conspicuousness of home-based consumption, they alter patterns of urban insecurities and they create new micro-societies.[56]

Regional differentiation in political, economic, and cultural matters has been increasing as well. In Europe, many of the newest nations in the European Union have only a few million people. In 1981, a reporter for the *Washington Post*, Joel Garreau, published *The Nine Nations of North America*. His North American "nations" included "Quebec," "New England," "The Foundry," "Ecotopia" (in the Pacific Northwest), "Mexamerica," "Dixie," and the "Bread Basket." Garreau argued that "each has its capital and distinctive web of power and influence.... Each has a peculiar economy; each commands a certain emotional allegiance from its citizens." Garreau suggested that "the more self-assured each of these Nine Nations becomes, the less willing it is to be dictated to by outsiders who show no interest in sharing—or even understanding—local values." Across North America, there was a diversity that "emphasizes the real, enduring, and basic economic and social differences of each region, manifested in attitudes towards everything from nuclear power to unions to abortion" to religion.[57]

In progressive economic thinking, there was a clear distinction between science and religion, between fact and value, between expertise and politics. In modern life, progressives believed, the trend of events was inexorably toward the dominance of science, fact, expertise. As this occurred, the world would inevitably converge toward one common set of social beliefs and governing arrangements, grounded in the objective truths of science. Yet Garreau was saying that, simply as a matter of his own investigations of North American trends, this was not happening. Contrary to earlier progressive expectations, the simple reality was that religious and other cultural differences among peoples and regions were persisting and in some cases even growing. As Buchanan suggested, the result was the erosion of the moral bonds that held together the American nation-state. A more effective politics and economics might require that sovereign boundaries and the institutions of governance be realigned in North America to fit those tighter regional and even local communities.

Pollution as Trespass

Murray Rothbard was the Karl Marx of the American libertarian movement (even as he lived much later, dying in 1995). Both heirs to the Jewish prophetic tradition, they delivered their messages in economic rather than biblical language. Rothbard, like Marx, wrote and spoke as though he was Moses handing down the Ten Commandments, seldom if ever showing a trace of doubt in his own pronouncements. Each was capable of both utter foolishness and brilliant insights. Their flamboyant and prophetic manner was offensive to conventional opinions, and neither Marx nor Rothbard was accepted by the mainstream economists of their times. The average American economist to this day may well have never heard of Murray Rothbard—and it is a virtual certainty that he or she was never assigned to read anything by Rothbard in graduate school.

Rothbard's special way of seeing the world—distinctive even by libertarian standards—is illustrated by his way of thinking about air, water, and other forms of pollution. As Rothbard declared—here invoking biblical phrasing—the core principle of libertarianism is "the command, 'Thou shall not interfere with A's property right.'" Reverting to more conventional language, he wrote that "the basic axiom of libertarian political theory holds that every man is a self-owner, having absolute jurisdiction over his own body. In effect, this means that no one else may justly invade, or aggress against, another's person"—or against their property. Thus as long as your actions do not do any harm to anyone else or their property, you are entirely free to do whatever you want. There is only one ethical commandment that justifies collective restraints on individual actions, potentially requiring the use of government coercive powers; as Rothbard declared, a "physical invasion" of another person's property "is the only human action that should be illegal and that justifies the use of physical violence to combat it."[58] Otherwise, anything goes; beyond the principle of noninterference with others, morality is strictly a personal matter (which is not to say that many people as individuals, including libertarians, might not voluntarily subscribe to strict biblical, secular humanist, or other possibly demanding ethical codes).

As limited as Rothbard's concept of public justice is, however, it has potentially radical implications for the environment. From a libertarian perspective, an act of pollution is an act of physical invasion—an act literally of trespass. As Rothbard declared, "If A is causing pollution of B's air and this can be proven beyond a reasonable doubt, then this is aggression and it should be enjoined and damages paid in accordance with strict liability."[59] Rothbard asserted this as an absolute requirement.* Hence, Rothbard the libertarian arrives at a rule for air, water, and other forms of pollution that would satisfy even the most ardent deep ecologist. Unless there is unanimous consent among those adversely affected by the emission of a pollutant, all air, water, and other forms of pollution must be strictly prohibited.†

---

* Actually, Rothbard did offer one qualification. If A was already polluting, and B was considering the possibility of locating near A, then A could "be said to have *homesteaded a pollution easement*," which would prevent B from pursuing a nuisance claim if B then affirmatively chose to move into the path of A's pollution. The application of this rule in practice, however, is likely to be problematic. What happens if a factory is emitting a serious pollutant over a wide surrounding area—might that mean that the presence of the factory would in effect prevent many other owners from making new uses of their properties (since the pollution levels might be unacceptable for these uses and they would be denied the opportunity to make a nuisance claim)? Rothbard makes an effort to address such issues but in the end is less than fully convincing.

† Such thinking became part of the wider political discussion in the United States with the entry of libertarian Ron Paul in the Republican race for the 2008 presidential nomination. In the fall of 2007, Paul declared—taking a harder line against pollution than any mainstream environmental leader would—that:

> nobody has the right to pollute their neighbors' air or water or land. People who pollute should be taken to court and closed down, but we have 150 years of traditions where they have been able to get away with this. We don't need government regulations to solve these problems. I grew up in Pittsburgh, where you couldn't even see the noon sun in the sky, and that whole city was cleaned up without the federal government needing to be involved. I think we would have been much better served from the start if people would have better understood the principles of private property [and the nuisance law limits to its use]. ("Election 08: Talk With the Candidates: Ron Paul," *Washington Post Online*, October 12, 2007, http://www.washingtonpost.com/wp-dyn/content/discussion/2007/10/01/DI2007100101451.html)

Rothbard gave special attention to the problem of air pollution. As he wrote in 1982, "Air pollution is a private nuisance generated from one person's landed property onto another and is an invasion of the airspace appurtenant to land and, often, of the person of the landowner." As a result, air pollution can "be considered a tort and subject to liability and injunction." The only defense of the air polluter, as with other forms of potential nuisance activities, is that any harm done to another person is so small that it does not rise to the level of a legitimate nuisance—in the case of some gaseous substances traveling through the air, for example, "the invisible and insensible crossing of another's air boundary . . . [may] not interfere with the [other] owner's use or enjoyment of his person or property"—and thus such substances would not be subject to a nuisance injunction to halt the offending activity.[60]

Rothbard's limits on pollution, to be sure, might virtually shut down modern society (thereby possibly appealing to some deep ecologists who would hope to maximize the total amount of wild nature in the world). Nuisance law is also applied after the fact, raising the possibility that a business might invest many millions of dollars in a new manufacturing plant, only to be told later by a judge that the plant had to be shut down as a nuisance. In the 1960s, the possibility arose that Los Angeles smog, chemical releases into the Hudson River, and many other forms pollution might actually be brought under control in the United States through newly vigorous court enforcement of nuisance laws. American industry reacted with alarm, generating pressures on Congress that helped to bring about the enactment of the Clean Air Act of 1970 and the Clean Water Act of 1972.[61] Rather than having widely varying pollution standards set by many individual local judges under nuisance law principles, American businesses wanted a single nationwide standard clearly set in advance—and thus also requiring the establishment of a national administrative agency, the Environmental Protection Agency, which was created in 1970. The passage of 1970s environmental legislation meant that a business could now negotiate its environmental approvals with the federal government in advance of any development and otherwise preempt the local (and highly unpredictable) application of nuisance law across many jurisdictions.

The point here is not that Rothbard—or deep ecologists—had the full answer. Nuisance law is well capable of addressing some local pollution problems and might be allowed a wider application, but it faces severe handicaps in any situation where there are many thousands of individual polluters and many millions of individuals affected by the air pollution (such as the smog in Los Angeles).[62] The collective action problems and burdens in attempting to deal with Los Angeles air pollution by means of nuisance law would have been immense. Yet it is important that both libertarians such as Rothbard and hard-core environmentalists can agree on an appropriate goal, whatever the practical limitations in pursuing it. All pollution, ideally, as they are saying, should be totally eliminated.

Rothbard had other equally unconventional views. Much as this book argues, he once wrote that "leaving out religious outlook . . . would disastrously skew any picture of the history of economic thought." In his economic thinking, Rothbard was a member of the Austrian school of economics (whose members also included Ludwig Von Mises and Friedrich Hayek), which is closely linked historically with a libertarian political philosophy. Rothbard explained that "it is no accident that the Austrian School . . . arose in a country that was not only solidly Catholic, but whose values and attitudes were still heavily influenced by Aristotelian and Thomist thought."[63] If Paul Watson saw appeals to natural law as providing a necessary defense of wild nature that would override any nation-state authority, Rothbard saw a similar role for the higher authority of natural law in protecting individual human freedoms against nation-state assaults.

The Protestant Reformation worked powerfully to advance individual liberties by establishing a new freedom of religion that was then transferred to other areas of individual relationships with the state. Always the contrarian, Rothbard emphasized, however, another side of Protestantism: its role in undermining the authority of natural law, as worked out over centuries by Roman Catholic theologians. Thus, as he wrote, "along with the absolute state, theories of absolutism arose and began to throw [Roman Catholic] natural law doctrines into the shade. The adoption of natural law theory, after all, meant that the state was bound to limit itself to the dictates of the natural or the divine law." But when the authority of natural law was denied, the power of the state became total: "The glorification of the state went hand in hand with a denial that human reason could come to know any natural law outside of positive edicts of the state." Without natural law and a corresponding rational basis for governmental actions that could limit the simple exercise of power, "justice has no rational foundation; it is purely mystical and solely a matter of faith." The Protestant way of thinking about God suggested that "[His] commands are merely arbitrary and mysterious, and not to be understood in terms of ethical content" as worked out by rational explication of natural laws.[64] As Rothbard wrote, it was Protestantism that was principally responsible for the rise of autocratic nation-states in Europe in the sixteenth and seventeenth centuries: "If reason cannot be used to frame an ethic [as in Thomist and other Scholastic thought], this means that Luther and Calvin had to, in essence, throw out natural law, and in doing so, they jettisoned the basic criteria developed over the centuries by which to criticize the despotic actions of the state. Indeed, Luther and Calvin, relying on isolated Biblical passages, rather than on an integrated philosophical system, opined that the powers that be are ordained of God, and that therefore the king, no matter how tyrannical, is divinely appointed and must always be obeyed."[65] Although Rothbard and Frank Knight are both important figures in the history of American libertarianism, they had diametrically opposite views in this one area—Knight seeing natural law as offering a mere pretense of rationality and being frequently used to justify state abuses of power.

For Rothbard, much like the Scholastics, an appropriate ethical system for society can be derived by processes of strictly rational analysis from initial assumptions that will be accepted by all people of good will. The proper study of economics, he argued, was thus based on "facts so general and universal and so deeply rooted in the nature of man and his world that everyone, upon learning or reading of them, would give his assent." The valid method of doing economics then consists of logically deriving the "deductive implications" of these facts and, since they will be known with certainty to be "true, their logical implications must be true as well."[66] Rothbard held that economic thought had reached a high point with the Salamanca school of Scholastic economics in sixteenth-century Spain, which produced key economic insights that were then lost until the rise of the Austrian school in the mid- to late nineteenth century.[67]

Many environmentalists are critical of the free market messages of Adam Smith and of mainstream economics. They might be surprised that Rothbard offered an even harsher judgment—if for somewhat different reasons—with respect to Smith. He wrote that, rather than the conventional view of Smith as the founder of modern economics, the truth "was virtually the reverse." In ignoring the more rational foundations of earlier Scholastic economic analyses, the fact was that Smith "tragically shunted economics on to a false path, a dead end from which the Austrians had to rescue economics a century later."[68] He considered that Smith's many economic confusions could ultimately be traced to a bias introduced by his Calvinist origins in Scotland. Smith's misguided labor theory of value, for example, was an implicit way of communicating—now in the disguise of an economic theory of value—the importance of hard work, as found in Calvinist thinking. As Rothbard wrote, he and other members of the Austrian school of economics were the heirs to: "the scholastics, and then France, Italy and Austria [which] were Catholic countries, and Catholicism emphasized consumption as the goal of production and consumer utility and enjoyment as, at least in moderation, valuable activities and goals. The British tradition, on the contrary, beginning with [Adam] Smith himself, was Calvinist, and reflected the Calvinist emphasis on hard work and labour toil as not only a good but a great good in itself, whereas consumer enjoyment is at best a necessary evil, a mere requisite to continuing labour and production."[69]

Rothbard also had a strong anarchist streak that sometimes went beyond even the views of many fellow libertarians in its resistance to any role for government.[70] In his opposition to economic religion, and the twentieth-century welfare and regulatory state that economic religion legitimized and promoted, Rothbard would have found common cause with many recent environmental prophets. In the end, he was, perhaps, more of an economic Calvinist than he realized. Indeed, there were deep and unresolved tensions between Rothbard's professed faith in a single universal natural law and his simultaneous extreme aversion to the exercise of any national or other governmental authority.

Although both Rothbard and Paul Watson look to natural law as a barrier to nation-state abuses, both leave out any mention of a God. Absent a God, they are forced to look to science—ecological science in Watson's case, economic science in Rothbard's—as the source of the religious authority for their understandings of natural law. The worship of science, however, is a centralizing influence that spawned many of the worst abuses both of wild nature and of individual liberty in the twentieth century. The scientific method itself is neutral with respect to the authority, or lack of such, of an ethical system—a problem for which Watson and Rothbard, both leaving God out of their messages, have no solution. The one way out, admittedly, would be to assume that, as with environmental creationists and so many other modern thinkers, they may be implicitly invoking the presence of a god, even as they say nothing directly about this and may even outwardly deny the existence of any god.

Environmentalism and the Market

The prospects for a greater decentralization of governing authority in the United States may depend on the degree to which environmentalists and libertarians find that they can work together in a common cause—spreading the message of a "new Calvinism" that once again rebels against a central religious authority, today the American nation-state, which is the church of the progressive gospel of efficiency. Yet, at present, environmentalists and libertarians mostly travel in different circles. Environmentalists react skeptically to libertarian proposals for the devolution and privatization of government functions. The practical result of giving wider scope to market forces, many environmentalists argue, would be the widespread destruction of nature. Surely, many people will think, this area of basic disagreement will pose an insuperable barrier to any joint efforts, whatever other commonalities may exist.

Yet, as libertarian thinkers such as John Baden and Richard Stroup have frequently pointed out, governments acting in the name of progressive religion have been responsible for many of the most environmentally destructive actions in the United States (see chap. 5).[71] It was not private business but the federal government that built many dams throughout the American West that were both economically wasteful and environmentally harmful. In the 1970s and 1980s many of the large timber sales on Rocky Mountain national forests were both money-losing propositions for the U.S. Forest Service and offensive to wilderness and other environmental values. Numerous agricultural wetlands around the United States have been filled in with the assistance of federal subsidy programs. Nuclear wastes for many years were dumped across the West by atomic bomb builders and testers. Around the world, the greatest destruction of the environment occurred in the former Soviet Union and other communist nations, where there were fewer political constraints to the all-out pursuit of economic progress.

In a 1991 book titled *Free Market Environmentalism* and many subsequent writings, Terry Anderson and Donald Leal argue that government regulation is not needed to resolve many environmental problems.[72] Environmental damages often occur because property rights are not adequately specified to include the full range of consequences of individual and group actions—a point emphasized by Garrett Hardin as well in his classic 1968 article titled "The Tragedy of the Commons."[73] Rather than imposing new government regulations with all the attendant political and bureaucratic problems, a better specification of property rights will often be a superior environmental solution.[74] Moreover, as Ronald Coase pointed out, bargaining in the private market may succeed in resolving many "externality" problems even within the framework of a less than ideal property rights regime.[75] Indeed, the most important consideration for Coase is that some set of property rights be well defined, letting the players in the market know clearly their initial bargaining positions, thereby facilitating their subsequent striking of a deal. It is governments that often fail to define rights adequately or in some cases even make matters worse by preventing private bargaining from occurring in the first place (holders of Western water rights, for example, were long prohibited from selling their rights to defenders of fishery and other "instream" uses that were not considered legally "beneficial").[76]

Historically, many pollution problems resulted from the free assignment of an indefinitely large number of "rights to pollute" to anyone who wanted them. If a resource is in fact scarce, and yet its use is made available to anyone at zero cost, there will always be large resulting misallocations and other economic failings.[77] Severe pollution in its various forms illustrates the point well. According to libertarian thinking, then, there are two main ways to establish tighter limits on environmentally polluting actions. First, the legal powers of individuals to sue for nuisance damages or for an injunction against an offending polluter could be expanded.[78] Second, the government could create new rights to pollute and then assign them in some fashion to individuals and businesses, which would own and be able to trade in the rights in a market. Although the rights are less than fully protected as private property, such "cap and trade" systems of pollution property rights have in fact been adopted in the United States for control of sulfur dioxide and nitrogen oxide air pollution and in Europe for imposing limits on emissions of greenhouse gases, among other important applications.[79]

The principle that plays such a prominent part in libertarian thinking—voluntary agreement as a guiding rule in individual and group relationships—is also surprisingly prominent in much of environmental thinking. The environmental assertion of the rights of NIMBY resistance is in essence a declaration for voluntary agreement as a central ordering principle in society—another way of making the libertarian demand that the coercive power of the state be curtailed in American life. In the future, finding an acceptable site for many NIMBY facilities is likely to prove practically feasible only with the provision of some form of monetary or other compensation to the surrounding community that would be adversely affected. That is to say, it will be necessary to "buy" from this community the permission to locate the facility. In this way, the environmental movement, if perhaps inadvertently, may be paving the way for further injecting new property rights and new market relationships—sometimes of a privately collective as well as individual character—into important parts of American life.[80] Local governments, for example, may end up being authorized to sell legally, and private firms to buy legally, the zoning changes necessary for a new development (buying and selling such changes would now usually be considered an illegal act of "bribery").[81]

Some deep ecologists might suggest that virtually all trading in goods and services in world markets should be halted, enforcing a new level of world autarky. Libertarians will object strongly to any such universal vision. Many libertarians would have little objection, however, to permitting a small private community to erect its own high barriers to trade, based on its own internal religious or other value system. Indeed, as suggested above, it is possible to imagine a world order in which the opportunity exists for every political jurisdiction to participate in international trade to a greater or lesser extent, leaving the actual degree of such participation as a matter strictly for local self-determination.

Conclusion

Almost five hundred years ago, the Protestant Reformation proclaimed a right of secession from the universal Church in Rome. Today, perhaps a new

Calvinism, drawing from current strands of economic and environmental Calvinism, will proclaim a new right of secession from the nation-state—the church of progressive economic religion headquartered in the United States in Washington, D.C. Calvinists have long been among the fiercest defenders historically of freedom from control by any central church authority, and now the most important churches are the nation-states of the world, legitimized by messages of economic religion. Religious secession from a "nation-state church" must include a geographic separation to go along with the assertion of new religious doctrines. As the scope for full worldwide freedom of religion is expanded to encompass secular forms of worship, regional and local sovereignty may flourish in the future.

CONCLUSION: RELIGIOUS CHALLENGES

With the arrival of the twenty-first century have come many strong reminders of the central importance of religion in human affairs. The struggle against terrorism has pitted the United States against an adversary that grounded its doctrines—however implausibly—in Islam, one of the major religions of the world. American politics has been filled with heated debates about abortion, stem cells, gay marriage, and other moral issues where positions are often shaped by religion. The Iraq war has been fought as a missionary crusade to spread "American religion" across the globe.

Yet the greatest novelty is not to be found in a revival of religion per se. Rather, the newest element is the turning back to Judaic, Christian, Islamic, and other traditional faiths. For much of the twentieth century, it looked as though the old-style religions might be fading. There were fierce religious struggles, but they typically involved secular religions rather than the traditional faiths of Western civilization (or at least so it seemed outwardly). World War II produced a death struggle between National Socialism in Germany and Marxist Socialism in the Soviet Union. Germany and the Soviet Union were in essence two vast and all-controlling national churches with their own well-developed theologies, inquisitions, crusades, and other state instruments of religious expression.

Confronting the horrors of the wars of Christian religion in the sixteenth and seventeenth centuries, Europe sought a more "rational"—a more peaceful—existence in the Enlightenment. After World War II, Europe repeated this experience in a secular religious fashion, turning away from its terrible religious wars of the first half of the century. In a first key step, six nations joined together to create the European Economic Community, linked by a common market in goods and services. Europeans increasingly renounced false economic prophets such as Karl Marx and turned to Adam Smith, John Maynard Keynes, and others in the British and American economic mainstream. English became the working language of Europe, partly reflecting the preeminence of English-speaking sources of the new universal messages of economic religion. The European Union today is held together above all by a shared economic faith—along with a commitment to individual rights and democracy that also traces significantly to Protestant England and its former colonies. Economic progress is the "rational" religion that now unites Europe. Indeed, Europe is more religiously unified at present than at any time since the medieval period, as economics has replaced the Roman Catholic Christianity of an earlier era.

The idea that secular religion played a central role in the history of the twentieth century, to be sure, is nothing new.[1] The powerful religious elements of socialism, communism, American progressivism (the "gospel of efficiency"), and many other secular creeds were obvious to anyone not specifically educated to believe otherwise. More recent is a growing understanding that traditional religion and secular religion are closely linked. The secular religions of the twentieth century were less novel than they claimed. Indeed, one might say that Christianity reappeared with a renewed energy in the twentieth century but in a new dress (or as many devout Christians would say, as new heresies). The various secular religions are proving on close study, and with the perspective of greater historical distance, to follow closely in the path of earlier branches of traditional Christianity. It can now be seen that the world wars and other fierce conflicts of the twentieth century were in part a secular reenactment—if on a much more destructive scale due to the "advances" of modern industry and technology—of the past European wars within Christian religion.

Indeed, these themes are increasingly being explored in a diverse body of scholarship. Some authors operate more in a spirit of intellectual curiosity. It has turned out not to be difficult to trace the connections between traditional Jewish and Christian religions and the secular religions of the modern age.[2] Whether old or new, religion in the Western world has been about an original creation, about the sources of sin in the world, and about salvation—in the hereafter or, more recently, in the arrival of a new heaven on earth. Almost all secular religions have absorbed from Judaism and Christianity the understanding that history is a continuing path from an original beginning to a final ending, and that the greater meaning of an individual's life is to be found in his or her place in this history.*

---

* Scientific utopianism is admittedly taking new forms. A virtual Christian heaven—characterized by eternal life, perfect happiness and rationality, and complete relief from all bodily limitations—is now projected by a leading American futurologist, Ray Kurzweil, based on the continuing exponential growth of computing power. Immortality right here on earth will be attainable by transferring the biologically encoded information of a person's brain into a specific computing machine, thus creating an exact mechanical replication of that individual's mind (minus the anxiety, fear, confusion, and other negative mental features that result from the current material limitations of life). As Kurzweil explains,

John Gray thus writes that the many modern political and economic "projects of universal emancipation are earthly renditions of the Christian promise of salvation." Indeed, "the idea of progress," based on modern advances in science and economics, "is a secular version of Christian eschatology. In Christianity, history cannot be senseless: it is a moral drama, beginning with a rebellion against God and ending with the Last Judgment. Christians therefore think of salvation as a historical event." This is in contrast, for example, to "Hindus and Buddhists, [for whom] it means liberation from time."[3]

Secular Eschatology

Igal Halfin is an Israeli historian who concludes, based on extensive archival research, that the "eschatological" elements of Russian communism, learned originally from Christianity, were decisive influences in determining the very categories of thought that shaped the former Soviet Union's government and economy in its early years. It was not economics that determined religion, as so many committed economic determinists have firmly believed, but actually the opposite. During the 1920s and 1930s, Soviet universities functioned as "a grand laboratory, designing techniques for the perfection of humanity." Life in revolutionary Russia was everywhere a reflection of "messianic aspirations," as the teachings of Marxist religion "shaped the identity of the Soviet citizen; it did not just coerce preexisting, fully formed citizens to adjust to a Soviet reality that was somehow external to them." Rather, for the communist faithful Marxism formed the basis for their very way of comprehending their own existence in the world and shaped their economic institutions.[4]

Marxism was, moreover, significantly derived from biblical sources. It was this feature that significantly explains its extraordinary spread across the world in the twentieth century. The communist gospel resonated especially in many

---

"Uploading a human brain means scanning all its salient details and then reinstantiating those details into a suitably powerful computational substrate. This process would capture a person's entire personality, memory, skills, and history," while allowing for the elimination of any less desirable elements in the reprogramming task. As a result, "future machines will be human," if without biological functions, representing the "next step in evolution." Attainment of a new, eternal heaven on earth (the "Singularity," as Kurzweil calls it), will "allow us to transcend these limitations of our biological bodies and brains. We will gain power over our fates. Our mortality will be in our own hands. We will be able to live as long as we want. . . . By the end of [the twenty-first] century, the nonbiological portion of our intelligence will be trillions of trillions of times more powerful than unaided human intelligence." We will be as God. See Ted Peters, "Transhumanism and the Posthuman Future: Will Technological Progress Get Us There?" *Global Spiral*, June 2008, http://www.metanexus.net/magazine/tabid/68/id/10546/Default.aspx. See also Ray Kurzweil, *The Singularity Is Near: When Humans Transcend Biology* (New York: Penguin, 2006).

Western cultures already imbued for millennia with its main themes. As Halfin reports, "Marxists would doubtless have renounced notions such as good, evil, messiah, and salvation as baseless religious superstitions that had nothing to do with the revolutionary experience. Yet, these concepts, translated into a secular key, continued to animate Communist discourse" in Russia for at least two decades after the 1917 revolution. Most Russian communists were nevertheless blind to the reality of the close "affinity" of Russian communism "with Christian messianism."[5] Yet, as described by Halfin, the parallels are obvious to us today:

> The Marxist concept of universal History was essentially inspired by the Judeo-Christian bracketing of historical time between the Fall of Adam and the Apocalypse. The Original Expropriation, at the beginning of time, represented a rupture in the timeless primitive Communism, which inaugurated History and set humanity on a course of self-alienation. The universal Revolution, an abrupt and absolute event, was to return humanity to itself in a fiery cataclysm. . . . Imbuing time with a historical teleology that gave meaning to events, Marxist eschatology described history as moral progression from the darkness of class society to the light of Communism.[6]

In 2000 another historian reached similar conclusions with respect to the implicit borrowings from Christian messages on which the Nazi regime in part rode to power in Germany. As Michael Burleigh comments, "Interest in political religions is currently undergoing a renaissance," partly reflecting the waning faith in the ability of economic religion and other strictly materialist understandings to explain the extraordinarily violent course of twentieth-century history. The leaders of both Nazi Germany and the Marxist Soviet Union "utilised sacred language and rites, even when they aggressively rejected religion" in any traditional form. As Burleigh finds, the popularity of Nazism partly reflected its wide use of "pseudo-liturgical rites and deliberate evocations of the Bible"; these practices were part of a wider European pattern in which "totalitarian ideologies themselves shadowed the belief patterns of conventional religion," all of them promising in new secular credos that "salvation would not be long in coming."[7]

Amid the social and economic chaos of Germany in the 1920s and 1930s, the "Nazi ideology offered redemption from a national ontological crisis." For German followers, "Nazism was not simply applied biology, but the expression of eternal scientific laws, revealed by God and in turn invested with sacred properties."[8] The swastika was the Nazi cross (also used historically as a religious symbol in Hinduism and Buddhism). Hitler promised a one-thousand-year reign of the Third Reich on earth—the Nazi millennium. It was all the prophetic destiny of the German people:

> Hitler assimilated biological notions of degeneration and purification to religious narratives of perdition and redemption. In the Wagnerian Bayreuth circle he found a suitably arty and elite coterie to deliver this specific mixture, namely an Aryan-Germanic mission to redeem Graeco-Roman civilization, to affirm a non-Jewish or deorientalized Christianity, and to lead the peoples into a "new, splendid and light-filled future." . . . Nazism was neither science run riot, . . . nor bastardized Christianity. . . . It was a creative synthesis of both. Armed with his religious science, Hitler was . . . God's partner in ordering and perfecting that part of mankind which concerned him.[9]

Psychological Religion

The increasing recognition of the large underlying Judeo-Christian influence in shaping secular religion has spawned another type of literature among the defenders of the historic Jewish and Christian faiths. For them, secular religion has cleverly and falsely stolen the authority of true religion. The twentieth century may have offered the greatest field for heresy in the Western world since the Roman Empire. Unlike other investigators motivated more by historical scholarly interests, however, these critics of secular religion are generally adherents of the traditional faiths. For them, unmasking the false claims of secular religion is a part of a wider agenda of restoring the valid Jewish and Christian understandings to their proper place in the world.

Sigmund Freud, no less than Marx, was a messiah of the modern age. Paul Vitz criticized this Freudian heresy in *Psychology as Religion*.[10] Vitz is a professor of psychology at New York University; as his career advanced, he turned to Christianity and found an increasing tension between his professional and his Christian lives. His own professional field of psychology, he now thinks, "has become a religion: a secular cult of the self." He labels this secular creed as the modern faith of "selfism," which assumes that "reward for the self (i.e., egoism) is the *only* functional ethical principle." In psychological religion, unlike Marxism, the focus thus is entirely on the personal and the prospects for achieving individual self-perfection (and in this respect psychological religion is less dangerous to the world, and may even encourage a libertarian outlook).

To maximize his or her enjoyments and satisfactions in life, a person should enter into a process of "self-actualization" and "self-realization," which ultimately serves to give order, intelligibility, and justification to individual actions. The ideal self-actualized type exhibits personal characteristics such as "acceptance of self and others," "an autonomous self independent of culture," "creativity," and "having 'peak' experiences." One might call the last being psychologically "born again." The secular religion of psychology has displaced Christianity as the leading source of authority and legitimacy in many areas of American private life and in some areas of public life—including the part "of the government bureaucracy that deals with social problems. It is certainly the controlling system [of belief] in the so-called 'helping professions'—clinical psychology, counseling, and social work."[11]

Psychological religion, like most other secular religions, poses as science. Yet, again like Marxism and other modern scientific faiths, it has the character and content of religion, something that has by now become apparent to all but the remaining true believers. As Vitz explains, "Clinical psychologists used to argue strenuously that their discipline was a bona fide science." Among many of them today, however, there is a growing acknowledgement in "describing psychology" that its "categories [are] indistinguishable from those used for religious cures and conversions."[12] The rituals of psychoanalysis, for example, are a variation on the historic Roman Catholic process of confession.

American Messianism

The United States has been a fertile ground for religion partly because it is not simply another historical and ethnic community gathered together in a particular geographic location. One hears frequently of "anti-Americanism" in the world but never of "anti-Englishism," "anti-Germanism," or "anti-Chineseism." Harvard political scientist Samuel Huntington wrote in 2004 that "becoming an American" is a process "comparable to conversion to a new religion and with similar consequences." For citizens, the American flag becomes "the equivalent of the cross for Christians." In the American civil religion, "Washington becomes Moses, Lincoln becomes Christ," the new savior who gave his life to save mankind (avoiding religious schism by preserving the union, the one true and valid church of the United States).[13]

Because the United States is the product of waves of immigration over several centuries, the national bonding agent has had to be a unifying secular faith.[14] No one Jewish, Christian, or any other traditional faith could hold Americans of so many races and backgrounds together. This integrating force, Huntington explains, had to be provided by "a nondenominational, national religion and, in its articulated form, not expressly a Christian religion." Its civil religion "converts Americans from religious people of many denominations into a [single] nation with the soul of a church." The unifying faith of the

United States, however, is secular only in outward appearance.* The reality, Huntington writes, is that the American nation-state in essence is "a church that is profoundly Christian in its origins, symbolism, spirit, accoutrements, and, most importantly, its basic assumptions about the nature of man, history, right and wrong. The Christian Bible, Christian references, biblical allusions and metaphors, permeate expressions of the [American] civil religion."[15]

It is not, to be sure, identical to Christianity. As Huntington notes, the American civil religion allows for the frequent use of the word "God," as on the nation's coins; however, "two words . . . do not appear in civil religion statements and ceremonies. They are 'Jesus Christ.'" This omission is of course of great religious significance. Many religions believe in a "god," but only Christianity believes in the divinity of Christ. Again, though, the reality can be deceptive; as Huntington finds, even with little explicit mention "the American civil religion is Christianity without Christ."[16] Admittedly, this may raise basic theological problems for those who think of themselves as being both great American national patriots and devout Christians—such people may in fact have ended up as deeply committed followers of two distinct, and in some ways perhaps conflicting, religions.

Sanford Levinson in 1988 published *Constitutional Faith*, a product, as he described it, of his own efforts to be both a "legal theologian" as well as a conventional law professor at the University of Texas.[17] Levinson explained that for most Americans the U.S. Constitution is seen—literally, not just metaphorically—as an American religious equivalent to the Christian Bible. The Constitution is the "sacred text" of the United States, the foundational document for the American "civil religion."[18] Quoting approvingly from a *Stanford Law Review* article on "The Constitution as Scripture," Levinson agrees that

---

* A leading historian of the American revolution, Gordon Wood, notes that "although some of the Founders . . . were fairly devout Christians, most leading Founders were not deeply religious men and few of them had much of a spiritual life." Indeed, "many of them shared the views of an enlightened speaker before the American Philosophical Society in 1793 who abhorred 'that gloomy superstition disseminated by ignorant illiberal preachers'" in the Christian churches of the time. As long ago as 1932, however, the American intellectual historian Carl Becker was pointing out that the Founders' rejection of traditional Christian religion was more superficial than real. Indeed, the leading thinkers of the eighteenth century took a vision of "life eternal in the Heavenly City of God," which they then "projected into the life of man on earth and identified with the desired and hoped-for regeneration of society." It was "to the future [that] the Philosophers therefore look, as to a promised land, a new millennium." If the goal was to displace traditional Christianity, they somehow understood that "the best hope . . . lay in recasting it, and in bringing it up to date" to fit the scientific expectations of the eighteenth century. In short, as Becker declared, "the task of the [Enlightenment] Philosophers was to present another interpretation of the past, the present, and the future state of mankind"—a seemingly new "religion of humanity" that in reality borrowed heavily from much older sources. See Gordon S. Wood, "Praying with the Founders," *New York Review of Books*, May 1, 2008, 54; and Carl L. Becker, *The Heavenly City of the Eighteenth-Century Philosophers* (1932; repr., New Haven: Yale University Press, 1968), 139, 118, 123, 122.

"America would have no national church . . . yet the worship of the Constitution would serve the unifying function of a national civil religion" for the people of the United States.[19]

As the ultimate adjudicators, the members of the Supreme Court not only dress and act like priests, but the American nation has in fact substituted a "priesthood of lawyers for a pontifical Court" in Rome. For Levinson, the contemporary legal debates about constitutional original intent versus a "living Constitution" reenact much older theological disagreements between Roman Catholicism and Protestantism. The Catholic Church historically saw Christianity as refined through the prism of centuries of church interpretation, papal encyclicals, the writings of Catholic scholars, church councils, and other historical events. For Protestants, the Catholic theology was heresy, the substituting of the writing and thinking of flawed human beings in place of God's directly revealed truths in the Bible. The real meaning of Christianity was to be found there by individual study alone—in combination with the Book of Nature, also a direct means of communication from God. According to Levinson, in the American law profession today there is a similar clash among "protestant" and "catholic" legal experts in which the new "protestant position is that it is the [U.S.] constitutional text alone, while the [new] catholic position is that the source of doctrine is the text of the Constitution plus unwritten tradition."[20]

Three years later, in my 1991 book *Reaching for Heaven on Earth: The Theological Meaning of Economics*, I found a similar "Protestant tradition" and "Roman tradition" that had also long shaped the understandings and interpretations of American economics.[21] Similar to Levinson's portrayal of the law, some of the most important schools of economics could be traced back to the medieval scholastics and the natural law teachings of the Roman Catholic Church, while other economic schools saw the world in less rational and more individualistic—more "Protestant"—terms. The historical success of Adam Smith was attributable partly to his skillful synthesis of these two central religious traditions of the West, now adapted in *The Wealth of Nations* to a Newtonian scientific vocabulary that had come to dominate European thinking in the eighteenth century.[22]

As illustrated by the method of analysis of this book, there has thus been a growing attention to the "theology" of secular religions. It is possible to focus on the assumptions and lines of reasoning of secular religions with critical analysis—a process of doing "secular theology." Such writings frequently agree that in one way or another modern religion is really old religion disguised in superficially new—typically scientific and economic—language. The modern age, in mostly failing to see these connections until fairly recently, has engaged in an act of religious self-deception on a grand scale. Although this is hardly unprecedented in human history, it does belie the many claims since the eighteenth century of the arrival of a new era of much greater human "enlightenment." Over the next three hundred years, the Enlightenment's grand claims and expectations held up well with respect to the scientific understanding of the workings of the natural world. In other domains, however—including the realms of human affairs within the province of the "social sciences," and in theology—human beings in the modern age have proved just as capable of acts of grand self-deception and folly as their predecessors.

Events in the American public arena are today shaped in significant part by the intellectual (or religious, as it turns out) disagreements and conflicts between leading secular religions. In the public arena the most important religious debate in the last part of the twentieth century was between economic and environmental religion—the new holy wars. As with other secular religions, the messages of economic and environmental religion are significantly derived from Christian sources. Yet again following the standard pattern, the traditional religious roots in both cases are frequently disguised by scientific claims and rhetoric—and therefore remain unacknowledged among perhaps the majority of contemporary followers in the economic and environmental gospels. Despite the secular framework of thought, true believers in both cases have been fighting about the real sources of sin in the world, how evil first arose, the decisive forces in shaping world history, and how the condition of human sinfulness might eventually be transcended—offering the latest prophesies for a new heaven (or conceivably a new hell) on earth.

The Fading of Economic Religion

When the American Economic Association was formed in 1885, many of the founding members were current or former Protestant ministers. One of the main economists involved, Richard Ely, was best known nationally at the time as a preacher in the social gospel movement. In his view, it was "as truly a religious work to pass good laws, as it is to preach sermons; as holy a work to lead a crusade against filth, vice, and disease in slums of cities . . . as it is to send missionaries to the heathen."[23] But Ely criticized many of his fellow social gospelers for their ambitious plans to cure all the ills of the world when these plans were not grounded in any adequate economic and other social science body of knowledge. To advance the mechanisms of economic progress, it would be necessary to turn to the scientific research of professional economists, as the formation of the American Economic Association would serve to encourage. Indeed, John R. Commons, John Bates Clark, and a number of other early American economists were also linked to the social gospel movement. Ely argued at one point that, as a religious subject, the field of economics should be placed within schools of theology.

The attempt to incorporate economics as an element within Protestant theology soon foundered, however, on the pluralism of American life: important economists who were Catholics and Jews rejected any close connections to Protestant religion. Yet the underlying religious element remained, even in ostensibly "secular" progressive thought, if now buried in more and more scientific camouflage.[24] By the second half of the twentieth century, economists had become the highest progressive priests of all, the only social science body with its own office in the White House, the Council of Economic Advisers, established by Congress in the Employment Act of 1946, responsible for overseeing the economic growth and development of the United States. Economists were the one professional discipline that produced the most important scientific knowledge, now capable of revealing how society's resources could be deployed with maximal efficiency, material production could thereby be maximized, and continuing rapid progress could then be made toward the elimination of scarcity and a new heaven on earth. American economists such as Paul Samuelson displaced the old Protestant language of good and evil with a new moral vocabulary of "efficient" and "inefficient"—the operative measure of the rate of movement along the redemptive path of economic progress.

At the beginning of the twenty-first century, however, economic religion is fading. Much of the technical body of economic research has been a practical failure in terms of providing a sound understanding of the actual workings of the American economic system.[25] It turns out that economics is a more complicated subject—at least when approached with strictly quantitative and other formal methods that emulate the methods of the physical sciences—than most twentieth-century economists understood. Even the premise that there are underlying laws that strictly control economic events, analogous to the physical laws of the universe, is an act of religious faith that now seems increasingly suspect. Economic events commonly reflect a wide range of human motivations, including some that are not entirely "rational" and thus are not subject to the rigorous predictability of outcomes in the natural world.

The more fundamental problem with economic religion, however, is moral and theological. The core tenet, that material progress will solve the problems of the human condition, did not fare well in the history of the twentieth century.[26] It is still possible to believe that economic progress is desirable, and most people do in fact hope for a high level of material comfort. But it has become much more difficult—and for large numbers of people it has become impossible—to believe that the full sources of human sinfulness lie in material causes and that the evils of the world can therefore be cured by economic solutions alone. The twentieth century was a period of extraordinary economic advance in Europe and the United States, and yet there often seemed little corresponding improvement in the ethical character of human behavior. Heaven on earth seems as remote today as ever—and some might suggest that the prospects have been receding, rather than advancing, partly owing to the large new dangers posed by the growing human powers to control nature.

The Environmental Gospel

In the public arena, where secular thought (or, as it might also be described, "implicit Christianity") dominates in the United States, the leading challenges to economic religion not surprisingly have come from other secular religions, especially environmental religion. The environmental gospel often distrusts science and is hostile to economics. Modern science and industry have combined to greatly increase the technological capacity of human beings to alter the natural world. Indeed, human beings in the past two hundred years, unlike any previous plant or animal species in the several-billion-year history of the planet, have suddenly and astonishingly acquired the actual physical capacity to remake the natural world as an act of deliberate, collective species choice. Previously, such powers were reserved to God alone, but the members of the human race now have the ability to "play God" with the world. The proper response to this brand-new circumstance in the history of the earth has posed religious questions of the most fundamental sort.

For environmental religion, the problem is that human beings have acquired divine powers but not divine wisdom. Even if, hypothetically, most individuals were exceptionally wise themselves, there would still be a large problem because collective decisions, now capable of altering the physical character of the whole world, must still be made through the very human processes of "politics." Worse yet, the rise of Islamic terrorism has shown how even small groups of people, operating outside any established nation-state political system, may increasingly be able to use the extraordinary powers of modern technology for malevolent purposes.

The Holocaust was the most powerful symbolic event of the twentieth century because it demonstrated with particular clarity that the widespread hopes for moral transformation based on material advance had been significantly misplaced. For many people it has not seemed possible to explain the terrible events in Nazi Germany by any appeal to adverse external factors in the social and economic environment. Environmentalism is perhaps a postmodern phenomenon in that it has turned to new ways of understanding and explaining the world that are outside the standard rationalism and economic determinism of the modern age. More ambivalent about science, environmentalism has been less overtly hostile to traditional religion (although it is often confused in its religious thinking). Indeed, many environmentalists now argue that the future defense of the natural world will require the creation of new "spiritual" values in society. They have little to say, however, about the possible original religious sources of these values, and few leading environmentalists in fact profess to be devout Christians, even as they show a deep commitment to implicit Christian themes of the past.

The appearance in 2004 of *Faith in Nature: Environmentalism as Religious Quest* therefore is noteworthy, offering there an interpretation of environmentalism as a secular religion following in the path of Christian religion. The author, Thomas Dunlap, is a historian at Texas A&M University who states that he is an environmentalist himself. He is also aware that many other environmentalists may be uncomfortable with his new line of religious analysis. Yet he thinks that intellectual honesty—and perhaps good political strategy in the long run—require seeing "environmentalism, its roots in the culture, its development as a movement in religious terms." To be sure, environmentalism "does not (necessarily) involve God (or gods) or devils, and afterlife, revelations from On High, prophets, or miracles." Nevertheless, environmentalism is very much a religion in helping its followers to "make (ultimate) sense of our lives in the context of the universe."[27]

Environmentalism is seeking to find new religious directions as Marxism, socialism, American progressivism, interest-group liberalism, and other secular religions of economic progress that dominated in the twentieth century have been fading.* Environmental religion is, moreover, derived in significant part from original Protestant (especially Calvinist) sources.

---

* Since the first Earth Day in 1970, April 22 has become a leading religious holiday in American life. Judged by media attention in April 2009, environmental religion is rapidly winning many new devout followers. The *New York Times Magazine* devoted most of its April 19 issue to "The Green Mind," asserting in one article that nature serves to enhance "the happiness of our everyday lives." "Real natural habitats," like many other religious surroundings, provide "significant sources of pleasure for modern humans." In an April 20 front-page article in the *Washington Post*, the sacrificial side of religion was instead emphasized. The *Post* reported that "across the Washington region, a few residents have embraced eco-friendly living with a fervor that makes Al Gore look like an oil company lobbyist. They give up everything from furnace heat (too many emissions) to store-bought meat (too much farming) to plans for a second child (too much of everything, given the average American's environmental impact)." One ten-year-old girl complained that her parents kept the heat at fifty-four degrees at night but acknowledged that she had grown used to it: "We've been green for a long time, . . . I don't even remember when we had the heat on all the time." A D.C.-area couple in a "green and greener marriage" could agree on "turning off most lights, turning down the heat and using a herd of sheep as a low-emissions mower," but the less-committed wife "said no to canning her own food and hand-grinding her own flour" (requests her husband had made). In one Washington marriage, the tensions could not be reconciled, leading to "at least one green divorce." It was reminiscent of tensions within Catholic and non-Catholic, kosher and nonkosher, and other mixed marriages of the past. See Paul Bloom, "Natural Happiness: The Self-Centered Case for Environmentalism," *New York Times Magazine*, April 19, 2009, 13; and David A. Fahrenthold, "D.C. Area Families Take Green to the Extreme: Eco-enthusiasts Step on Some Toes in a Bid to Reduce their Carbon Imprints," *Washington Post*, April 20, 2009, A1.

Dunlop writes that for the past 150 years, "Americans who failed to find God in church took terms and perspectives from Christian theology into their search for ecstatic experiences in nature. Environmentalism's rhetorical strategies, points of view, and ways of thought remain embedded in this evangelical Protestant heritage, which forms the unacknowledged ground of many environmental attitudes and arguments."[28]

Most environmentalists embrace Darwin, but many react to being in the presence of the natural world with powerful feelings of religious reverence and awe. Rather than scientific objectivity or value-neutrality, these feelings more closely resemble the feelings long experienced in Protestant religion in encountering "the creation" in nature. It is difficult not to conclude that the sources are the same—that many leading environmentalists are in fact "environmental creationists," even as they might be disconcerted by the suggestion of close parallels between their own beliefs and old-fashioned Protestant creationism. In visiting places in nature "untouched by human hand" (however illusory this perception may often be), the evidence, including their own personal testimonies, strongly suggests the experiencing of a direct connection to God—it is just that many environmentalists are unwilling to say so explicitly.

Secular Religion and Christianity

The rise of modern science posed a great challenge to traditional Christian religion. Since the Enlightenment, and partly as a result of this challenge, Christian messages increasingly have been found outside the traditional religious forms. By the twentieth century, secular religions were more influential—more capable of dispensing social authority and legitimacy—throughout much of the Western world. This development can be seen in several lights. The spread of secular religion might be seen as a valid new expression of Christianity—in the same religious category as, say, the emergence of Protestantism during the sixteenth century. Or secular religion might instead be seen as a great new heresy that falsely distorts and caricatures a valid Christian message. Or secular religion might be a seen as brand-new religion altogether, even as it borrows heavily from traditional Christian sources—in the same category, say, as Islam, which represented an offshoot from Judeo-Christian history in the seventh century.

The 2009 Religious Identification Survey showed that the number of Americans who say that they have no religious identification has risen from 8 percent in 1990 to 15 percent in 2009. In response to this new data, *Newsweek* magazine published a feature story on "The End of Christian America." Jon Meacham, the author, found that "while we remain a nation decisively shaped by religious faith, our politics and our culture are, in the main, less influenced by movements and arguments of an explicitly Christian character than they were even five years ago." Meacham interviewed the Reverend Albert Mohler Jr.—president of the Southern Baptist Theological Seminary, one of the largest in the world, and a "starch, unflinchingly conservative Christian"—who found the latest survey results to be deeply depressing.[29] As Meacham reported:

> Then came the point he could not get out of his mind: while the unaffiliated have historically been concentrated in the Pacific Northwest, the report said, "this pattern has now changed, and the Northeast emerged in 2008 as the new stronghold of the religiously unidentified." As Mohler saw it, the historic foundation of America's religious culture was cracking.
>
> "That really hit me hard," he told me last week. "The Northwest was never as religious, never as congregationalized, as the Northeast, which was the foundation, the home base, of American religion. To lose New England struck me as momentous." Turning the report over in his mind, Mohler posted a despairing online column on the eve of Holy Week lamenting the decline—and, by implication, the imminent fall—of an America shaped and suffused by Christianity. "A remarkable culture-shift has taken place around us," Mohler wrote. "The most basic contours of American culture have been radically altered. The so-called Judeo-Christian consensus of the last millennium has given way to a post-modern, post-Christian, post-Western cultural crisis which threatens the very heart of our culture." When Mohler and I spoke in the days after he wrote this, he had grown even gloomier. "Clearly, there is a new narrative, a post-Christian narrative, that is animating large portions of this society," he said from his office on campus in Louisville, Ky.[30]

The new poll data further affirmed a trend that had been apparent since at least the 1960s. As Meacham wrote, the term post-Christianity "was popularized during what scholars call the 'death of God' movement of the mid-1960s—a movement that is, in its way, still in motion. Drawing from Nietzsche's 19th-century declaration that 'God is dead,' a group of Protestant theologians held that, essentially, Christianity would have to survive without an orthodox understanding of God."[31] Perhaps that is what has been happening. While orthodox forms of Christianity might be losing followers, new and unorthodox (heretical for some people) forms such as environmental religion were booming. Perhaps the rise of economic religion in the twentieth century in the United States and then the rapidly growing influence of environmental religion since the 1960s should be understood in these terms. These religious developments may not have represented the emergence of two new religions, but conceivably the rise of unconventional forms of Christianity—an outcome in practice by which it might be possible increasingly for the Christian religion to "survive [and even thrive] without an orthodox understanding of God."

Church and State

However one sees it, secular religion became the most powerful religious force in western Europe and the United States in the twentieth century. The nation-states of the West had their state religions, turning the apparatus of the nation-state into a secular state church. In some nations the punishments for heresy were no less severe in the twentieth century than in the medieval Christian period, while in other nations heretics no longer feared for their lives, although they often paid other high prices, such as the loss of a job or the scorn of their neighbors. Religion—now in its new secular forms—was as central to the tasks of governance, the organization of society, and the moral judgments of people as it had ever been in the Christian past. The nation-state in practice amounts to a secular theocracy. Even as Marxism had collapsed at the end of the century and other progressive economic gospels were coming under increasing challenge, new secular religious contenders were emerging in their place, including environmental religion.

If secular religion is taken seriously as a genuine form of religion—and it is difficult to see how it might not be—some political and religious conundrums will be posed. If Americans wish to maintain the traditional separation of church and state, much of the modern welfare and regulatory state—which now amounts to a new "secular religious church"—would have to be dismantled and privatized. Libertarians might find this a happy prospect, but it is perhaps equally or more likely that the principle of separation of church and state will have to be abandoned in the United States.

That will, however, create its own large complications. What is the justification for religious coercion? When the state is a church, tax collections become coercive tithes. This problem could be ameliorated if the United States broke into a number of smaller sovereign jurisdictions. A state religion is less objectionable when the citizens of the state are more religiously homogeneous; there is less need for religious coercion in collecting taxes when you and I share the same faith and thus give more willingly. Perhaps an American right of free secession will have to be constitutionally recognized. When a state becomes a church, secession becomes the operative means of exiting from the church, asserting a full freedom of religion that now involves geographic as well as doctrinal dimensions. Protestants asserted this right five hundred years ago with respect to the Roman Catholic Church; perhaps a similar, new "protestant" right of free geographic secession from the state, directed against the nation-states (the new "Romes" of our time), will be required. The economic Calvinist Frank Knight probably would have approved, as his libertarian disciple James Buchanan has offered many sharp criticisms of the modern Leviathan as found in the American nation-state—and, in fact, has proposed the urgent need to break it apart into many smaller independent parts.[32]

Blending Old and New

Although it is hardly the first to make the argument, this book further documents that Christian ideas and messages in the twentieth century had a greater influence and a more powerful impact on the world when they were expressed outside a traditional Christian language and institutional setting. Indeed, many of the leading prophets of an essentially Christian worldview did not recognize the actual roots of their thinking; some of them even denied any connection with Christianity. Within institutional Christianity, for its part, many leaders were equally oblivious to the implicit Christian content of secular religions such as the progressive economic and the environmental gospels.

An obvious question is why this large lack of awareness has persisted over such a long period of time. One possibility is that much of the Christian message strikes many modern observers as true and valid, even as they wish to disassociate themselves from the many religious wars, doctrinal feuds, hypocritical priesthoods, and other historical baggage of two thousand years of official Christian church history. Another factor may be that the pace of scientific and other discoveries in the modern era has been so rapid that official sources of Christian thought have struggled to keep pace, leaving a common impression that Christianity is an outdated—and often confused—religious force in the world.* Partly reflecting a lack of religious knowledge and introspection

---

* Writing in the journal *First Things*—which describes itself as a "survey of religion, culture, and public life"—the University of Delaware physicist Stephen Barr comments that:

Wolfhart Pannenberg, one of the great figures of German Protestant theology, turns eighty this year. . . . Pannenberg may be the only major systematic theologian of modern times to have studied and written extensively on the natural sciences. Why this should be so in the Age of Science is not altogether clear. After all, the greatest systematic theologian of the Middle Ages, Thomas Aquinas, studied the leading science of his day, and the Aristotelianism on which he drew was considered to be a scientific system as well as a philosophy.

A lot has happened since then, of course—the Scientific Revolution and Isaac Newton, in particular—and, in the view of Pannenberg, Christian theology has never quite recovered. Nor

on their own part, a brand-new religion may have seemed necessary to many modern observers to match the extraordinary pace of change of modern times in general. As a result, many secular religions may have emerged, including some explored in this book, to fill the bill.

As also examined in this book, whatever difficulties Christianity may have experienced in its encounter with modern science and the many other startling events of the modern age, secular religion has been at least equally flawed in terms of the religious quality of its thought—its theological rigor and coherence. The events of the twentieth century may thus have set the stage for a new period of religious ferment and renewal—perhaps already becoming visible in what Robert Fogel has referred to as "the fourth great awakening," which came into view in the last few decades of the century.[33] Institutional Christianity may need to recover some of the social influence and vitality that has shifted to the secular recasting of many of its main messages; whereas secular religions may need to study more closely the past centuries of Christian religion, in which many of the same theological issues and questions have already been explored in greater depth and with greater sophistication.

It would be folly at this point—and it is certainly not the purpose of this book—to try to predict the ultimate outcome of such a potential religious synthesis. It is in any case likely to evolve gradually and slowly, rather than spring from any single grand pronouncement.

Conclusion

This book finds that the leading secular movements of our times are essentially religious in character, drawing on the various Christian traditions that produced Western civilization. The two most important secular movements of the late twentieth century were "economic religion" and "environmental religion," both of them "religions" in the sense that they have comprehensive worldviews and myths that provide human beings with the deepest sense of meaning. The story of "economic religion" is that human beings can produce an ideal world, or heaven on earth, by ending material poverty though productivity, efficiency, and scientific management. The "religion of environmentalism" has emerged to protest economic religion, however, and has fought this counter-battle by presenting its own worldview and religious story. This message says that we once had an ideal world, or Eden, which was destroyed

---

will it, he thinks, unless more effort is expended by theologians to come to terms with modern scientific ideas. (Stephen M. Barr, "Theology After Newton," *First Things* 187 [November 2008]: 29)

by progress, economic growth, and industry, and that we must repent and return to Eden. In other words, as I have argued in this book, the clash between "economic religion" and "environment religion" took place in the late twentieth century on the same scale as the clash of Roman Catholicism and Protestantism in the sixteenth and seventeenth centuries, minus the bloodshed, of course. Their conflict has shaped our social debate on the place of human beings in the natural world and our hopes for material and spiritual well-being—the new holy wars of our time.

It is time to take secular religion seriously. It is real religion. In the twentieth century it showed greater energy, won more converts, and had more impact on the Western world than the traditional institutional forms of Christianity. If this is more widely recognized, however, some difficult challenges will be posed for the conventional pieties of our times. The task of more fully integrating Jewish, Christian, economic, sociological, Americanist, psychological, environmental, and still other vital religions into the full domain of world theology is just beginning.

NOTES

Preface

1. "The Exhibition of 1851," The Speech of H.R.H. The Prince Albert, K.G., F.R.S., at The Lord Mayor's Banquet, in the City of London, October 1849, printed in *Illustrated London News*, October 11, 1849, http://pages.zoom.co.uk/leveridge/albert.html.

2. Alejandro R. Roces, "Disasters Are Getting Worse," *Philippine Star*, July 3, 2007, 11.

3. See Robert H. Nelson, *Reaching for Heaven on Earth: The Theological Meaning of Economics* (Lanham, Md.: Rowman and Littlefield, 1991); and Robert H. Nelson, *Economics as Religion: From Samuelson to Chicago and Beyond* (University Park: Pennsylvania State University Press, 2001).

4. Jesse H. Ausubel, "The Liberation of the Environment," *Daedalus* 125 (Summer 1996): 14.

5. See Robert H. Nelson, "Sustainability, Efficiency, and God: Economic Values and the Sustainability Debate," *Annual Review of Ecology and Systematics* 26 (1995); and Robert H. Nelson, "The Gospel According to Conservation Biology," *Philosophy and Public Policy Quarterly* 27 (Summer–Fall 2007).

6. On the powerful implicit normative elements in "scientific" economics, see Donald N. Mc-Closkey, "The Rhetoric of Economics," *Journal of Economic Literature* 21 (June 1983); and many subsequent writings, most recently Deirdre N. McCloskey, *The Bourgeois Virtues: Ethics for an Age of Commerce* (Chicago: University of Chicago Press, 2006).

7. Frank R. Baumgartner, "Punctuated Equilibrium Theory and Environmental Policy," in *Punctuated Equilibrium and the Dynamics of U.S. Environmental Policy*, ed. Robert Repetto (New Haven: Yale University Press, 2006), 42.

8. Helen Ingram and Leah Fraser, "Path Dependency and Adroit Innovation: The Case of California Water," in Repetto, *Punctuated Equilibrium and the Dynamics of U.S. Environmental Policy*, 81. See also Barbara Gray, "Framing of Environment Disputes," in *Making Sense of Intractable Environmental Conflicts: Concepts and Cases*, ed. Roy J. Lewick, Barbara Gray, and Michael Elliott (Washington, D.C.: Island Press, 2003).

9. Paul Tillich, *Theology of Culture* (New York: Oxford University Press, 1959).

10. William Grassie, "The New Sciences of Religion," *Zygon* 43 (March 2008): 128, 130.

11. Ibid., 134.

12. Max L. Stackhouse, *Globalization and Grace* (New York: Continuum, 2007), 55, 31. See also Robert H. Nelson, "God and Globalization: A Review Essay," *Review of Faith and International Affairs* 6 (December 2008).

13. See Thomas R. Dunlop, "Environmentalism, a Secular Faith," *Environmental Values* 15, no. 3 (2006): 322, 325.

14. Paul C. Vitz, *Psychology as Religion: The Cult of Self-Worship* (Grand Rapids, Mich.: Eerdmans, 1977). See also William M. Epstein, *Psychotherapy as Religion: The Civil Divine in America* (Reno: University of Nevada Press, 2006).

15. John Gray, "An Illusion with a Future," *Daedalus* 133 (Summer 2004): 12.

16. Gregory Clark, *A Farewell to Alms: A Brief Economic History of the World* (Princeton: Princeton University Press, 2007), 195, 1, 33.

17. See, among many possible examples, Leo Marx, *The Machine in the Garden: Technology and the Pastoral Ideal in America* (New York: Oxford University Press, 1964); Roderick Nash, *Wilderness and the American Mind* (New Haven: Yale University Press, 1967); and Francis Fukuyama, *Our Posthuman Future: Consequences of the Biotechnology Revolution* (New York: Farrar, Straus and Giroux, 2002).

18. Daniel J. Fiorino, *The New Environmental Regulation* (Cambridge: MIT Press, 2006), 186.

19. Richard J. Lazarus, *The Making of Environmental Law* (Chicago: University of Chicago Press, 2004), 190, 254.

20. For more on the religious background I brought to these issues, see Robert H. Nelson, "The Theology of Economics," in *Faithful Economics: The Moral Worlds of a Neutral Science*, ed. James W. Henderson and John Pisciotta (Waco: Baylor University Press, 2005).

21. Robert H. Nelson, "Unoriginal Sin: The Judeo-Christian Roots of Ecotheology," *Policy Review*, no. 53 (Summer 1990).

22. Nelson, *Economics as Religion*.

23. A less comprehensive treatment is found, for example, in Robert H. Nelson, "Environmental Religion: A Theological Critique," *Case Western Reserve Law Review* 25 (Fall 2004).

24. See Robert H. Nelson, *Reaching for Heaven on Earth*. See also Robert H. Nelson, "Scholasticism Versus Pietism: The Battle for the Soul of Economics," *Econ Journal Watch* 1 (December 2004), http://www.econjournalwatch.org/pdf/NelsonCharacterIssues1December2004.pdf.

25. The urgent need to rethink environmentalism is argued in Ted Nordhaus and Michael Shellenberger, *Break Through: From the Death of Environmentalism to the Politics of Possibility* (New York: Houghton Mifflin, 2007).

26. Robert H. Nelson, "What Is 'Economic Theology'?" *Princeton Seminary Bulletin* 25 (February 2004).

Acknowledgments

1. See Herman Daly and Joshua Farley, *Ecological Economics: Principles and Applications* (Washington, D.C.: Island Press, 2003).

2. See D. N. McCloskey, "The Rhetoric of Economics," *Journal of Economic Literature* 21 (June 1983); and D. N. McCloskey, *The Rhetoric of Economics* (Madison: University of Wisconsin Press, 1985). See, more recently, D. N. McCloskey, *The Bourgeois Virtues: Ethics for an Age of Commerce* (Chicago: University of Chicago Press, 2006).

Introduction

Adapted from Robert H. Nelson, "Environmental Religion: A Theological Critique," *Case Western Reserve Law Review* 55 (Fall 2004).

1. See John B. Cobb Jr., *Sustaining the Common Good: A Christian Perspective on the Global Economy* (Cleveland, Ohio: Pilgrim Press, 1994), 49, 28, 40.

2. J. R. McNeill, *Something New Under the Sun: An Environmental History of the Twentieth-Century World* (New York: Norton, 2000), 334–35.

3. See Roger S. Gottlieb, ed., *This Sacred Earth: Religion, Nature, Environment* (New York: Routledge, 1996).

4. Cited in Roderick Nash, *Wilderness and the American Mind*, rev. ed. (New Haven: Yale University Press, 1973), 126.

5. See Steven C. Rockefeller and John C. Elder, eds., *Spirit and Nature: Why the Environment Is a Religious Issue* (Boston: Beacon Press, 1992), 1. See also Theodore Roszak, *The Voice of the Earth* (New York: Simon and Schuster, 1992), 101–3.

6. William Cronon, foreword to Thomas R. Dunlap, *Faith in Nature: Environmentalism as Religious Quest* (Seattle: University of Washington Press, 2004), xi–xii.

7. Stephen Fox, *The American Conservation Movement: John Muir and His Legacy* (Madison: University of Wisconsin Press, 1985); see also Rice Odell, *Environmental Awakening: The New Revolution to Protect the Earth* (Cambridge, Mass.: Ballinger, 1980).

8. Richard L. Revesz and Michael A. Livermore, *Retaking Rationality: How Cost-Benefit Analysis Can Better Protect the Environment and Our Health* (New York: Oxford University Press, 2008).

9. See Richard D. Morgenstern, ed., *Economic Analyses at EPA: Assessing Regulatory Impact* (Washington, D.C.: Resources for the Future, 1997); and Winston Harrington, Richard D. Morgen-

stern, and Thomas Sterner, eds., *Choosing Environmental Policy: Comparing Instruments and Outcomes in the United States and Europe* (Washington, D.C.: Resources for the Future, 2004).

10. See Norman Miller, *Environmental Politics: Interest Groups, the Media, and the Making of Policy* (New York: Lewis Publishers, 2002).

11. Samuel P. Hays, *Conservation and the Gospel of Efficiency: The Progressive Conservation Movement, 1890–1920* (Cambridge: Harvard University Press, 1959).

12. Samuel Haber, *Efficiency and Uplift: Scientific Management in the Progressive Era, 1890–1920* (Chicago: University of Chicago Press, 1964), ix.

13. Dwight Waldo, *The Administrative State: A Study of the Political Theory of American Public Administration* (1948; repr., New York: Holmes and Meier, 1984), 19–20.

14. J. B. Bury, *The Idea of Progress* (1932; repr., Westport, Conn.: Greenwood Press, 1982), 4.

15. See Robert H. Nelson, *Economics as Religion: From Samuelson to Chicago and Beyond* (University Park: Pennsylvania State University Press, 2001).

16. James Hastings Nichols, *History of Christianity, 1650–1950: Secularization of the West* (New York: Ronald Press, 1956), 243.

17. Alasdair MacIntyre, *Marxism and Christianity* (Notre Dame: University of Notre Dame Press, 1984), 6.

18. John Maynard Keynes, "Economic Possibilities for Our Grandchildren" (1930), in *Essays in Persuasion* (New York: Norton, 1963), 369, 371–72.

19. Michael A. Bernstein, *A Perilous Progress: Economists and Public Purpose in Twentieth-Century America* (Princeton: Princeton University Press, 2001).

20. Cited in John McPhee, *Encounters with the Archdruid* (New York: Farrar, Straus and Giroux, 1971), 159.

21. Jesse H. Ausubel, "Renewable and Nuclear Heresies," *International Journal of Nuclear Governance, Economy, and Ecology* 1, no. 3 (2007).

22. Robert Royal, *The Virgin and the Dynamo: The Use and Abuse of Religion in Environmental Debates* (Grand Rapids, Mich.: Eerdmans, 1999), 14.

23. See William C. Dennis, "Wilderness Cathedrals and the Public Good," *Freeman*, May 1987; and John Copeland Nagle, "The Spiritual Values of Wilderness," *Environmental Law* 35 (Fall 2005).

24. Editorial, "Stalled Chesapeake Cleanup: Back to the Future on Cleaning the Bay," *Washington Post*, November 25, 2008, A14.

25. Rachel Carson, *Silent Spring* (New York: Fawcett Crest, 1962).

26. See Francis Fukuyama, *Our Posthuman Future: Consequences of the Biotechnology Revolution* (New York: Farrar, Straus and Giroux, 2002).

27. Kenneth E. Boulding, *Beyond Economics: Essays on Society, Religion, and Ethics* (Ann Arbor: University of Michigan Press, 1970), 211.

28. Robert H. Nelson, "Is 'Libertarian Environmentalist' an Oxymoron? The Crisis of Progressive Faith and the Environmental and Libertarian Search for a New Guiding Vision," in *The Next West: Public Lands, Community, and Economy in the American West*, ed. John A Baden and Donald Snow (Washington, D.C.: Island Press, 1997).

29. James C. Scott, *Seeing Like a State: How Certain Schemes to Improve the Human Condition Have Failed* (New Haven: Yale University Press, 1998).

30. Kevin Phillips, *The Cousins' Wars: Religion, Politics, and the Triumph of Anglo-America* (New York: Basic Books, 1999).

31. Mark Stoll, *Protestantism, Capitalism, and Nature in America* (Albuquerque: University of New Mexico Press, 1997), 49.

32. Alister McGrath, *The Reenchantment of Nature: The Denial of Religion and the Ecological Crisis* (New York: Doubleday, 2002), 79, 80.

33. Bjorn Lomborg, *The Skeptical Environmentalist: Measuring the Real State of the World* (New York: Cambridge University Press, 2001), 3–42; and Gregg Easterbrook, *A Moment on the Earth: The Coming Age of Environmental Optimism* (New York: Viking, 1995).

34. Deut. 28, 29 (*The Way: An Illustrated Edition of the Living Bible* [Wheaton, Ill.: Tyndale House Publishers, 1989]).

35. Robert Mendelson, "The Peculiar Economics of Global Warming," *The Milken Institute Review* (Second Quarter, 2000): 35. See also Robert Mendelson, *The Greening of Global Warming* (Washington, D.C.: AEI Press, 1999); Robert Mendelson and James Neumann, eds., *The Impact of Climate Change on the United States Economy* (New York: Cambridge University Press, 2004); and Robert Mendelson, ed., *Global Warming and the American Economy: A Regional Assessment of Climate Change Impacts* (Northampton, Mass.: Edward Elgar, 2001).

36. Shannon Petersen, *Acting for Endangered Species: The Statutory Ark* (Lawrence: University of Kansas Press, 2007).

37. Steve Bruce, *God Is Dead: Secularization in the West* (Malden, Mass.: Blackwell, 2002).

38. I have already mentioned Marxism. See also, for example, Paul C. Vitz, *Psychology as Religion: The Cult of Self Worship*, 2d ed. (Grand Rapids, Mich.: Eerdmans, 1994). For a broader treatment, see Frank E. Manuel and Fritzie P. Manuel, *Utopian Thought in the Western World* (Cambridge: Harvard University Press, 1979). See also Nelson, *Economics as Religion*; and Robert H. Nelson, *Reaching for Heaven on Earth: The Theological Meaning of Economics* (Lanham, Md.: Rowman and Littlefield, 1991).

39. Henry David Thoreau, *Walden* (New York: Oxford University Press, 1997). For the theological transition from older New England theology to Thoreau, Emerson, and transcendentalism, see Perry Miller, *Errand into the Wilderness* (Cambridge: Harvard University Press, 1975).

40. Paul H. Santmire, *The Travail of Nature: The Ambiguous Ecological Promise of Christian Theology* (Minneapolis: Augsburg Fortress Publishers, 1985), 63.

41. The quotes from Muir are cited in Nash, *Wilderness and the American Mind*, 125–26.

42. Nash, *Wilderness and the American Mind*, 125–26.

43. Holmes Rolston III, "Caring for Nature: From Fact to Value, from Respect to Reverence," *Zygon* 39 (June 2004): 296.

44. Cited in Colman McCarthy, "The Noah Movement," *Washington Post*, February 10, 1996, A23.

45. Cited in "Babbitt Says Falcon May Leave Endangered List," *Washington Post*, August 26, 1998, A2.

46. Herman E. Daly, "The Lurking Inconsistency," *Conservation Biology* 13 (August 1999): 693.

47. A. N. Whitehead, *Science and the Modern World* (1925; repr., New York: Free Press, 1967), 76.

48. Timothy George, *Theology of the Reformers* (Nashville: Broadman and Holman, 1999).

Introduction to Part I

1. Ray Squitieri, "The Good News and the Bad News from Washington," in *Painting the White House Green: Rationalizing Environmental Policy Inside the Executive Office of the President*, ed. Randall Lutter and Jason F. Shogren (Washington, D.C.: Resources for the Future, 2004), 172–74. For a similar view, see also Robert H. Nelson, *Reaching for Heaven on Earth: The Theological Meaning of Economics* (Lanham, Md.: Rowman and Littlefield, 1991), chaps. 1, 3.

2. Quoted in Christopher Manes, *Green Rage: Radical Environmentalism and the Unmaking of Civilization* (Boston: Little, Brown, 1990), 31.

3. Bryan G. Norton, "Thoreau's Insect Analogies: Or, Why Environmentalists Hate Mainstream Economists," *Environmental Ethics* 13 (Fall 1991): 250.

4. Bill Devall and George Sessions, *Deep Ecology: Living as if Nature Mattered* (Salt Lake City: Peregrine Smith Books, 1985), 115, 135.

5. Paul Josephson, *Industrialized Nature: Brute Force Technology and the Transformation of the Natural World* (Washington, D.C.: Island Press, 2002).

6. Paul Oslington, "The Necessity of a Theological Economics," paper presented to the annual meeting of the American Economic Association, Chicago, Ill., January 1998.

7. Cardinal Joseph Ratzinger, *"In the Beginning . . .": A Catholic Understanding of the Story of the Creation and the Fall* (1986; repr., Huntington, Ind.: Our Sunday Visitor, 1990), 53, 51.

Chapter 1

Adapted from Robert H. Nelson, "What Is 'Economic Theology'?" *Princeton Seminary Bulletin* 25 (February 2004). A full exploration of the religious status of economics is contained in Robert H.

Nelson, *Economics as Religion: From Samuelson to Chicago and Beyond* (University Park: Pennsylvania State University Press, 2001).

1. Sallie McFague, "New House Rules: Christianity, Economics, and Planetary Living," *Daedalus* 30 (Fall 2001): 8.

2. William J. Baumol, "On My Attitudes: Sociopolitical and Methodological," in *Eminent Economists: Their Life Philosophies*, ed. Michael Szenberg (New York: Cambridge University Press, 1992), 51.

3. Richard T. Ely, *Social Aspects of Christianity and Other Essays* (New York: Thomas Y. Crowell, 1889), 15, 53, 73.

4. This is a main theme of Robert H. Nelson, *Reaching for Heaven on Earth: The Theological Meaning of Economics* (Lanham, Md.: Rowman and Littlefield, 1991).

5. Sidney Fine, *Laissez Faire and the General-Welfare State: A Study of Conflict in American Thought, 1865-1901* (Ann Arbor: University of Michigan Press, 1964), 381.

6. Arthur J. Vidich and Sanford M. Lyman, *American Sociology: Worldly Rejections of Religion and their Directions* (New Haven: Yale University Press, 1985), 134.

7. Robert William Fogel, *The Fourth Great Awakening and the Future of Egalitarianism* (Chicago: University of Chicago Press, 2000), 122, 124.

8. See Dorothy Ross, *The Origins of American Social Science* (New York: Cambridge University Press, 1991); John Rutherford Everett, *Religion in Economics: A Study of John Bates Clark, Richard T. Ely, and Simon N. Patten* (1946; repr., Philadelphia: Porcupine Press, 1982); and Robert M. Crunden, *Ministers of Reform: The Progressives' Achievement in American Civilization, 1889-1920* (Chicago: University of Illinois Press, 1984).

9. Michael A. Bernstein, *A Perilous Progress: Economists and Public Purpose in Twentieth-Century America* (Princeton: Princeton University Press, 2001).

10. See, for example, Crunden, *Ministers of Reform*.

11. See Nelson, *Reaching for Heaven on Earth*; and Nelson, *Economics as Religion*. See also, for example, Robert H. Nelson, "Economic Religion Versus Christian Values," *Journal of Markets and Morality* 1 (October 1998); Robert H. Nelson, "Does 'Existence Value' Exist? An Essay on Religions, Old and New," *Independent Review* 1 (Spring 1997); Robert H. Nelson, "Sustainability, Efficiency, and God: Economic Values and the Sustainability Debate," *Annual Review of Ecology and Systematics* 26 (1995); and Robert H. Nelson, "Economics as Religion," in *Economics and Religion: Are They Distinct?* ed. H. Geoffrey Brennan and A. M. C. Waterman (Boston: Kluwer Academic, 1994).

12. R. A. Mundell, "A Reconsideration of the Twentieth Century," *American Economic Review* 90 (June 2000): 327, 331.

13. Charles L. Schultze, "The Role and Responsibilities of the Economist in Government," *American Economic Review* 72 (May 1982): 62.

14. Paul A. Samuelson, *Economics* (New York: McGraw-Hill, 1948), 127, 602. McGraw-Hill later reprinted the original *Economics* to celebrate its fiftieth anniversary.

15. Gregory Clark, *A Farewell to Alms: A Brief Economic History of the World* (Princeton: Princeton University Press, 2007), 3.

16. Gary Becker, "Milton Friedman," in *Remembering the University of Chicago: Teachers, Scientists, and Scholars*, ed. Edward Shils (Chicago: University of Chicago Press, 1991), 145-46.

17. Albert O. Hirschman, "How Keynes Was Spread from America," *Challenge*, November-December 1988, 6.

18. Edward Shils, "Harry Johnson," in Shils, *Remembering the University of Chicago*, 201, 209.

19. Joseph E. Stiglitz, *Wither Socialism?* (Cambridge: MIT Press, 1994), 201.

20. Ibid., 5.

21. See Eirik G. Furubotn and Rudolf Richter, *Institutions and Economic Theory: The Contribution of the New Institutional Economics* (Ann Arbor: University of Michigan Press, 1997).

22. See Martin Wolf, "Seeds of Its Own Destruction," *Financial Times*, March 8, 2009.

23. Samuelson, *Economics*, 482.

24. Ibid., 153.

25. See the journal *First Things*, edited by Richard Neuhaus (http://www.firstthings.com/).

26. Observation of G. K. Chesterton, quoted in Michael Novak, "The Nation with the Soul of a Church," in *A Public Philosophy Reader*, ed. Richard J. Bishirjian (New York: Arlington House, 1978), 92.

27. Fogel, *The Fourth Great Awakening*, 3-4.

28. Patricia Dalton, "We've Gotta Have It: But We Don't Need It and It's Consuming Us," *Washington Post*, November 28, 2004, B1.

29. Robert J. Samuelson, "It's Not the Economy, Stupid," *Washington Post*, January 7, 1994, A19.

Chapter 2

Adapted from Robert H. Nelson, "Anti-terrorism and Economic Theology: An Exercise in Comparative Theology," paper presented at the third annual meeting of the Association for the Study of Religion, Economics, and Culture, Kansas City, Mo., October 22–24, 2004.

1. Leszek Kolakowski, *Why Is There Something Rather Than Nothing? 23 Questions from Great Philosophers* (New York: Basic Books, 2007).

2. Max Weber, *The Protestant Ethic and the Spirit of Capitalism* (1905; repr., New York: Charles Scribner, 1958).

3. Robert Putnam, *Making Democracy Work: Civic Traditions in Modern Italy* (Princeton: Princeton University Press, 1993).

4. Eirik G. Furubotn and Rudolf Richter, *Institutions and Economic Theory: The Contribution of the New Institutional Economics* (Ann Arbor: University of Michigan Press, 1997).

5. Douglass C. North, *Institutions, Institutional Change, and Economic Performance* (New York: Cambridge University Press, 1990).

6. Laurence R. Iannaccone, "Introduction to the Economics of Religion," *Journal of Economic Literature* 36 (September 1998).

7. Corry Azzi and Ronald Ehrenberg, "Household Allocation of Time and Church Attendance," *Journal of Political Economy* 83 (February 1975).

8. Robert B. Ekelund and others, *Sacred Trust: The Medieval Church as an Economic Firm* (New York: Oxford University Press, 1996).

9. Robert B. Ekelund Jr., Robert F. Hebert, and Robert D. Tollison, *The Marketplace of Christianity* (Cambridge: MIT Press, 2006).

10. A. M. C. Waterman, "Economics as Theology: Adam Smith's Wealth of Nations," *Southern Economic Journal* 68 (April 2002).

11. Robert H. Nelson, *Economics as Religion: From Samuelson to Chicago and Beyond* (University Park: Pennsylvania State University Press, 2001); and Robert H. Nelson, *Reaching for Heaven on Earth: The Theological Meaning of Economics* (Lanham, Md.: Rowman and Littlefield, 1991).

12. "God Is Not a Republican, or a Democrat," statement of religious leaders printed in the *Christian Century*, September 21, 2004, 26.

13. Quoted in Laurie Goodstein, "After the Attacks: Finding Fault," *New York Times*, September 15, 2001, A15.

14. Goodstein, "After the Attacks."

15. Robin Allen, "Aden Port Stagnates While Yemenis Dither," *Financial Times*, June 10, 2003.

16. "Experts Warn of More Attacks," *New Zealand Herald*, August 7, 2003.

17. "Markets and Schools Can Defeat Terror," *Weekend Australian*, August 9, 2003.

18. Gordon Brown, "Drugs Are Just the Start," *Guardian*, August 28, 2003.

19. Thomas L. Friedman, "Connect the Dots," *New York Times*, September 25, 2003.

20. Quoted in "Lula Sticks to the Right," *Buenos Aires Herald*, July 15, 2006, 6.

21. Quoted in Louise Continelli, "Feed Hungry to Cut Terrorism Threat, Activist Urges," *Buffalo News*, September 10, 2003.

22. Lawrence Wright, *The Looming Tower: Al-Qaeda and the Road to 9/11* (New York: Knopf, 2006), 301, 304.

23. See Alberto Abadie, "Poverty, Political Freedom, and the Roots of Terrorism" (working paper 10859, National Bureau of Economic Research, October 2004).

24. President George W. Bush, "Remarks on the War on Terror," Oak Ridge National Laboratory, Oak Ridge, Tennessee, July 12, 2004.

25. President George W. Bush, "Results in Iraq: 100 Days Toward Security and Freedom," White House Release, August 8, 2003.

26. President George W. Bush, "State of the Union Address," Washington, D.C., January 20, 2004.

27. President George W. Bush, "Remarks on Operation Iraqi Freedom," Ford Community and Performing Arts Center, Dearborn, Michigan, April 28, 2003.

28. Wilfred M. McClay, "The Soul of a Nation," *Public Interest* (Spring 2004): 13.

29. Quoted in "Graham Creates Controversy," *Daily Beacon*, August 27, 2002, http://www.daily beacon.utk.edu/article.php/6806 (accessed September 27, 2004).

30. Franklin Graham, "My View of Islam," *The Wall Street Journal*, December 3, 2001.

31. "Franklin Graham Speaks Out on Radical Islam," transcript from *Christian World News*, October 4, 2002.

32. Bernard Lewis, "The Revolt of Islam," *New Yorker*, November 19, 2001.

33. "God Is Not a Republican, or a Democrat," 26.

34. Stanley Hauerwas, *Against the Nations: War and Survival in a Liberal Society* (Notre Dame: University of Notre Dame Press, 1992), 6.

35. Second Vatican Council, "Decree Concerning the Pastoral Office of Bishops in the Church," Rome, October 28, 1965, quoted in U.S. Conference of Catholic Bishops, *Readings on Catholics in Political Life* (Washington, D.C.: 2006), x.

36. McClay, "The Soul of a Nation," 6.

37. This argument is developed at length in Nelson, *Reaching for Heaven on Earth*. See also Robert H. Nelson, "Scholasticism Versus Pietism: The Battle for the Soul of Economics," *Econ Journal Watch* 1 (December 2004), http://www.econjournalwatch.org/pdf/NelsonCharacterIssues1December2004.pdf.

38. Eli Berman and David D. Laitin, "Religion, Terrorism, and Public Goods: Testing the Club Model," *Journal of Public Economics* 92 (October 2008).

Chapter 3

Adapted from Robert H. Nelson, "Does 'Existence Value' Exist? An Essay on Religions, Old and New," *Independent Review* 1 (Spring 1997).

1. Barton H. Thompson Jr., "What Good Is Economics?" *University of California Davis Law Review* 37 (November 2003): 176, 177, 197, 179.

2. Robert C. Mitchell and Richard T. Carson, *Using Surveys to Value Public Goods: The Contingent Valuation Method* (Washington, D.C.: Resources for the Future, 1989).

3. John McPhee, *Encounters with the Archdruid* (New York: Farrar, Straus and Giroux, 1971), 74.

4. Bryan G. Norton, "Thoreau's Insect Analogies: Or Why Environmentalists Hate Mainstream Economists," *Environmental Ethics* 13 (Fall 1991).

5. Stanley Lebergott, "Long-Term Trends in the U.S. Standard of Living," in *The State of Humanity*, ed. Julian L. Simon (Cambridge, Mass.: Blackwell, 1995), 149.

6. J. Moltmann, "The Destruction and Healing of the Earth: Ecology and Theology," in *God and Globalization*, vol. 2, *Theological Ethics and the Spheres of Life*, ed. Max Stackhouse and D. Browning (Harrisburg, Pa.: Trinity, 2001), 279.

7. John V. Krutilla, "Conservation Reconsidered," *American Economic Review* 57 (September 1967).

8. Mitchell and Carson, *Using Surveys to Value Public Goods*.

9. *State of Ohio v. U.S. Department of the Interior*, 880 F.2d 432 (D.C. Cir. 1989).

10. John Terborgh, "A Matter of Life and Death," *New York Review of Books*, November 5, 1992, 6.

11. Henry D. Jacoby, "What Is Nature Worth?" paper delivered at the First Abraham Kuyper Consultation on "Common Grace: Theology, Ecology, and Technology," Princeton Theological Seminary, Princeton, N.J., February 2, 2002, 11, 12.

12. Walter J. Mead, "Review and Analysis of Recent State-of-the-Art Contingent Valuation Studies," in *Contingent Valuation: A Critical Assessment, Washington, D.C., April 2 and 3, 1992* (Cambridge, Mass.: Cambridge Economics).

13. Roger Bate, *Pick a Number: A Critique of Contingent Valuation Methodology and Its Application in Public Policy* (Washington, D.C.: Competitive Enterprise Institute, February 1994); William H. Desvousges and others, "Contingent Valuation: The Wrong Tool to Measure Passive-Use Losses," *Choices* 8 (Second Quarter, 1993); Steven F. Edwards, "Rethinking Existence Values," *Land Economics* 68

(February 1992); Donald H. Rosenthal and Robert H. Nelson, "Why Existence Values Should Not Be Used in Cost-Benefit Analysis," *Journal of Policy Analysis and Management* 11 (Winter 1992); Raymond J. Kopp, "Why Existence Value Should Be Used in Cost-Benefit Analysis," *Journal of Policy Analysis and Management* 11 (Winter 1992); John Quiggin, "Existence Value and Benefit-Cost Analysis: A Third View," *Journal of Policy Analysis and Management* 12 (Winter 1993); Alan Randall, "Passive-Use and Contingent Valuation—Valid for Damage Assessment," *Choices* 8 (Second Quarter, 1993); and Richard Stewart, *Natural Resource Damages: A Legal, Economic, and Policy Analysis* (Washington, D.C.: National Legal Center for the Public Interest, 1995).

14. Anonymous, "'Ask a Silly Question, . . . ': Contingent Valuation of Natural Resource Damages," *Harvard Law Review* 105 (June 1992); and Charles J. DiBona, "Assessing Environmental Damage," *Issues in Science and Technology* 9 (Fall 1992).

15. Matthew F. Child, "The Thoreau Ideal as a Unifying Thread in the Conservation Movement," *Conservation Biology* 23 (April 2009).

16. Jerry A. Hausman, ed., *Contingent Valuation: A Critical Assessment* (New York: North Holland, 1993).

17. Richard T. Carson and others, "A Contingent Valuation Study of Lost Passive Use Values Resulting from the Exxon Valdez Oil Spill," Report to the Attorney General of Alaska, Natural Resource Damage Assessment Inc. (La Jolla, Calif., November 1992).

18. Kenneth Arrow and others, "Report of the NOAA Panel on Contingent Valuation," *Federal Register* 4601 (January 15, 1993).

19. Paul R. Portney, "The Contingent Valuation Debate: Why Economists Should Care," *Journal of Economic Perspectives* 8 (Fall 1994).

20. Jacoby, "What Is Nature Worth?" 20.

21. Paul Milgrom, "Is Sympathy an Economic Value? Philosophy, Economics, and the Contingent Valuation Method," in Hausman, *Contingent Valuation.*

22. Ron Arnold, *At the Eye of the Storm: James Watt and the Environmentalists* (Chicago: Henry Regnery, 1982), 123.

23. Brooke Williams, "Love or Power?" *Northern Lights* 7 (Fall 1991).

24. Robert Royal, *The Virgin and the Dynamo: Use and Abuse of Religion in Environmental Debates* (Grand Rapids, Mich.: Eerdmans, 1999).

25. McPhee, *Encounters with the Archdruid,* 84.

26. Roderick Nash, *Wilderness and the American Mind* (New Haven: Yale University Press, 1973), 126; Muir quoted on p. 125.

27. Roger G. Kennedy, "The Fish That Will Not Take Our Hooks," *Wilderness* (Spring 1995): 28.

28. Mark Sagoff, "On the Expansion of Economic Theory: A Rejoinder," *Economy and Environment* (Summer 1994): 7–8. See also Mark Sagoff, "On the Economic Value of Ecosystem Services," *Environmental Values* 17, no. 2 (2008).

Chapter 4

Adapted from Robert H. Nelson, "Sustainability, Efficiency, and God: Economic Values and the Sustainability Debate," *Annual Review of Ecology and Systematics* 26 (1995).

1. Frank Ackerman and Lisa Heinzerling, *Priceless: On Knowing the Price of Everything and the Value of Nothing* (New York: New Press, 2004).

2. Paul R. Portney, "EPA and the Evolution of Federal Regulation," in *Public Policies for the Environment,* ed. Paul R. Portney (Washington, D.C.: Resources for the Future, 1990).

3. Larry E. Ruff, "The Economic Common Sense of Pollution," *Public Interest* (Spring 1970); and Allen V. Kneese and Charles L. Schultze, *Pollution, Prices, and Public Policy* (Washington, D.C.: Brookings Institution, 1975).

4. Robert H. Nelson, "The Economics Profession and the Making of Public Policy," *Journal of Economic Literature* 25 (March 1987).

5. Carl Kaysen, "Model-Makers and Decision-Makers: Economists in the Public Policy Process," *Public Interest* (Summer 1968): 83.

6. Charles L. Schultze, *Politics and Economics of Public Spending* (Washington, D.C.: Brookings Institution, 1968), 2–3.

7. Charles L. Schultze, "The Role and Responsibilities of the Economist in Government," *American Economic Review* 72 (May 1982). See also Daniel W. Bromley, "The Ideology of Efficiency: Searching for a Theory of Policy Analysis," *Journal of Environmental Economics and Management* 19 (January 1990).

8. Henry D. Jacoby, "What Is Nature Worth?" paper delivered at the First Abraham Kuyper Consultation on "Common Grace: Theology, Ecology, and Technology," Princeton Theological Seminary, Princeton, N.J., February 2, 2002, 4.

9. Herbert A. Simon, "The Failure of Armchair Economics," *Challenge*, November–December, 1986.

10. William R. Allen, "Economics, Economists, and Economic Policy: Modern American Experiences," *History of Political Economy* 9 (Spring 1977).

11. Alec Cairncross, "Economics in Theory and Practice," *American Economic Review* 75 (May 1985): 4.

12. Carol H. Weiss, "Research for Policy's Sake: The Enlightenment Function of Social Research," *Policy Analysis* 3, no. 4 (1977): 544.

13. D. N. McCloskey, *The Rhetoric of Economics* (Madison: University of Wisconsin Press, 1985).

14. Robert M. Solow, *Sustainability: An Economist's Perspective* (Woods Hole, Mass.: Woods Hole Oceanographic Institution, 1991); reprinted in Robert M. Solow, "Sustainability: An Economist's Perspective," in *Economics of the Environment: Selected Readings*, ed. Robert N. Stavins, 4th ed. (New York: Norton, 2000).

15. Ibid., 132.

16. Ibid.

17. Ibid., 133.

18. Ibid., 134–35.

19. Ibid., 134.

20. Robert M. Solow, *Growth Theory: An Exposition* (New York: Oxford University Press, 1970).

21. William Nordhaus, *A Question of Balance: Weighing the Options on Global Warming Policies* (New Haven: Yale University Press, 2008).

22. Freeman Dyson, "The Question of Global Warming," *New York Review of Books*, June 12, 2008.

23. William Nordhaus, "Letter," *New York Review of Books*, September 25, 2008, 92.

24. Ibid., 93.

25. Ibid.

26. Bjorn Lomborg, *Solutions for the World's Biggest Problems: Costs and Benefits* (New York: Cambridge University Press, 2007).

27. Dyson, "The Question of Global Warming," 45.

28. Nordhaus, "Letter," 92.

29. See also Robert H. Nelson, "Global Warming and Religion: Climate Policy as Applied Theology," in *The Global Warming Debate: Science, Economics, and Policy* (Great Barrington, Mass.: American Institute for Economic Research, 2008).

30. John A. McPhee, *Encounters with the Archdruid* (New York: Farrar, Straus and Giroux, 1971).

31. Paul R. Ehrlich, *The Population Bomb* (New York: Ballantine Books, 1968).

32. Robert Costanza, *Ecological Economics: The Science and Management of Sustainability* (New York: Columbia University Press, 1991).

33. Federico Mayor, "Foreword," in *Environmentally Sustainable Economic Development: Building on Brundtland*, ed. Robert Goodland and others (New York: United Nations Educational, Scientific, and Cultural Organization, 1991), 3.

34. World Commission on Environment and Development, *Our Common Future* (New York: Oxford University Press, 1987).

35. "Introduction," in *Environmentally Sustainable Economic Development: Building on Brundtland*, ed. Robert Goodland and others (New York: United Nations Educational, Scientific, and Cultural Organization, 1991), 11, 12.

36. Harold J. Barnett and Chandler Morse, *Scarcity and Growth: The Economics of Natural Resource Availability* (Baltimore: Johns Hopkins University Press for Resources for the Future, 1963); and World

Resources Institute, *World Resources, 1994–95: People and the Environment* (New York: Oxford University Press, 1994).

37. World Bank, *World Development Report, 1992: Development and the Environment* (New York: Oxford University Press, 1992), 9.

38. Herman Daly and Joshua Farley, *Ecological Economics: Principles and Applications* (Washington, D.C.: Island Press, 2003).

39. Letter to supporters of The Land Institute (located in Salinas, Kans.), from Wes Jackson, president, October 2004.

Chapter 5

Adapted from Robert H. Nelson, "All in the Name of Progress: An Essay-Review of Paul R. Josephson's *Industrialized Nature*," *Politics and the Life Sciences* 23 (October 2005).

1. James C. Scott, *Seeing Like a State: How Certain Schemes to Improve the Human Condition Have Failed* (New Haven: Yale University Press, 1998).

2. Ibid., 89–90.

3. See Judith Shapiro, *Mao's War Against Nature: Politics and the Environment in Revolutionary China* (New York: Cambridge University Press, 2001).

4. See Randal O'Toole, *The Best-Laid Plans: How Government Planning Harms Your Quality of Life, Your Pocketbook, and Your Future* (Washington, D.C.: Cato Institute, 2007).

5. Charles L. Schultze, *The Public Use of Private Interest* (Washington, D.C.: Brookings Institution, 1977), 72, 21.

6. See Stephen A. Marglin, *The Dismal Science: How Thinking Like an Economist Undermines Community* (Cambridge: Harvard University Press, 2008).

7. Anonymous, "'Ask a Silly Question . . . ': Contingent Valuation of Natural Resource Damages," *Harvard Law Review* 105 (June 1992).

8. Paul Josephson, *Industrialized Nature: Brute Force Technology and the Transformation of the Natural World* (Washington, D.C.: Island Press, 2002), 255, 256, 257, 256.

9. Ibid., 257.

10. Ibid., 28, 64.

11. Ibid., 64, 64–65.

12. Ibid., 65, 19, 31, 33, 65.

13. Ibid., 44, 45, 47.

14. Gifford Pinchot, *The Fight for Conservation* (Seattle: University of Washington Press, 1967), 95.

15. Charles Howard Hopkins, *The Rise of the Social Gospel in American Protestantism, 1865–1915* (New Haven: Yale University Press, 1940), 320–21.

16. Josephson, *Industrialized Nature*, 10, 10–11, 10.

17. Ibid., 174, 176, 174, 175.

18. Ibid., 185.

19. Ibid., 12.

20. Ibid., 194–95.

21. Ibid., 180.

22. See, for example, J. R. McNeill, *Something New Under the Sun: An Environmental History of the Twentieth Century World* (New York: Norton, 2000).

23. See A. Dan Tarlock, "Can Cowboys Become Indians? Protecting Western Communities as Endangered Cultural Remnants," *Arizona State Law Journal* 31 (Summer 1999).

Introduction to Part II

1. Karl Polanyi, *The Great Transformation: The Political and Economic Origins of our Time* (1944; repr., Boston: Beacon Press, 1957).

2. Carl L. Becker, *The Heavenly City of the Eighteenth-Century Philosophers* (New Haven: Yale University Press, 1932).

3. Jean Starobinski, *Jean-Jacques Rousseau: Transparency and Obstruction*, trans. Arthur Goldhammer (1971; repr., Chicago: University of Chicago Press, 1988), 29, 3.

4. Ibid., 112, 16.

5. Edward Norman, *Secularization: New Century Theology* (New York: Continuum, 2002).

6. Mark Stoll, *Protestantism, Capitalism, and Nature in America* (Albuquerque: University of New Mexico Press, 1997), 52.

7. Donald Worster, *The Wealth of Nature: Environmental History and the Ecological Imagination* (New York: Oxford University Press, 1993), 196.

8. Ibid., 197–98.

9. Ibid., 198.

10. Ibid., 199.

11. Clarence Faust and Thomas Johnson, eds., *Jonathan Edwards: Representative Selections* (New York: American Book Company, 1935), 60–61.

12. Worster, *The Wealth of Nature*, 200.

13. See Robert H. Nelson, "Bruce Babbitt, Pipeline to the Almighty," *Weekly Standard*, June 24, 1996.

14. Worster, *The Wealth of Nature*, 189.

15. Transcript of James Gustave ("Gus") Speth *On Point* interview, April 22, 2008, http://www.eenews.net/tv/video_guide/786 (accessed April 25, 2008).

16. See also Deepak Lal, "Eco-fundamentalism," *International Affairs* 71, no. 3 (July 1995).

17. See Robert H. Nelson, *Reaching for Heaven on Earth: The Theological Meaning of Economics* (Lanham, Md.: Rowman and Littlefield, 1991).

18. See Robert H. Nelson, "Scholasticism Versus Pietism: The Battle for the Soul of Economics," *Econ Journal Watch* 1 (December 2004), http://www.econjournalwatch.org/pdf/NelsonCharacterIssues 1December2004.pdf.

Chapter 6

Partially adapted from Robert H. Nelson, "Unoriginal Sin: The Judeo-Christian Roots of Ecotheology," *Policy Review* 53 (Summer 1990).

1. John Courtney Murray, *We Hold These Truths: Catholic Reflections on the American Proposition* (New York: Sheed and Ward, 1960), 201, 112.

2. Donald Worster, *The Wealth of Nature: Environmental History and the Ecological Imagination* (New York: Oxford University Press, 1993), 195.

3. Muir, as quoted in Worster, *The Wealth of Nature*, 195.

4. Worster, *The Wealth of Nature*, 195.

5. Robert Royal, *The Virgin and the Dynamo: The Use and Abuse of Religion in Environmental Debates* (Grand Rapids, Mich.: Eerdmans, 1999), 12.

6. Worster, *The Wealth of Nature*, 195.

7. Ibid., 193, 196.

8. Karl R. Popper, *The Open Society and Its Enemies*, vol. 1, *The Spell of Plato* (1962; repr., Princeton: Princeton University Press, 1971). See also Robert H. Nelson, *Reaching for Heaven on Earth: The Theological Meaning of Economics* (Lanham, Md.: Rowman and Littlefield, 1991).

9. Bill Devall and George Sessions, *Deep Ecology: Living as if Nature Mattered* (Salt Lake City: Peregrine Smith Books, 1985), 48.

10. Neil Everndon, "Beyond Ecology," quoted approvingly in Devall and Sessions, *Deep Ecology*, 48.

11. Dave Foreman, "The Destruction of Wilderness," *Earth First! The Radical Environmental Journal* (December 1989): 20.

12. Ibid.

13. Craig Canine, "Wes Jackson," *Smithsonian*, November 2005, 81.

14. Wes Jackson, quoted in ibid., 81.

15. Canine, "Wes Jackson," 81.

16. Wes Jackson, quoted in ibid., 81.

17. David W. Orr, "Armageddon Versus Extinction," *Conservation Biology* 19 (April 2005): 290.

18. Ibid.

19. See Mark Dowie, *Losing Ground: American Environmentalism at the Close of the Twentieth Century* (Cambridge: MIT Press, 1995).

20. Donald R. McGregor, "Public Response to Y2K: Social Amplification and Risk Adaptation: Or, 'How I Learned to Stop Worrying and Love Y2K,'" in *The Social Amplification of Risk*, ed. Nick Pidgeon, Roger E. Kasperson, and Paul Slovic (New York: Cambridge University Press, 2003), 256.

21. Bill McKibben, *The End of Nature* (New York: Random House, 1989), 50.

22. Ibid., 216.

23. David Brower, comments cited in John McPhee, *Encounters with the Archdruid* (New York: Farrar, Straus and Giroux, 1971), 83.

24. Interview with Foreman, cited in Douglas S. Looney, "Protection or Provocateur," *Sports Illustrated*, May 27, 1991.

25. Captain Paul Watson, "On the Precedence of Natural Law," speech to the sixth Western Public Interest Law Conference at the University of Oregon Law School, *Journal of Environmental Law and Litigation* 3 (1988): 82.

26. Anne Petermann, "Tales of a Recovering Misanthrope," *Earth First! The Radical Environmental Journal* 19 (June–July 1999): 3.

27. The Pianka speech and the reaction are described in Cathy Young, "Environmentalism and the Apocalypse," *Boston Globe*, April 17, 2006, A15.

28. Kate Soper, *What Is Nature?* (Cambridge, Mass.: Blackwell Publishers, 1995), 19.

29. William Cronon, "Getting Back to the Wrong Nature," *Utne Reader*, May–June 1996, 78, 76, 78.

30. McKibben, *The End of Nature*, 186, 180.

31. Quoted in "Bulletin Board," *High Country News*, September 23, 1991, 16.

32. William Cronon, "The Trouble with Wilderness; or, Getting Back to the Wrong Nature," in *Uncommon Ground: Rethinking the Human Place in Nature*, ed. William Cronon (New York: Norton, 1996).

33. See Robert H. Nelson, *A Burning Issue: A Case for Abolishing the U.S. Forest Service* (Lanham, Md.: Rowman and Littlefield, 2000).

34. Bruce N. Ames and Lois Gold, "Environmental Pollution and Cancer: Some Misconceptions," in *Phantom Risk*, ed. Kenneth R. Foster, David E. Bernstein, and Peter W. Huber (Cambridge: MIT Press, 1993).

35. Lynn White Jr., "The Historical Roots of Our Ecological Crisis," *Science* 155 (March 10, 1967).

36. J. R. McNeill, *Something New Under the Sun: An Environmental History of the Twentieth-Century World* (New York: Norton, 2000), 337.

37. Julianne Lutz Newton and Eric T. Freyfogle, "Sustainability: A Dissent," *Conservation Biology* 19 (February 2005): 25.

38. Ibid.

39. Soper, *What Is Nature?* 160–61.

40. George M. Marsden, *Jonathan Edwards: A Life* (New Haven: Yale University Press, 2003), 221–22.

41. Jonathan Edwards, "Sinners in the Hands of an Angry God," quoted in Marsden, *Jonathan Edwards*, 223.

42. Marsden, *Jonathan Edwards*, 224, 353.

Chapter 7

Partially adapted from Robert H. Nelson, "Environmental Calvinism: The Judeo-Christian Roots of Environmental Theology," in *Taking the Environment Seriously*, ed. Roger E. Meiners and Bruce Yandle (Lanham, Md.: Rowman and Littlefield, 1993).

1. Mark Stoll, "Creating Ecology: Protestants and the Moral Community of Creation," in *Religion and the New Ecology: Environmental Responsibility in a World in Flux*, ed. David M. Lodge and

Christopher Hamlin (Notre Dame: University of Notre Dame Press, 2006), 57. See also Mark Stoll, *Protestantism, Capitalism, and Nature in America* (Albuquerque: University of New Mexico Press, 1997).

2. Ibid., 54. See also Mark Stoll, "Green Versus Green: Religions, Ethics, and the Bookchin-Foreman Dispute," *Environmental History* 6 (July 2001): 414.

3. J. Baird Callicott and Michael P. Nelson, "Introduction," in *The Great New Wilderness Debate*, ed. Callicott and Nelson (Athens: University of Georgia Press, 1998), 5.

4. I first used the characterization "Calvinism minus God," in Robert H. Nelson, "Calvinism Minus God: Environmental Restoration as a Theological Concept," in *Saving the Seas: Values, Scientists, and International Governance*, ed. L. Anathea Brooks and Stacy D. VanDeveer (College Park, Md.: Maryland Sea Grant College, 1997). See also Robert H. Nelson, "Calvinism Minus God," *Forbes*, October 5, 1998.

5. John Calvin, *Calvin's Institutes: A New Compend*, ed. Hugh T. Kerr (Louisville, Ky.: Westminster/John Knox Press, 1989), 26–27, 99.

6. Ibid., 43.

7. Ibid., 24.

8. Ibid., 25–26.

9. Ibid., 65, 56, 110, 115.

10. Ibid., 99, 41–42.

11. J. Baird Callicott, "That Good Old-Time Wilderness Religion," in Callicott and Nelson, *The Great New Wilderness Debate*, 389.

12. Max Weber, *The Protestant Ethic and the Spirit of Capitalism* (1905; repr., New York: Scribner, 1958).

13. R. H. Tawney, *Religion and the Rise of Capitalism: A Historical Study* (New York: Harcourt, Brace, 1926), 105.

14. Weber, *The Protestant Ethic and the Spirit of Capitalism*, 163.

15. Ernst Troeltsch, *Protestantism and Progress: A Historical Study of the Relation of Protestantism to the Modern World*, trans. W. Montgomery (1912; repr., Boston: Beacon Press, 1958), 86–87.

16. For more on the large "Roman" influences in the United States during the twentieth century, see Robert H. Nelson, *Reaching for Heaven on Earth: The Theological Meaning of Economics* (Lanham, Md.: Rowman and Littlefield, 1991), chaps. 5, 6.

17. See David Gelernter, *Americanism: The Fourth Great Western Religion* (New York: Doubleday, 2007).

18. Perry Miller, *Errand into the Wilderness* (1956; repr., New York: Harper and Row, 1964), 11–12.

19. Catherine Albanese, *Nature Religion in America: From the Algonkian Indians to the New Age* (Chicago: University of Chicago Press, 1990), 37.

20. See Sigurd Olson, "Why Wilderness?" in Callicott and Nelson *The Great New Wilderness Debate*.

21. Roderick Nash, *Wilderness and the American Mind* (New Haven: Yale University Press, 1973), 37.

22. Lynn White Jr., "The Historical Roots of our Ecological Crisis," *Science* 155 (March 10, 1967).

23. John Preston, *Saints Qualification* (1633), quoted in Miller, *Errand into the Wilderness*, 77.

24. Quoted in E. Brooks Holifield, *Theology in America: Christian Thought from the Age of the Puritans to the Civil War* (New Haven: Yale University Press, 2003), 33.

25. Holifield, *Theology in America*, 33.

26. Miller, *Errand into the Wilderness*, 77.

27. Cotton Mather, *The Christian Philosopher: A Collection of the Best Discoveries in Nature, with Religious Improvements* (1721), quoted in Albanese, *Nature Religion in America*, 41.

28. Jonathan Edwards, *The Images and Shadows of Things Divine*, ed. Perry Miller (New Haven: Yale University Press, 1948), 69.

29. Ibid., 61.

30. George M. Marsden, *Jonathan Edwards: A Life* (New Haven: Yale University Press, 2003), 77.

31. Ibid., 78.

32. Ibid., 79.

33. Jonathan Edwards, "Sinners in the Hands of an Angry God," quoted in Callicott and Nelson, *The Great New Wilderness Debate*, 26.

34. See Robert H. Nelson, "Calvinism Minus God," *Forbes*, October 5, 1998.

35. Perry Miller, *Errand into the Wilderness*, 184–85.

36. Robert D. Richardson Jr., *Emerson: The Mind on Fire* (Berkeley and Los Angeles: University of California Press, 1995).

37. Ralph Waldo Emerson, as quoted in Arthur A. Ekirch Jr., *Man and Nature in America* (New York: Columbia University Press, 1963), 51.

38. See Ralph Waldo Emerson, "Nature," in *Ralph Waldo Emerson: Selected Essays, Lectures and Poems*, ed. Robert D. Richardson Jr. (New York: Bantam Books, 1990), 17–18, 32. See also Richardson, *Emerson*, 224–34.

39. Ekirch, *Man and Nature in America*, 48, 47, 49, 51, 49, 48.

40. Ibid., 53.

41. Robert D. Richardson Jr., *Henry David Thoreau: A Life of the Mind* (Berkeley and Los Angeles: University of California Press, 1986).

42. Mark Sagoff, *The Economy of the Earth: Philosophy, Law, and the Environment*, 2d ed. (New York: Cambridge University Press, 2008), 111.

43. Henry David Thoreau, *The Maine Woods*, in *A Week on the Concord and Merrimack Rivers; Walden; The Maine Woods; Cape Cod* (New York: Library of America, 1985), 683.

44. Ibid., 712.

45. Linnie Marsh Wolfe, "Introduction," to John Muir, *John of the Mountains: The Unpublished Journals of John Muir*, ed. Linnie Marsh Wolfe (1938; repr., Madison: University of Wisconsin Press, 1979), xii, xi.

46. Muir, *John of the Mountains*, 94–95.

47. Ibid, 83–84.

48. Ibid., 97–98, 99, 86.

49. Ibid., 92.

50. Ibid., 89.

51. Joseph Sax, *Mountains Without Handrails: Reflections on the National Parks* (Ann Arbor: University of Michigan Press, 1980), 104.

52. Eugene Cittadino, "Ecology and American Social Thought," in *Religion and the New Ecology: Environmental Responsibility in a World of Flux*, ed. David M. Lodge and Christopher Hamlin (Notre Dame: University of Notre Dame Press, 2006), 104.

53. Among his many writings, see Edward Abbey, *Desert Solitaire: A Season in the Wilderness* (New York: Ballantine Books, 1968).

54. Dave Foreman, *Confessions of an Eco-Warrior* (New York: Harmony Books, 1991).

55. Susan Zakin, *Coyotes and Town Dogs: Earth First! and the Environmental Movement* (New York: Viking, 1993), 259. See also Alston Chase, *In a Dark Wood: The Fight Over Forests and the Tyranny of Ecology* (Boston: Houghton Mifflin, 1995).

56. Martha F. Lee, *Earth First! Environmental Apocalypse* (Syracuse: Syracuse University Press, 1995), x.

57. Earth First! took its inspiration in part from Edward Abbey, *The Monkey Wrench Gang* (New York: Avon, 1976).

58. Dave Foreman, "Statement of Principles," as cited in Lee, *Earth First!* 39.

59. Lee, *Earth First!* 39, 40.

60. Ibid., 40–42.

61. Ibid., 17, 42, 43.

62. Anonymous, "Ele! Mellonkemmi, Greetings Earthfriends," *Earth First! Newsletter*, August 1981, cited in Lee, *Earth First!* 43.

63. Christopher Manes, *Green Rage: Radical Environmentalism and the Unmaking of Civilization* (Boston: Little, Brown, 1990), 8.

64. See Steven Chase, ed., *Defending the Earth: A Dialogue Between Murray Bookchin and Dave Foreman* (Boston: South End Press, 1991).

65. Dave Foreman, *Rewilding North America: A Vision for Conservation for the 21st Century* (Washington, D.C.: Island Press, 2004).

Introduction to Part III

1. Elizabeth A. Johnston, "Losing and Finding Creation in the Christian Tradition," in *Christianity and Ecology: Seeking the Well-Being of Earth and Humans* (Cambridge: Harvard University Press, 2000).

2. I first used the phrase "environmental creationism" in print in Robert H. Nelson, "Environmental Creationism," *Forbes*, April 8, 1996.

3. Max Oelschlaeger, *Caring for Creation: An Ecumenical Approach to the Environmental Crisis* (New Haven: Yale University Press, 1994); and Carol S. Robb and Carl J. Casebolt, eds., *Covenant for a New Creation: Ethics, Religion, and Public Policy* (Maryknoll, N.Y.: Orbis, 1991).

4. Peter Borelli, "The Ecophilosophers," *The Amicus Journal* (Spring 1988): 35.

5. "Inside the World's Last Eden: A Personal Journal to a Place No Human Has Ever Seen," *Time*, July 13, 1992; and John McCormick, *Reclaiming Paradise: The Global Environmental Movement* (Bloomington: University of Indiana Press, 1989).

6. Gustav Niebuhr, "Black Churches' Efforts on Environmentalism Praised by Gore," *Washington Post*, December 3, 1993, A13.

7. David Remnick, "Talk of the Town," *New Yorker*, March 5, 2007, 34.

8. Bruce Babbitt, "Our Covenant: To Protect the *Whole* of Creation," circulated to top staff of the Department of the Interior through the e-mail system, December 14, 1995. This speech was delivered on various occasions, including to the League of Conservation Voters in New York City in early December 1995.

9. Lara Lutz, "Environmental Stewardship Growing Presence in Churches," *Bay Journal*, February 2006, http://www.bayjournal.com/article.cfm?article=2728 (accessed March 23, 2009).

10. Cited in Lutz, "Environmental Stewardship Growing Presence in Churches."

11. Lutz, "Environmental Stewardship Growing Presence in Churches."

12. Cited in ibid.

13. David M. Lodge and Christopher Hamlin, "Preface," in *Religion and the New Ecology*, ed. Lodge and Hamlin (Notre Dame: University of Notre Dame Press, 2006), xi.

14. William Cronon, "Introduction: In Search of Nature," in *Uncommon Ground: Rethinking the Human Place in Nature*, ed. Cronon (New York: Norton, 1996), 26.

15. William Cronon, "The Trouble with Wilderness; or, Getting Back to the Wrong Nature," in Cronon, *Uncommon Ground*, 69.

Chapter 8

This chapter is newly written.

1. Thomas R. Dunlap, *Faith in Nature: Environmentalism as Religious Quest* (Seattle: University of Washington Press, 2004), 38.

2. Mark Sagoff, "Environmentalism: Death and Resurrection," *Philosophy and Public Policy Quarterly* 27 (Summer–Fall 2007).

3. Eugene Cittadino, "Ecology and American Social Thought," in *Religion and the New Ecology: Environmental Responsibility in a World of Flux*, ed. David M. Lodge and Christopher Hamlin (Notre Dame: University of Notre Dame Press, 2006), 73.

4. Ibid.

5. Donald Worster, *Nature's Economy: A History of Ecological Ideas*, 2d ed. (New York: Cambridge University Press, 1994), 209.

6. Ibid., 210.

7. Ibid.

8. Quoted in ibid., 216.

9. Frederic E. Clements, *Plant Succession: An Analysis of the Development of Vegetation* (Washington, D.C.: Carnegie Institution, 1916), 124–25.

10. Worster, *Nature's Economy*, 214–15.

11. Ibid., 211.

12. Max Oelschlaeger, *The Idea of Wilderness* (New Haven: Yale University Press, 1991), 205.

13. See Curt Meine, *Aldo Leopold: His Life and Work* (Madison: University of Wisconsin Press, 1988); and Julianne Lutz Newton, *Aldo Leopold's Odyssey: Rediscovering the Author of "A Sand County Almanac"* (Washington, D.C.: Island Press, 2006).

14. Aldo Leopold, *A Sand County Almanac* (1949; repr., New York: Oxford University Press, 1968).

15. See Robert H. Nelson, "The Religion of Forestry: Scientific Management," *Journal of Forestry* 97 (November 1999).

16. Aldo Leopold, "The Conservation Ethic," in Aldo Leopold, *The River of the Mother of God and Other Essays*, ed. Susan L. Flader and J. Baird Callicott (Madison: University of Wisconsin Press, 1991), 188.

17. Aldo Leopold, "Marshland Elegy," in *A Sand County Almanac* (1949; repr., New York: Oxford University Press, 1968), 100.

18. Oelschlaeger, *The Idea of Wilderness*, 238.

19. Cittadino, "Ecology and American Social Thought," 94.

20. Leopold, "The Community Concept," in *A Sand County Almanac,* 203–4.

21. Aldo Leopold, "Engineering and Conservation," in *The River of the Mother of God and Other Essays*, 254.

22. Oelschlaeger, *The Idea of Wilderness*, 230.

23. Ibid., 232–33.

24. Aldo Leopold, *Game Management* (New York: C. Scribner's Sons, 1933).

25. Dunlap, *Faith in Nature*, 65, 167.

26. Robert H. Nelson, *Reaching for Heaven on Earth: The Theological Meaning of Economics* (Lanham, Md.: Rowman and Littlefield, 1991), 176–84.

27. See Philip Mirowski, *More Heat Than Light: Economics as Social Physics, Physics as Nature's Economics* (New York: Cambridge University Press, 1989); and Philip Mirowski, *Against Mechanism: Protecting Economics from Science* (Totowa, N.J.: Rowman and Littlefield, 1988).

28. See Mirowski, *More Heat Than Light*.

29. Donald Worster, *The Wealth of Nature: Environmental History and the Ecological Imagination* (New York: Oxford University Press, 1993), 159.

30. Quoted in Worster, *The Wealth of Nature*, 175.

31. See Robert H. Nelson, *A Burning Issue: A Case for Abolishing the U.S. Forest Service* (Lanham, Md.: Rowman and Littlefield, 2000), chap. 2.

32. Eugene Pleasants Odum, *Fundamentals of Ecology* (Philadelphia: Saunders, 1953); and Paul A. Samuelson, *Foundations of Economic Analysis* (1947; repr., New York: Atheneum, 1965).

33. Eugene Pleasants Odum, "The Strategy of Ecosystem Development," *Science* 164 (April 18, 1969): 266.

34. Worster, *The Wealth of Nature*, 160.

35. Ibid.

36. Ibid., 161.

37. Odum, "Strategy of Ecosystem Development," 266.

38. Worster, *Wealth of Nature*, 163.

39. R. V. O'Neill, "Perspectives on Economics and Ecology," *Ecological Applications* 6, no. 4 (1996): 1033. See also Robert V. O'Neill, "Is It Time to Bury the Ecosystem Concept? (With Full Military Honors, Of Course!)," *Ecology* 82, no. 12 (2001).

40. Cittadino, "Ecology and American Social Thought," 105.

41. Mark Stoll, "Edward O. Wilson: The Science of Religion, the Religion of Science, and the Biologist's 'Inner Baptist,'" in *Eminent Lives in Twentieth Century Science and Religion*, ed. Nicolaas A. Rupke (New York: Peter Lang, 2007).

42. Edward O. Wilson, *Sociobiology: The New Synthesis* (Cambridge: Harvard University Press, 1975).

43. Edward O. Wilson, *The Diversity of Life*, 2d ed. (New York: Norton, 1989); and E. O. Wilson, ed., *Biodiversity* (Washington, D.C.: National Academy Press, 1988).

44. Stephen Jay Gould, "Prophet for the Earth: A Review of Edward O. Wilson's *The Diversity of Life*," *Environmental Law* 24, no. 2 (1994): 818.

45. Edward O. Wilson, "The Diversity of Life," *Discover*, September 1992, 47.

46. Ibid., 51, 47, 51, 48.

47. Ibid., 67.

48. Ibid., 68.

49. Alister McGrath, *The Reenchantment of Nature: The Denial of Religion and the Ecological Crisis* (New York: Doubleday, 2002), 181.

50. Gould, "Prophet for the Earth," 819.

51. Stoll, "Edward O. Wilson," 11.

52. Daniel B. Botkin, *Discordant Harmonies: A New Ecology for the Twenty-first Century* (New York: Oxford University Press, 1990), vii.

53. Ibid., 194.

54. Ibid., vii.

55. Ibid., 188–89.

56. See also A. Dan Tarlock, "Beyond the Balance of Nature: Environmental Law Faces the New Ecology," *Duke Environmental Law and Policy Forum* 7 (Fall 1996).

57. Allan K. Fitzsimmons, *Defending Illusions: Federal Protection of Ecosystems* (Lanham, Md.: Rowman and Littlefield, 1999).

58. Ibid., 29–30.

59. Ibid., 28, 27.

60. Ibid., 32, 14.

61. Secretary of the interior Bruce Babbitt, quoted in ibid., 16.

62. For the new view, see Charles C. Mann, *1491: New Revelations of the Americas Before Columbus* (New York: Knopf, 2005).

63. Robert Royal, *1492 and All That: Political Manipulations of History* (Washington, D.C.: Ethics and Public Policy Center, 1992).

64. Robert H. Nelson, *Public Lands and Private Rights: The Failure of Scientific Management* (Lanham, Md.: Rowman and Littlefield, 1995).

65. Ed Marston, "Ecotage Isn't a Solution, It's Part of the Problem," *High Country News*, June 19, 1989, 15.

Chapter 9

This chapter is newly written.

1. *Congressional Record*, 95th Cong., 2d sess., 124 (1978): S 10973.

2. Ibid.

3. Jamie Sayen, "And I Will Be Heard: Abolitionism and Preservationism in Our Time," in *Wild Earth: Wild Ideas for a World Out of Balance*, ed. Tom Butler (Minneapolis: Milkweed Editions, 2002), 124.

4. John Micklethwait, "The Culture Wars Go Global," *Economist*, special issue, *The World in 2008*, December 2007, 26.

5. See Jason Annan, "Is Environmentalism the New State Religion?" in *The Market Meets the Environment: Economic Analysis of Environmental Policy*, ed. Bruce Yandle (Lanham, Md.: Rowman and Littlefield, 1999).

6. See Christian Smith, ed., *The Secular Revolution: Power, Interests, and Conflict in the Secularization of American Public Life* (Berkeley and Los Angeles: University of California Press, 2003).

7. Willett Kempton, James S. Boster, and Jennifer A. Hartley, *Environmental Values in American Culture* (Cambridge: MIT Press, 1995), 215.

8. Ibid., 211, 226, 102, 214.

9. Ibid., 207, 209, 218.

10. Ibid., 220.

11. Ibid., 260.

12. Ibid., 265.

13. Ibid., 178.

14. Ibid., 91.

15. Ibid., 92.

16. Ibid.

17. Ibid., 113–14.

18. Ibid., 115, 223, 224.

19. Max Oelschlaeger, *Caring for Creation: An Ecumenical Approach to the Environmental Crisis* (New Haven: Yale University Press, 1994), 5.

20. Ibid., 6, 112.

21. See, for example, John B. Cobb Jr., *A Theology of Ecology: Is It Too Late?* (Denton, Tex.: Environmental Ethics Books, 1995).

22. Oelschlaeger, *Caring for Creation*, 100.

23. Ibid., 101.

24. Ibid., 101, 103.

25. See also Michael B. Barkley, *Environmental Stewardship in the Judeo-Christian Tradition: Jewish, Catholic, and Protestant Wisdom on the Environment* (Grand Rapids, Mich.: Actor Institute, 2000).

26. Oelschlaeger, *Caring for Creation*, 128, 131, 132, 133, 137, 131.

27. Ibid., 145.

28. Ibid., 145, quoting James Nash.

29. Ibid., 145.

30. Ibid., 115, 108, 102, 96.

31. Ibid., 114, 76, 83, 102, 4, 83.

32. Ibid., 90, 200.

33. See Richard D. Land and Louis A. Moore, eds., *The Earth Is the Lord's: Christians and the Environment* (Nashville: Broadman Press, 1992).

34. E. O. Wilson, *The Creation: An Appeal to Save Life on Earth* (New York: Norton, 2006).

35. Ibid., 3, 4, 106

36. Ibid., 4, 5.

37. Ibid., 99, 92, 12.

38. Ibid., 9.

39. Ibid., 10.

40. Ibid., 10, 7, 10, 123.

41. Ibid., 89–90.

42. Ibid., 168.

43. See Robert Whelan, Joseph Kirwan, and Paul Haffner, *The Cross and the Rain Forest: A Critique of Radical Green Spirituality* (Grand Rapids, Mich.: Eerdmans, 1996).

44. S. M. Hutchens, "The Evangelical Ecologist," *New Atlantis* 18 (Fall 2007): 94–97.

45. Alister McGrath, *The Reenchantment of Nature: The Denial of Religion and the Ecological Crisis* (New York: Doubleday, 2002), ix, x. See also Alister E. McGrath, *Theology: The Basics* (Malden, Mass.: Blackwell, 2004).

46. McGrath, *The Reenchantment of Nature*, 17.

47. Ibid., 19.

48. Quoted in McGrath, *The Reenchantment of Nature*, 18.

49. Quoted in McGrath, *The Reenchantment of Nature*, 16.

50. McGrath, *The Reenchantment of Nature*, 158, 16.

51. Ibid., 17.

52. Ibid., 21–22.

53. Ibid., 160.

54. See Mario Livio, *Is God a Mathematician?* (New York: Simon and Schuster, 2009).

55. Quoted in McGrath, *The Reenchantment of Nature*, 160.

56. McGrath, *The Reenchantment of Nature*, 94.

57. Ibid., 12.

58. See Carol S. Robb and Carl J. Casebolt, eds., *Covenant for a New Creation: Ethics, Religion, and Public Policy* (Maryknoll, N.Y.: Orbis, 1991).

59. I first raised this question in Robert H. Nelson, "Religion as Taught in the Public Schools," *Forbes*, July 7, 1997.

Chapter 10

This chapter is newly written.

1. Connie Barlow, "Rewilding for Evolution," in *Wild Earth: Wild Ideas for an Earth Out of Balance*, ed. Tom Butler (Minneapolis: Milkweed Editions, 2002), 86.

2. Dave Foreman, *Rewilding North America: A Vision for Conservation in the 21st Century* (Washington, D.C.: Island Press, 2004).

3. Reed F. Noss and J. Michael Scott, "Ecosystem Protection and Restoration: The Core of Ecosystem Management," in *Ecosystem Management: Applications for Sustainable Forest and Wildland Resources*, ed. Mark S. Boyce and Alan Haney (New Haven: Yale University Press, 1997); and John McCormick, *Reclaiming Paradise: The Global Environmental Movement* (Bloomington: Indiana University Press, 1989).

4. See Robert Royal, *1492 and All That: Political Manipulations of History* (Washington, D.C.: Ethics and Policy Center, 1992).

5. Ibid., 88.

6. Barlow, "Rewilding for Evolution," 87.

7. Robert V. O'Neill, "Is It Time to Bury the Ecosystem Concept? (With Full Military Honors, Of Course!)," *Ecology* 82, no. 12 (2001).

8. Robert B. Keiter, *Keeping Faith with Nature: Ecosystems, Democracy, and America's Public Lands* (New Haven: Yale University Press, 2003).

9. See also Mark S. Boyce and Alan Haney, eds., *Ecosystem Management: Applications for Sustainable Forest and Wildlife Resources* (New Haven: Yale University Press, 1997).

10. Keiter, *Keeping Faith with Nature*, 327, 2.

11. Ibid., 2, 12.

12. John L. Matthews, "The Conservation of Our Natural Resources," *Atlantic Monthly*, May 1908.

13. See Samuel P. Hays, *Conservation and the Gospel of Efficiency: The Progressive Conservation Movement, 1890–1920* (Cambridge: Harvard University Press, 1959).

14. Jill Lepore, "Our Own Devices: Does Technology Drive History?" *New Yorker*, May 12, 2008, 118, 119.

15. Keiter, *Keeping Faith with Nature*, 13, 12, 14, 24–25, 25.

16. Paul W. Taylor, *Respect for Nature: A Theory of Environmental Ethics* (Princeton: Princeton University Press, 1986), 3.

17. Keiter, *Keeping Faith with Nature*, 128.

18. Ibid., 324–25.

19. Ibid., 325.

20. Ibid., 147.

21. John Wesley Powell, *Report on the Lands of the Arid Region of the United States*, quoted in ibid., 136.

22. See Charles E. Kay and Randy T. Simmons, eds., *Wilderness and Political Ecology: Aboriginal Influences and the Original State of Nature* (Salt Lake City: University of Utah Press, 2002).

23. See Charles C. Mann, *1491: New Revelations of the Americas Before Columbus* (New York: Knopf, 2005).

24. Keiter, *Keeping Faith with Nature*, 144, 145.

25. See also Steven L. Yaffee, "Three Faces of Ecological Management," *Conservation Biology* 13 (August 1999).

26. Robert H. Nelson, "Mythology Instead of Analysis: The Story of Public Forest Management," in *Forestlands: Public and Private*, ed. Robert T. Deacon and M. Bruce Johnson (San Francisco: Pacific Institute for Public Policy Research, 1985).

27. Robert H. Nelson, "Ineffective Laws and Unexpected Consequences: A Brief Review of Public Land History," chap. 1 in Nelson, *Public Lands and Private Rights: The Failure of Scientific Management* (Lanham, Md.: Rowman and Littlefield, 1995).

28. Kim Todd, "Conservation Quandary: Researchers Face the Prospect of Killing One Owl to Save Another," *High Country News* 40 (August 4, 2008): 11.

29. Ibid., 12.

30. Ibid., 11.

31. Ibid., 15.

32. Ibid., 16.

33. Ibid., 15.

34. See Nelson, "Ineffective Laws and Unexpected Consequences."

35. See Douglas Fox, "Identity Crisis," *Conservation Magazine*, April–June 2008, 23, 26.

36. Ibid., 23, 26.

37. Robert Elliot, "Faking Nature," *Inquiry* 25, no. 1 (1982).

38. Robert Elliot, *Faking Nature: The Ethics of Environmental Restoration* (New York: Routledge, 1997).

39. Eric Katz, "The Big Lie: Human Restoration of Nature," in *Research in Philosophy and Technology*, vol. 12 (Stamford, Conn.: JAI Press, 1991).

40. Elliot, *Faking Nature*, 97.

41. Ibid., 98, 83.

42. Andrew Curry, "Creationist Beliefs Persist in Europe," *Science* 323 (February 27, 2009): 1159.

43. Elliot, *Faking Nature*, 89.

44. Ibid., 115, 112.

45. Ibid., 95–96, 95, 92.

46. See Michael Thompson, Richard Ellis, and Aaron Wildavsky, *Cultural Theory* (Boulder, Colo.: Westview Press, 1990), 25–37; and Keith Thomas, *Man and the Natural World: Changing Attitudes in England, 1500–1800* (New York: Oxford University Press, 1983).

47. Kate Soper, *What is Nature?* (Cambridge, Mass.: Blackwell, 1995), 2.

48. Ibid., 254.

49. Pope John Paul II, *Encyclical Letter—Evangelium Vitae* [Gospel of life], March 25, 1995, 62, 71, 64.

50. Quoted in Pope John Paul II, *Evangelium Vitae*, 52.

51. Soper, *What is Nature?* 6, 7.

52. Ibid., 13.

53. Ibid., 160.

54. Ibid., 255, 207.

55. Ibid., 255–56, 257.

56. See Robert H. Nelson, *A Burning Issue: A Case for Abolishing the U.S. Forest Service* (Lanham, Md.: Rowman and Littlefield, 2000); and Roger A. Sedjo, "Does the Forest Service Have a Future?" *Regulation* (Spring 2000).

57. See Robert H. Nelson, "The Gospel According to Conservation Biology," *Philosophy and Public Policy Quarterly* 27 (Summer–Fall 2007).

58. David Takacs, *The Idea of Biodiversity: Philosophies of Paradise* (Baltimore: Johns Hopkins University Press, 1996), 246.

59. Ibid., 42.

60. Ibid., 79.

61. Edward O. Wilson, *The Diversity of Life*, 2d ed. (New York: Norton, 1989).

62. Takacs, *The Idea of Biodiversity*, 195.

63. Ibid., 74, 75, 81, 82.

64. Ibid., 79.

65. Ibid., 76.

66. Ibid., 75.

67. Ibid., 115, 116, 115.

68. Ibid., 167.

69. Ibid., 177–78.

70. Bryan G. Norton, *Why Preserve Natural Variety?* (Princeton: Princeton University Press, 1992); and Bryan G. Norton, ed., *The Preservation of Species: The Value of Biological Diversity* (Princeton: Princeton University Press, 1988).

71. Takacs, *The Idea of Biodiversity*, 230.

72. Ibid., 237, 239, 243.

73. Ibid., 247, 248, 247.

74. Ibid., 254, 262, 262–63, 265.

75. Ibid., 266–67.

76. Ibid., 268.

77. Ibid., 270, 337.

78. Eugene Cittadino, "Ecology and American Social Thought," in *Religion and the New Ecology: Environmental Responsibility in a World of Flux*, ed. David M. Lodge and Christopher Hamlin (Notre Dame: University of Notre Dame Press, 2006), 93.

79. I review the large scientific failings of the neoclassical economics prevailing in the American economics profession from the 1950s to the 1970s, as described in a large economic literature since then, in Robert H. Nelson, *Economics as Religion: From Samuelson to Chicago and Beyond* (University Park: Pennsylvania State University Press, 2001), 52–81.

80. Daniel B. Botkin, *Discordant Harmonies: A New Ecology for the Twenty-first Century* (New York: Oxford University Press, 1990).

81. Eugene Cittadino, "Ecology and American Social Thought," 93.

82. Ibid., 101.

83. F. Foster and J. Aber, "Background and Framework for Long-Term Ecological Research," in *Forests in Time: The Environmental Consequences of 1,000 Years of Change in New England*, ed. David R. Foster and John D. Aber (New Haven: Yale University Press, 2004), 5–6.

84. D. Foster and others, "The Environmental and Human History of New England," in Foster and Aber, *Forests in Time*, 64, 62.

85. Ibid., 43–44.

86. Herman E. Daly, "The Lurking Inconsistency," *Conservation Biology* 13 (August 1999).

87. See Marc K. Landy, Marc J. Roberts, and Stephen R. Thomas, *The Environmental Protection Agency: Asking the Wrong Questions, from Nixon to Clinton* (New York: Oxford University Press, 1994).

Chapter 11

Adapted from Robert H. Nelson, "Environmental Colonialism: 'Saving' Africa from Africans," *Independent Review* 8 (Summer 2003). I gained firsthand exposure to African environmental issues in 1999 when, as part of my sabbatical year from the University of Maryland, I spent six months as a visiting research associate at the Center for Applied Social Science (CASS) at the University of Zimbabwe in Harare. I have since been back to Africa for multiple visits, most frequently to Tanzania.

1. See Bjorn Lomborg, *The Skeptical Environmentalist: Measuring the Real State of the World* (New York: Cambridge University Press, 2001).

2. For reviews of the history of American environmental policy, see Daniel J. Fiorino, *The New Environmental Regulation* (Cambridge: MIT Press, 2006); Richard J. Lazarus, *The Making of Environmental Policy* (Chicago: University of Chicago Press, 2004); and James Salzman and Barton H. Thompson, *Environmental Law and Policy* (New York: Foundation Press, 2003). For a more critical view, see David Schoenbrod, *Saving Our Environment From Washington: How Congress Grabs Power, Shirks Responsibility, and Shortchanges the People* (New Haven: Yale University Press, 2005).

3. See Richard N. L. Andrews, *Managing the Environment, Managing Ourselves: A History of American Environmental Law* (New Haven: Yale University Press, 1999), chap. 7.

4. See Mark Spence, *Dispossessing the Wilderness: Indian Removal and the Making of the National Parks* (New York: Oxford University Press, 1999); and Karl Jacoby, *Crimes Against Nature: Squatters, Poachers, Thieves, and the Hidden History of American Conservation* (Berkeley and Los Angeles: University of California Press, 2001).

5. Paul Sutter, *Driven Wild: How the Fight Against Automobiles Launched the Modern Wilderness Movement* (Seattle: University of Washington Press, 2002), 11.

6. Ibid., 11–12.

7. Alston Chase, *Playing God in Yellowstone: The Destruction of America's First National Park* (Boston: Atlantic Monthly Press, 1986).

8. Sutter, *Driven Wild*, 12.

9. John Reader, *Africa: A Biography of the Continent* (New York: Vintage Books, 1999).

10. Raymond Bonner, *At the Hand of Man: Peril and Hope for Africa's Wildlife* (New York: Knopf, 1993), 7, 286.

11. See also Martha Honey, "Tanzania: Whose Eden Is It?" chap. 6 in *Ecotourism and Sustainable Development: Who Owns Paradise?* 2d ed. (Washington, D.C.: Island Press, 2008).

12. Jonathan S. Adams and Thomas O. McShane, *The Myth of Wild Africa: Conservation Without Illusion* (Berkeley and Los Angeles: University of California Press, 1996).

13. Quoted in Adams and McShane, *The Myth of Wild Africa*, 15.

14. Roderick P. Neumann, *Imposing Wilderness: Struggles Over Livelihood and Nature Preservation in Africa* (Berkeley and Los Angeles: University of California Press, 1998), 18.

15. Ibid.

16. Mafigeni Safari and Tours (promotional advertisement), Duiwelskloof, South Africa, http://www.mafigeni.co.za/more_info-tanzania.htm (accessed August 14, 2002).

17. Reader, *Africa*, 600.

18. Ibid.

19. Helge Kjekshus, *Ecology Control and Economic Development in East African History: The Case of Tanganyika, 1850–1950* (1977; repr., London: James Curry, 1996), 178.

20. Quoted in ibid.

21. Reader, *Africa*, 589, 590.

22. A. D. Graham, *The Gardeners of Eden* (London: Allen and Unwin, 1973), 27.

23. Reader, *Africa*, 592.

24. Kjekshus, *Ecology Control and Economic Development in East African History*, 181.

25. Adams and McShane, *The Myth of Wild Africa*, 47.

26. John M. MacKenzie, *The Empire of Nature: Hunting, Conservation, and British Imperialism* (Manchester: Manchester University Press, 1988).

27. Adams and McShane, *The Myth of Wild Africa*, 48.

28. Royal National Parks Department, *Report* (1955), as quoted in ibid., 48.

29. Adams and McShane, *The Myth of Wild Africa*, 49.

30. John McPhee, *Encounters with the Archdruid* (New York: Farrar, Straus and Giroux, 1971).

31. Adams and McShane, *The Myth of Wild Africa*, 53.

32. Ibid.

33. Barnabas Dickson, "Global Regulation and Communal Management," in *Endangered Species, Threatened Convention: The Past, Present and Future of CITES*, ed. Jon Hutton and Barnabas Dickson (London: Earthscan Publications, 2000), 176.

34. Dan Brockington, *Fortress Conservation: The Preservation of the Mkomazi Game Reserve, Tanzania* (Bloomington: Indiana University Press, 2002).

35. Jean-Francois Bayart, Stephen Ellis, and Beatrice Hibou, *The Criminalization of the State in Africa* (Bloomington: Indiana University Press, 1999).

36. Brockington, *Fortress Conservation*, 10.

37. Ibid., 56.

38. Ibid., 73.

39. Tanzania Wildlife Division, as quoted in Brockington, *Fortress Conservation*, 80.

40. Brockington, *Fortress Conservation*, 80.

41. Ibid., 126.

42. Ibid.

43. Neumann, *Imposing Wilderness*, 13, 9.

44. Ibid., 141.

Introduction to Part IV

1. David Van Biema, "Mother Teresa's Crisis of Faith," *Time*, August 23, 2007.

2. Frank H. Knight and Thornton W. Merriam, *The Economic Order and Religion* (1945; repr., Westport: Greenwood Press, 1979).

3. Frank H. Knight, "The Role of Principles in Economics and Politics," *American Economic Review* 41 (March 1951), reprinted in Frank H. Knight, *On the History and Method of Economics* (Chicago: University of Chicago Press, 1956), 252.

4. E . Brooks Holifield, *Theology in America: Christian Thought from the Age of the Puritans to the Civil War* (New Haven: Yale University Press, 2003), 41.

Chapter 12

Adapted from Robert H. Nelson, "Frank Knight and Original Sin," chap. 5 in *Economics as Religion: From Samuelson to Chicago and Beyond* (University Park: Pennsylvania State University Press, 2001). See also Robert H. Nelson, "Frank Knight and Original Sin," *Independent Review* 6 (Summer 2001).

1. John Maynard Keynes, *The General Theory of Employment, Interest, and Money* (New York: Harcourt, Brace, 1936).

2. See J. Patrick Raines and Clarence R. Jung, "Knight on Religion and Ethics as Agents of Social Change," *American Journal of Economics and Sociology* 45 (October 1986): 430–31.

3. George J. Stigler, autobiographical statement in *Lives of the Laureates: Thirteen Nobel Economists*, 3d ed., ed. William Breit and Roger W. Spencer (Cambridge: MIT Press, 1995), 98.

4. William S. Kern, "Frank Knight on Preachers and Economic Policy: A 19th Century Antireligionist, He Thought Religion Should Support the Status Quo," *American Journal of Economics and Sociology* 47 (January 1988).

5. Don Patinkin, *Essays On and In the Chicago Tradition* (Durham: Duke University Press, 1981), 46.

6. Frank H. Knight, "Pragmatism and Social Action," *International Journal of Ethics* 46 (January 1936), reprinted in Frank. H. Knight, *Freedom and Reform: Essays in Economics and Social Philosophy* (Indianapolis: Liberty Press, 1982), 52.

7. Frank H. Knight, *Risk, Uncertainty, and Profit* (1921; repr., New York: Harper and Row, 1965). This was Knight's first book, based on his doctoral dissertation.

8. Razeen Sally, "The Political Economy of Frank Knight: Classical Liberalism from Chicago," *Constitutional Political Economy* 8, no. 2 (1997).

9. Richard Schlatter, *Private Property: The History of an Idea* (1951; repr., New York: Russell and Russell, 1973), 35.

10. Richard T. Ely, *Social Aspects of Christianity and Other Essays* (New York: Crowell, 1889), 1, 6–7.

11. Charles Howard Hopkins, *The Rise of the Social Gospel in American Protestantism, 1865–1915* (New Haven: Yale University Press, 1940).

12. Frank H. Knight, "Ethics and Economic Reform," *Economica* 6 (February 1939), reprinted in Knight, *Freedom and Reform*, 126, 127, 129, 130–31.

13. Knight, *Freedom and Reform*, 63.

14. Ibid., 63–64.

15. Ibid, 131.

16. Ibid., 67.

17. Frank H. Knight, "Liberalism and Christianity," in Frank H. Knight and Thornton W. Merriam, *Economic Order and Religion* (New York: Harper and Brothers, 1945), 100.

18. Kern, "Frank Knight on Preachers and Economic Policy."

19. Frank H. Knight, "The Rights of Man and Natural Law," *Ethics* 44 (January 1944), reprinted in Knight, *Freedom and Reform*, 332.

20. Knight, "Ethics and Economic Reform," 125.

21. Knight, "The Rights of Man and Natural Law," 320.

22. Knight, "Pragmatism and Social Action," 53.

23. Frank H. Knight, "Salvation by Science: The Gospel According to Professor Lundberg," *Journal of Political Economy* 55 (December 1947), reprinted in Frank H. Knight, *On the History and Method of Economics* (Chicago: University of Chicago Press, 1956).

24. Daniel J. Hammond, "Frank Knight's Antipositivism," *History of Political Economy* 23 (1991).

25. Frank H. Knight, "The Role of Principles in Economics and Politics," *American Economic Review* 41 (March 1951), reprinted in Frank H. Knight, *On the History and Method of Economics* (Chicago: University of Chicago Press, 1956), 277.

26. Ibid., 275.

27. Frank H. Knight, "The Limitations of Scientific Method in Economics," in *The Ethics of Competition and Other Essays* (1935; repr., New Brunswick, N.J.: Transactions Publishers, 1997).

28. Frank H. Knight, "Free Society: Its Basic Nature and Problem," *Philosophical Review* (January 1948), reprinted in Knight, *Essays on the History and Method of Economics*, 299.

29. Richard A. Gonce, "Frank H. Knight on Social Control and the Scope and Method of Economics," *Southern Economic Journal* 38 (April 1972).

30. Frank H. Knight, "Abstract Economics as Absolute Ethics," *Ethics* 76 (April 1966): 166.

31. Paul A. Samuelson, *Economics* (New York: McGraw-Hill, 1948); and Paul A. Samuelson, *Foundations of Economic Analysis* (Cambridge: Harvard University Press, 1947).

32. Knight, "Salvation by Science," 229, 235.

33. Ibid., 230.

34. Knight, "The Role of Principles in Economics and Politics," 261, 258, 260.

35. Frank H. Knight, "Economic Psychology and the Value Problem," *Quarterly Journal of Economics* 39 (May 1925), reprinted in Knight, *The Ethics of Competition*.

36. Ibid., 279.

37. Knight, "Free Society," 299.

38. See John Kohl, "Christianity: Protestantism," in *Encyclopedia of the World's Religions*, ed. R. C. Zaehner (New York: Barnes and Noble, 1997), 101.

39. Ross B. Emmett, "Frank Knight: Economics Versus Religion," in *Economics and Religion: Are They Distinct?* ed. H. Geoffrey Brennan and A. M. C. Waterman (Boston: Kluwer Academic Publishers, 1994), 118–19.

40. James M. Buchanan, "Frank H. Knight," in *Remembering the University of Chicago: Teachers, Scientists, and Scholars*, ed. Edward Shils (Chicago: University of Chicago Press, 1991), 247, 246. See also James M. Buchanan, "The Economizing Element in Knight's Ethical Critique of Capitalist Order," *Ethics* 98 (October 1987).

41. For a full exploration of the Puritan mentality, see Michael Walzer, *The Revolution of the Saints: A Study in the Origins of Radical Politics* (New York: Atheneum, 1974). See also Duncan B. Forrester, "Martin Luther and John Calvin," in *History of Political Philosophy*, ed. Leo Strauss and Joseph Cropsey (Chicago: University of Chicago Press, 1981).

42. Knight, "Liberalism and Christianity," 39.

43. Knight, "The Role of Principles in Economics and Politics," 273, 269, 262.

44. A classic study of the powerful role of Calvinist (and Quaker) religion in American life is found in E. Digby Baltzell, *Puritan Boston and Quaker Philadelphia: Two Protestant Ethics and the Spirit of Class Authority and Leadership* (New York: Free Press, 1979).

45. Paula Baker, *The Moral Frameworks of Public Life: Gender, Politics, and the State in Rural New York, 1870–1930* (New York: Oxford University Press, 1991), 14.

46. Frank H. Knight, "The Ethics of Competition," *Quarterly Journal of Economics* 37 (August 1923), reprinted in Knight, *The Ethics of Competition*, 33.

47. Paul K. Conkin, *Puritans and Pragmatists: Eight Eminent American Thinkers* (Bloomington: Indiana University Press, 1976), 3–4.

48. Patinkin, *Essays On and In the Chicago Tradition*, 34.

49. Richard Boyd, "Frank Knight's Pluralism," *Critical Review* 11 (Fall 1997): 537.

50. For further discussion of these theological traditions, see Robert H. Nelson, *Reaching for Heaven on Earth: The Theological Meaning of Economics* (Lanham, Md.: Rowman and Littlefield, 1991).

51. Boyd, "Frank Knight's Pluralism," 537.

52. See Knight, "The Ethics of Competition"; and Frank H. Knight, "Ethics and the Economic Interpretation," *Quarterly Journal of Economics* 36 (May 1922), reprinted in Knight, *The Ethics of Competition*.

53. Knight, "Liberalism and Christianity," 71.

54. Knight, "Ethics and Economic Reform," 84.

55. Frank H. Knight, "Social Science," *Ethics* 51 (January 1941), reprinted in Knight, *On the History and Method of Economics*, 134.

56. Knight, "Ethics and Economic Reform," 55.

57. Raines and Jung, "Knight on Religion and Ethics as Agents of Social Change."

58. Knight, "The Role of Principles in Economics and Politics," 266.

59. See "Introduction: The Market Paradox," in Nelson, *Economics as Religion*.

60. Knight, "Free Society," 295.

61. Knight, "Ethics and Economic Reform," 73.

62. Frank H. Knight, "Social Science and the Political Trend," *University of Toronto Quarterly* 3 (1934), reprinted in Knight, *Freedom and Reform*, 39-40.

63. Knight, "The Role of Principles in Economics and Politics," 265.

64. Conkin, *Puritans and Pragmatists*, 18.

65. Ernest Troeltsch, *Protestantism and Progress: A Historical Study of the Relation of Protestantism to the Modern World*, trans. W. Montgomery (1912; repr., Boston: Beacon Press, 1958), 125-26.

Chapter 13

Partially adapted from Robert H. Nelson, "Is 'Libertarian Environmentalist' an Oxymoron? The Crisis of Progressive Faith and the Environmental and Libertarian Search for a New Guiding Vision," in *The Next West: Public Lands, Community, and Economy in the American West*, ed. John A. Baden and Donald Snow (Washington, D.C.: Island Press, 1997). This chapter also draws on themes that I first developed in Robert H. Nelson, *Reaching for Heaven on Earth: The Theological Meaning of Economics* (Lanham, Md.: Rowman and Littlefield, 1991).

1. See William Tucker, *Progress and Privilege: America in the Age of Environmentalism* (Garden City, N.Y.: Doubleday, 1982).

2. See Robert J. Duffy, *The Green Agenda in American Politics: New Strategies for the Twenty-First Century* (Lawrence: University Press of Kansas, 2003).

3. Criticisms of environmental thinking are found in Peter Huber, *Hard Green: Saving the Environment from the Environmentalists: A Conservative Manifesto* (New York: Basic Books, 1999); Martin W. Lewis, *Green Delusions: An Environmentalist Critique of Radical Environmentalism* (Durham: Duke University Press, 1992); and Charles T. Rubin, *The Green Crusade: Rethinking the Roots of Environmentalism* (New York: Free Press, 1994).

4. See Ted Nordhaus and Michael Shellenberger, *Break Through: From the Death of Environmentalism to the Politics of Possibility* (New York: Houghton Mifflin, 2007).

5. Richard J. Lazarus, *The Making of Environmental Law* (Chicago: University of Chicago Press, 2004), 27-28.

6. David Schoenbrod, *Saving Our Environment From Washington: How Congress Grabs Power, Shirks Responsibility, and Shortchanges the People* (New Haven: Yale University Press, 2005), 192.

7. See Robert Nozick, "A Framework for Utopia," chap. 10 in *Anarchy, State, and Utopia* (New York: Basic Books, 1974).

8. See also Robert H. Nelson, "The Right of Free Secession," chap. 8 in *Reaching for Heaven on Earth*.

9. See Stephen Skowronek, *Building a New American State: The Expansion of National Administrative Capacities, 1877-1920* (New York: Cambridge University Press, 1982); Robert H. Weibe, *The Search for Order, 1877-1920* (New York: Hill and Wang, 1967); and Richard Hofstadter, *The Age of Reform: From Bryan to F.D.R.* (New York: Vintage Books, 1955).

10. See Dwight Waldo, *The Administrative State: A Study of the Political Theory of American Public Administration* (1948; repr., New York: Holmes and Meier, 1984).

11. Eliza Wing-Yee Lee, "Political Science, Public Administration, and the Rise of the American Administrative State," *Public Administration Review* 155 (November-December 1995): 543.

12. Editorial, *First Things* 1 (April 1990): 8.

13. William A. Schambra, "Progressive Liberalism and American 'Community,'" *Public Interest* (Summer 1985): 36.

14. See Brian Doherty, *Radicals for Capitalism: A Freewheeling History of the Modern American Libertarian Movement* (New York: Public Affairs, 2007).

15. Harry C. Boyte, *The Backyard Revolution: Understanding the New Citizen Movement* (Philadelphia: Temple University Press, 1980).

16. Mark Sagoff, *Price, Principle, and the Environment* (New York: Cambridge University Press, 2004), 74.

17. Mark Sagoff, *The Economy of the Earth: Philosophy, Law, and the Environment*, 2d ed. (New York: Cambridge University Press, 2008).

18. James M. Buchanan, *What Should Economists Do?* (Indianapolis: Liberty Press, 1979), 24, 145.

19. Ibid., 157, 173.

20. Ibid., 281.

21. See Nelson, *Reaching for Heaven on Earth*, 288–96.

22. Buchanan, *What Should Economists Do?* 280, 90–91, 216, 88.

23. See Robert H. Nelson, "Scholasticism Versus Pietism: The Battle for the Soul of Economics," *Econ Journal Watch* 1 (December 2004), http://www.econjournalwatch.org/pdf/NelsonCharacter Issues1December2004.pdf.

24. Buchanan, *What Should Economists Do?* 211.

25. Ibid., 229, 228–29, 111, 110.

26. Ibid., 228–29, 110–11.

27. See also George Sessions, ed., *Deep Ecology for the 21st Century: Readings on the Philosophy and Practice of the New Environmentalism* (Boston, Mass.: Shambhala Publication, 1995); and David Landis Barnhill and Roger S. Gottlieb, eds., *Deep Ecology and World Religions: New Essays on Sacred Ground* (Albany: State University of New York Press, 2001).

28. Bill Devall and George Sessions, *Deep Ecology: Living as if Nature Mattered* (Salt Lake City: Peregrine Smith Books, 1985), 48, 56.

29. Ibid., 56, 57, 48.

30. Ibid., 35, 21.

31. Ibid., 43, 145.

32. Ibid., 151, 61, 151, 107.

33. Ibid., 115, 125.

34. Ibid., 169, 20, 18–19.

35. Buchanan, *What Should Economists Do?* 228.

36. Ernest Callenbach, *Ecotopia* (1975; repr., New York: Bantam, 1977), 5.

37. Colman McCarthy, "'I'm a pacifist because I'm a violent son of a bitch': A Profile of Stanley Hauerwaus," *Progressive* 67 (April 2003): 23.

38. Stanley Hauerwas, *Against the Nations: War and Survival in a Liberal Society* (Notre Dame: University of Notre Dame Press, 1992), 6, 7.

39. This is a main theme of Nelson, *Reaching for Heaven on Earth*.

40. Hauerwas, *Against the Nations*, 8, 14.

41. Ibid., 110, 111, 117, 122, 127.

42. Ibid., 123.

43. Ibid., 128, 129, 196.

44. Captain Paul Watson, "On the Precedence of Natural Law," *Journal of Environmental Law and Litigation* 3 (1988).

45. Ibid., 79, 85.

46. Ibid., 82.

47. Ibid., 81–82.

48. Ibid., 83, 82.

49. Ibid., 86.

50. Ibid.

51. Ibid., 89.

52. Ibid.

53. Norman Macrae, *The 2025 Report: A Concise History of the Future, 1975–2025* (New York: Macmillan, 1984), 132, 124.

54. Ibid., 115.

55. Robert H. Nelson, *Private Neighborhoods and the Transformation of Local Government* (Washington, D.C.: Urban Institute Press, 2005).

56. Chris Webster and Georg Glasze, "Conclusion: Dynamic Urban Order and the Rise of Residential Clubs," in *Private Cities: Global and Local Perspectives*, ed. George Glasze, Chris Webster, and Klaus Frantz (New York: Routledge, 2006), 222.

57. Joel Garreau, *The Nine Nations of North America* (New York: Avon Books, 1982), 1, 8.

58. Murray N. Rothbard, "Law, Property Rights, and Air Pollution," *Cato Journal* 2 (Spring 1982): 57, 60, 61.

59. Ibid., 77.

60. Ibid., 98.

61. See Richard J. Lazarus, *The Making of Environmental Law* (Chicago: University of Chicago Press, 2004); and Daniel J. Fiorino, *The New Environmental Regulation* (Cambridge: MIT Press, 2006).

62. See Elizabeth Brubaker, *Property Rights in the Defense of Nature* (Toronto: Earthscan, 1995).

63. Murray N. Rothbard, *An Austrian Perspective on the History of Economic Thought*, vol. 1, *Economic Thought Before Adam Smith* (Brookfield, Vt.: Edward Elgar, 1995), xiii.

64. Ibid., 71.

65. Ibid., 137.

66. Murray N. Rothbard, *An Austrian Perspective on the History of Economic Thought*, vol. 2, *Classical Economics* (Brookfield, Vt.: Edward Elgar, 1995), 12, 13.

67. See Alejandro A. Chafuen, *Faith and Liberty: The Economic Thought of the Late Scholastics* (Lanham, Md.: Lexington Books, 2003).

68. Rothbard, *Classical Economics*, xi.

69. Ibid., xii.

70. See Murray N. Rothbard, *Power and Market: Government and the Economy* (Kansas City, Kans.: Sheed, Andrews, and McMeel, 1970).

71. John Baden and Richard Stroup, eds., *Bureaucracy Versus Environment: The Environmental Costs of Bureaucratic Governance* (Ann Arbor: University of Michigan Press, 1981).

72. Terry L. Anderson and Donald R. Leal, *Free Market Environmentalism* (San Francisco: Pacific Research Institute for Public Policy, 1991). See also Terry L. Anderson and Donald Leal, *Enviro-Capitalists: Doing Good While Doing Well* (Lanham, Md.: Rowman and Littlefield, 1997).

73. Garrett Hardin, "The Tragedy of the Commons," *Science* 162 (1968).

74. Terry L. Anderson and Fred S. McChesney, *Property Rights: Cooperation, Conflict, and Law* (Princeton: Princeton University Press, 2003). See also Robert J. Smith, "Resolving the Tragedy of the Commons by Creating Private Property Rights in Wildlife," *Cato Journal* 1 (Fall 1981).

75. Ronald A. Coase, "The Problem of Social Cost," *Journal of Law and Economics* 3 (October 1960).

76. See Richard Wahl, *Markets for Federal Water: Subsidies, Property Rights, and the Bureau of Reclamation* (Washington, D.C.: Resources for the Future, 1989).

77. J. H. Dales, *Pollution, Property, and Prices* (Toronto: University of Toronto Press, 1968).

78. See Brubaker, *Property Rights in the Defense of Nature*.

79. Wallace E. Oates, "From Research to Policy: The Case of Environmental Economics," *University of Illinois Law Review* 2000, no. 1 (2000).

80. See Robert H. Nelson, "Private Rights to Government Actions: How Modern Property Rights Evolve," *University of Illinois Law Review* 1986, no. 2 (1986).

81. Robert H. Nelson, *Zoning and Property Rights* (Cambridge: MIT Press, 1977); and Robert H. Nelson, *Private Neighborhoods and the Transformation of Local Government* (Washington, D.C.: Urban Institute Press, 2005).

Conclusion

1. See Raymond Aron, "The Future of Secular Religions" (July 1944), reprinted in Raymond Aron, *The Dawn of University History: Selected Essays from a Witness to the Twentieth Century* (New York: Basic Books, 2002).

2. See Michael Allen Gillespie, *The Theological Origins of Modernity* (Chicago: University of Chicago Press, 2008).

3. John Gray, "An Illusion with a Future," *Daedalus* 133 (Summer 2004): 11. See also John Gray, *Heresies: Against Progress and Other Illusions* (London: Granta Books, 2004).

4. Igal Halfin, *From Darkness to Light: Class, Consciousness, and Salvation in Revolutionary Russia* (Pittsburgh: University of Pittsburgh Press, 2000).

5. Ibid., 39.

6. Ibid., 40.

7. Michael Burleigh, *The Third Reich: A New History* (New York: Hill and Wang, 2000), 11, 12. See also Michael Burleigh, *Earthly Powers: The Clash of Religion and Politics in Europe, from the French Revolution to the Great War* (New York: HarperCollins, 2006); and Michael Burleigh, *Sacred Causes: The Clash of Religion and Politics from the Great War to the War on Terror* (New York: HarperCollins, 2007).

8. Burleigh, *The Third Reich*, 12, 13.

9. Ibid., 13–14.

10. Paul C. Vitz, *Psychology as Religion: The Cult of Self-Worship*, 2d ed. (Grand Rapids, Mich.: Eerdmans, 1994). See also William M. Epstein, *Psychotherapy as Religion: The Civil Divine in America* (Reno: University of Nevada Press, 2006).

11. Vitz, *Psychology as Religion*, xii, 32, xi, 10, 144.

12. Ibid., 41.

13. Samuel P. Huntington, *Who Are We? Challenges to America's National Identity* (New York: Simon and Schuster, 2004), 191, 127, 106.

14. David Gelernter, *Americanism: The Fourth Great Religion* (New York: Doubleday, 2007).

15. Huntington, *Who Are We?* 106.

16. Ibid.

17. Sanford Levinson, *Constitutional Faith* (Princeton: Princeton University Press, 1988), 27.

18. Ibid., 121.

19. Thomas C. Grey, "The Constitution as Scripture," *Stanford Law Review* 37 (November 1984): 18, quoted in ibid., 55.

20. Ibid., 47, 27, 29.

21. Robert H. Nelson, *Reaching for Heaven on Earth: The Theological Meaning of Economics* (Lanham, Md.: Rowman and Littlefield, 1991).

22. Ibid., 95–106.

23. Richard T. Ely, *Social Aspects of Christianity and Other Essays* (New York: Crowell, 1889), 73.

24. Arthur J. Vidich and Stanford M. Lyman, *American Sociology: Worldly Rejections of Religion and Their Directions* (New Haven: Yale University Press, 1985).

25. See Douglass C. North, *Understanding the Process of Economic Change* (Princeton: Princeton University Press, 2005).

26. Robert J. Samuelson, *The Good Life and Its Discontents: The American Dream in the Age of Entitlement, 1945–1995* (New York: Times Books, 1995).

27. Thomas R. Dunlap, *Faith in Nature: Environmentalism as Religious Quest* (Seattle: University of Washington Press, 2004), 5.

28. Ibid., 167.

29. Jon Meacham, "The End of Christian America," *Newsweek*, April 13, 2009.

30. Ibid.

31. Ibid.

32. James M. Buchanan, *The Limits of Liberty: Between Anarchy and Leviathan* (Chicago: University of Chicago Press, 1975).

33. Robert William Fogel, *The Fourth Great Awakening and the Future of Egalitarianism* (Chicago: University of Chicago Press, 2000).

INDEX